Portrait of Britain
Vol 4

Portrait of Britain Vol 4
First edition

Published in 2022
by Hoxton Mini Press, London
Copyright © Hoxton Mini Press 2022
All rights reserved

All images © The Photographers

Front cover image by Sirli Raitma
Back cover image by Ali Wright
Introduction by Jess Phillips
Sequence by Friederike Huber
Design by Daniele Roa
Copy-editing by Florence Filose
Production by Anna De Pascale

With thanks to Shaz Madani for initial
series design and Héloise Winstone for
production support.

A CIP catalogue record for this book
is available from the British Library

ISBN 978-1-914314-13-1

Printed and bound by OZGraf, Poland

Hoxton Mini Press is an environmentally
conscious publisher, committed to offsetting
our carbon footprint. The offset for this book
was purchased from Stand For Trees.

For every book you buy from our website,
we plant a tree:
www.hoxtonminipress.com

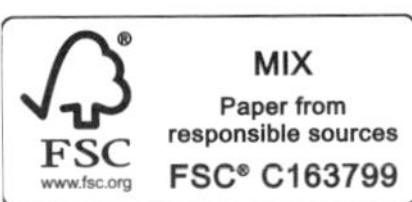

Portrait of Britain

Vol 4

HOXTON MINI PRESS

Note from the Publisher

My gran, when she was alive, used to occasionally wear big sunglasses. You know the kind, the ones that can be worn over at least two other glasses and protect from both the sun and large flying objects. The woman on the front of this year's edition reminds me a little of her and yet in so many ways is different. This woman (who is called Eha, p.330) reminds me of how we once imagined the future might look when the phrase 'silver surfer' was first coined and we were still using dial-up. And yet this is now; this technology is real. Is she playing an immersive alien shoot-'em-up or face-timing her grandchildren? Perhaps both at once.

The phrase 'the new normal', which Jess Phillips so eloquently explores overleaf, but which can so often feel overused, is now more relevant than ever. In a world that has been shattered by the pandemic, the constant evolution of technology promises to bring some of those broken pieces back together: Zoom, Instagram, Facebook, Meta… Whatever your tastes, there is a way to stay connected.

But are we actually more connected, or are we further apart? Does virtual working work? Is social media isolating? How do we survive without physical intimacy?

This is the fourth book in this series and over and over I see one theme emerge above all others: the need for genuine human connection. Touch, love, togetherness. These books celebrate that above all else.

I miss my gran.

Martin Usborne
Co-founder, Hoxton Mini Press

A New Normal

Britain in 2021 is a paradox. A country and a people striving every day to get back to the way things were, at the same time as trying desperately to forge a different future. We want both to regress and progress. We are both angry and grateful, certain but unsure, militant and cowed by our shared experience – which was not shared equally. It never is.

We remain as a nation very much under the shadow of what went before, always waiting for the news to turn sour, for our liberty and freedom to once again be sacrificed in the trade-off for our lives. 2021 has been a sort of half-life of hope and fear metred out in equal portions, so that we all feel as if the outcome was a nil-nil draw.

I am struck by how well this is summed up by the portrait of John in this collection (p.34), a former scientist who helped create the contraceptive pill. As a feminist, the creation of the contraceptive pill speaks of freedom. For women its invention meant a different, more liberated future. In 2021 we have been reminded quite how much our freedom and liberty relies on people in clean white lab coats and goggles;

it has been a shot in the arm for many who have burst their blister packs without a second thought to who created the pills within. John the scientist was the future once. Yet in this image John sits in his home that is a time capsule of the kind of 1960s décor that used to be available in the local Woolworths, but is now traded as vintage one-offs in fancy boutiques. To me, this paradox of a scientist who screams freedom and future sat in the past is very 'Britain in 2021'.

This collection includes images of such hope for a return to the life that we once took for granted. Portraits of babies born into the captivity of the pandemic (p.88 and p.320) or the image of children playing with their long unseen friends in a garden in Gravesend, Kent (p.198), remind me of that feeling of breathing out when we could finally be unmasked and hold our people close. Back to normal. Lovely, comfy normal.

But a jarring contrast to this relief is never more than a few pages away: images of resistance and protest that slap in our face that normal isn't good enough. Normal meant that you were

more likely to die from Covid or face police brutality or inaction if you were Black or Asian (p.306). Normal meant that the pandemic only aided the existing epidemic of male violence against women and girls (p.308).
In 2021 Britons took to the streets and demanded the new. Going back cannot be enough; for many people being asked to be grateful for the basics made normal seem oppressive.

As a politician during this historic time, I have seen the pandemic used as an excuse for inaction and a tool to make the populous feel ungrateful for asking for anything other than a vaccine. We have been told to praise our rulers because of the things that they did right, and to cut them some slack for the things that have gone wrong – even if they were going wrong long before we could all name the different variants of concern. So much slack has been cut, the benefit of the doubt has been in oversupply.

The image of Dr Mavi (p.318) was taken in the Birmingham hospital that serves my people. I have mixed feelings about it because I have watched my family be fixed there and also said a final goodbye. I've felt grateful for good service and warmth at the same time as wanting to rant at length about waiting times or rubbish car-parking for my dying mother. Dr Mavi tells us how the pandemic stretched and challenged staff. The pressure is clear. And yet he says: 'Medical students were stepping up as doctors, consultants were working in different specialities and there was no sense of hierarchy. That completely went. And morale was so high.' Through the hell, working differently – breaching through what was considered normal – made it better.

Back to normal can never be enough, no matter how much we crave it when it's gone. The Britain in this book is one that makes me feel bold; these faces make me certain that we won't settle. We have all learnt a new resilience which I have no doubt will help us as the shadow shrinks and we ask for a new, better normal.

Jess Phillips MP, 2021

Portraits

AISHA
by Andrea Thomson
Edinburgh

Aisha and I met on Instagram, then met up
in real life to take some photos. She's a pretty
extraordinary woman. She is from Nigeria and
is studying Architecture at Edinburgh on a
full scholarship. She's also the first ever Black
woman elected Vice President Welfare of
Edinburgh University Students' Association
in its 438 years of existence.

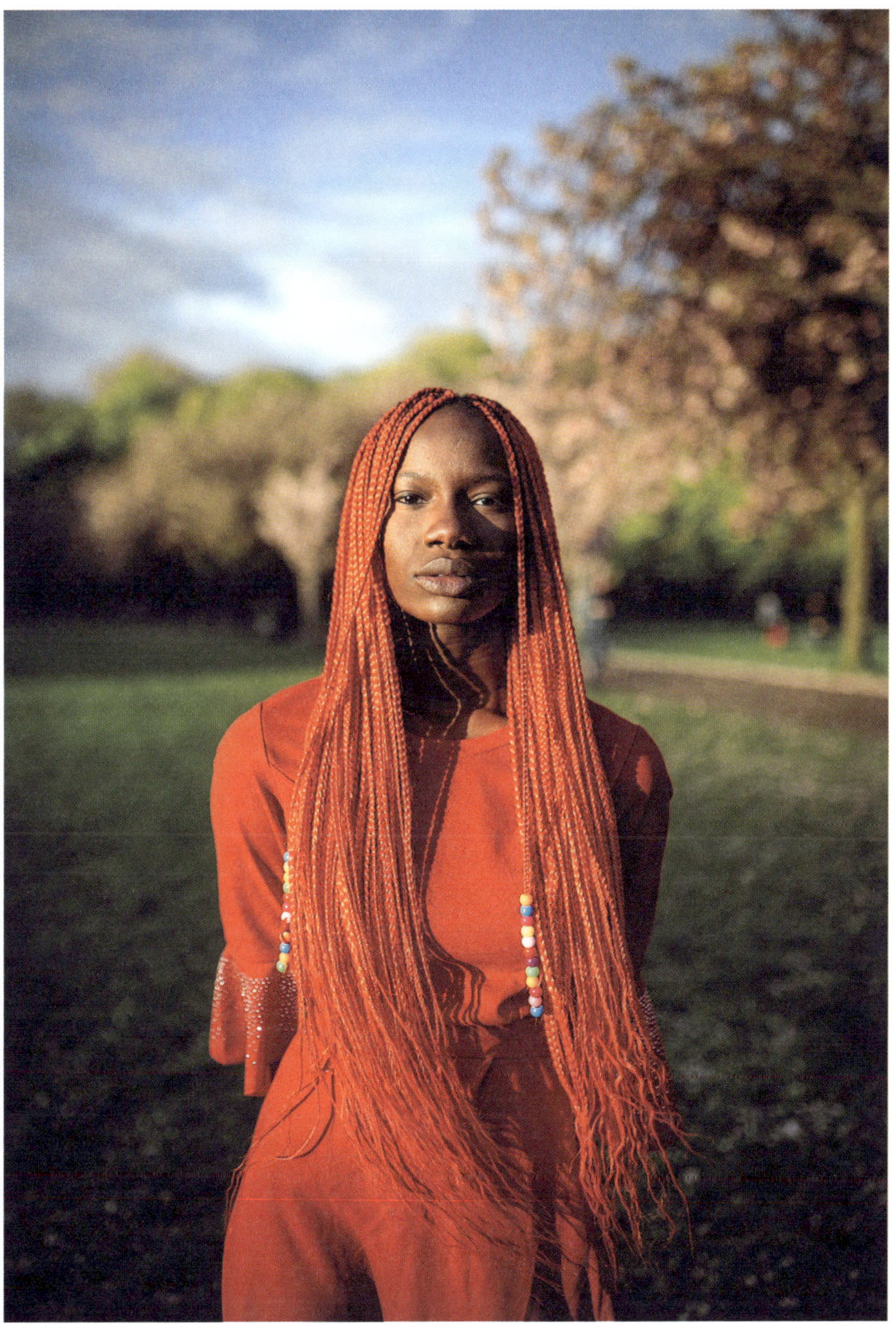

TOM
by Raphaël Neal
London

Tom is a young make-up artist living in Croydon.
I am making a series called 'New Waves' about
teenagers and the inevitable consequences
climate change will have on their mental and
physical health. In this portrait, I tried to
evoke the sweat, pleasure and underlying
worry of a UK heatwave.

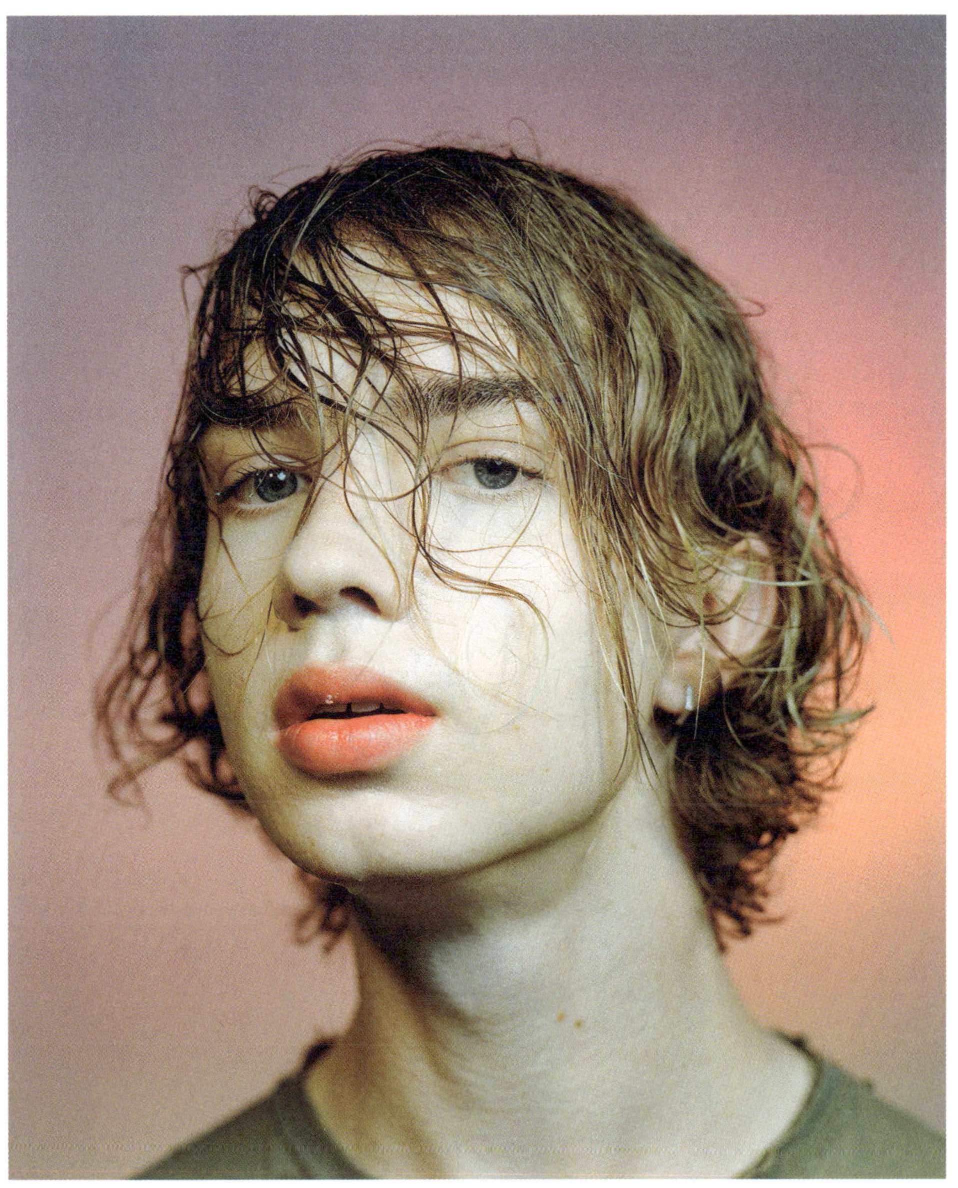

FREEDOM
by Celie Nigoumi
Frome, Somerset

Beth is an acting student at RADA. She is their first
student who uses a wheelchair, which has meant they
have had to look at different and inclusive ways
of offering a classical actor's training. I wanted to
photograph Beth in nature as, having myself
grown up being a carer for a disabled parent,
I've seen how enjoying nature is a luxury that
disabled people are often excluded from
by lack of accessibility.

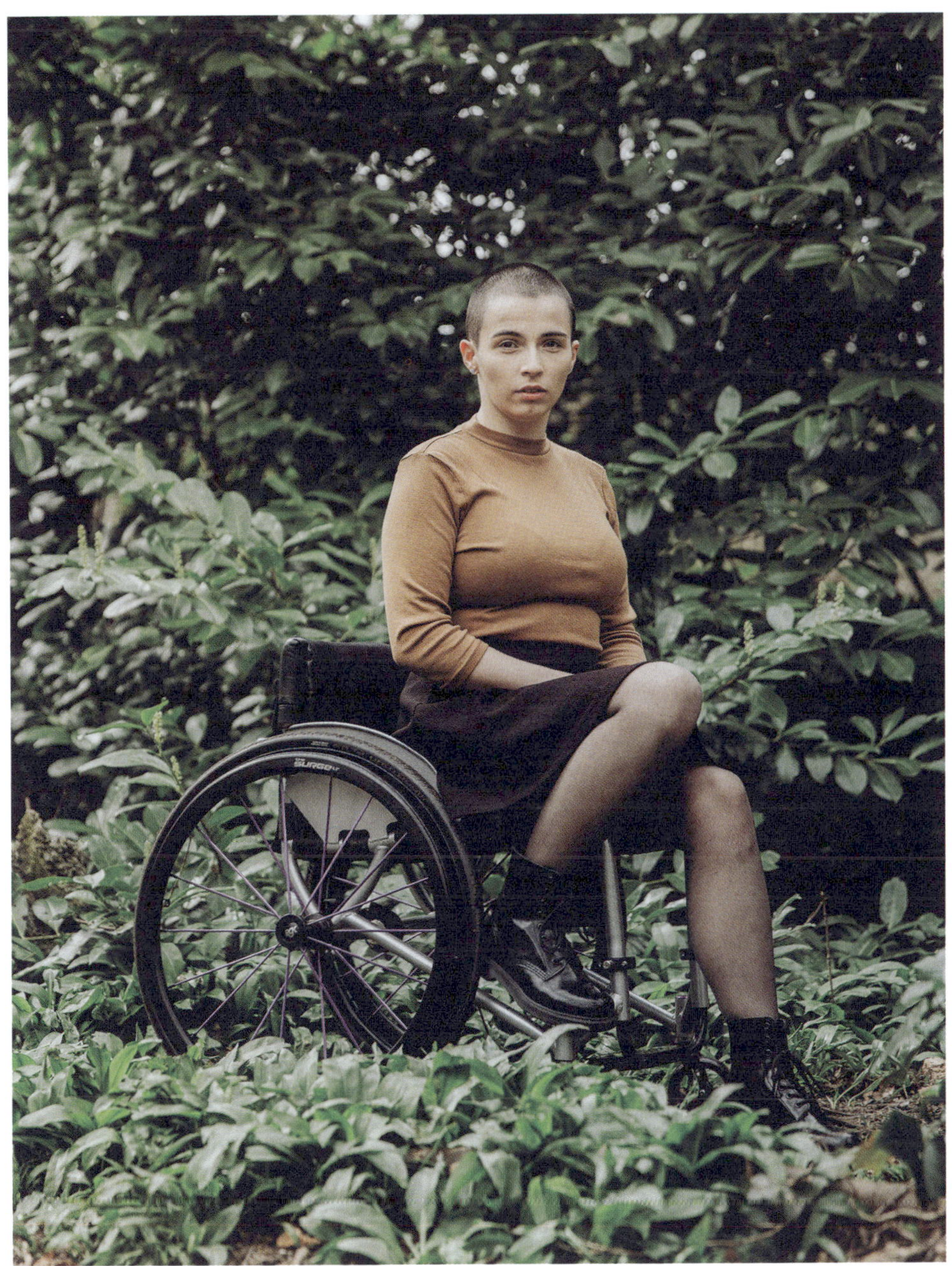

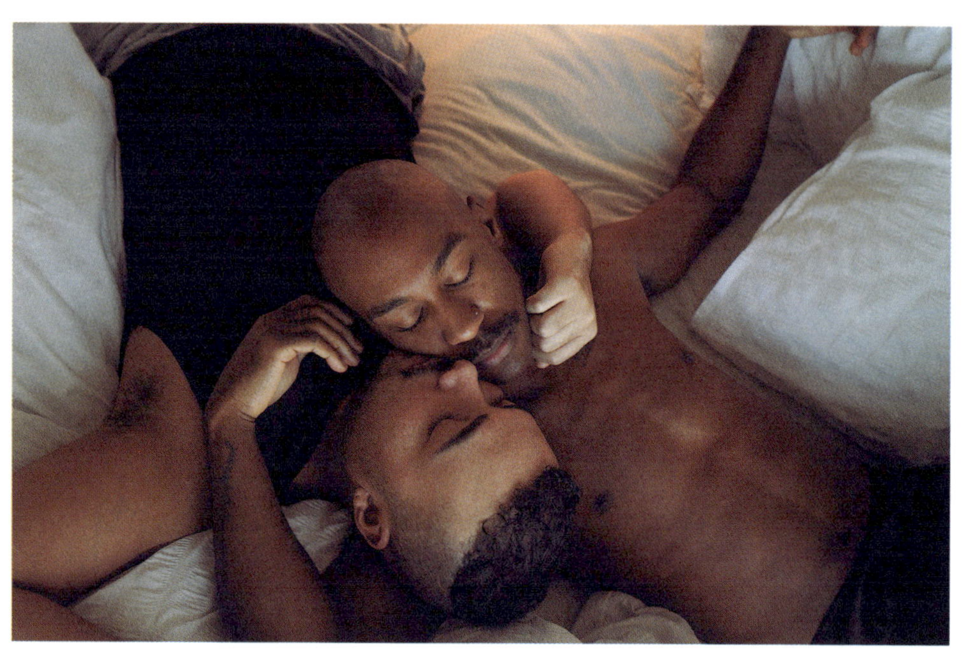

INTIMACY
by Ryan Edy
London

I took this photo of Joshua and Dale during
lockdown. I wanted to capture a moment of true
intimacy between them on camera. Intimacy is normally
something we just 'feel', so in pictures it can look forced
and contrived from not being authentic. To portray the
couple being truly themselves I spent as much time
as possible with them in their home, until they'd
almost forgotten I was there.

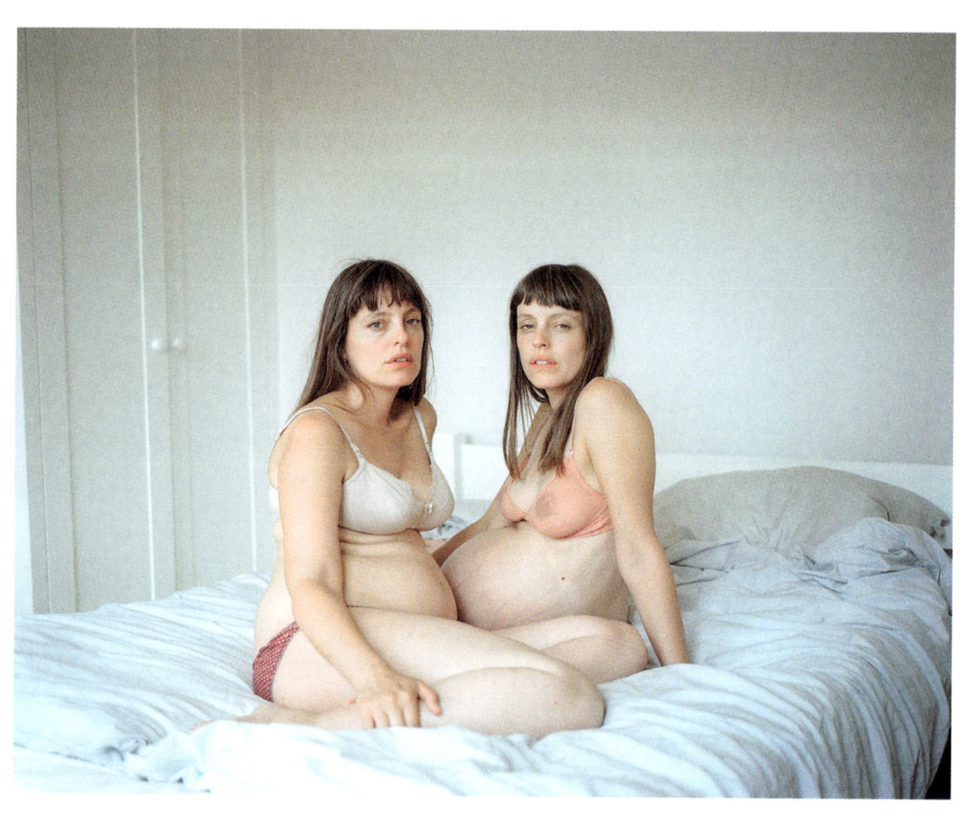

TWINS EXPECTING
by Imogen Freeland
London

Photographing these twin sisters, Tessa and Melanie,
while they were both pregnant at the same time felt like
capturing a piece of magic – their individual journeys
to motherhood both completely unique and
yet miraculously in sync.

MAYSA
by Christopher James Owens
Kingston upon Hull, East Yorkshire

'I never had a hobby before other than reading
but during lockdown my mum took me and my sisters
to the park to watch the grown-up kids skating.
When we got home, we looked up female skaters and
there weren't many and not ones that looked like us.
My mum says never judge a book by its cover,
some people would look at us and think we can't
skate, but we can. We are talented, Muslim,
British and proud.' – Maysa

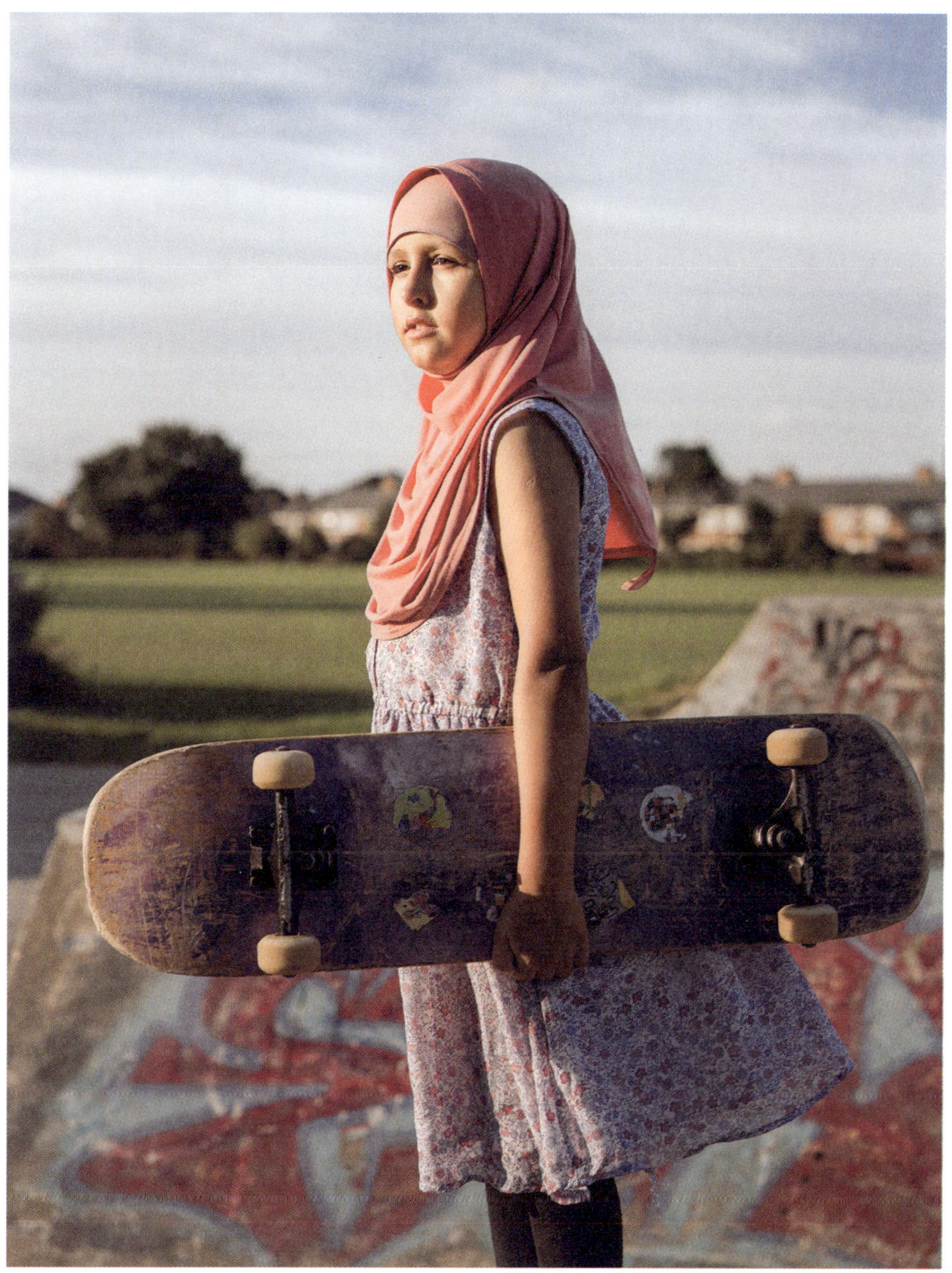

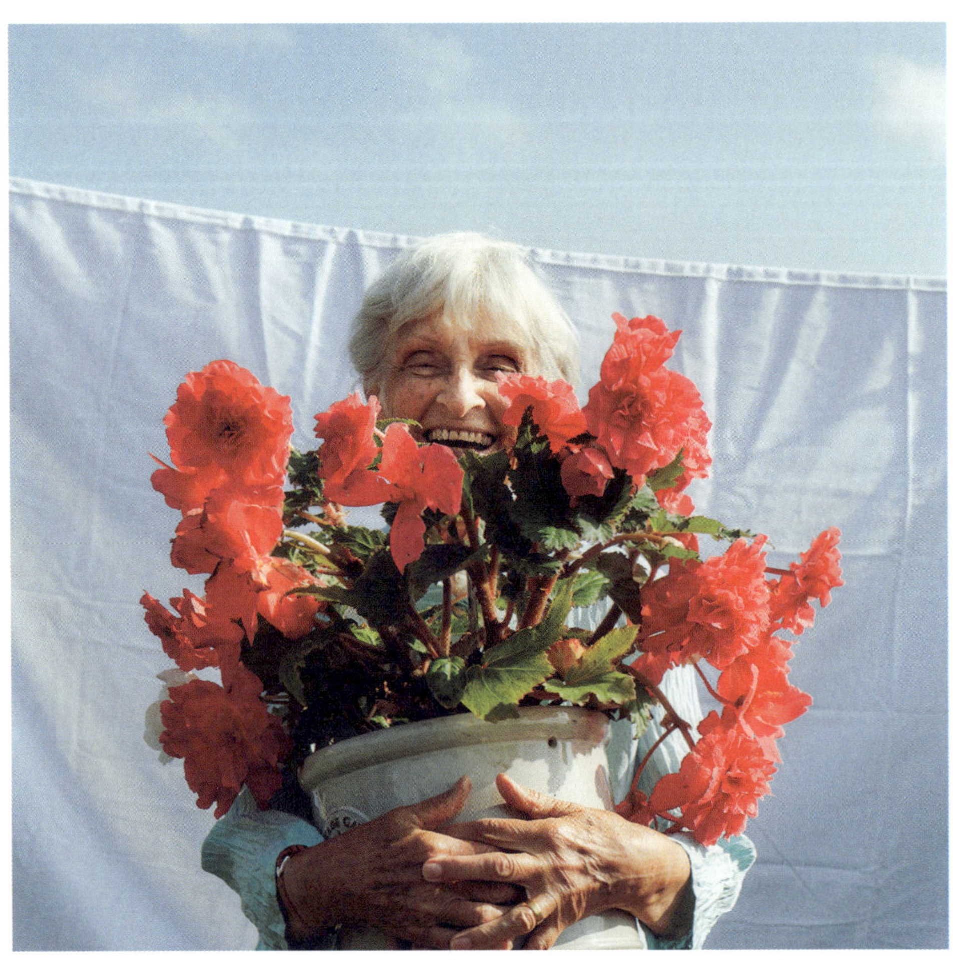

GRANDMA JACKY
by Caitlin Chescoe
Twyning, Gloucestershire

The day I took this photo was the first time my
sister and I had seen our grandma in nine months
because of the Covid-19 lockdowns. It was
a moment we had all been dreaming of.

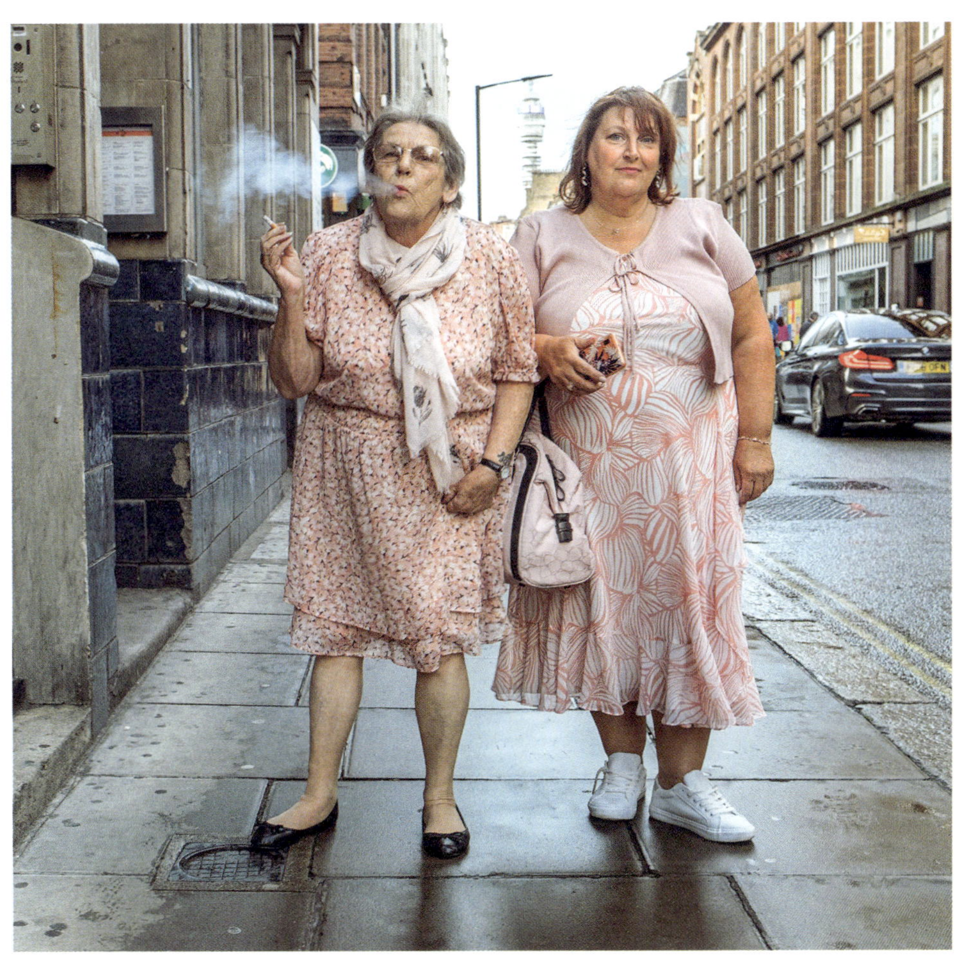

JULIE AND BRENDA
by Steve Reeves
London

Julie and her mum Brenda live in Barrow, but were
taking a weekend break in London together. They told
me that now lockdown has ended, they intend to
have some fun and try new things.

AT HOME WITH SAMUEL
by Francis Augusto
London

This is my little brother, Samuel, who is 12 years old.
During the first lockdown, I decided to pick up my
camera again and I asked Sam if he would be
up for being photographed. He was a little nervous
at first, but eventually got into it.

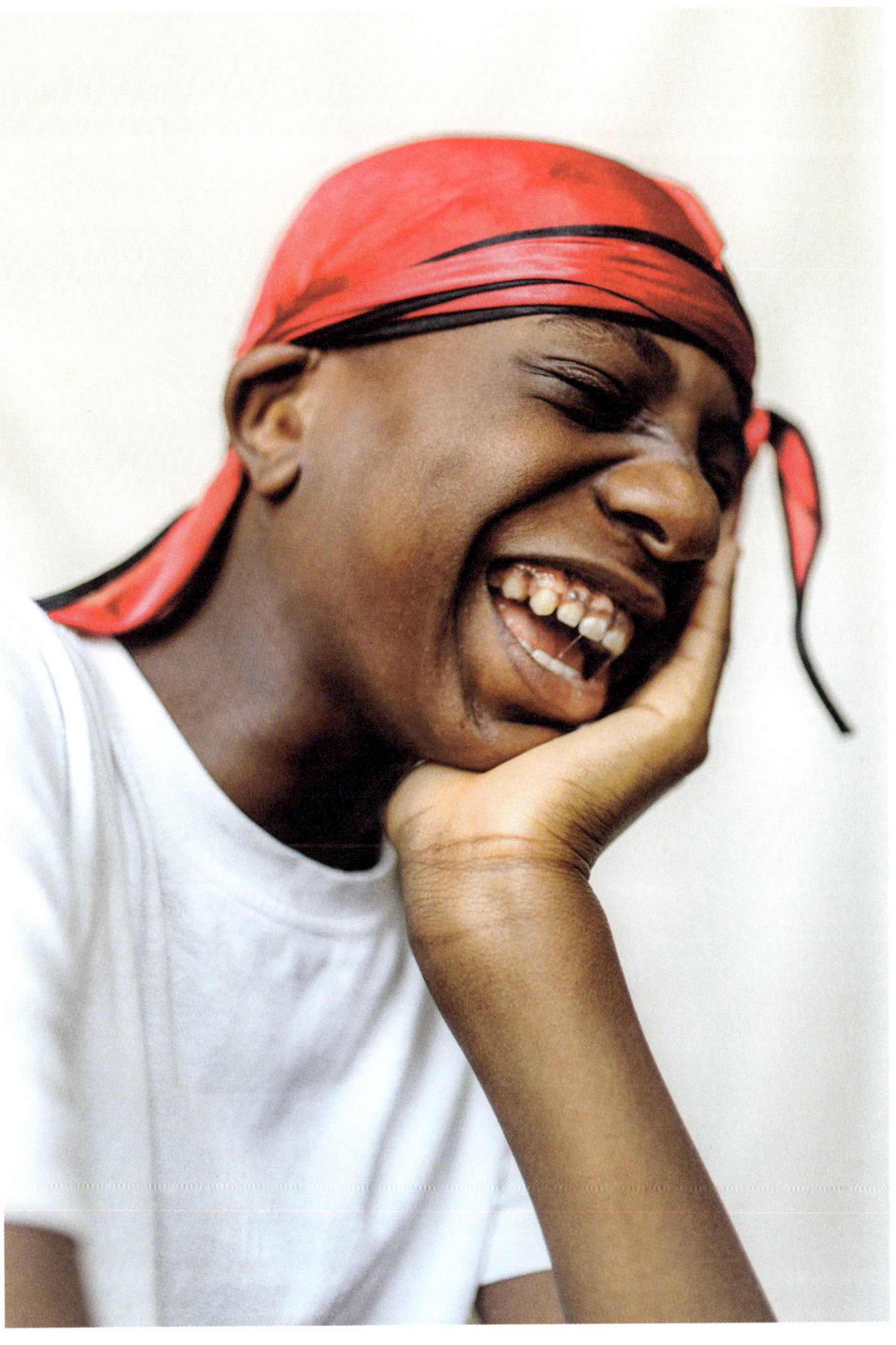

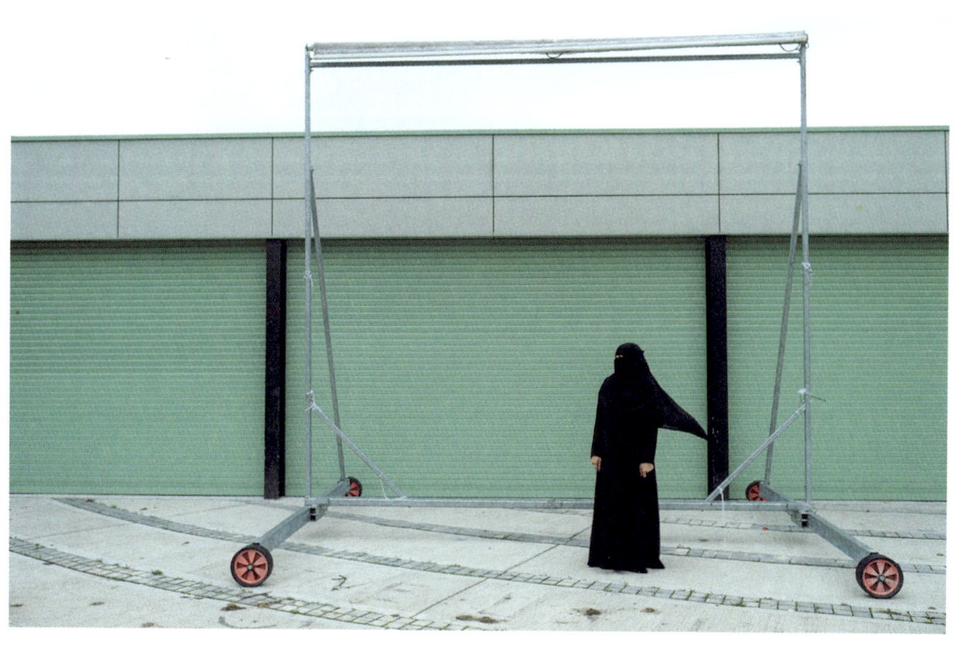

GEOMETRY
by Robert Huggins
London

I saw the mother in this photo at Hackney Marshes,
she was taking her son to football. As she walked in front
of the cricket pavilion, I was struck by the geometric
composition of the scene and started to frame this image
in my head. After a quick chat about photography,
she agreed to let me take it.

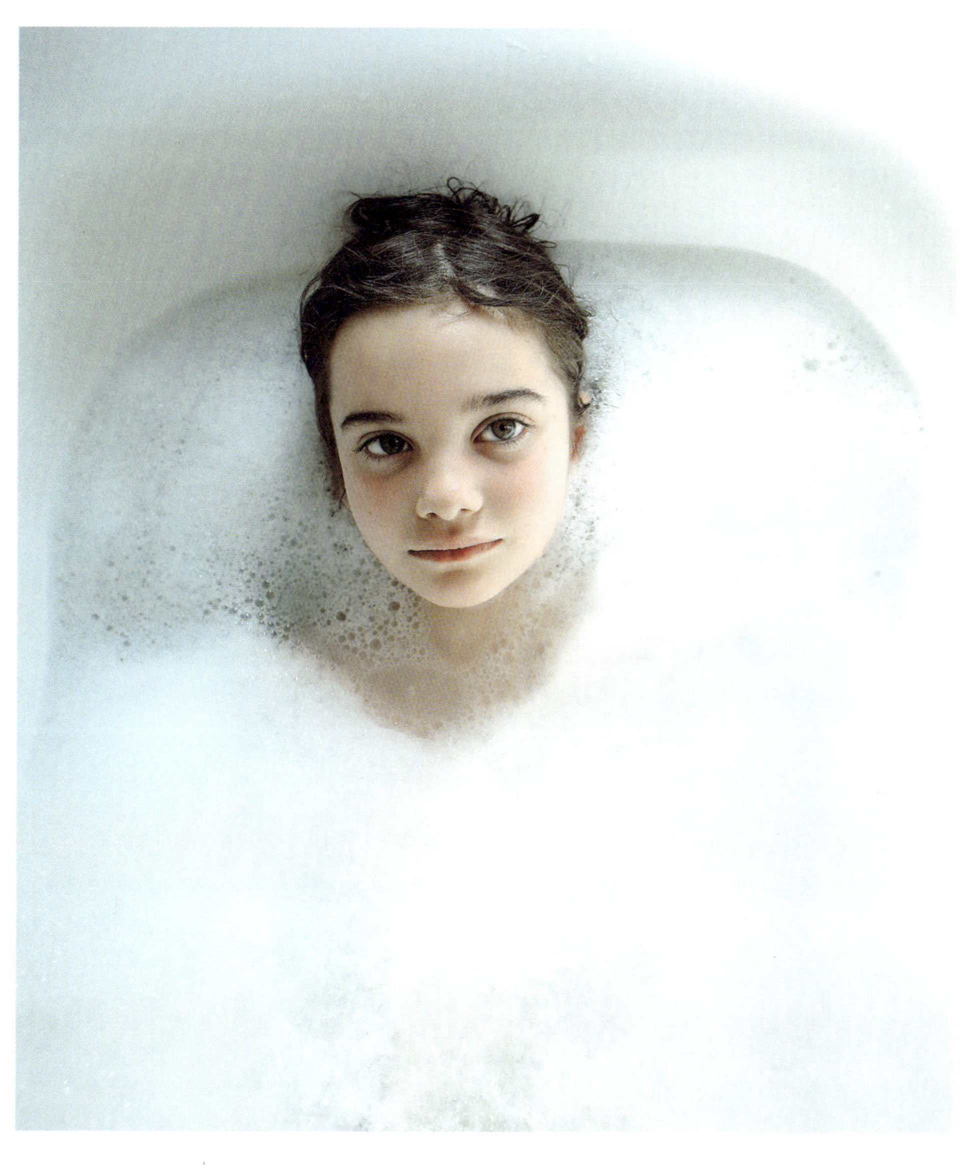

A POCKET OF CALM
by Natalia Zapala-Movshovitz
London

THE LONGING TO START SCHOOL
by Mauro Arena
London

I took this photo of my daughter Matilde during
the first lockdown. Matilde's behaviour was changing,
she was showing signs of stress and frustration at not
being able to leave home to play with her friends.
I wanted to portray her in her school uniform as
a way of capturing our hope for a swift
return to school and normal life.

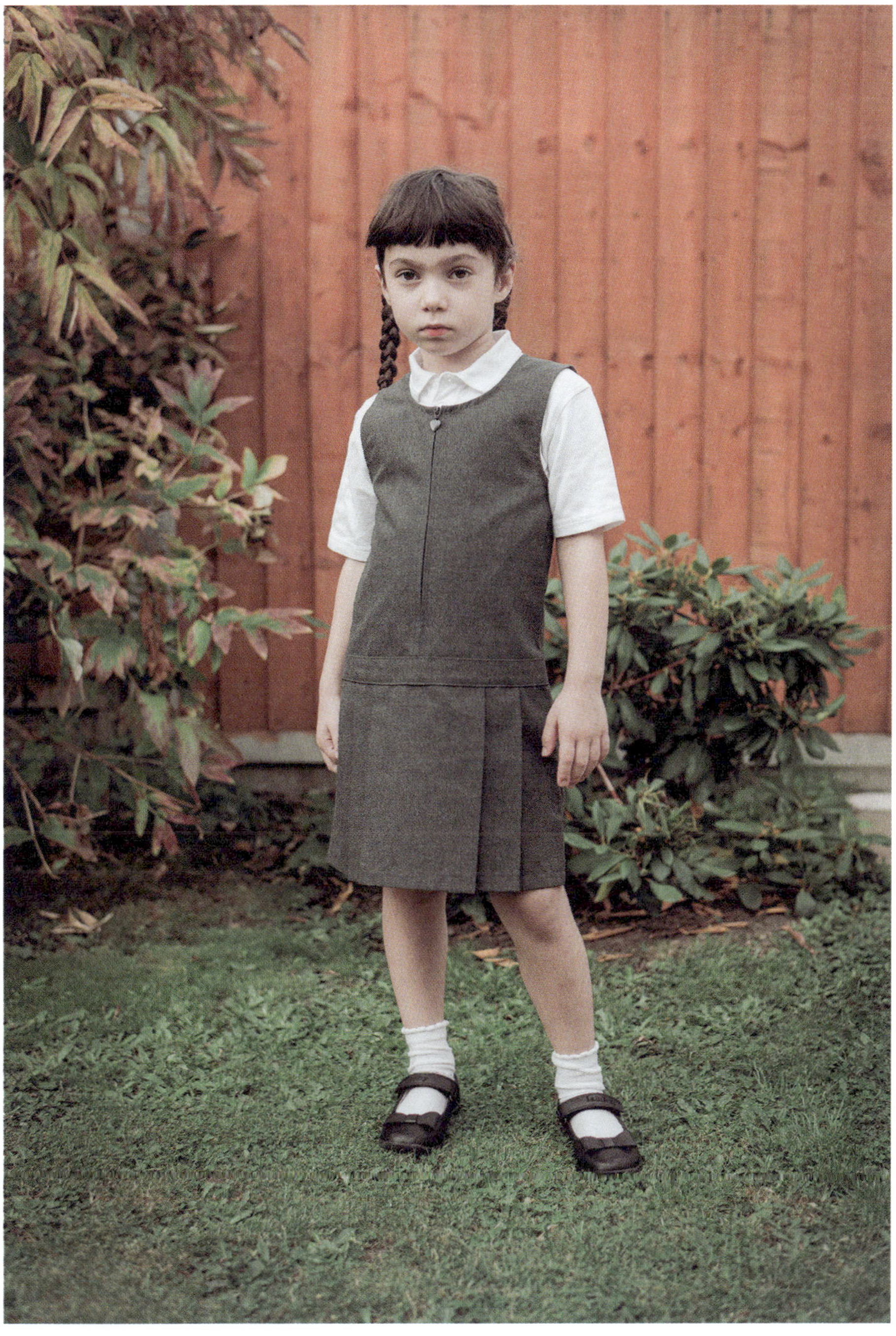

FISHMONGERS OF PORTOBELLO
by Charlotte Cullen
Edinburgh

During the third lockdown in January, I was
walking past my local fishmonger in Portobello when
I asked if I could take this photo. The streets around
felt empty, but James (*right*) and his colleagues were
still going to work, putting themselves at risk
to provide for others.

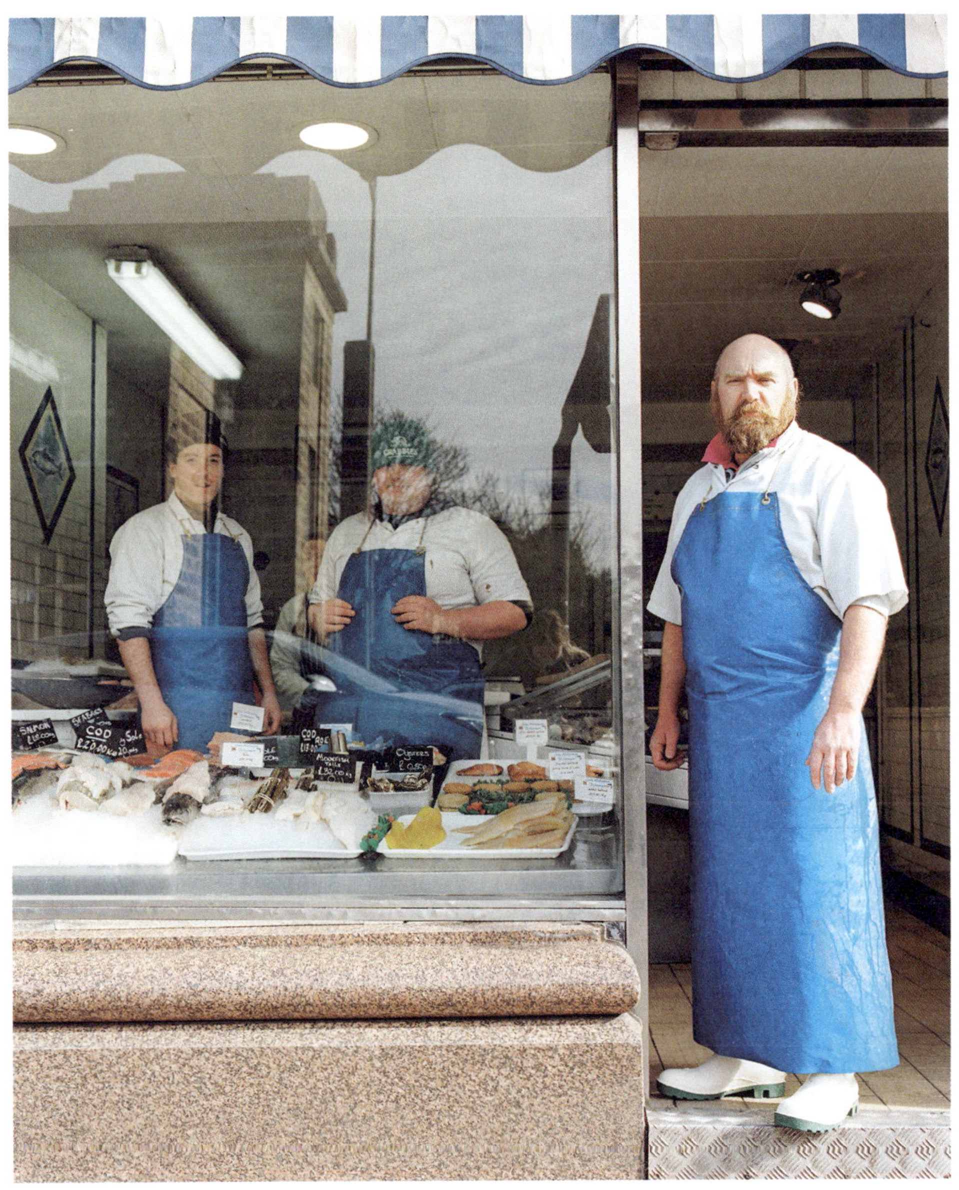

JAVARN
by Ellie Laycock
London

Javarn is part of the St Matthew's Project
Under 10s football team. The project started as
a regular kickabout on a Brixton estate in 2004,
and now offers trips, training and support to over
200 young people in Lambeth every week. I wanted
to take portraits of the Under 10s team in the
style of their footballing heroes, the kind you would
see on FIFA cards or in high-end sports brand
advertising, as I knew they would enjoy
seeing themselves that way.

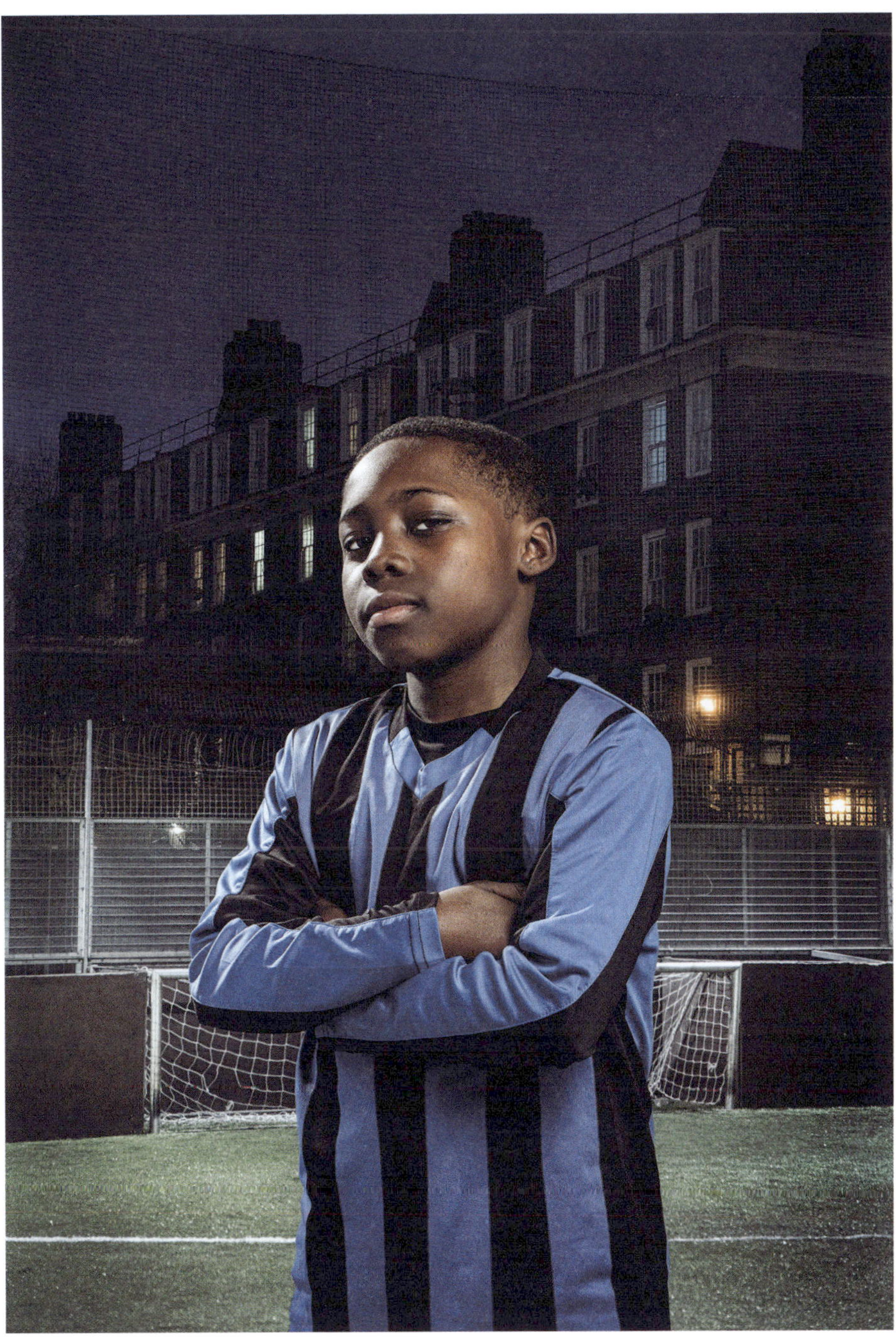

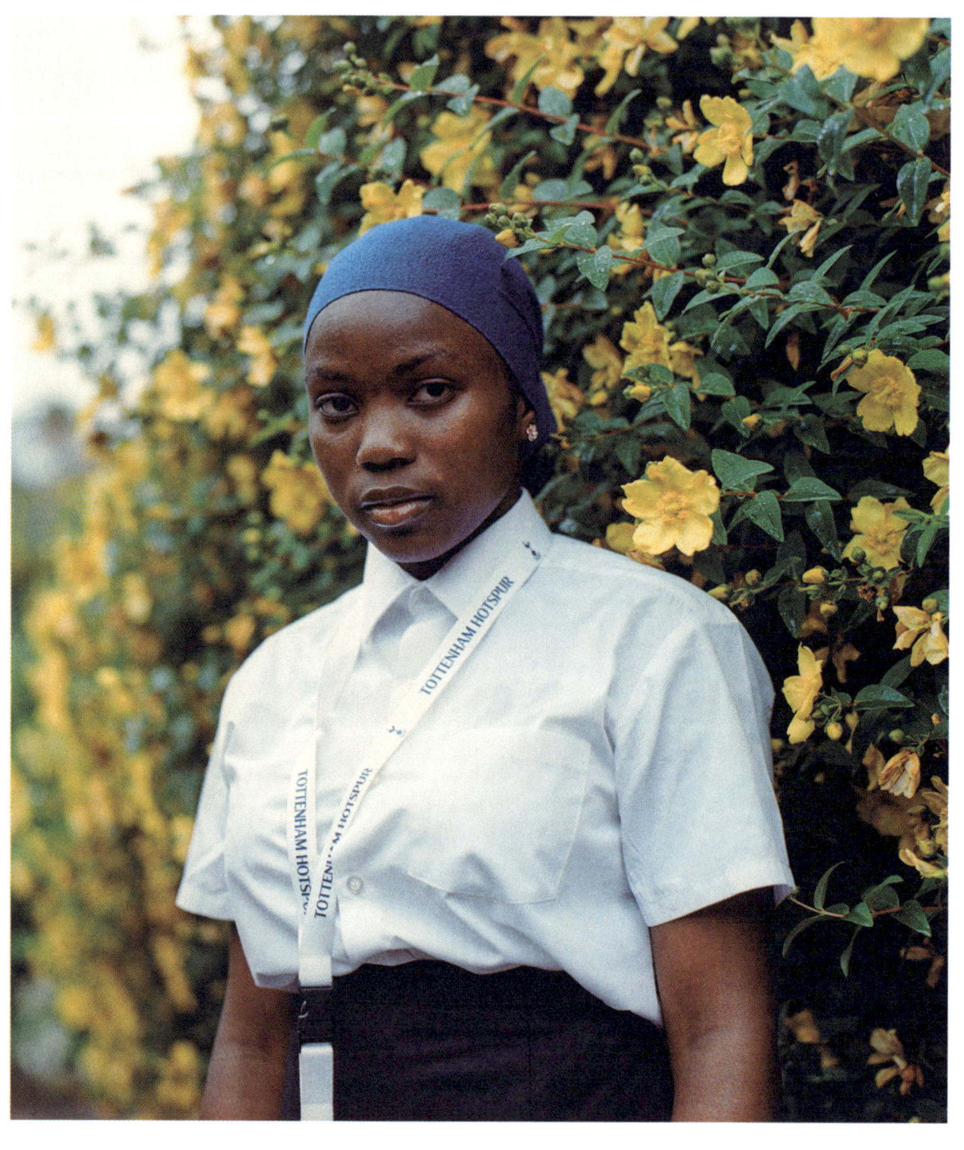

SALMA
by Ross Cooke
Manchester

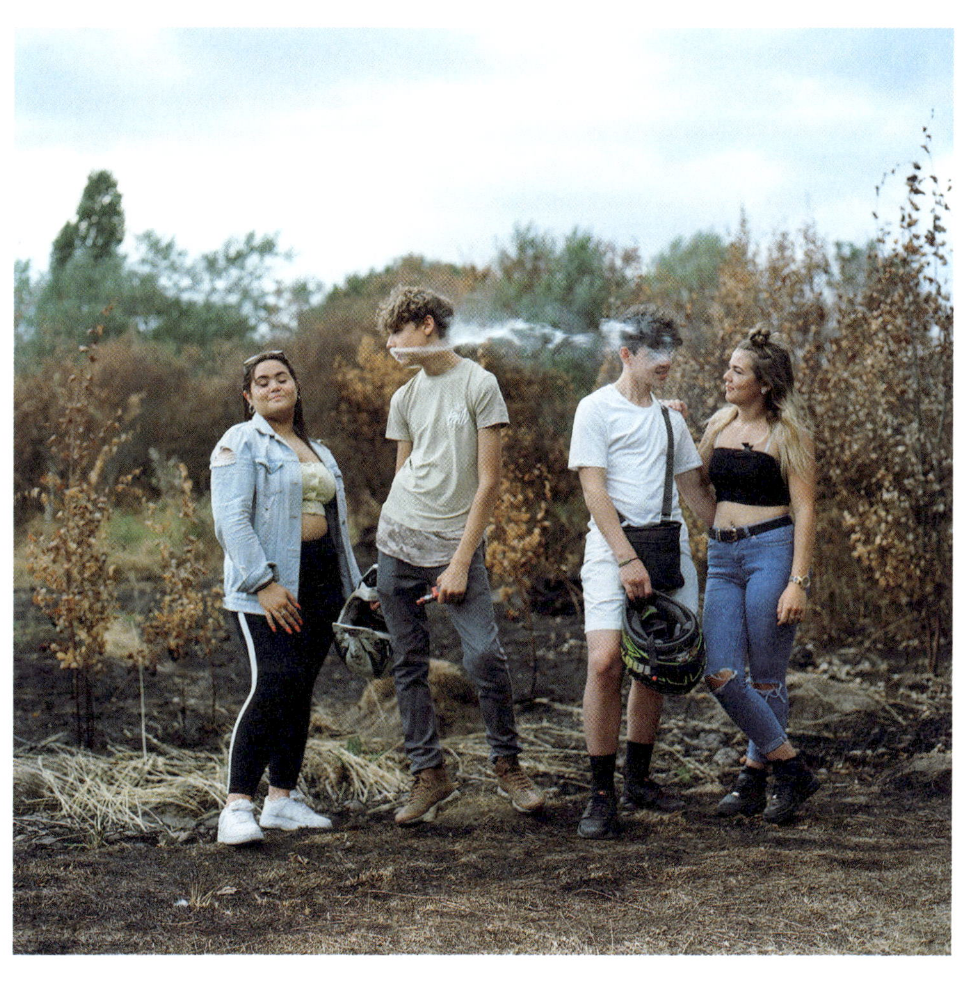

FERN, CALLUM, ASH AND SOPHIE
by Laura Pannack
Tipton, West Midlands

JOHN IN HIS LIVING ROOM
by Hannah Maule-ffinch
London

John is a former scientist who helped create
the contraceptive pill. I was using John's home
for a commercial shoot (he hasn't changed the décor
in many, many years) and he allowed me to
take his portrait before we started.

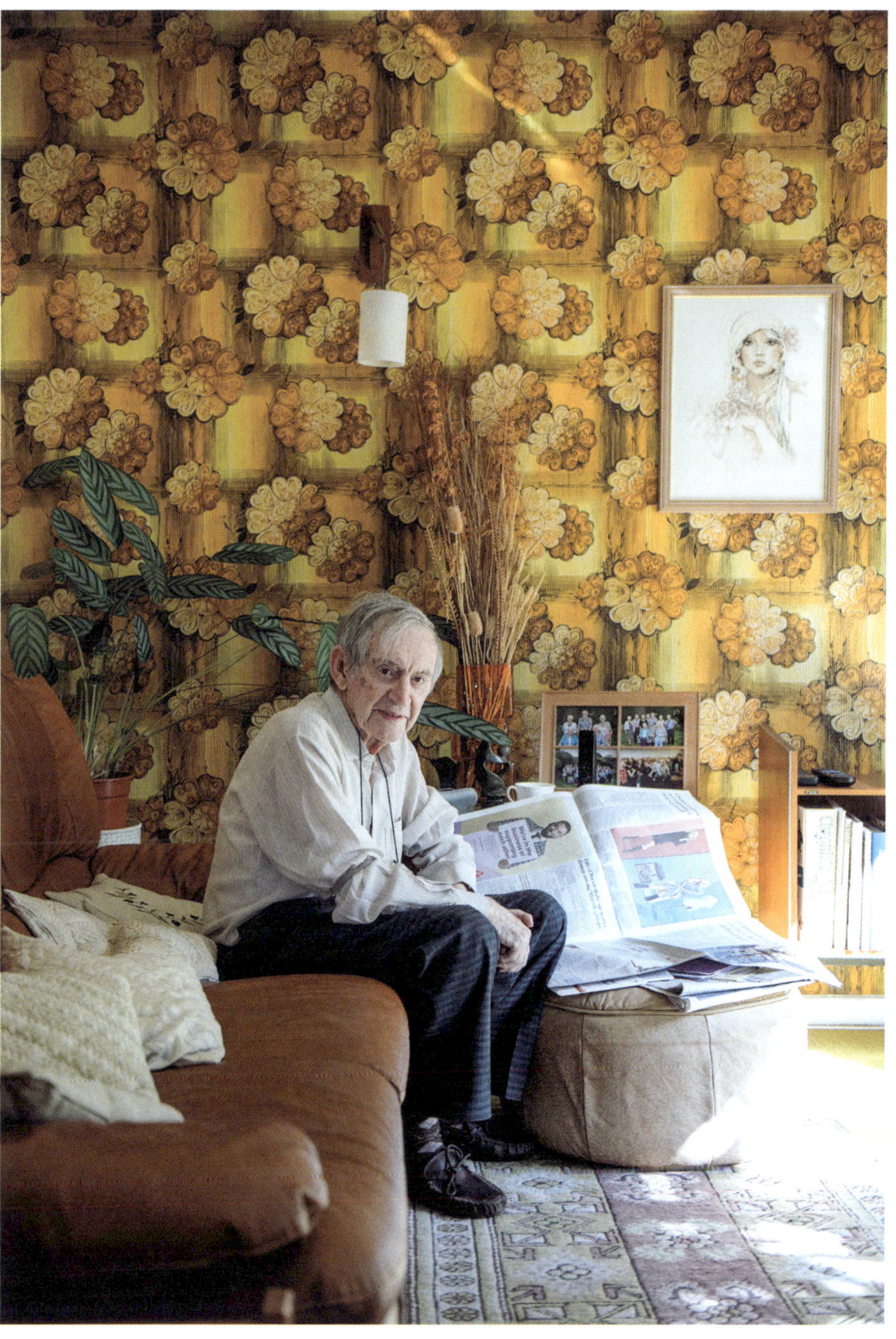

JESSICA AND THE GOWER
by Marksteen Adamson
Gower Peninsula, Swansea

I took a group of young adults down to the
Gower Peninsula in Wales to escape inner-city
distractions, explore nature and learn to swim.
Jessica, who lives in Hackney, has been a young carer
since childhood and is now also an ambassador for
Action For Children. This trip to the sea was
a chance to reflect and renew confidence.

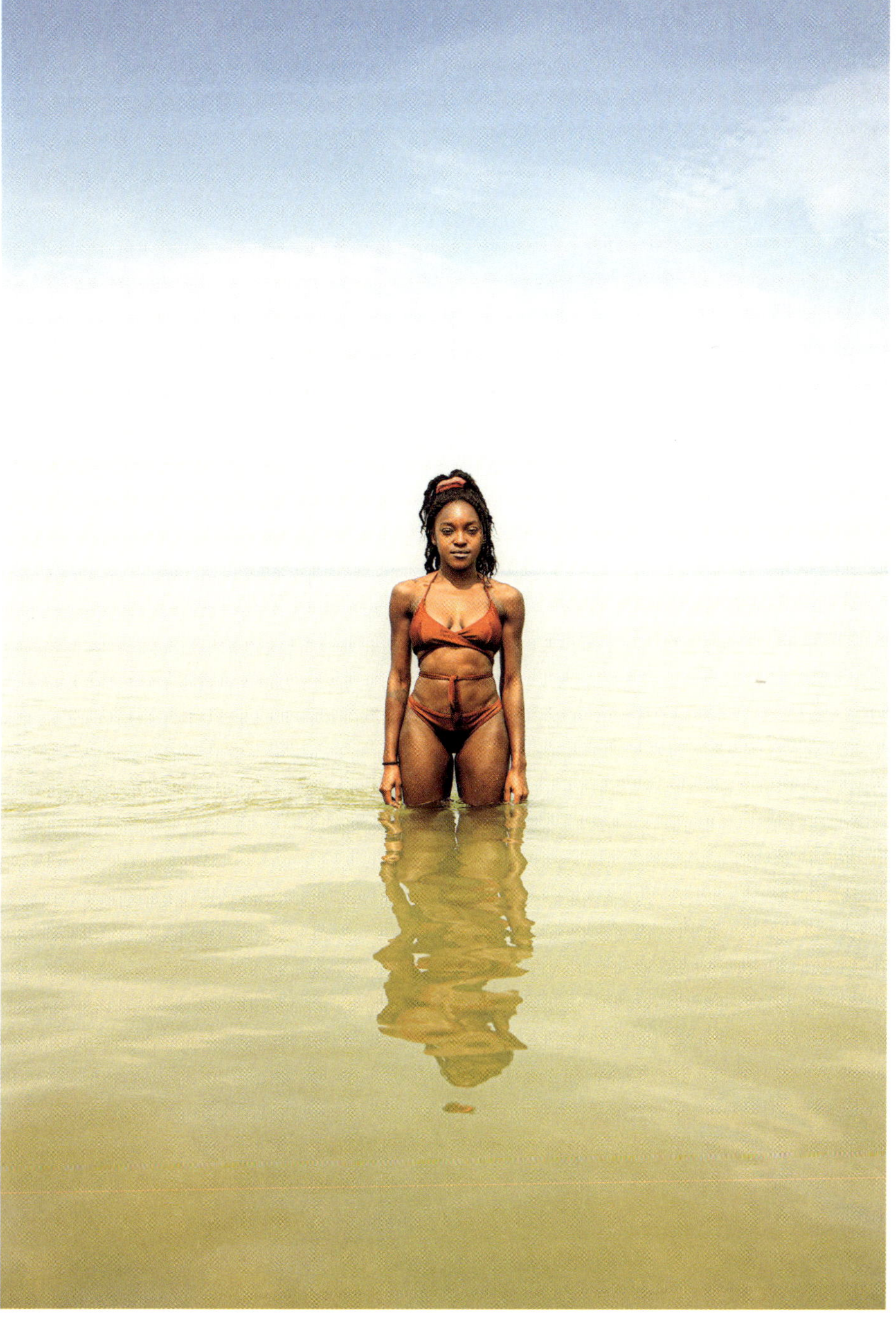

LONDON'S BEST DRESSED MAN
by Robin Sinha
London

This is Jama Elmi, I took his portrait after
encountering him by chance in Leicester Square –
his vibrant attire immediately caught my eye.
After posing for this photo, he wished me good day
and told me to Google 'London's Best Dressed Man'.
That evening, I did, and guess who I saw.
I learnt that Jama is a support worker in Acton
who tries to bring joy to his patients through
his flamboyant wardrobe.

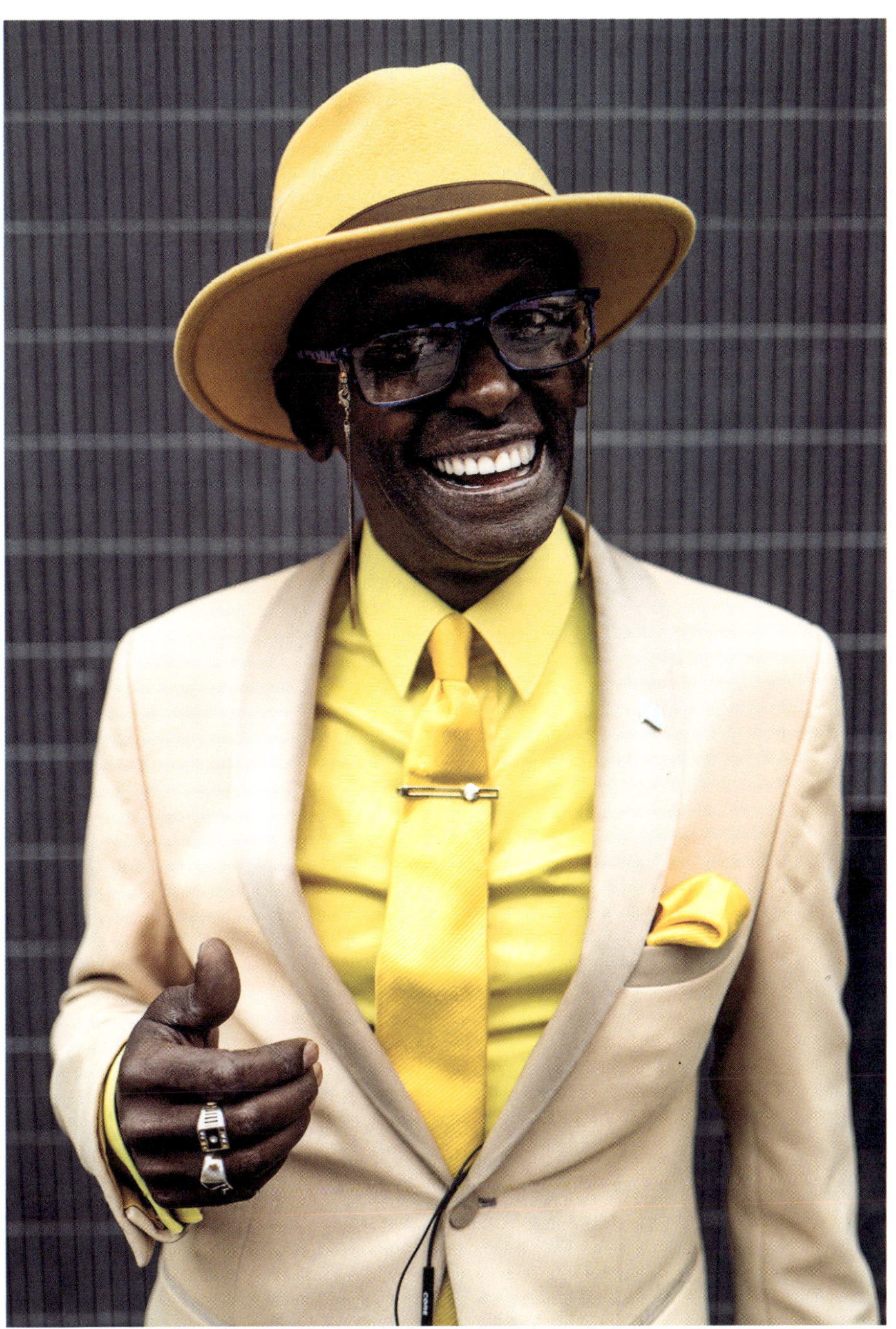

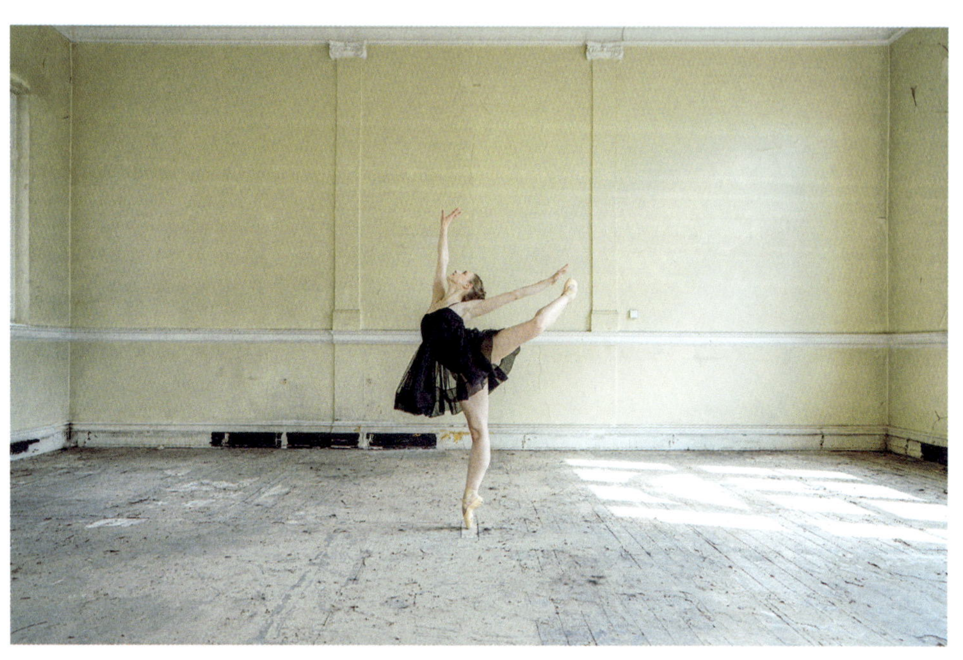

NATASCHA MAIR
by Rory Rae
London

My friend Natascha Mair is a principal ballerina
in the English National Ballet. Natascha and I had just
finished creating a video of her dancing at the now derelict
Fulham Town Hall and I took the opportunity to make
this portrait. I liked the contrast of the faded grandeur
of the assembly hall with her elegant pose.

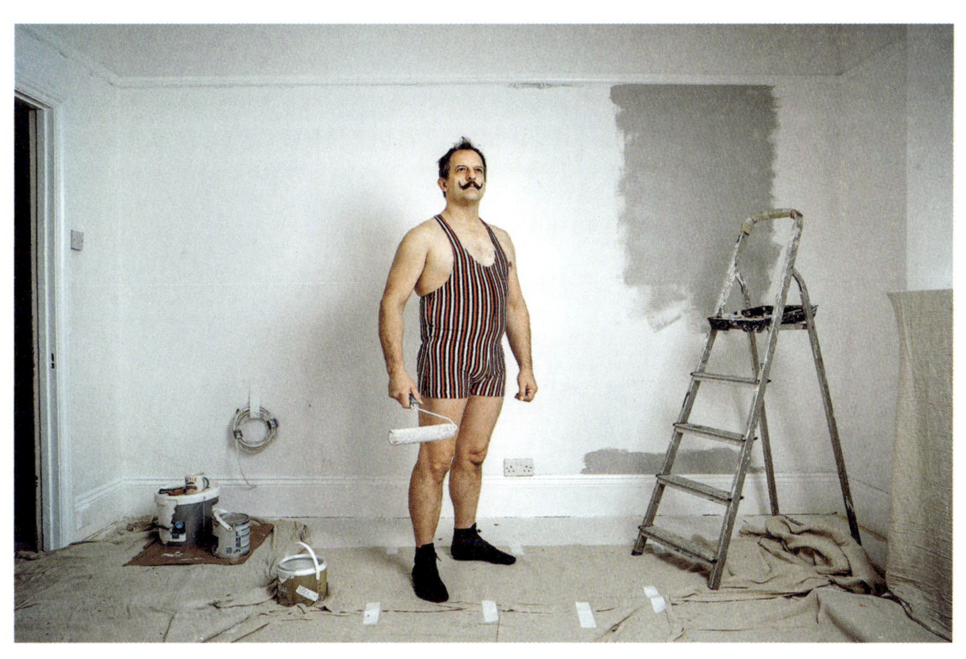

DAVID – ALL DRESSED UP AND
NOWHERE TO GO
by Joe Short
Bristol

David Downie is an acrobat who, having lost his audience
during lockdown, started renovating houses instead:
'With my acrobatics it's entirely spontaneous, so without
the audience's interaction there is no show. Everybody
has been fixing up their homes so I was able to find work
painting and decorating. It's kept the money coming in,
but I've desperately missed performing.'

EMBRACE YOUR THIRTIES
by Celie Nigoumi
Frome, Somerset

Here, Samie is celebrating her 38th birthday.
Not a common milestone, or one that women are
supposed to be particularly joyful about, but
Samie embraces ageing every year.

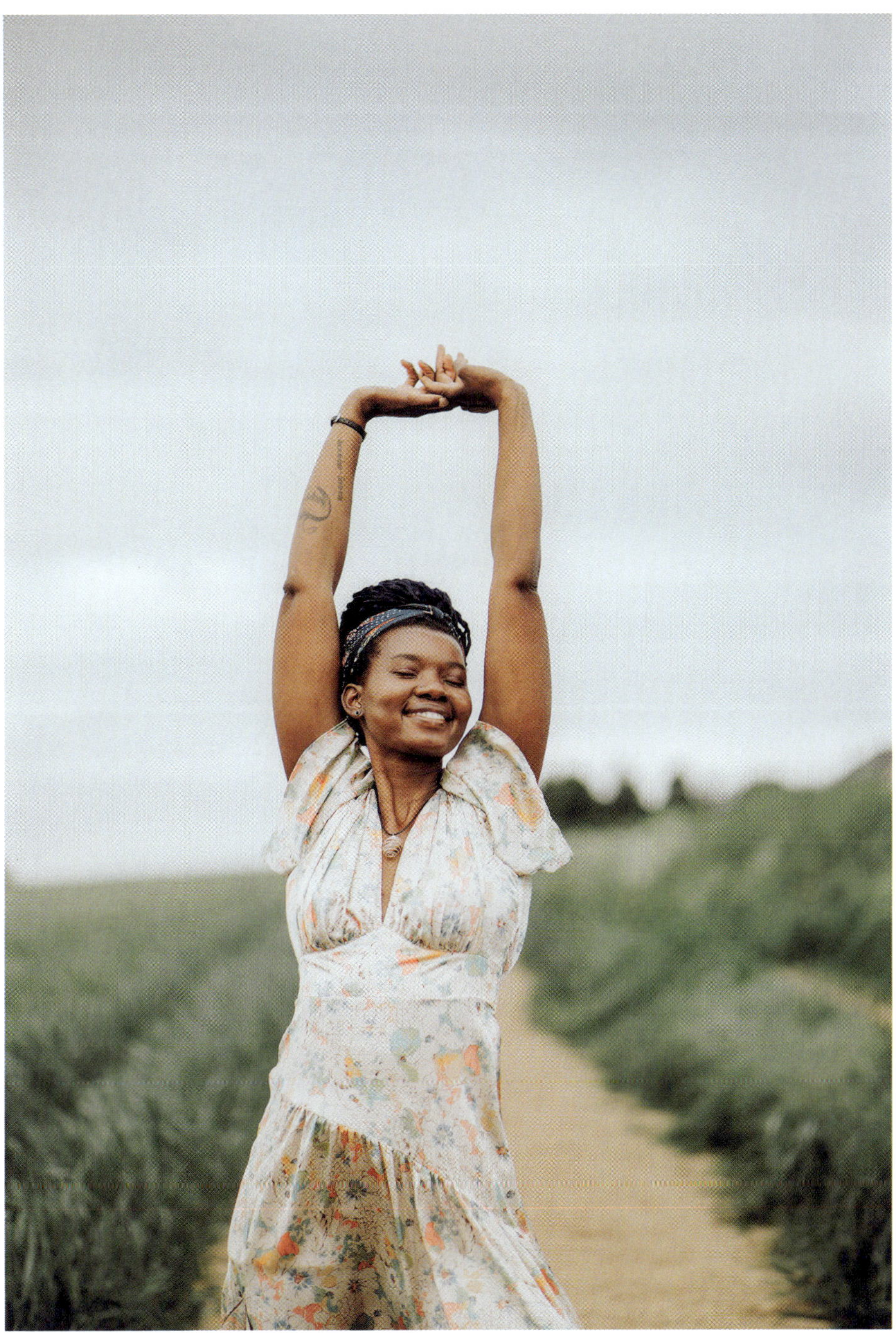

MAUDE STYLED BY MAUDE
by Imogen Freeland
Cambridge

This image is part of a series I made with my
nine-year-old niece, Maude, while we spent lockdown
at her grandparents' house. The idea for the series
was that she could style herself (with a little help
from me) using whatever clothing and objects
she found around the house. Each time we made a
photo, Maude experimented with a new persona.

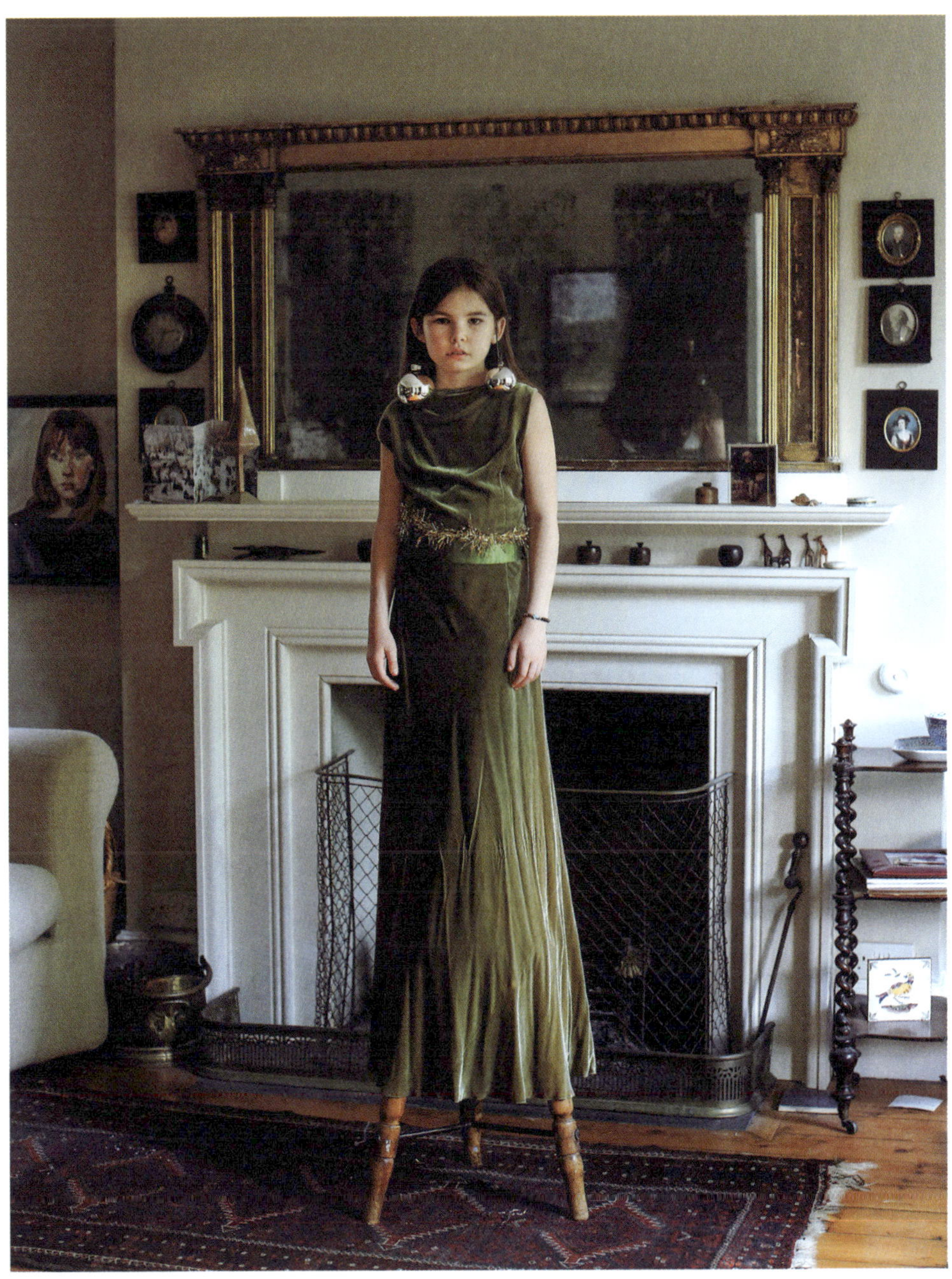

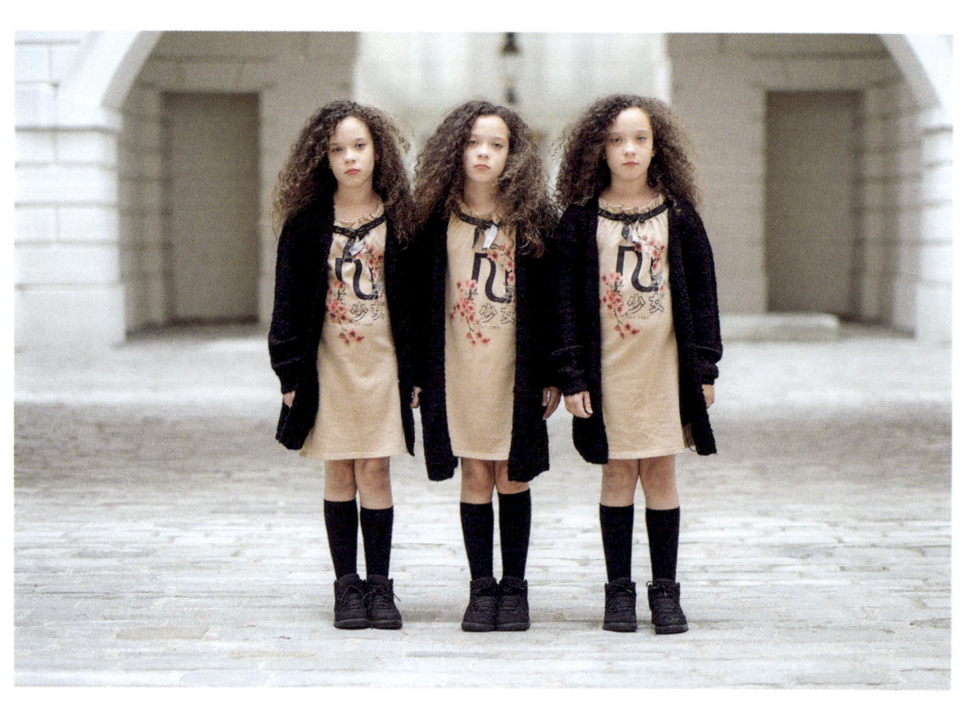

FRANKIE P, BILLIE P AND ASHLEE P
by Peter Zelewski
London

Frankie, Billie, and Ashlee are 10-year-old identical triplets.
Identical triplets are extremely rare, occurring in only
one in 200 million births. These triplets are so identical
that even their own mother sometimes can't tell them apart.

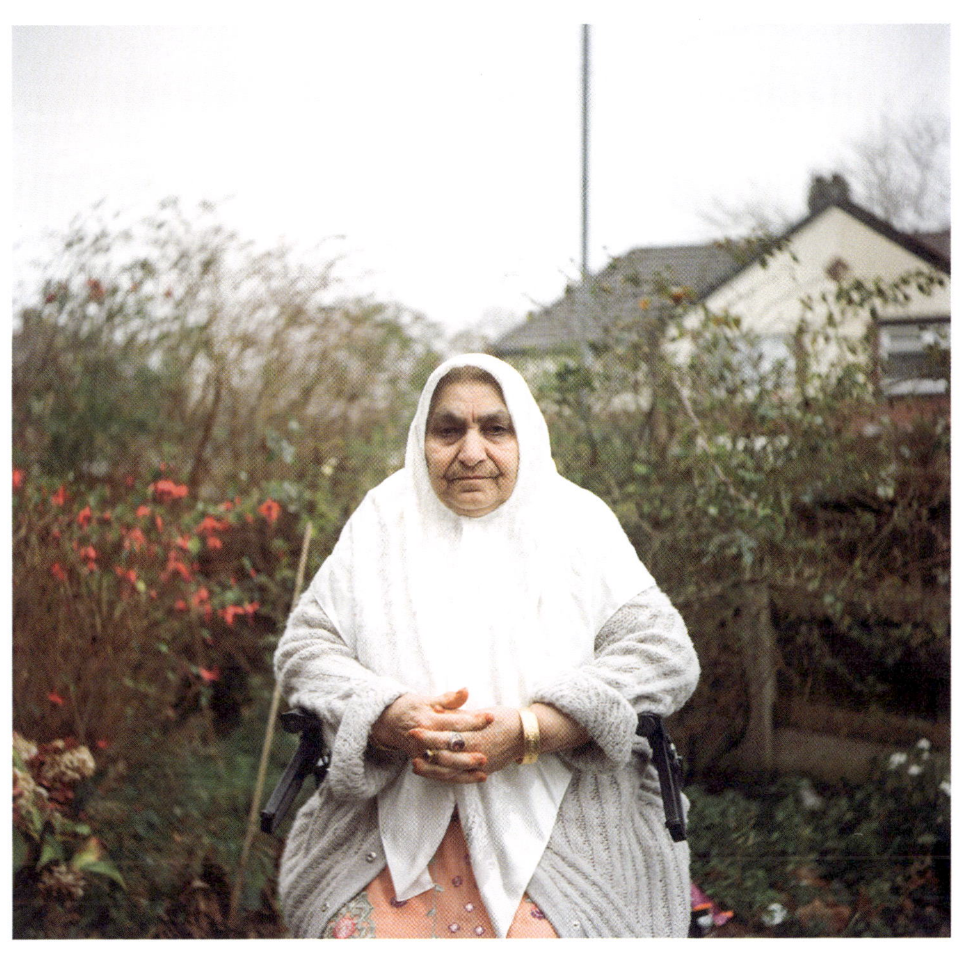

PORTRAIT OF HALIMA JABEEN
IN HER FRONT GARDEN
by Maryam Wahid
Ashton-under-Lyne, Greater Manchester

I was commissioned to photograph Halima for
The Tape Letters, a project capturing the stories
of people who used cassette tapes to send messages to
their loved ones in Pakistan in the late 70s and 80s.

GLENDA IN THE MIST
by Charlie Clift
London

I had gone to take a portrait of the actor
Glenda Jackson for BAFTA. I arrived early, and
found there was an unusual mist hanging over
Blackheath. I was worried that if I waited until
the agreed time, we'd miss this opportunity to shoot
against this ethereal landscape so I knocked
on Glenda's door. Five minutes later she walked
out, wearing the most splendid red coat.

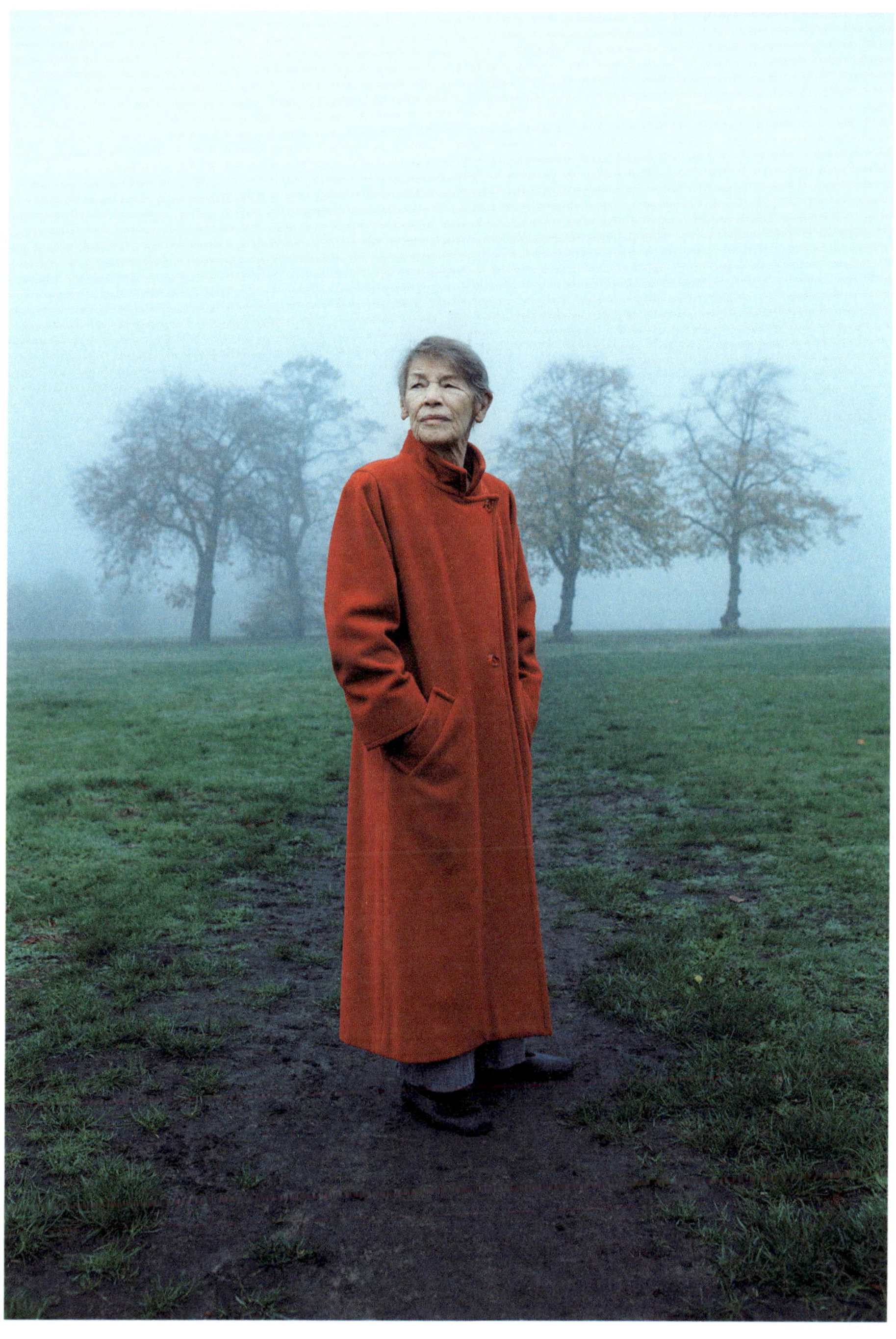

SAM AND GARY, PROUD LIONS
by Ali Wright
London

I took this photo of partners Sam and Gary a
few hours before the kick-off of the Euro 2020 final.
Together they founded Charlton Invicta, Europe's
first LGBTQ+ football team to be affiliated with a
professional club (Charlton Athletic). 'Everything we
do is to create a safe, welcoming and inclusive space
for LGBTQ+ people in football.' – Sam (*left*)

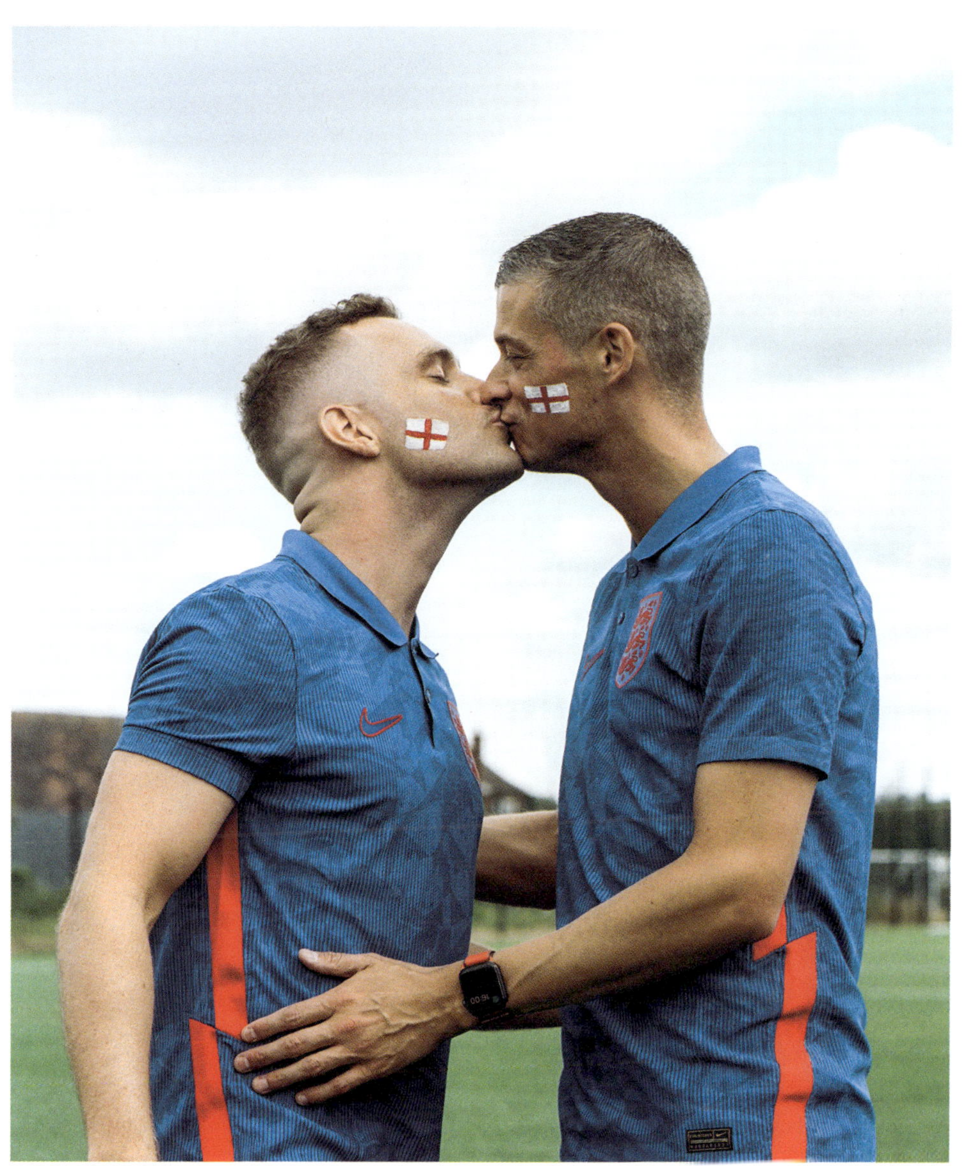

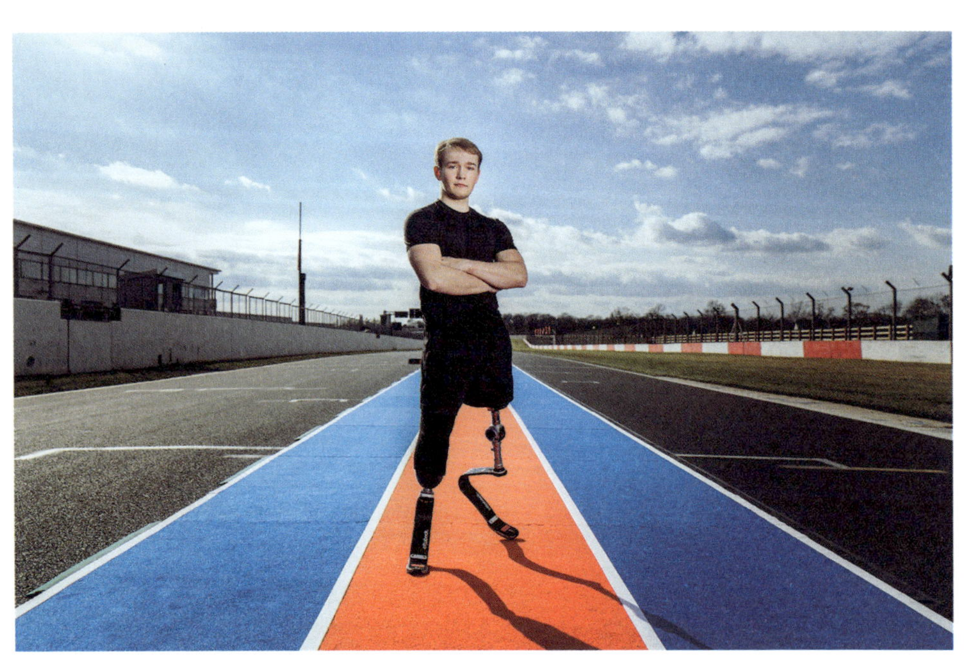

UNTITLED
by Patch Dolan
Donington Park, Leicestershire

Four years to the day since Billy Monger (*pictured*) lost his
legs during an F4 race at Donington Park, he returned to
the track to learn how to run on blades – with the help of
double Paralympic sprint champion, Jonnie Peacock.

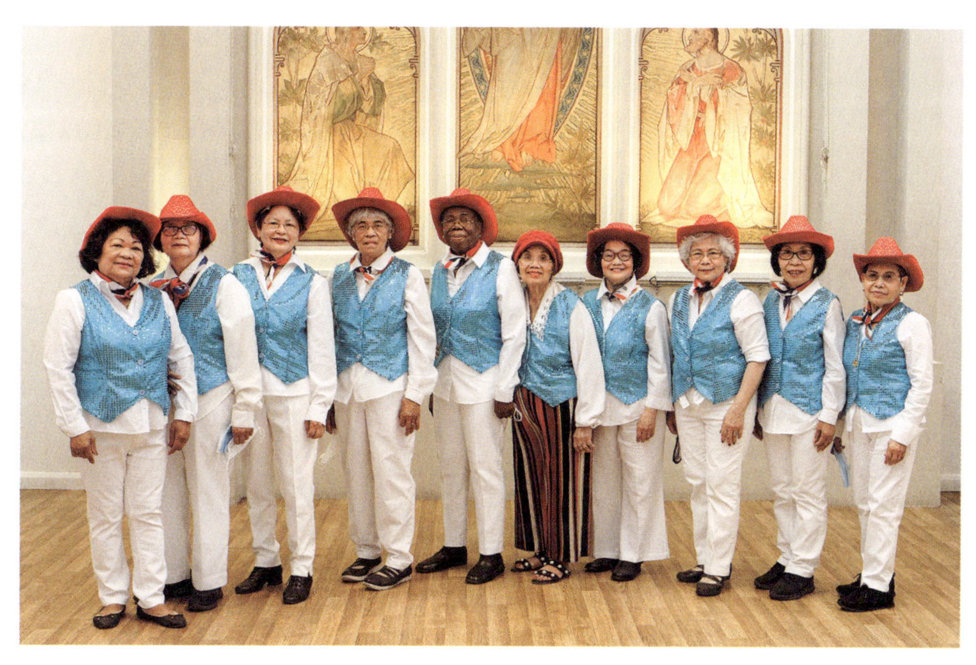

DANCING LADIES
by Natasha Durlacher
London

This dance troupe, who are all over the age of 75,
formed around 20 years ago. Over lockdown they
rehearsed together on Zoom, then as restrictions eased
they began performing outside on the Lisson Green Estate
so isolating and vulnerable residents could watch
through their windows.

MOTHER'S LAND
by Ayesha Jones
Borth, Ceredigion

Growing up, I spent my summer holidays in Wales
with my grandparents; it was the place I always
escaped to when I needed a break. As an adult,
I connected with a group that helps people of the
African diaspora find their ancestral roots, and moved
to Burkina Faso. I got married there and had my son,
but things went down a dark path and I prayed every
day to be back in Wales where my son would be safe.
This image represents making it home.

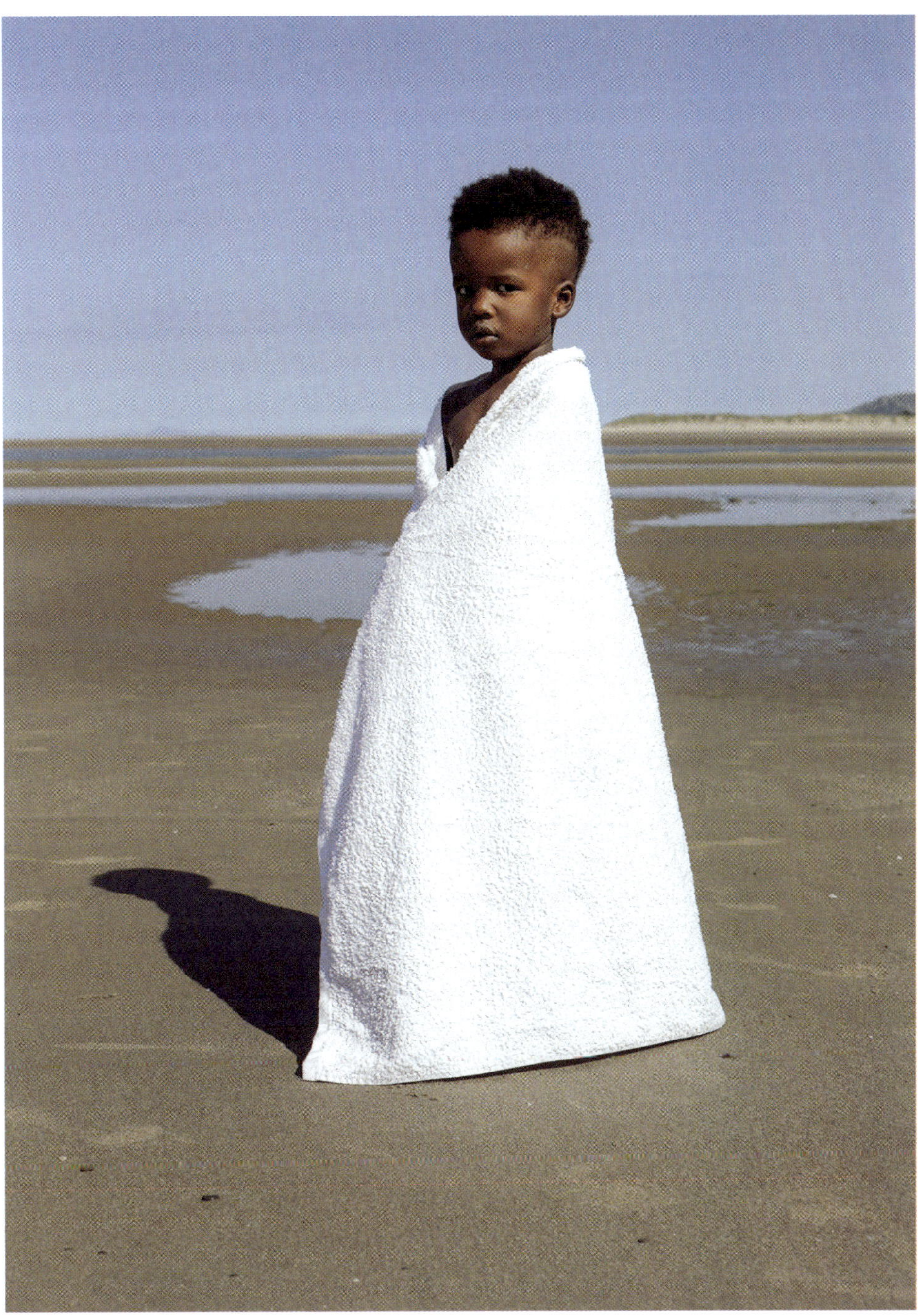

THE REAL CATWALK
by Daniele Fummo
London

I met Monique Dior (*pictured*) on a sunny day
in Trafalgar Square, where she was taking part in
The Real Catwalk – a runway show that celebrates
every kind of body and welcomes people of any
gender, race, ability, sexuality and size.

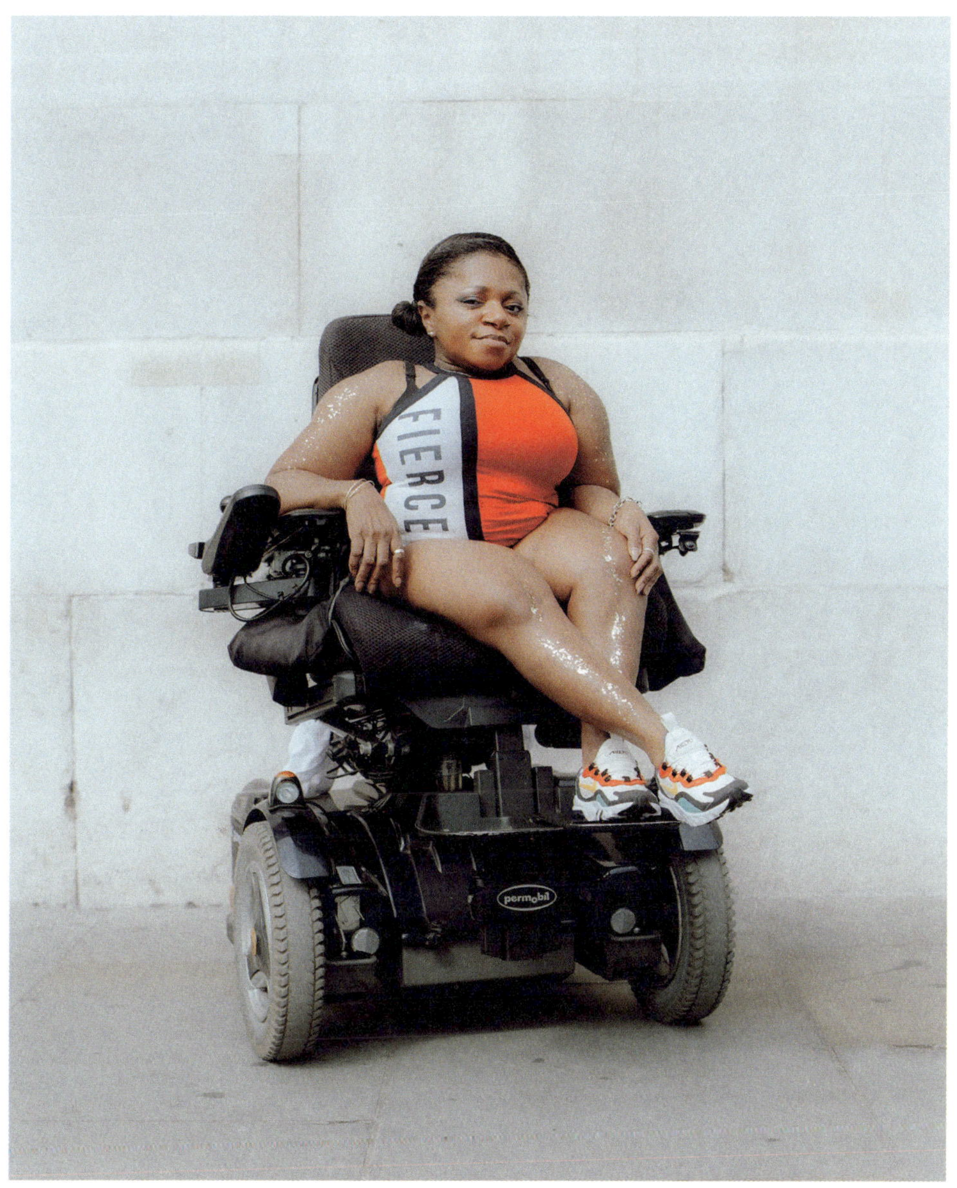

FIERCE
permobil

MICHAELA COEL AT THE BAFTAS
by Charlie Clift
London

At the 2021 BAFTAs, Michaela Coel's television
series *I May Destroy You* won four awards.
When Michaela arrived at my backstage studio
to have her portrait taken, she had just won
Best Actress and was deep in thought. It was
an honour to capture her in that moment.

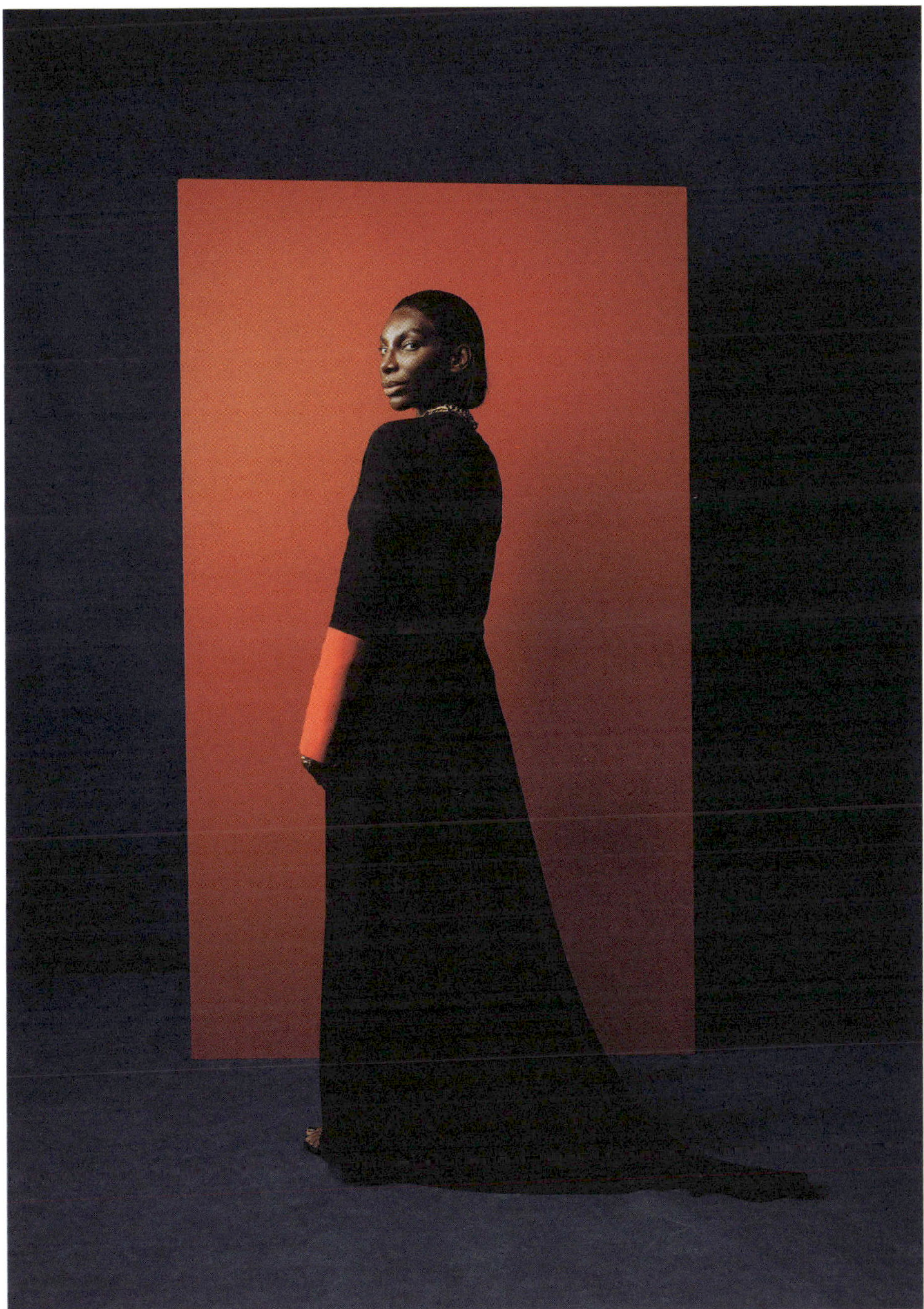

EMILIA
by Craig Fleming
Bude, Cornwall

Emilia is my girlfriend's daughter. We were all on a
caravan holiday together; I was watching TV and she'd
just finished her dog jigsaw. I turned to talk to her
and noticed how beautiful the light was, so grabbed
my camera and fired off a few frames.

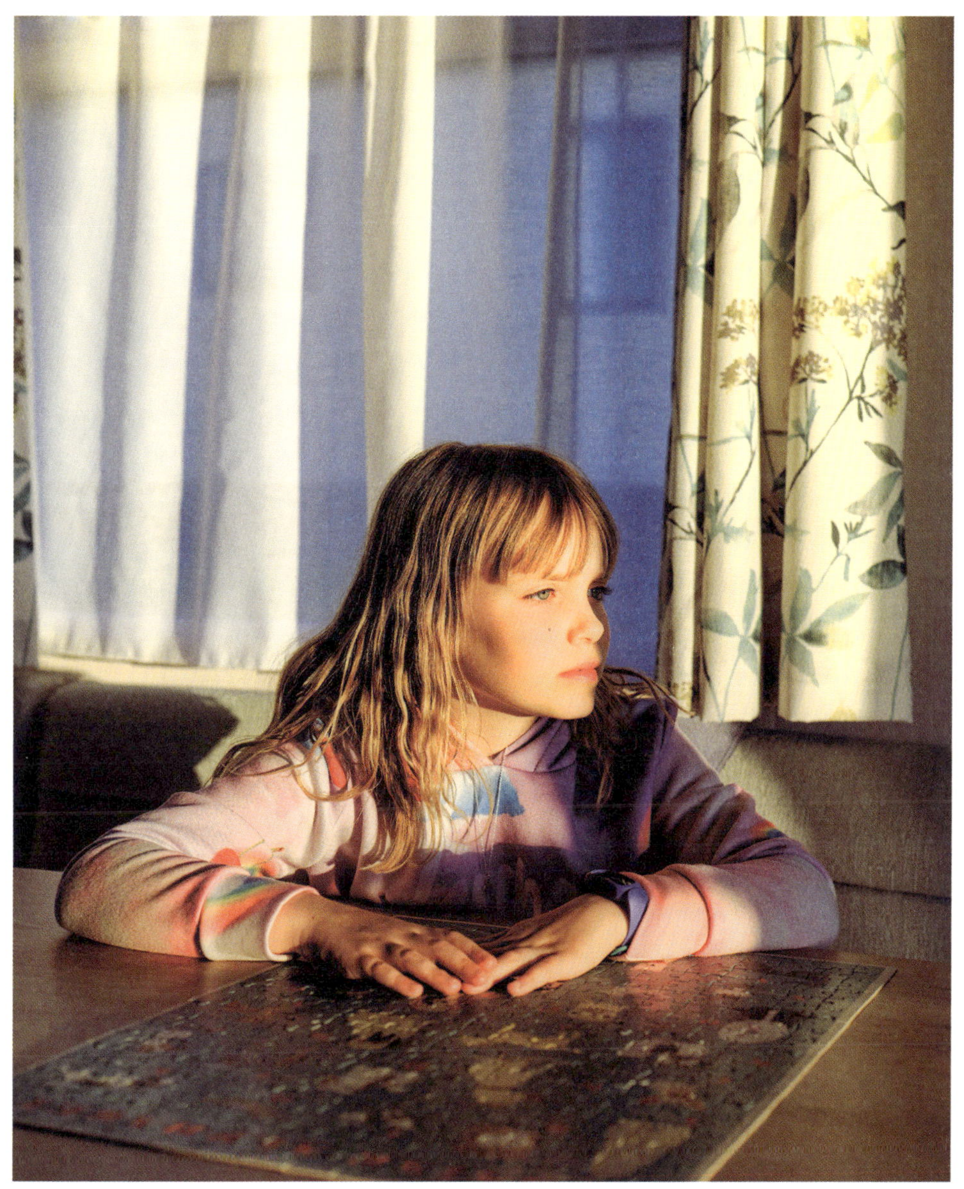

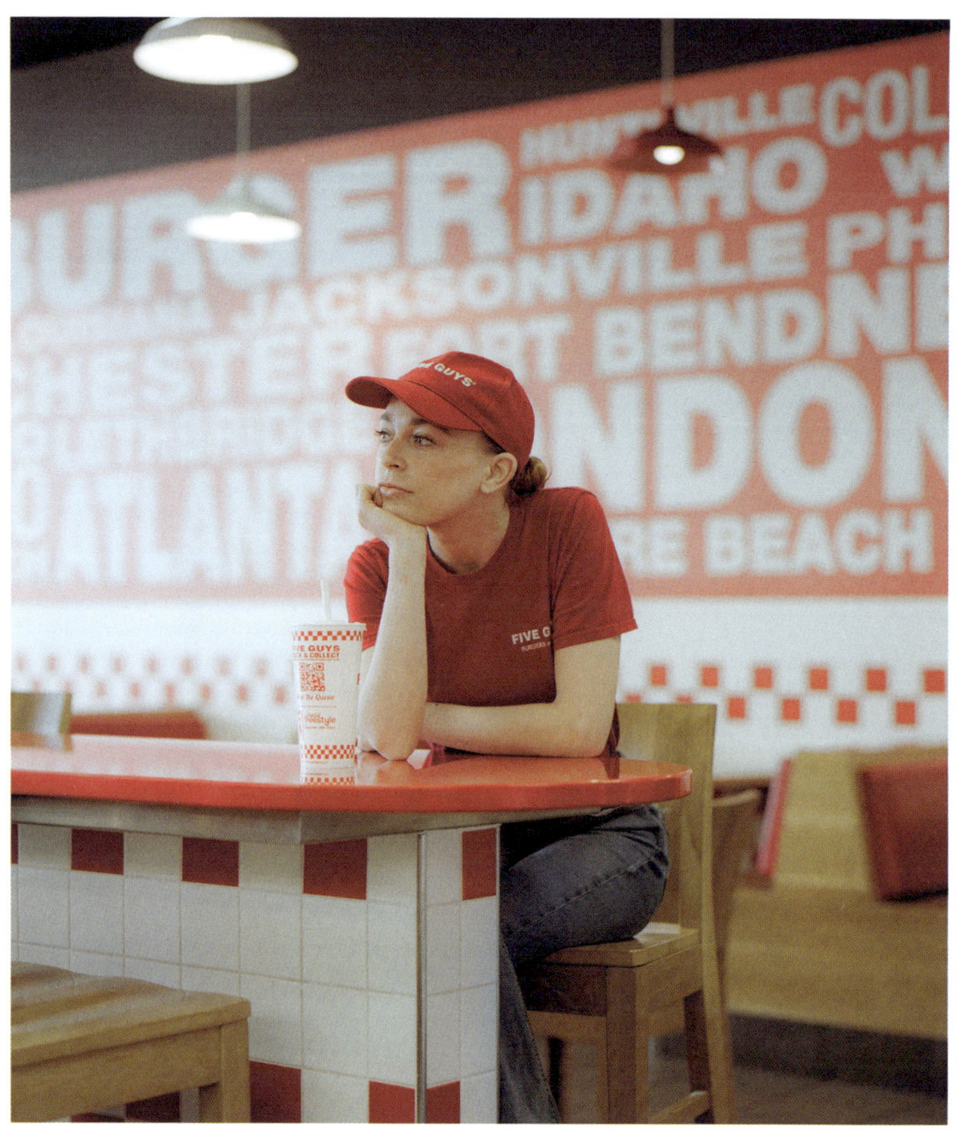

VIOLET
by Benjamin Brooks
Brighton, East Sussex

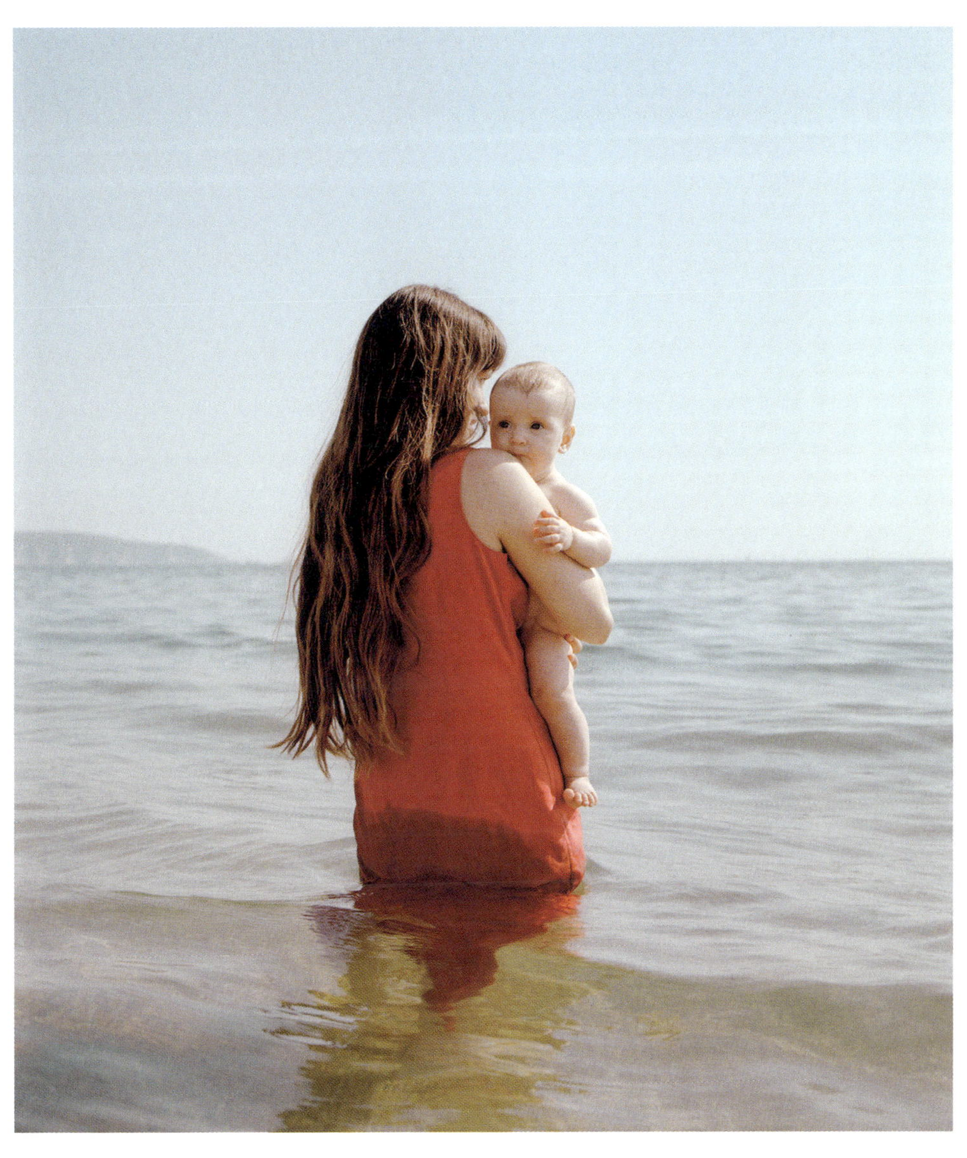

KNEE-DEEP
by Laima Arlauskaite
Milford-on-Sea, Hampshire

KIYAH-LEI
by Jay Fenwick
Gerrards Cross, Buckinghamshire

As with most of my subjects, it was the first time
I had met Kiyah-Lei when I took this photograph
of her. We were working on a fashion shoot in a forest
during one of the lockdowns, so we were all pleased
to be outside in the fresh air. Kiyah-Lei was quite
shy initially (understandable when someone is pointing
a camera at you) but as we began to ramble about
in the ferns taking pictures, she became more
comfortable and I thought she projected such
inner strength in this photo.

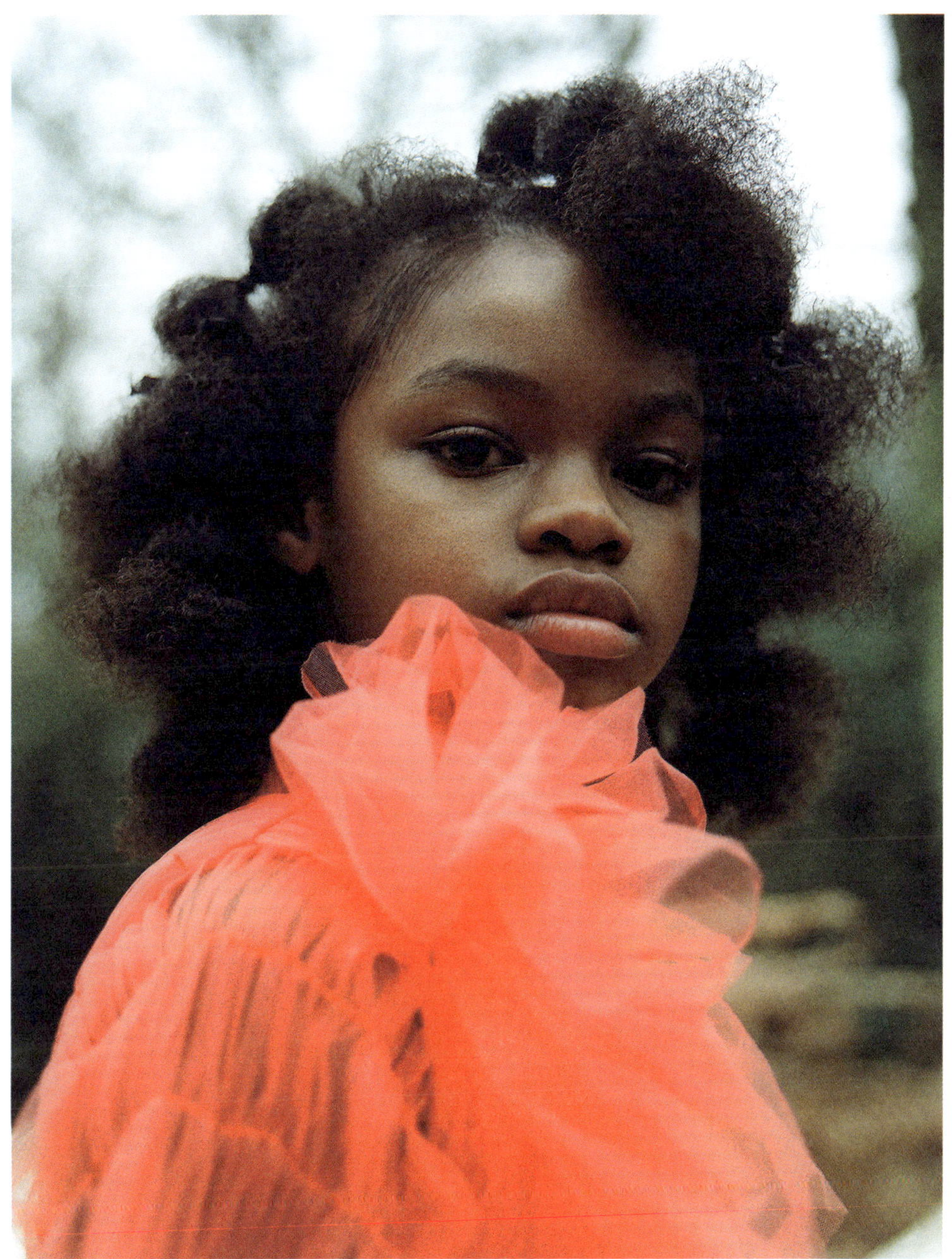

LOCKDOWN HOMESCHOOL 2.0
by Andrea Thomson
Edinburgh

I took this photo of my eldest son during the first
day of 'school' in the second lockdown. My sons had
moved their bunk-bed mattresses onto the floor
to create one giant bed, and slept that way together for
many months. Under the circumstances, I let them –
and it made a good spot for school Teams calls.

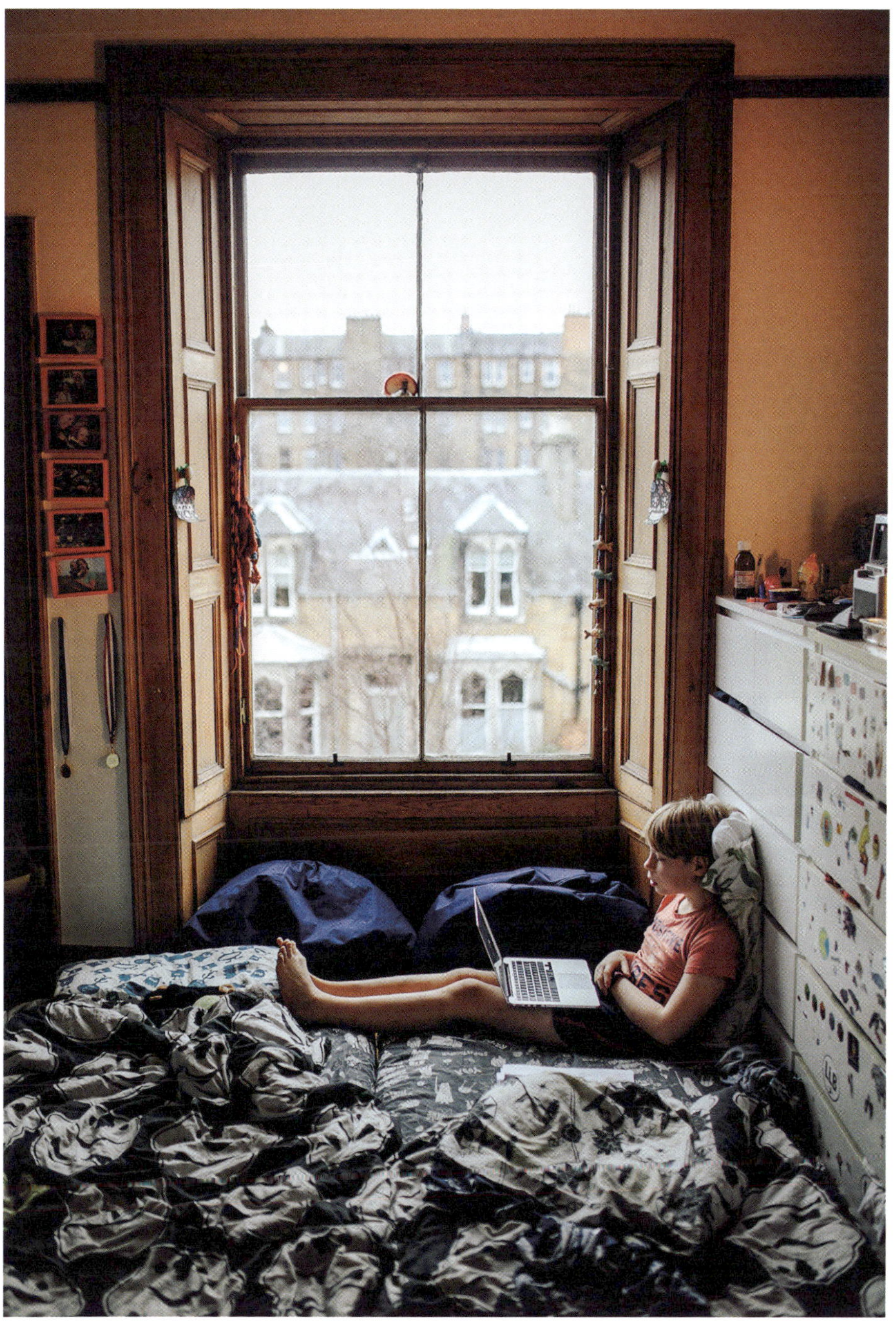

CHARLIE
by Craig Fleming
Sheffield, South Yorkshire

I've been photographing my niece Charlie
since she was born, but she's now approaching an
age where she's starting to feel more self-conscious.
I was using this screen to diffuse the harsh sunlight
as I took her portrait, but I dropped it;
Charlie picked it up and did this.

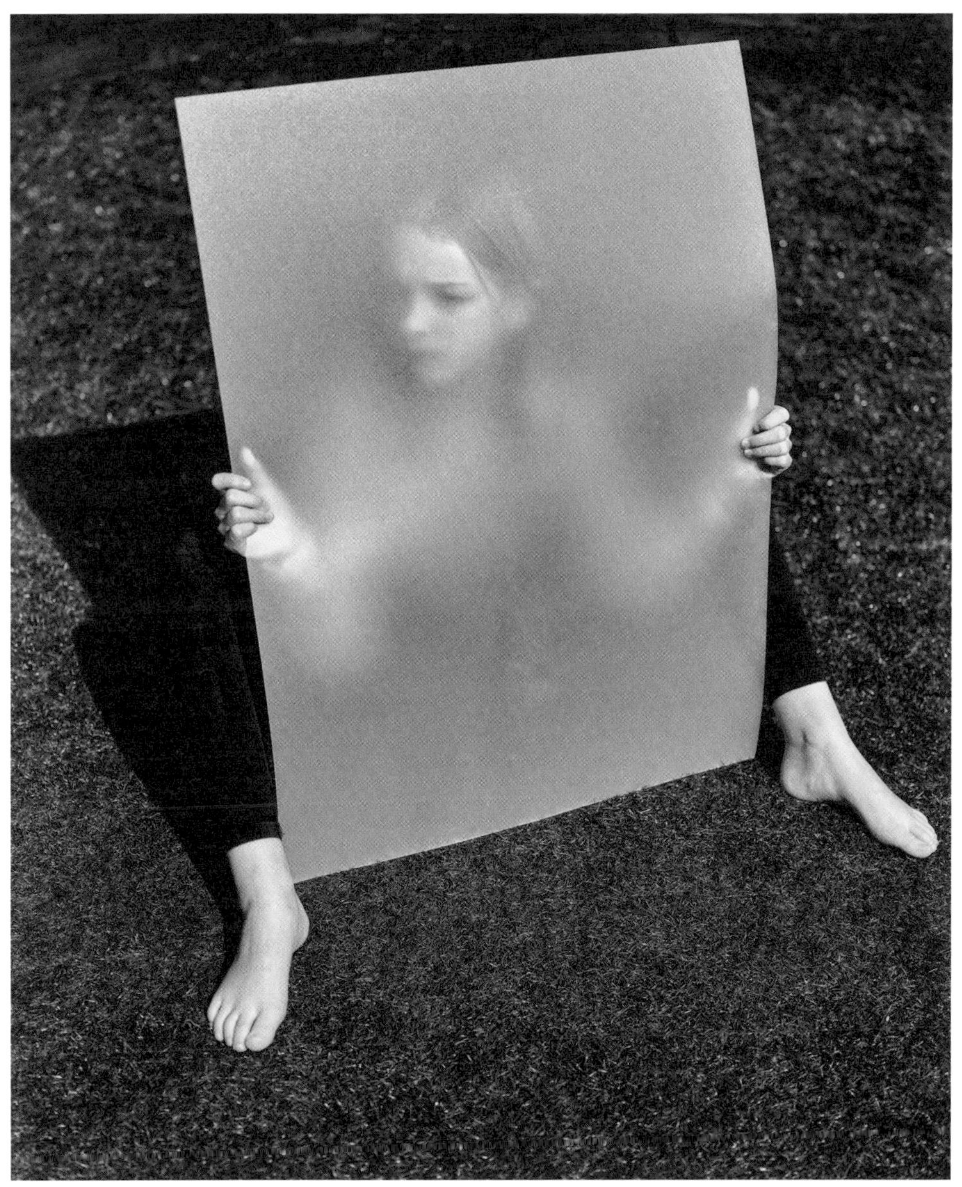

HANNEKE DYE, PORTRAIT OF
A HOLOCAUST SURVIVOR
by Carolyn Mendelsohn
Hebden, North Yorkshire

Hanneke Dye was born in secret on
10th February 1943, in a small village near
Breda in the Netherlands where her Jewish parents
were in hiding. Her mother had to give birth to
her in complete silence, with no painkillers, in case
people heard and informed the Nazis. In this portrait,
Hanneke is holding a photograph of herself as
a newborn baby with her mother.

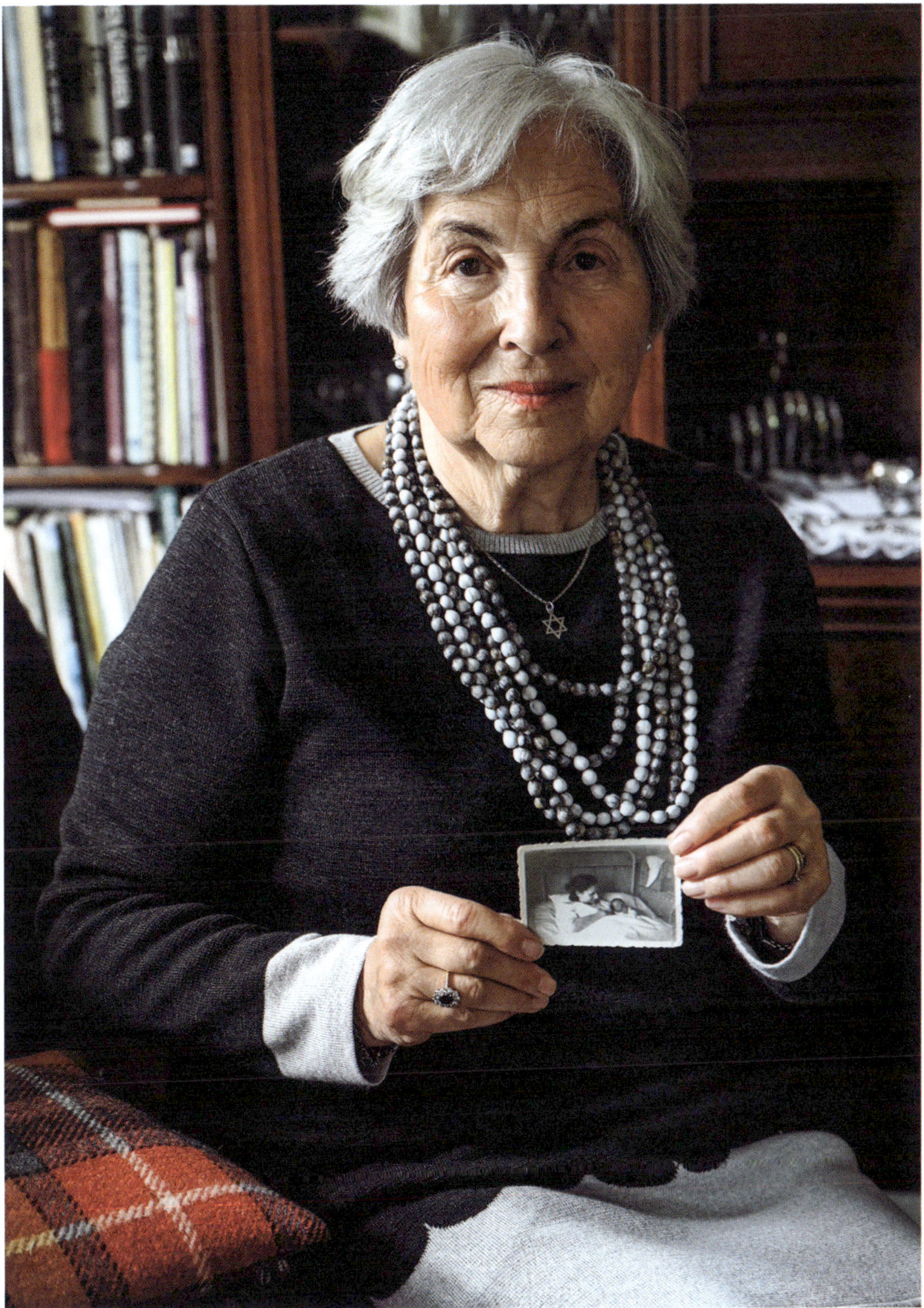

REBECCA
by Nicola Stead
Glasgow

I met Rebecca at the Govan food bank. As a
single mum with three kids, the pandemic has been
a struggle for her. She told me she had a lot of anxiety
around the safety of her children, which she has had to
hide from them. Rebecca has been using the food bank
throughout the pandemic and she described how
the volunteers there have really gone the extra mile,
even delivering food to her door when she
was too sick to make it along.

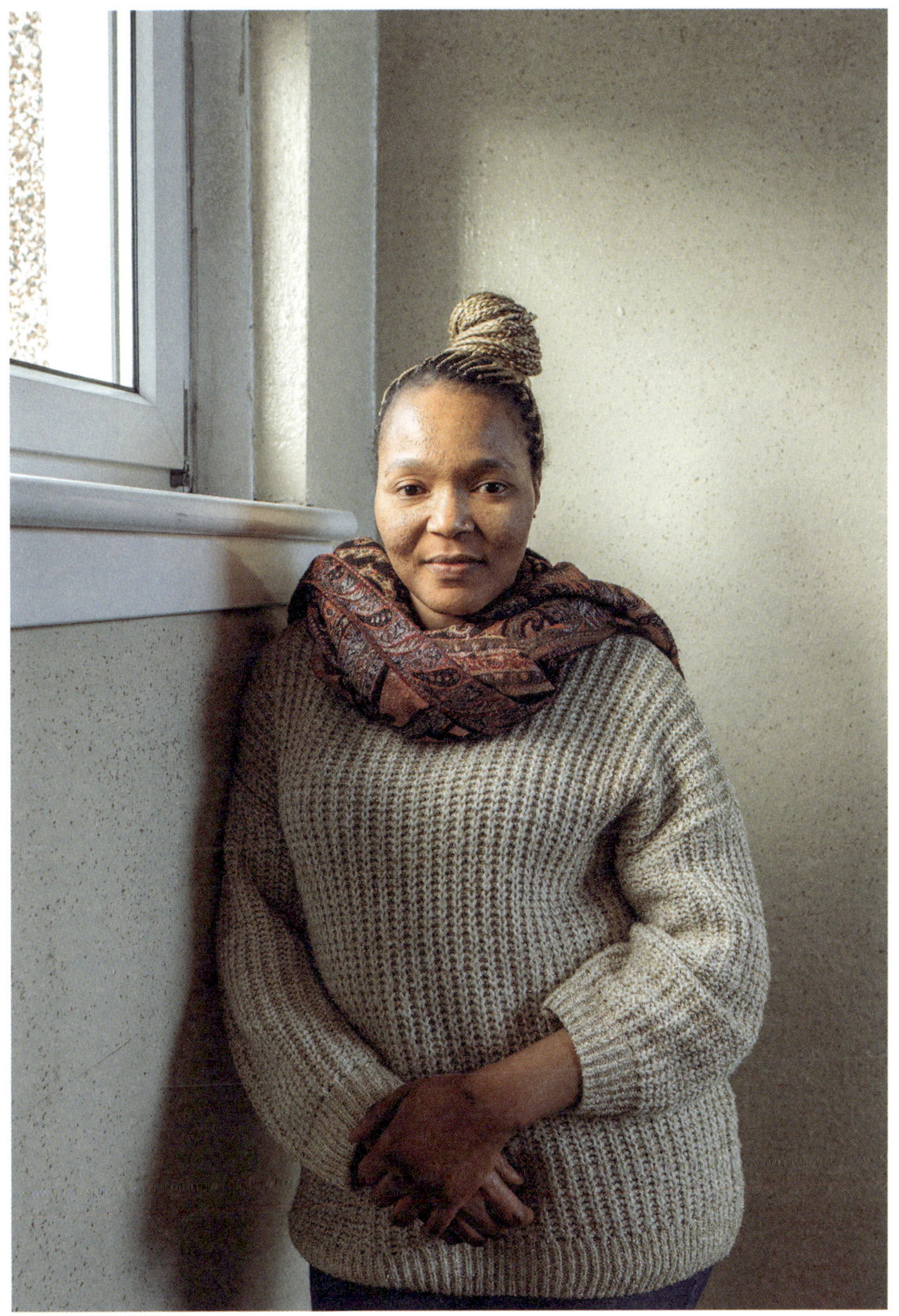

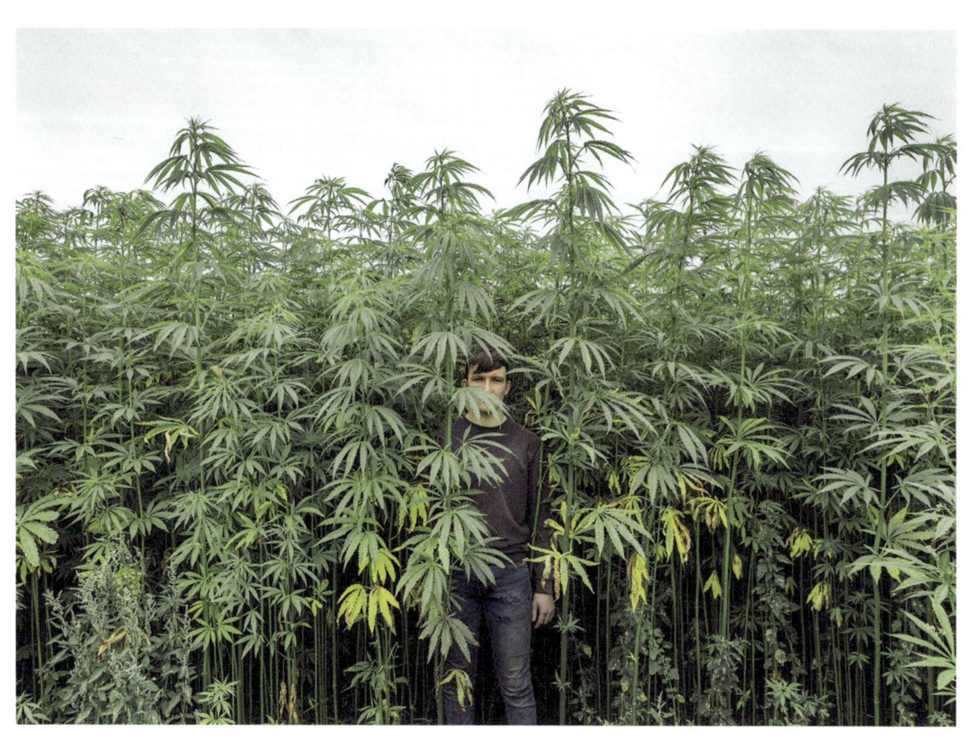

BENJAMIN AT HIS PARENTS' FARM
by James Deavin
Undisclosed location, East Yorkshire

While researching a new project on farming, I came across
this family-run hemp farm in Yorkshire. They invited me
to come and visit and meet the family – three generations
of hemp farmers, the youngest of whom is 16-year-old
Benjamin. He works at the farm when he has time
between studying, and showed me round.

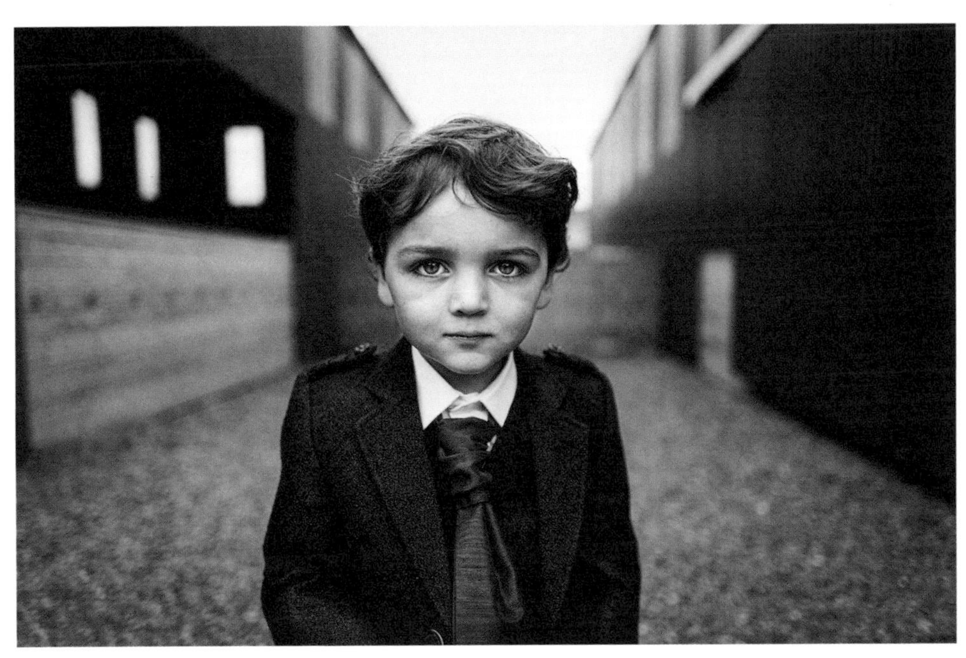

THE BAIRN AND THE BARN
by Paul Reid
Maybole, South Ayrshire

This little boy was attending a wedding I was working
at as a photographer. He was just standing there seeming
so small in between the two sides of the barn.
He looked directly at me and I knew I was about
to capture something truly special; I felt as
though he was looking into my very soul.

37 WEEKS
by Kat Green
Margate, Kent

Laura Jean commissioned me to take her portrait
when she was 37 weeks pregnant with her first child.
I wanted to portray her confidence as a woman
and a mum to be, proud of her body for
what it had achieved.

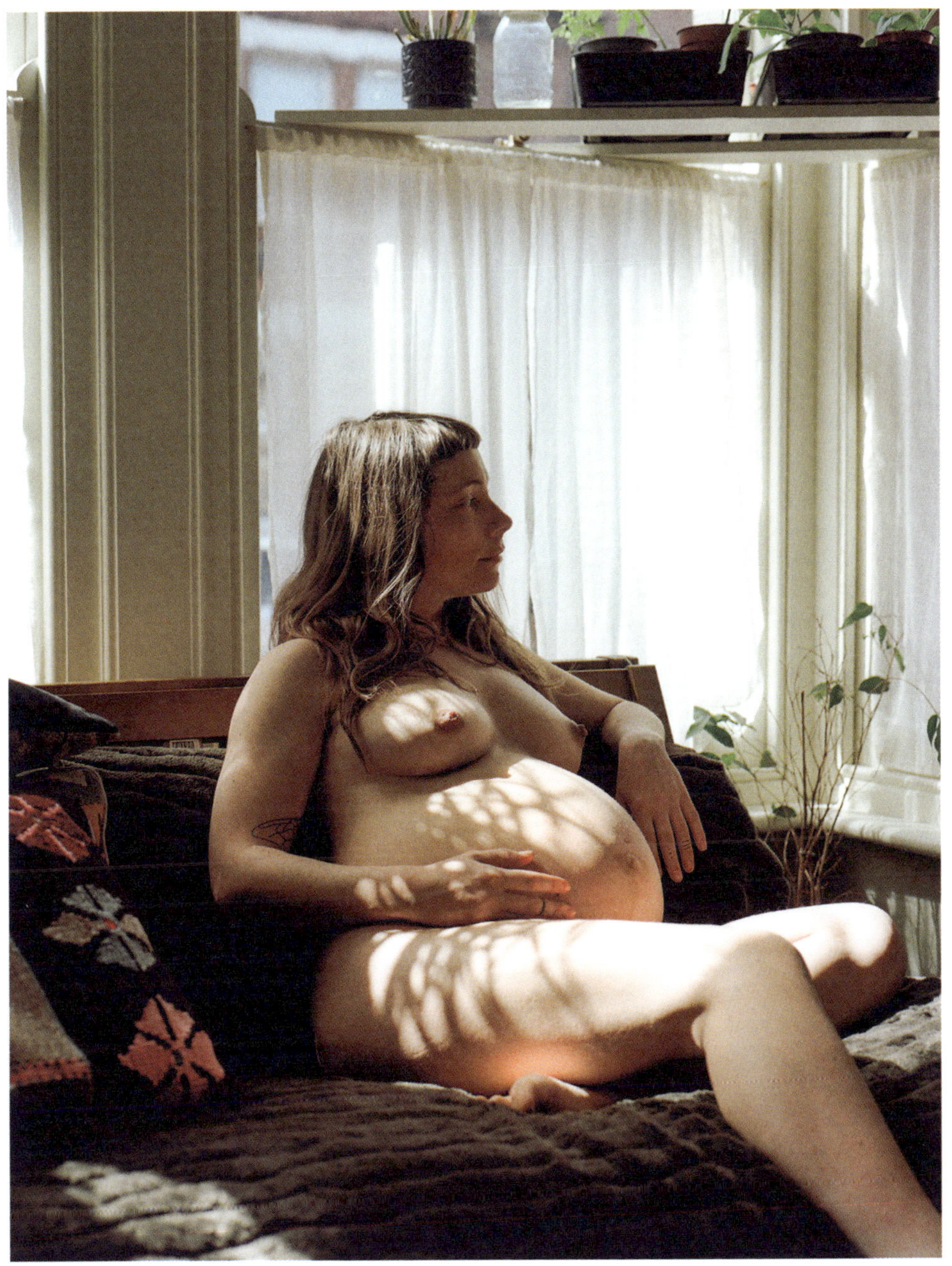

BARBELINE, TEXTILE DESIGNER
by Polly Braden
London

Barbeline grew up in care and had her son, Elijah,
when she was 18. She was with his dad for two years.
She told me, 'Elijah's dad wasn't happy that I didn't
have to rely on him. I'm always able to get on
by myself.' Barbeline set up a business producing
designs for clothes, cushions and wallpaper in 2012.

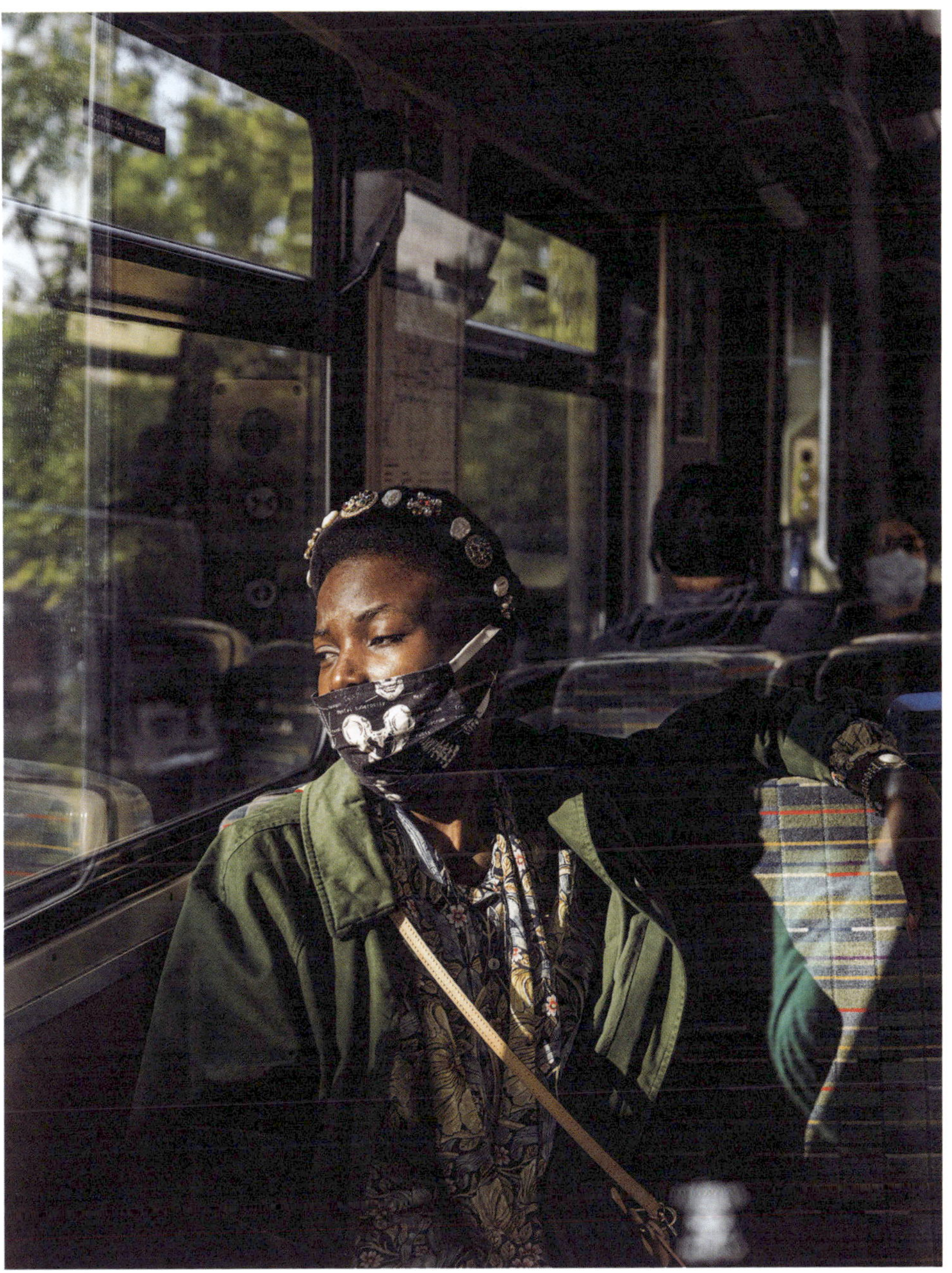

THE CALM BEFORE THE STORM
by JJ Jordan
London

Marija Malenica (*pictured*) is a Croatian,
European and World Kickboxing Champion who
lives and trains in London. Boxing has given Marija
self-confidence, though she admitted to me that she has
many fears outside of the sport. In this portrait, I tried
to capture both her fragility and her inner power.

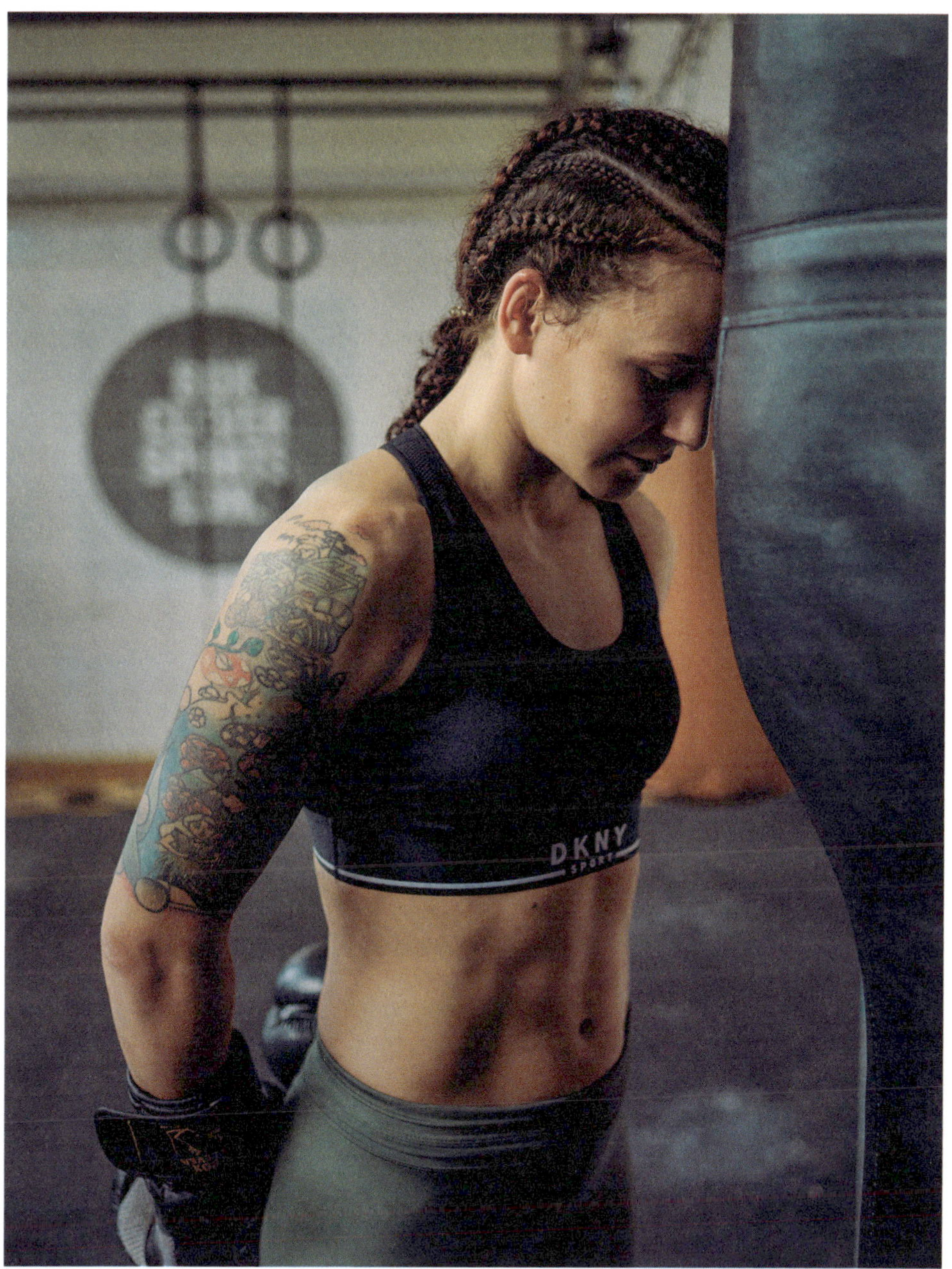

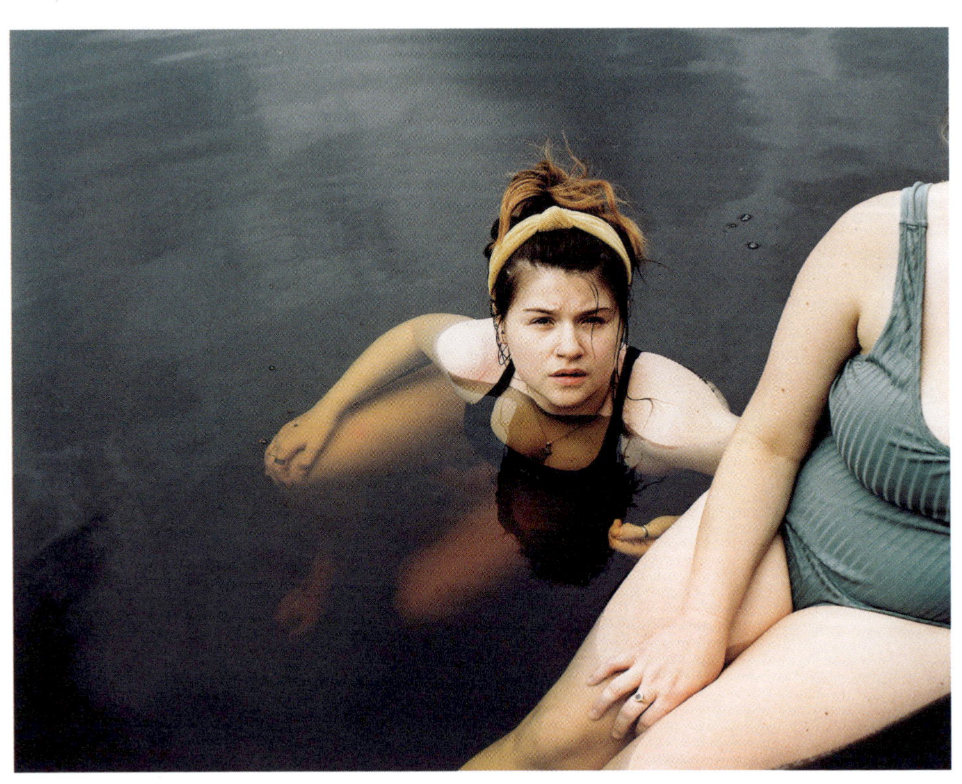

ALICE
by Lily Miles
Boyne Water, Shropshire

Alice is one of my group of friends from university.
We all got into wild swimming while we were studying,
and now we always try to scope out the nearest bit
of water for a dip when we're together. Alice always
seems to be the first one in; she tests the temperature
for the rest of us and I admire this bravery.

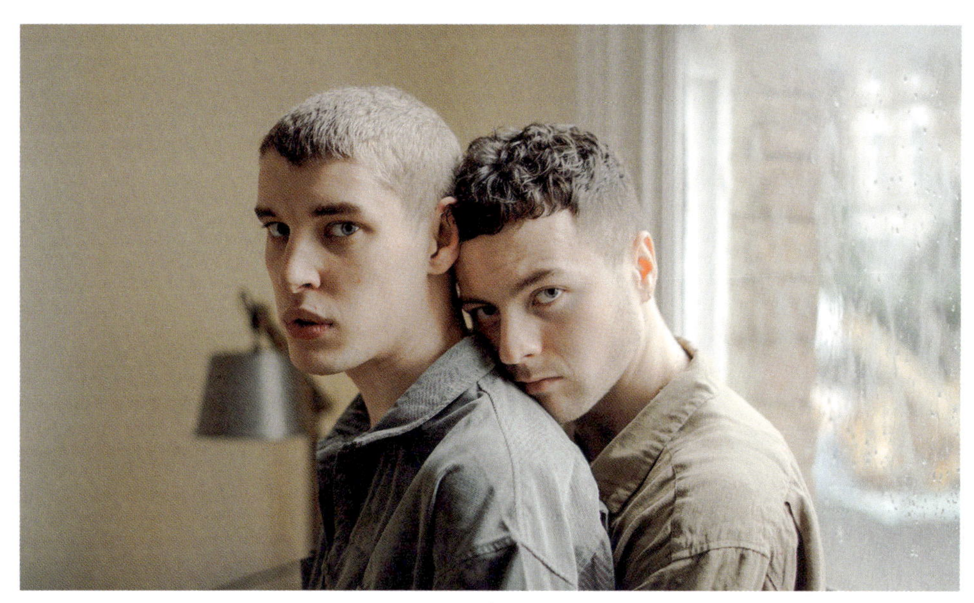

RYAN AND CONOR AT HOME
by Harry Rose
London

Ryan (*left*) and Conor are a gay couple living and
working in London. Ryan is a male model and a disability
activist and campaigner. Living with cerebral palsy, he is
on a mission to make the fashion world a more accessible
and diverse place. Conor is a professional photographer,
who has photographed Ryan for multiple large campaigns.

KAVITA
by Sarah M. Lee
London

I saw Kavita, who is a student, in Hyde Park
and she let me take her portrait while she waited
for a friend near Speakers' Corner. I asked her what
her hopes for the future were and she replied,
'Pure happiness.'

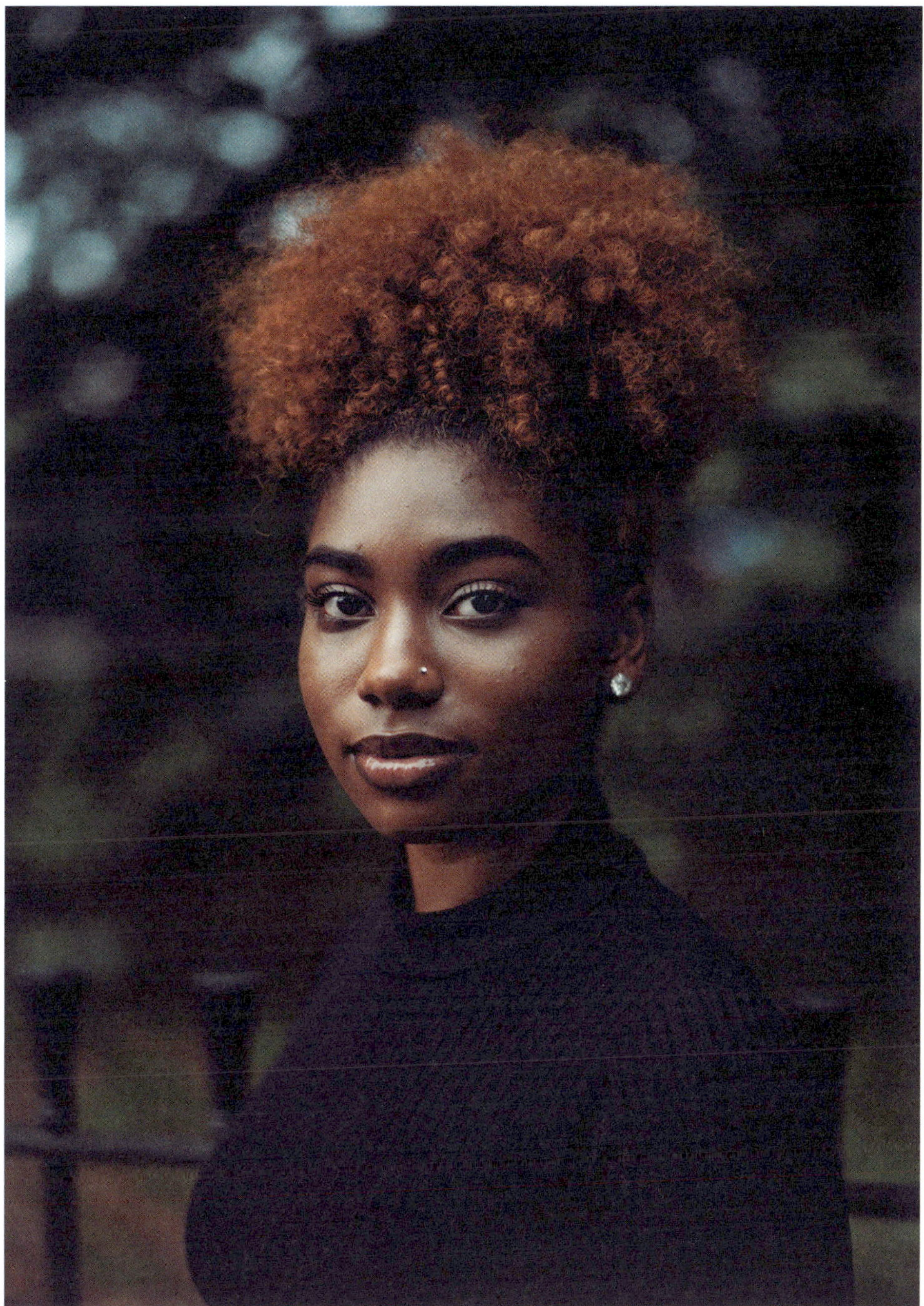

FINDING HOME?
by Lee Brodhurst-Hooper
Undisclosed location, Kent

After splitting up with his wife, Geoff (*pictured*)
only had two options: go into temporary
accommodation and give up his beloved dog,
or find his own alternative situation. He chose
the latter and he and his dog Sunny now live
off-grid in a secret camp surrounded by trees,
next to some cliffs on the Kent coast.

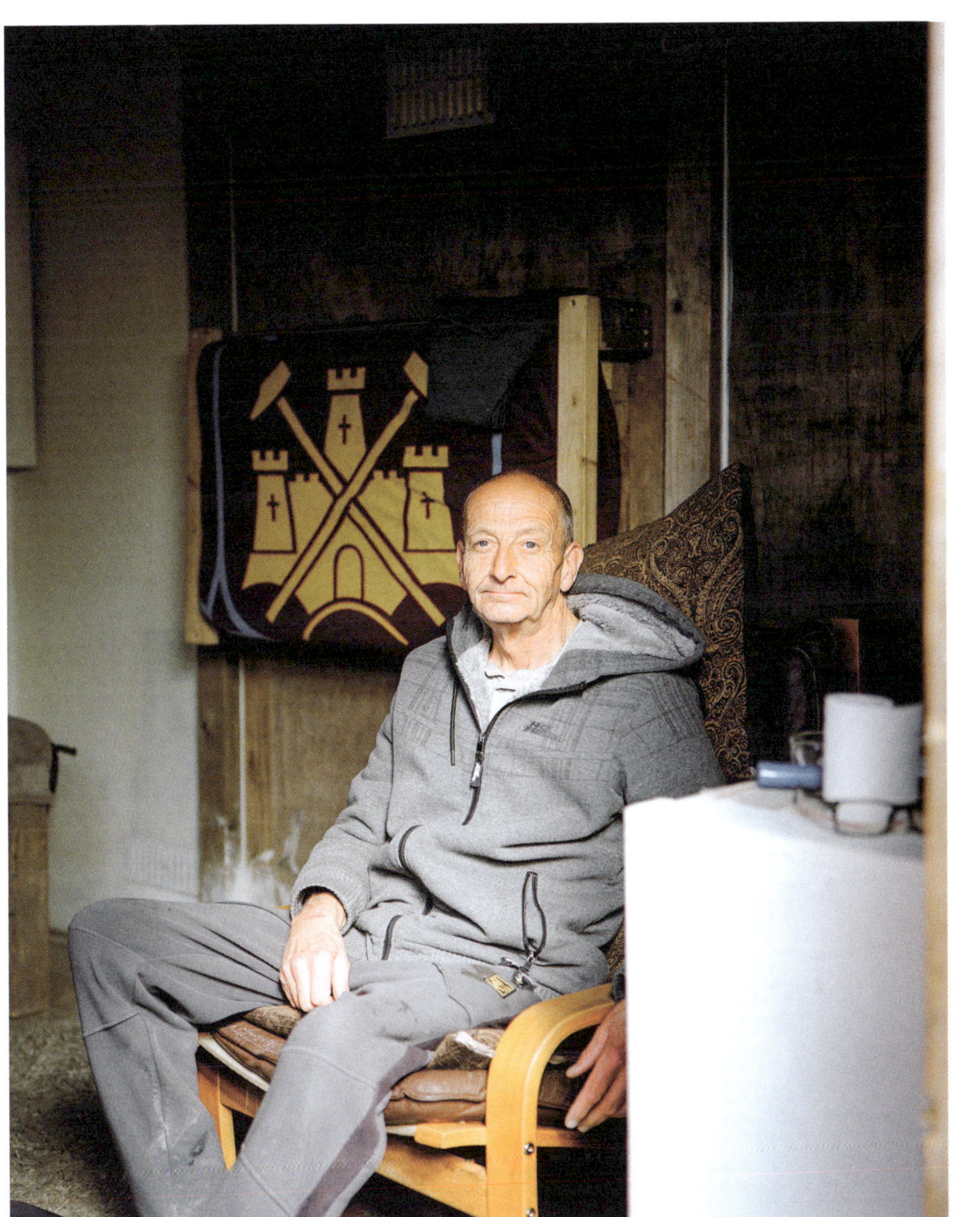

LOCKDOWN MOTHER
by Ella Brolly
Edinburgh

This is my best friend Maud with her son, Fred,
who is my godson. Fred was born right at the
beginning of the pandemic and Maud went through
a turbulent break-up with Fred's father shortly after.
I saw Fred and Maud battle through lockdowns,
sofa-surfing and court cases together, while Maud
managed the trials and tribulations of being a
27-year-old single mother with grace, love and
a smile on her face. In this photo they are back
in their home after many long months.

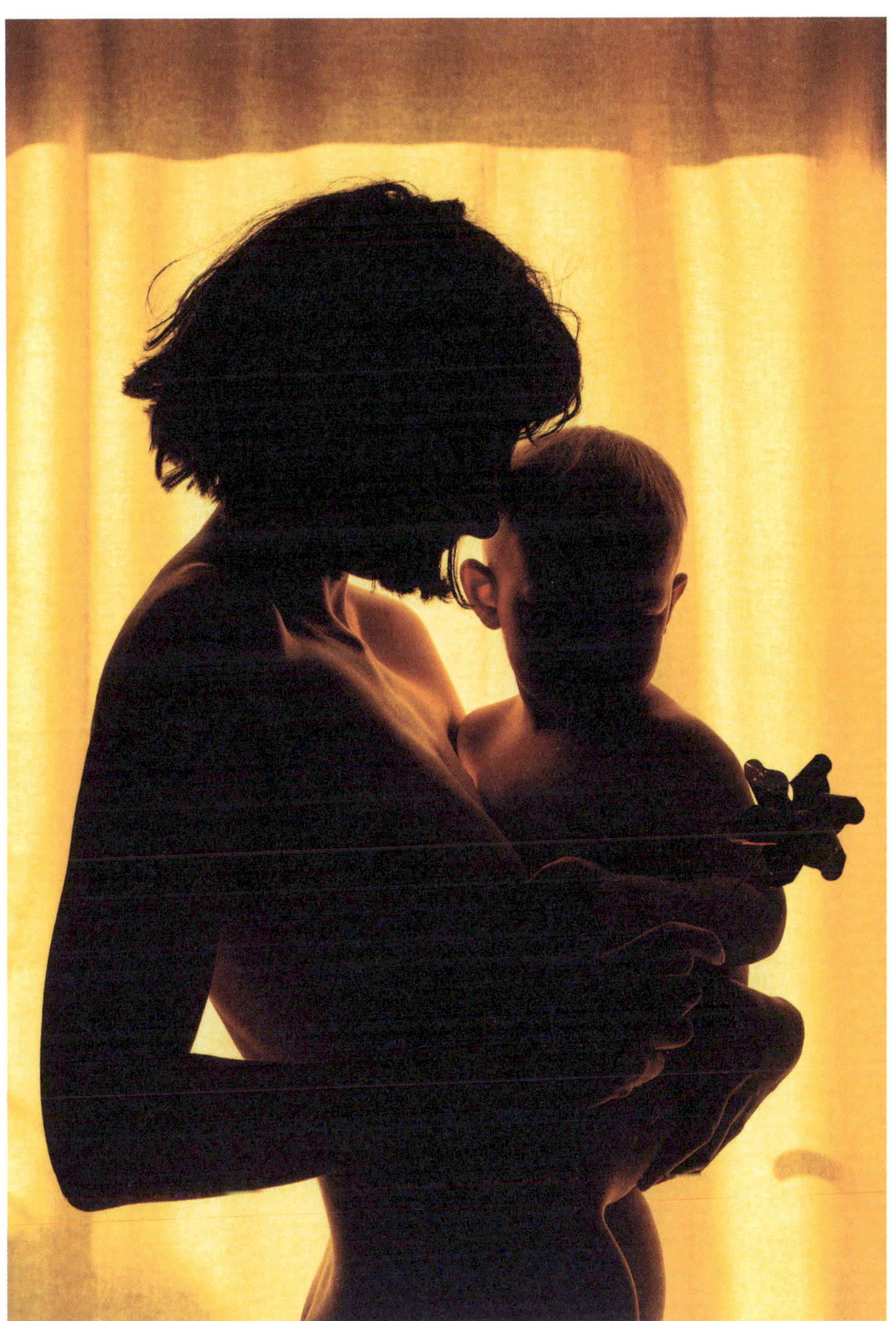

FISAYO AKINADE
by Phil Sharp
London

I took this photo of the actor Fisayo Akinade in
July 2021, but I first photographed Fisayo back
in 2014 when he had just started his career. There's
a real joy in photographing the same person
years apart; I'm hoping Fisayo comes back
to sit again in another seven years.

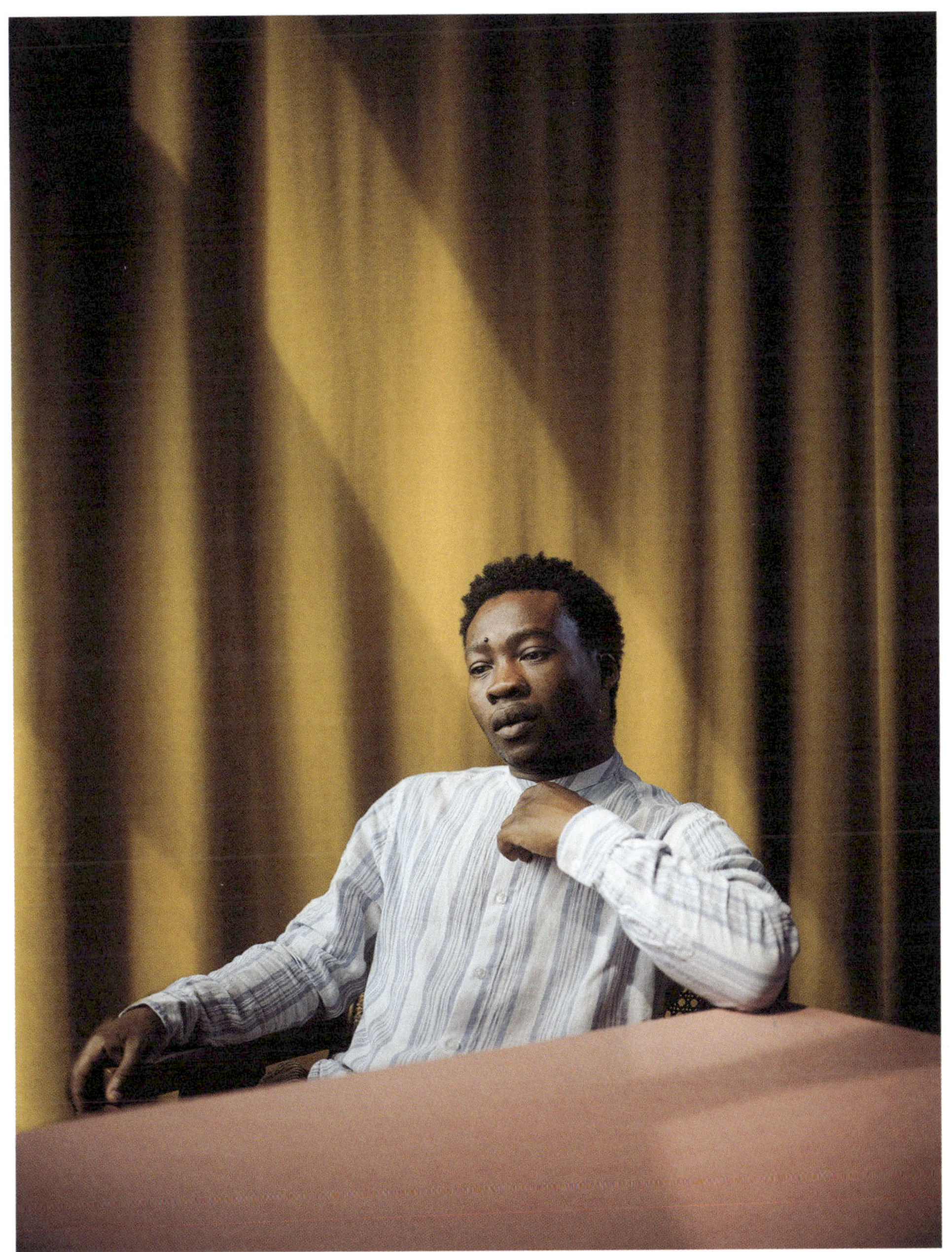

ANOTHER YEAR OLDER
by Clair Robins
Leicester

Covid seemed to make a year of my daughter's life
disappear. One minute she was in primary school
in Year 6, running into class in a gingham dress,
the next she was finishing Year 7 at secondary school.
Looking at this photo I hardly recognise her.

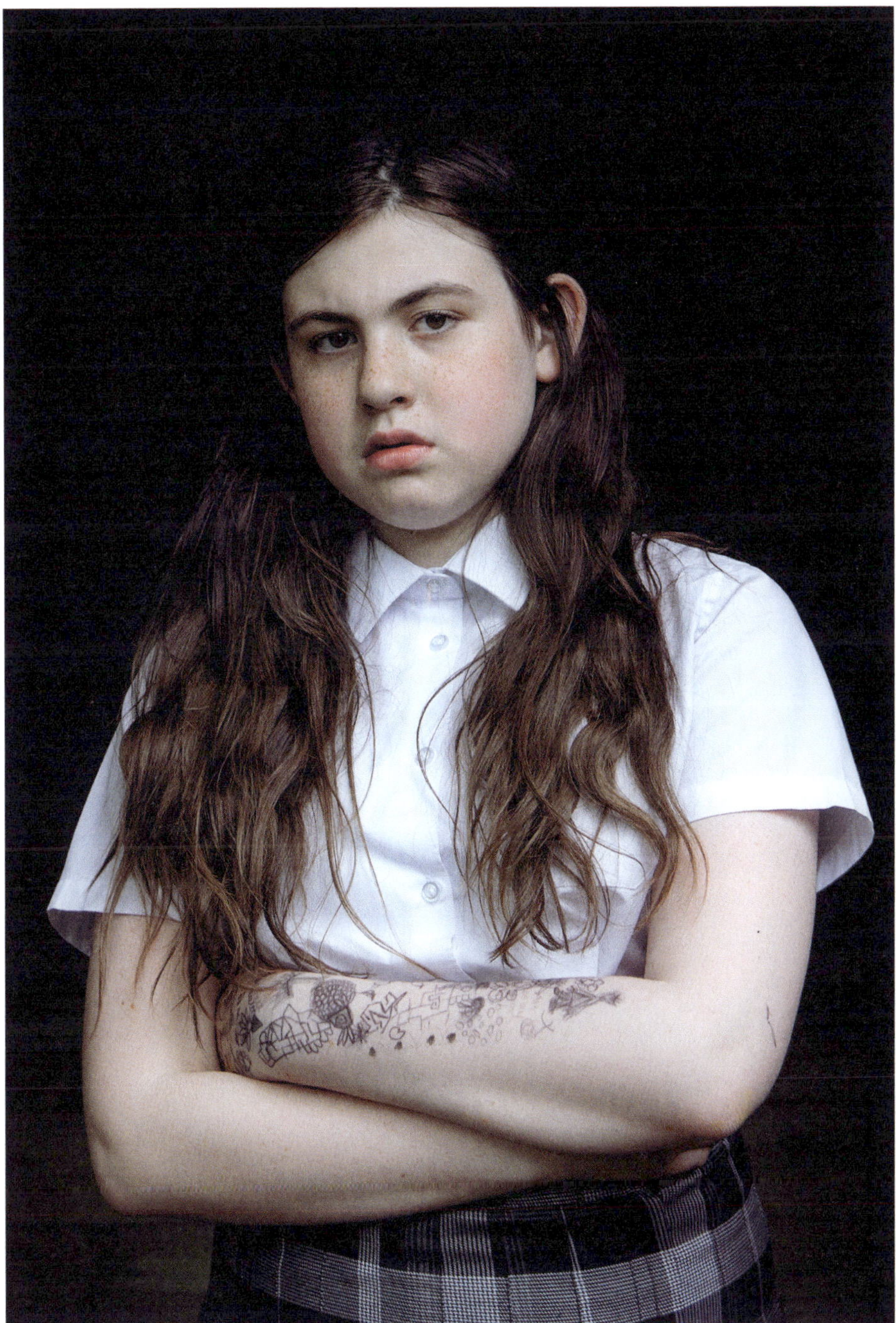

FIRST (PROPER) HUG
by Clair Robins
Leicester

Lockdown had prevented my daughter (*right*)
from seeing her best friend for weeks. After a lot
of 'screen time', this was their first proper hug.

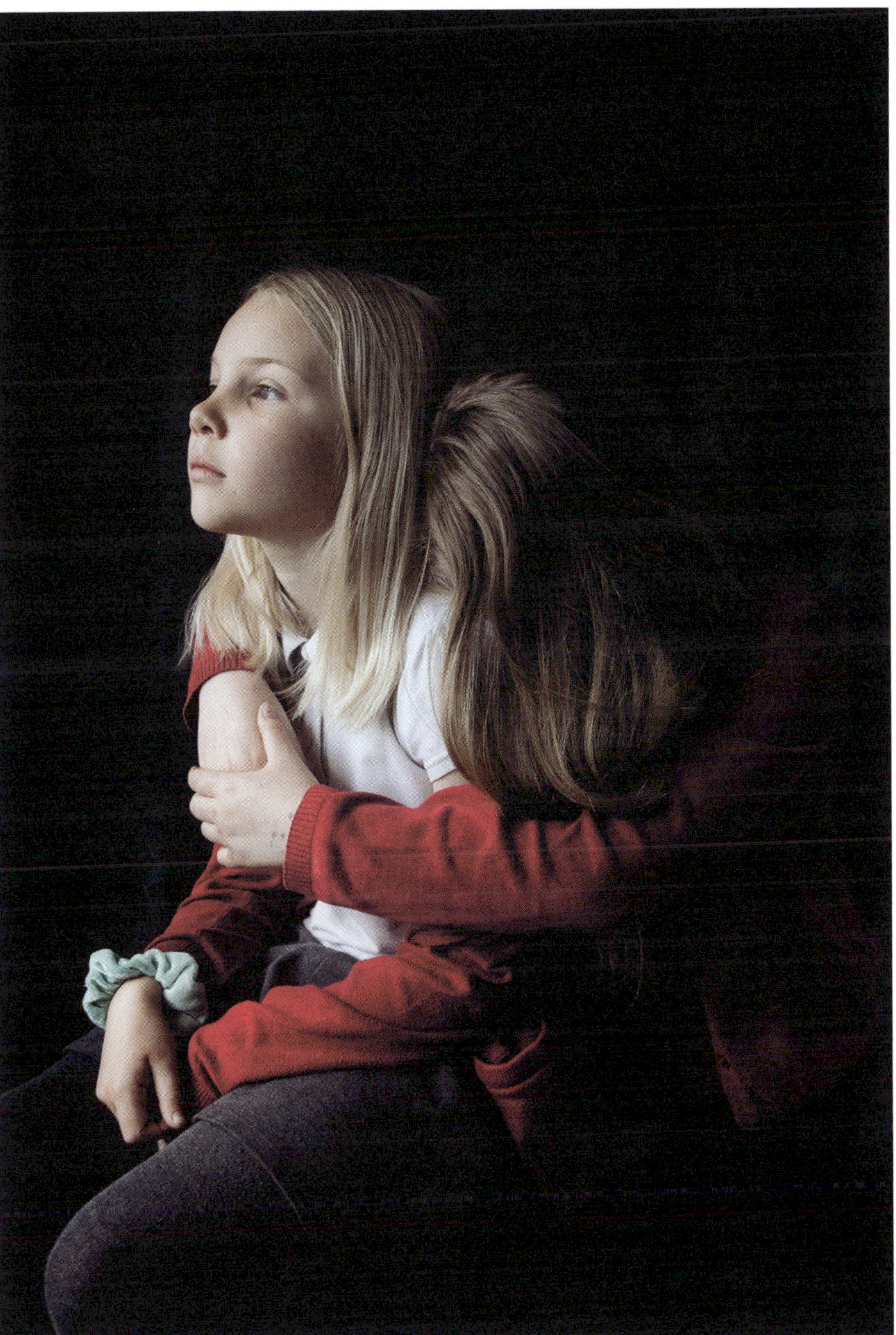

WILLIAM
by Lauren Norris
Falmouth, Cornwall

I lived with Will while at university in Falmouth.
He always agreed to model for shoots for my degree –
and he made the best coffee.

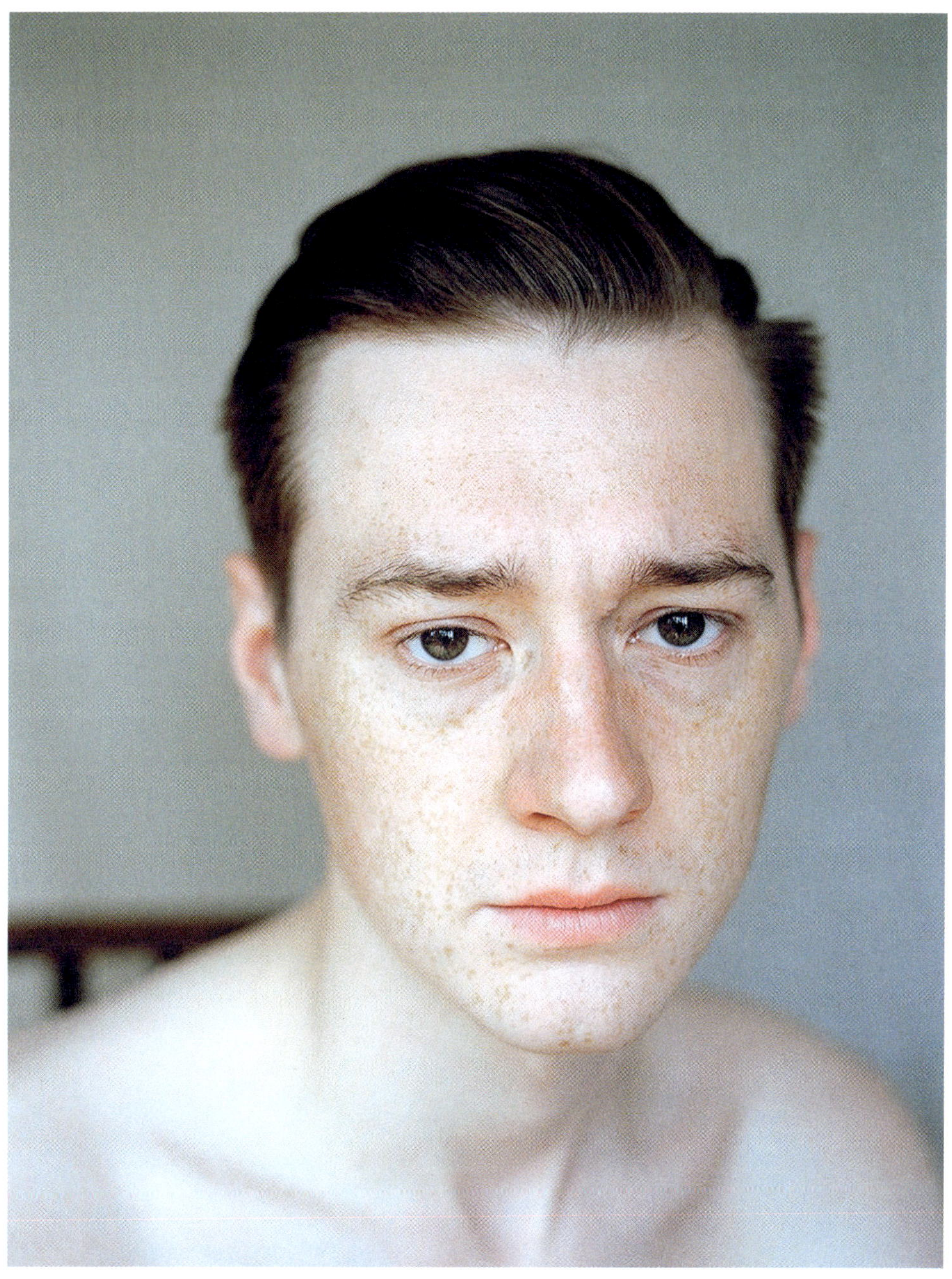

SILVER (THEY/HE)
by Emil Lombardo
London

During the third lockdown, I cycled to different
parts of London to photograph trans and non-binary
people outside of their homes. Silver was one of
the amazing, beautiful people I met; they are a
talented drag king who performs in queer venues
across the city. Silver was a couple of months post
top surgery when I took this photo, and this was
the first time they had taken their shirt off in public.

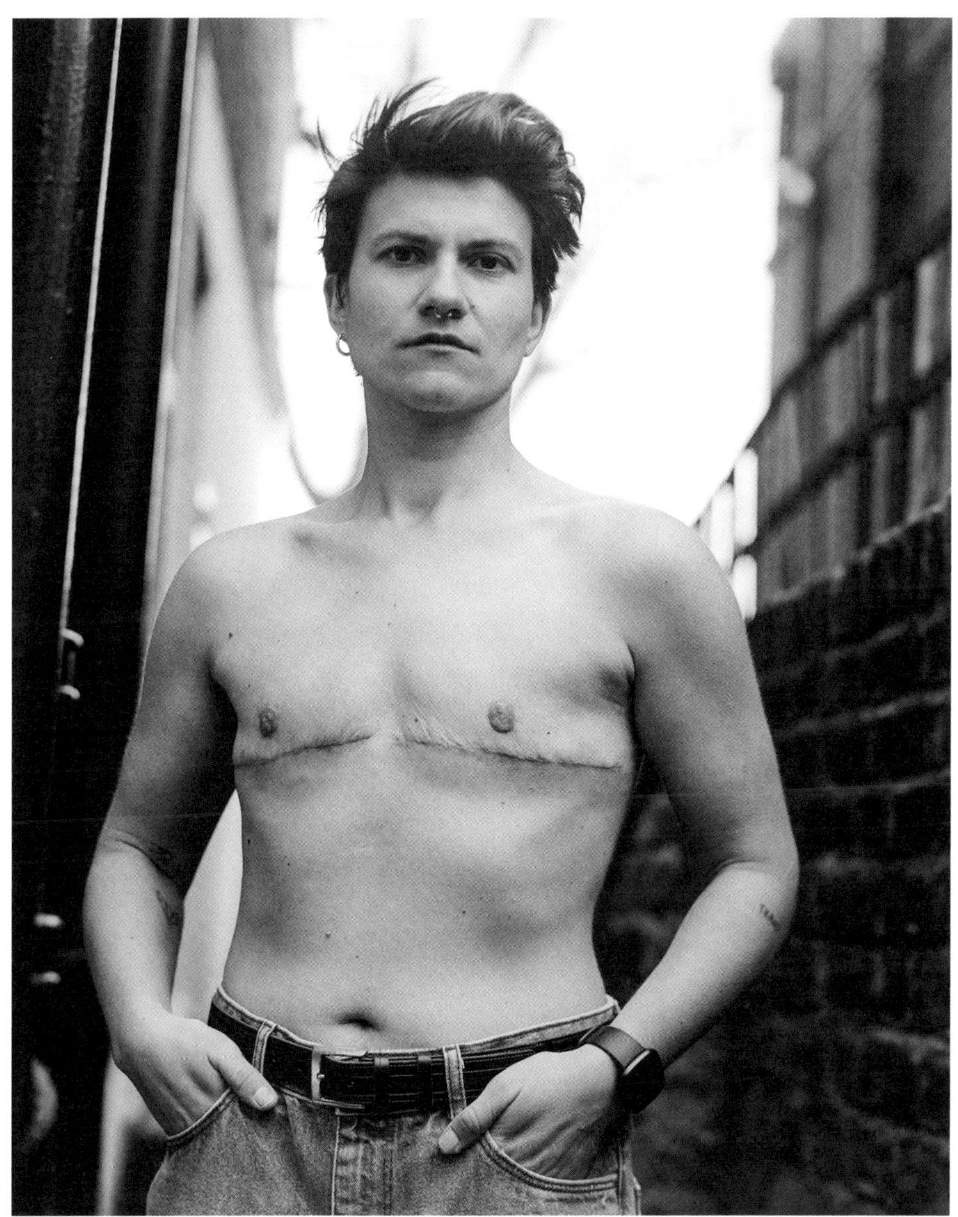

PAUL WELLER
by Phil Fisk
Ripley, Surrey

I went to photograph Paul Weller at his studio for
the *Observer New Review*. I was a little nervous
before I arrived because I thought that having a
photographer in his music space might annoy him.
I was so wrong. The door opened, I got the loveliest
welcome and my first proper handshake since
the first lockdown. Paul was a childhood hero
of mine, and has now become a beacon of hope
for me in getting older with style and a
never-waning sense of adventure.

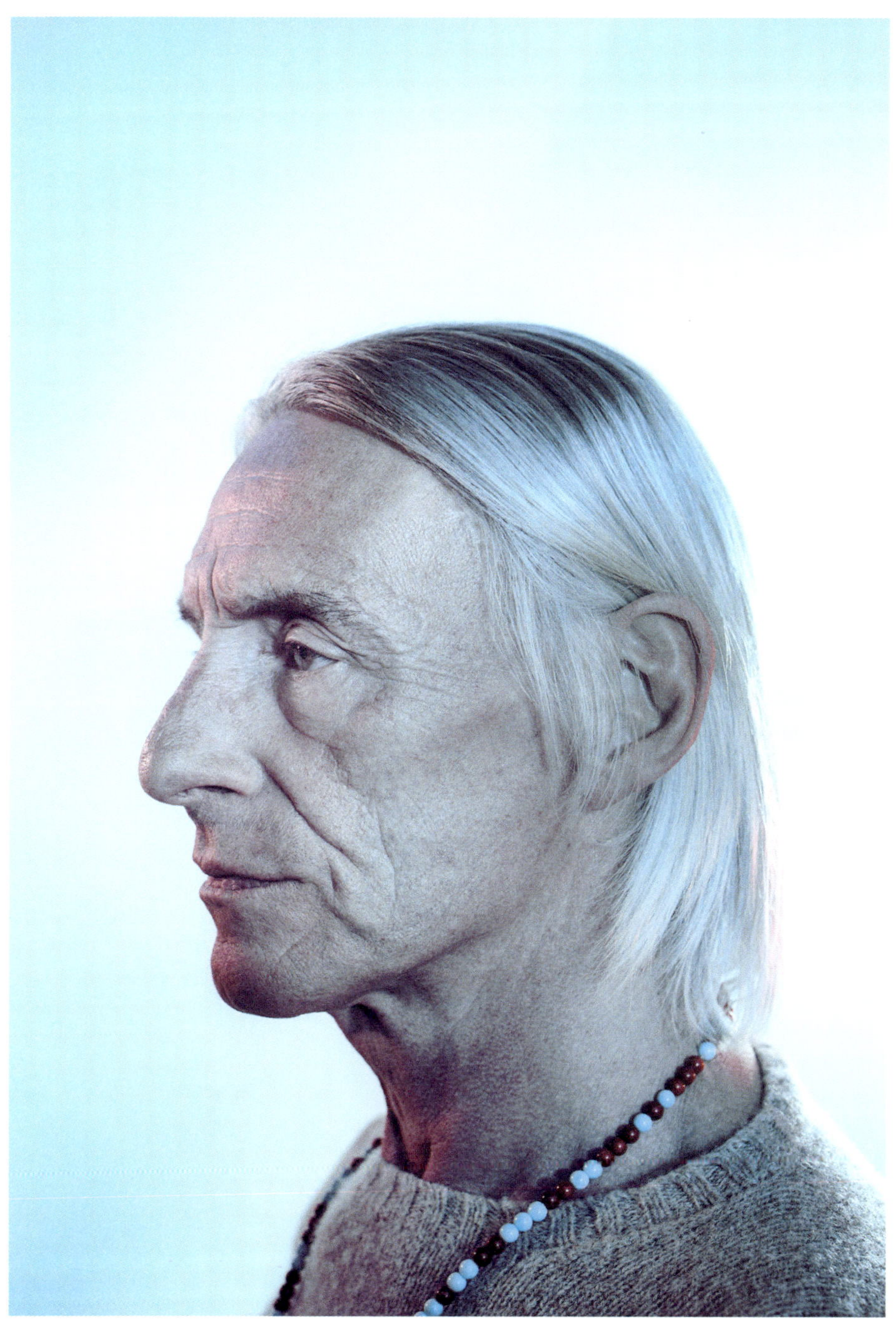

60 MILES BY ROAD OR RAIL
by Christian Sinibaldi
Northampton

I was commissioned to photograph Ghulam Hussain
Khan (*left*) and Perveen Khan as part of '60 Miles
by Road or Rail', a community project celebrating the
heritage of Northampton and its residents.
I was introduced to the couple by one of the project
co-ordinators, Subika, who calls them 'Uncle
and Auntie'. Although they are not related to her
by blood, they play a huge part in Subika's life and
are important members of the local community.

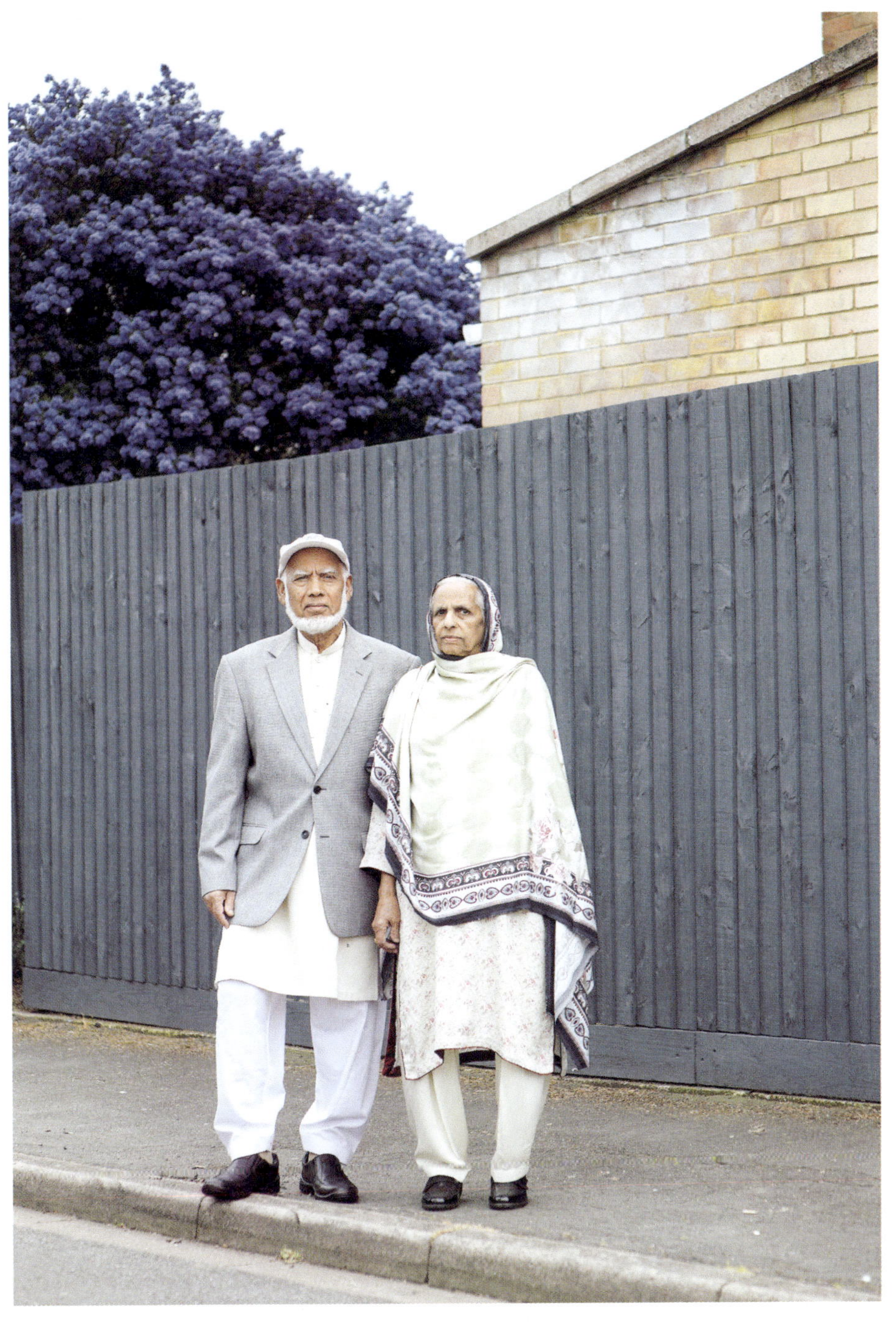

MICHAEL
by Rhiannon Adam
Trusthorpe, Lincolnshire

I spotted Michael from a distance, cradling
a roll-up between his stained fingers and
looking at it ponderously. It was as though he
was contemplating the last cigarette he was ever
going to have, leaning against the railings of a bridge.
He seemed out of place, like a still from an American
road movie. The light was low and glowing, and
I knew I couldn't miss this chance to ask
to take his photo.

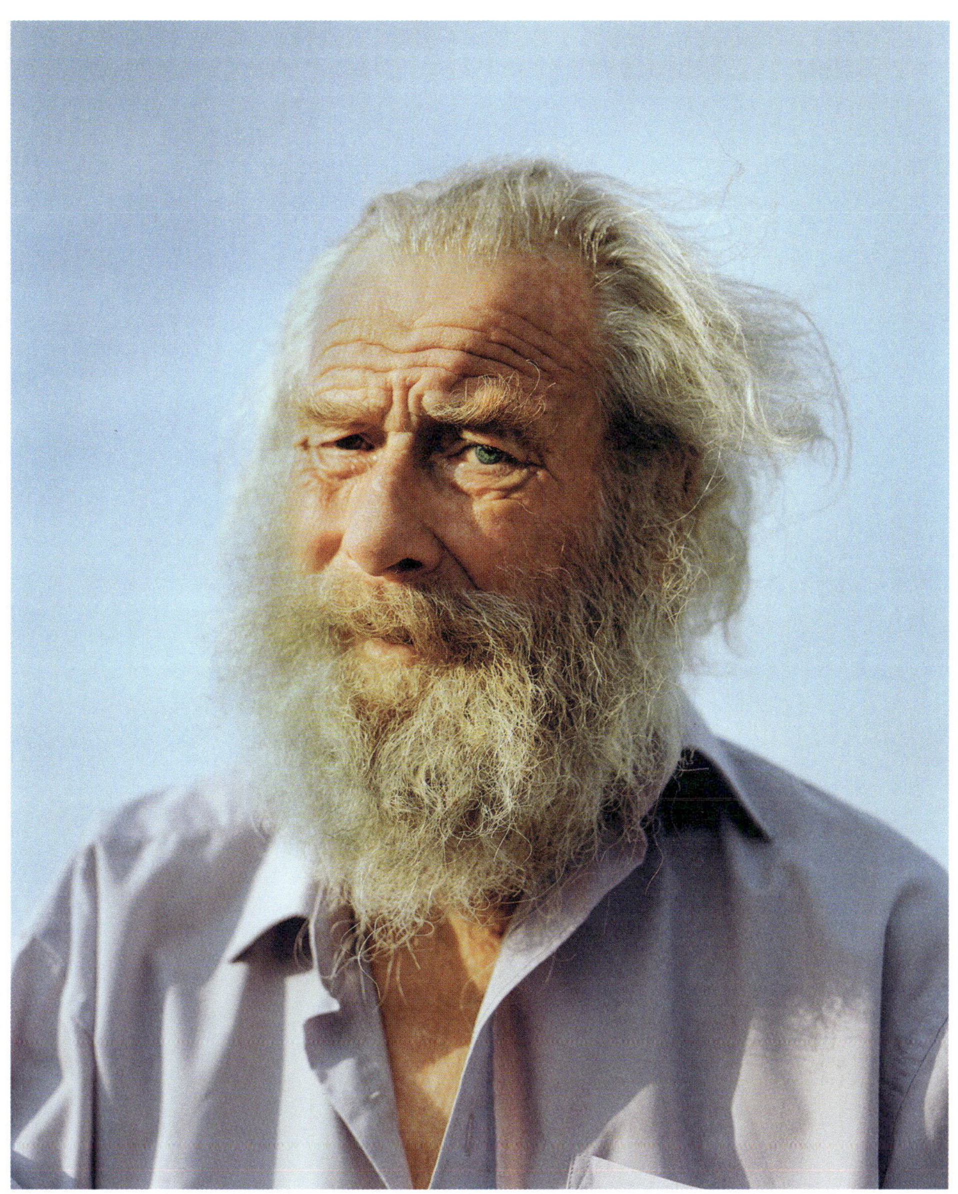

JOSEPH
by Craig Fleming
Stockport, Greater Manchester

Joseph is part of an online drama group for
young people and adults with learning difficulties
called 'Down the Lens', run by Emily Curtis.
I was commissioned by Emily to photograph her
students for a project exploring how they would like
to be seen versus how they feel they are actually seen.
Even with this important subject matter, it was
one of the most fun shoots I've undertaken.

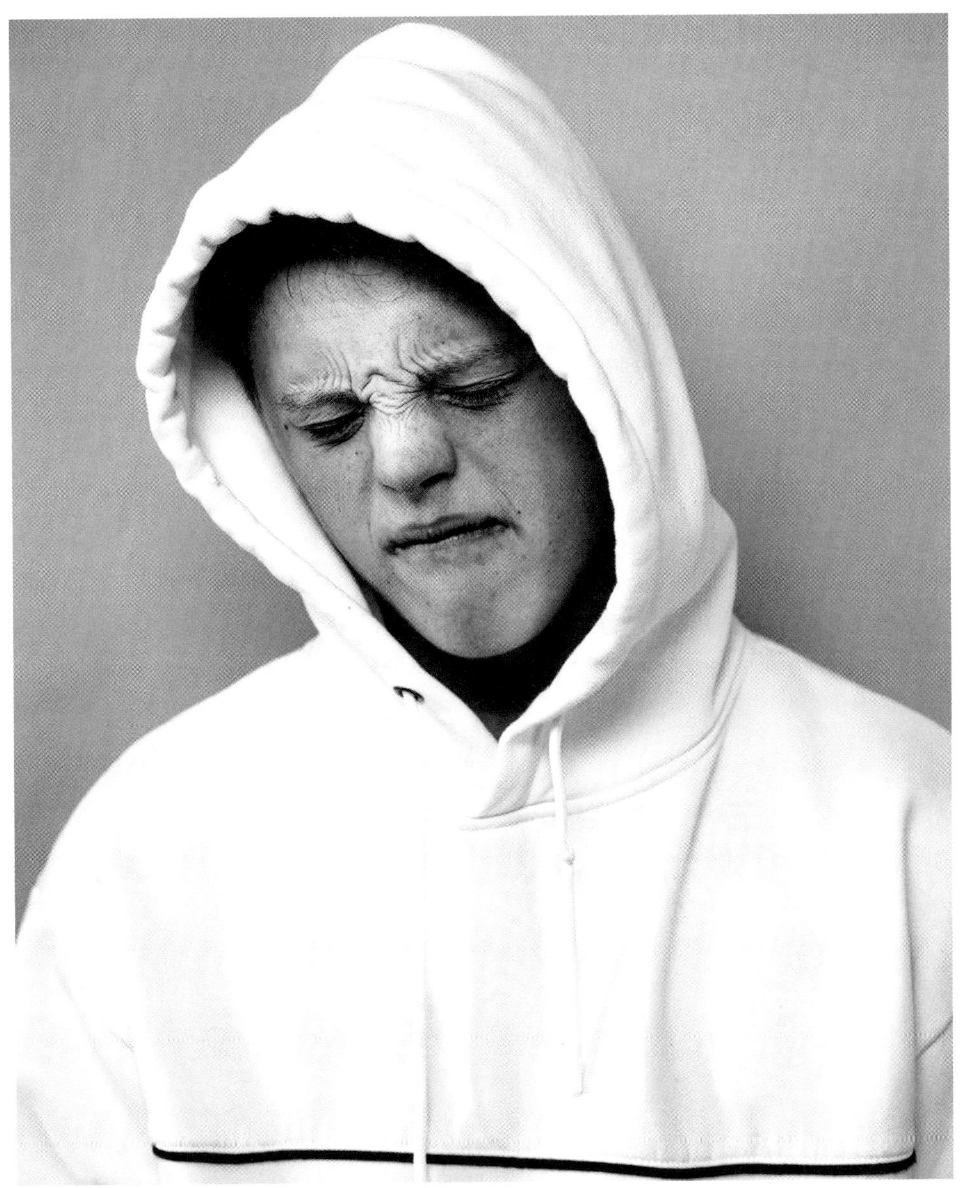

THE GREEDY GULL
by Lorraine Poole
Girvan, South Ayrshire

I took my parents on holiday to Scotland recently.
We were staying by the sea, so one evening I drove
us into town to pick up some fish and chips.
I parked the car so we had a wonderful view of
the shore and we dived into our newspaper-wrapped
delicacies. A minute later, I noticed this huge
seagull sitting on my sunroof staring down at my
dad's dinner. My dad, Bill, hadn't noticed at
all until I took this photo on my phone.

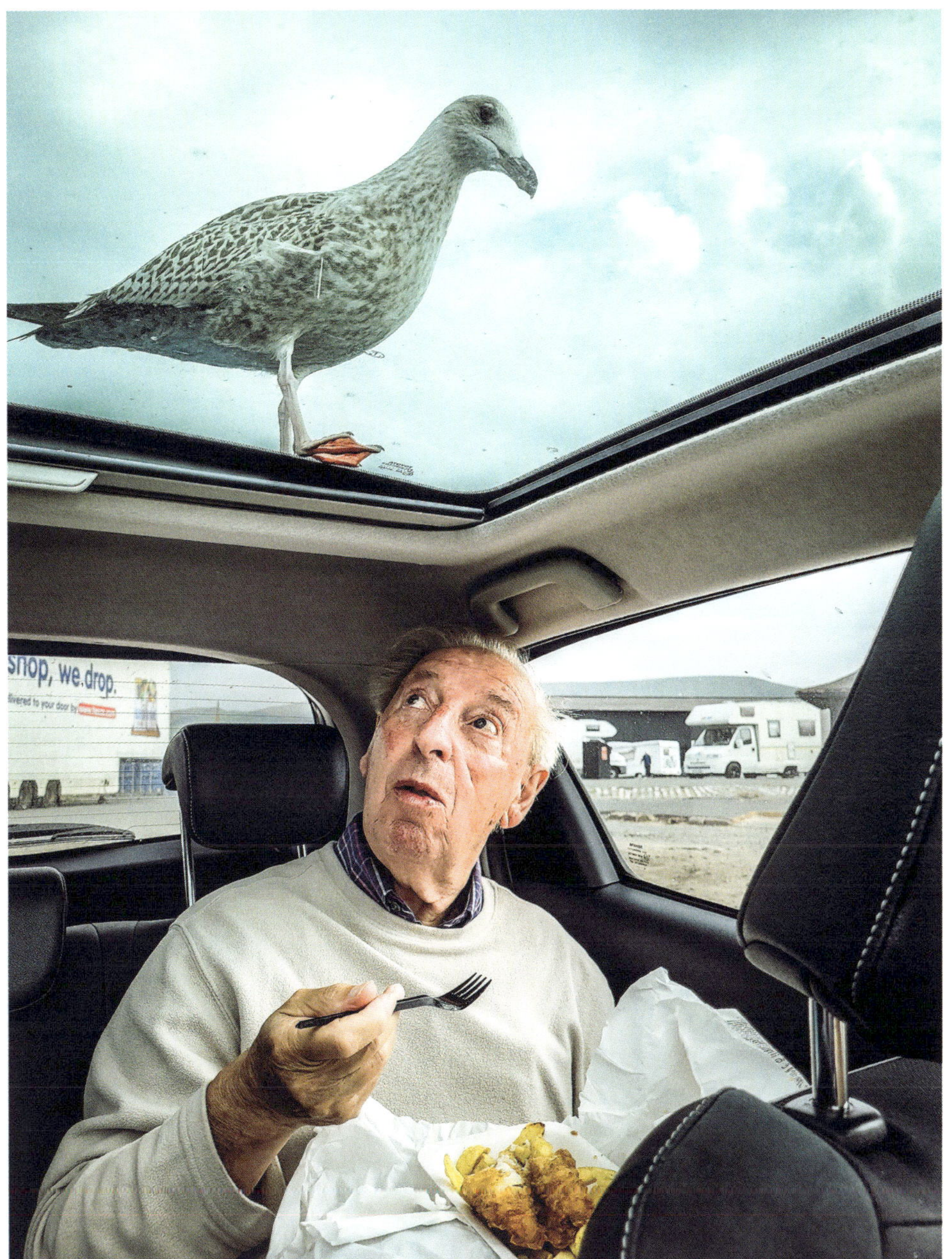
snop, we.drop.

MAN'S BEST FRIEND
by Joshua Atkins
Chatham, Kent

This gentleman asked me if I could take a photograph
of him and his dog, in exchange for a kiss
from my girlfriend. (He had had a lot to drink.)
He lifted the dog in the air after this, but
I preferred the tender moment.

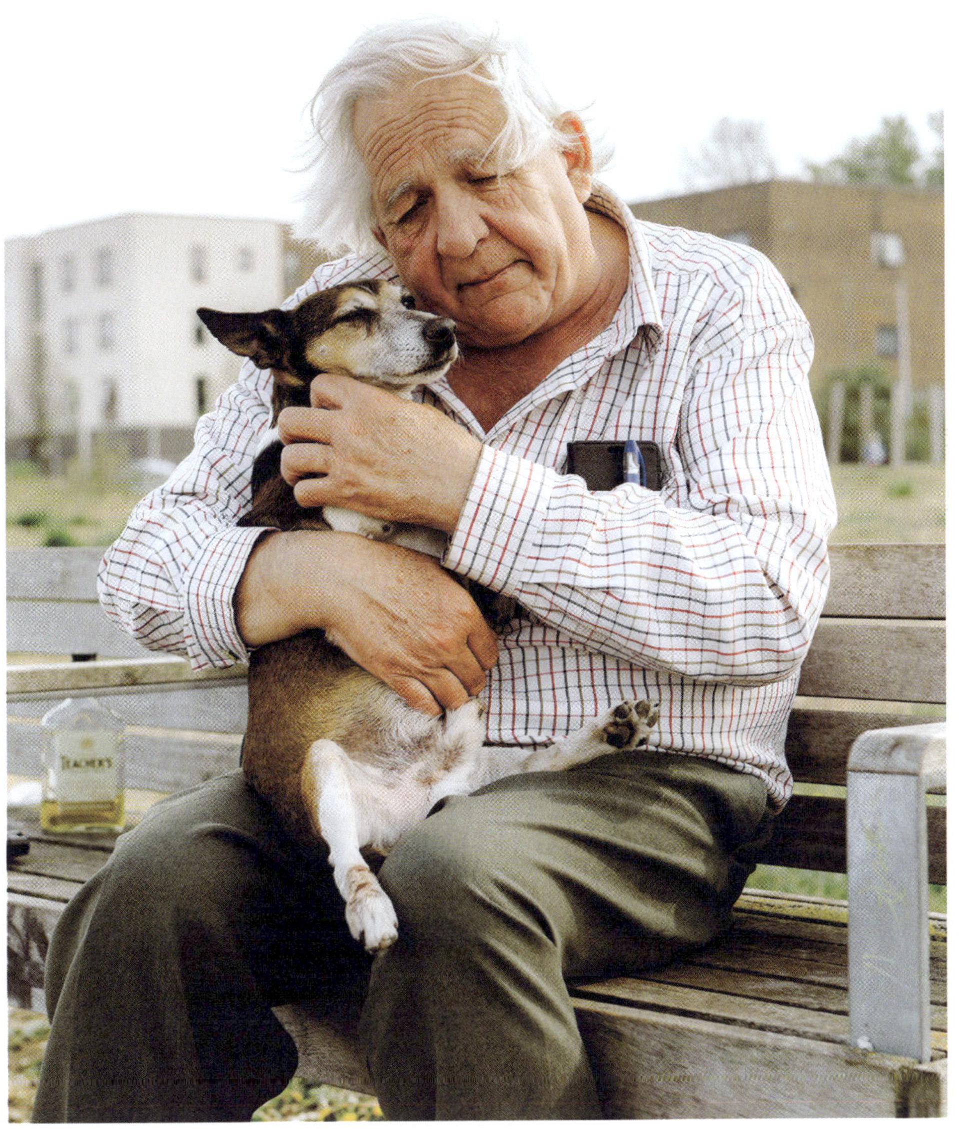

MIRIAM MARGOLYES
by Mark Harrison
London

Miriam enjoys life to the max; she's one of my
favourite people to spend time with. I had gone to
photograph her for the *Radio Times* – this is an
outtake from the shoot in her kitchen.

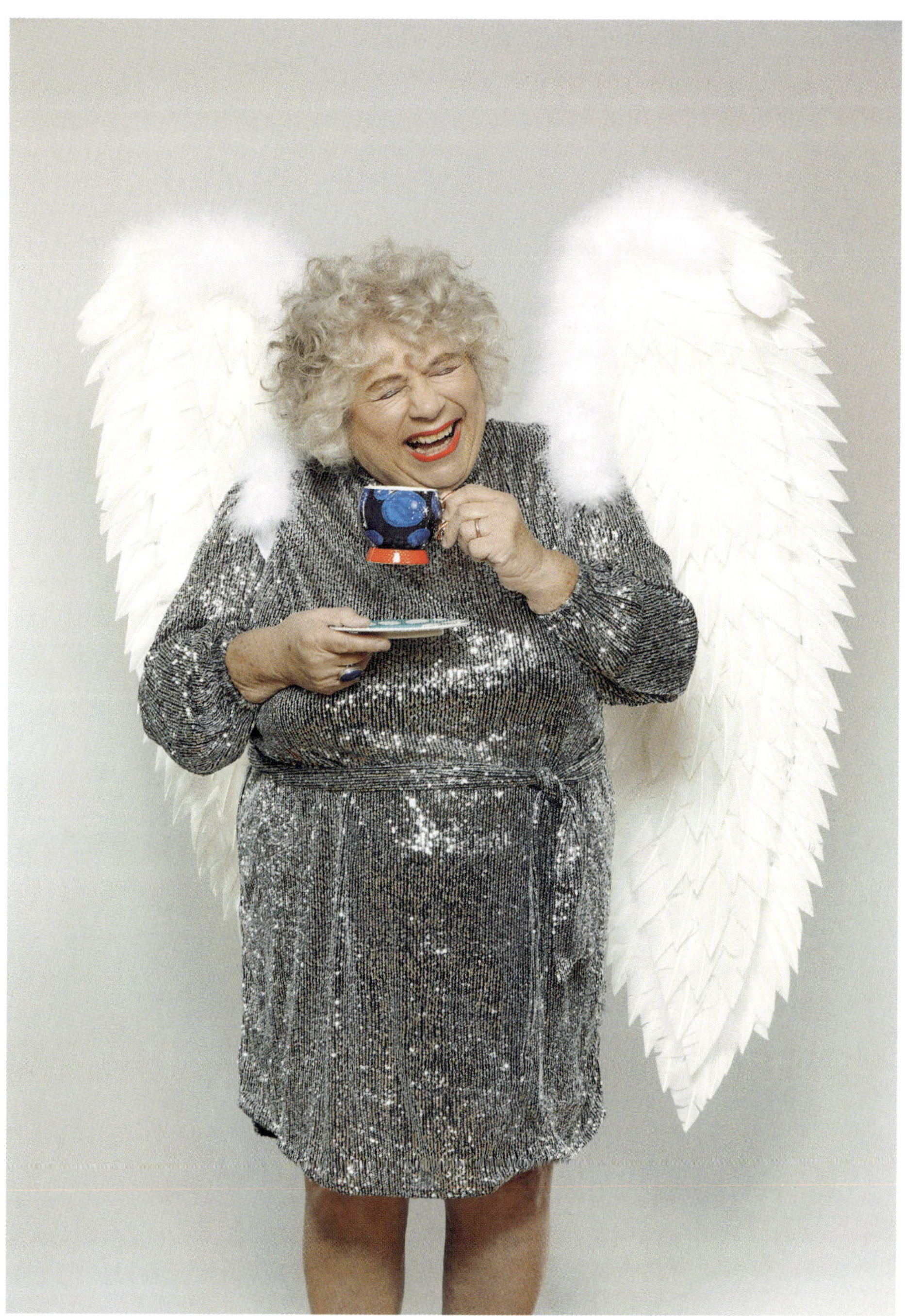

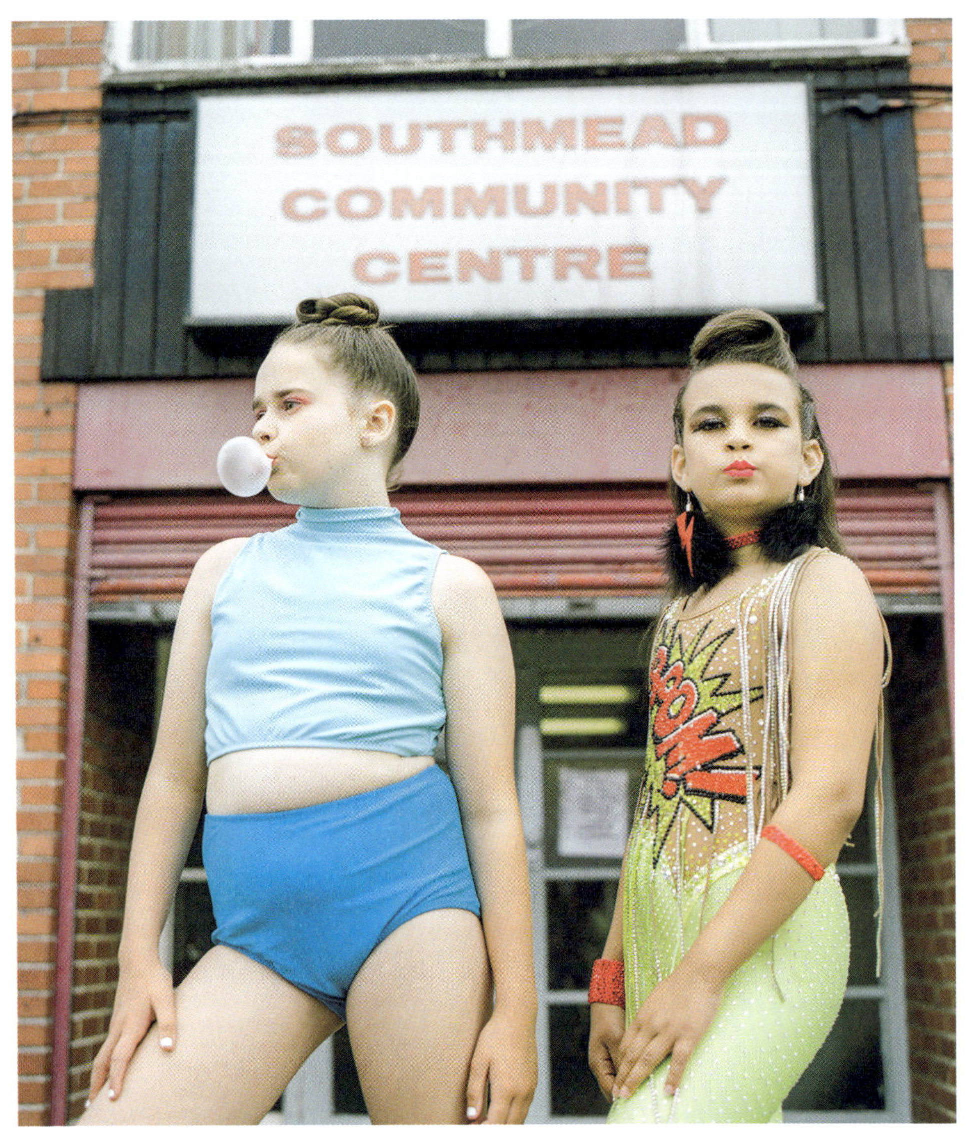

LEXI AND LILY, FAST AND FUSION
by Lucy Werrett
Bristol

114

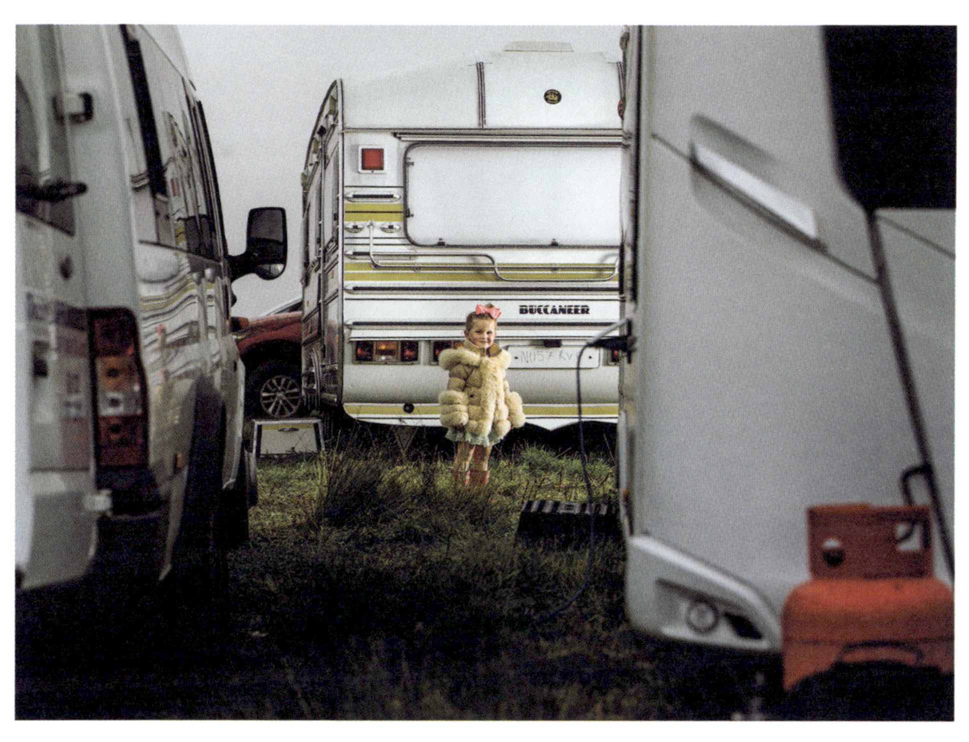

JOSIE
by Tim Fisher
Appleby-in-Westmorland, Cumbria

Josie was visiting the annual Appleby Horse Fair
for the first time, to meet up with her friends and
extended family.

JUNE
by Steve Reeves
London

I saw June walking through Covent Garden.
I loved the way that her blue scarf complimented
the sky, so asked if I could take her picture. She told
me she has lived in Soho for the last 35 years, and
worked in publishing before she retired. She was born
in Clapham but spent many years living in France,
which explained her slight accent. When I asked
June her age, she said 'that's a secret'.

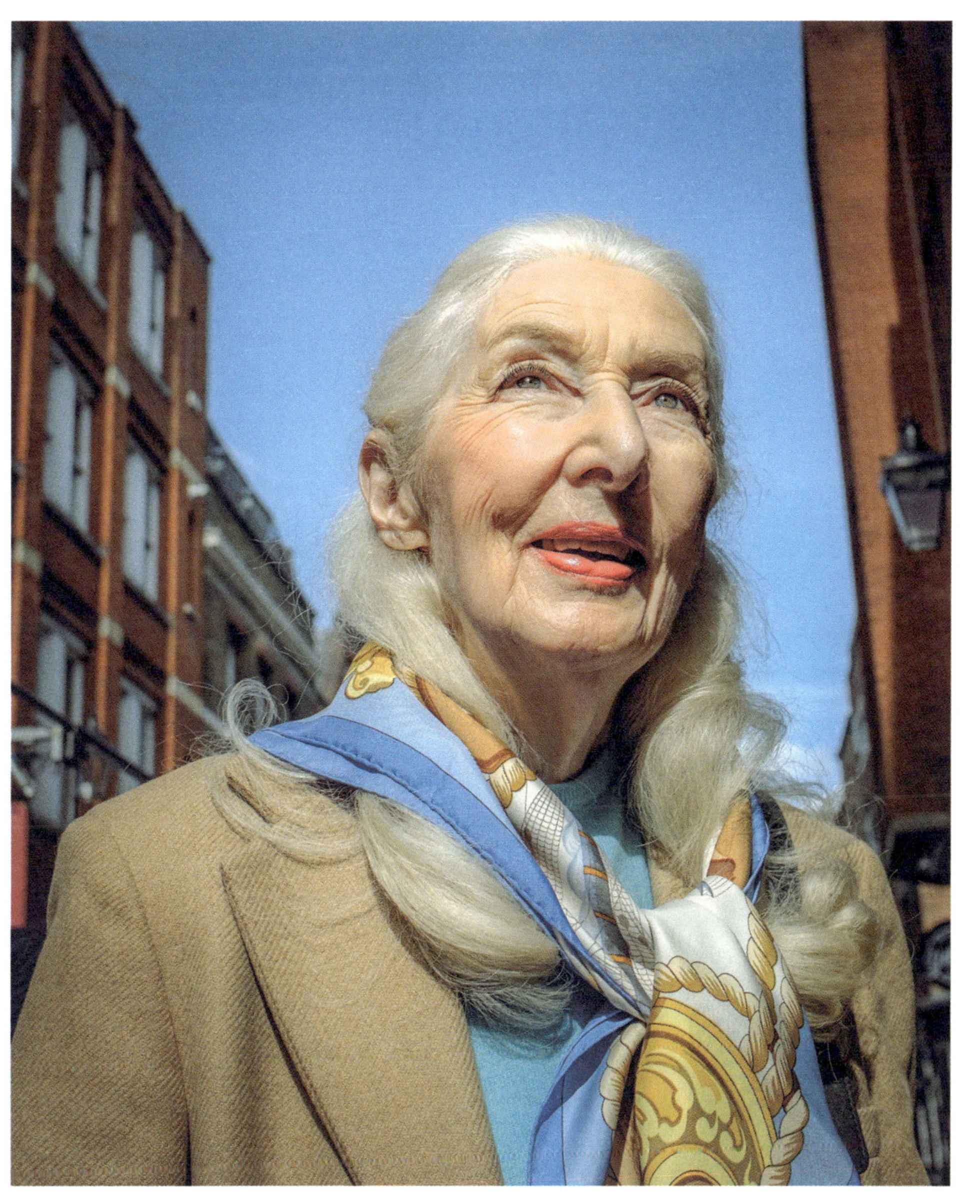

WENDY
by Curtis Hughes
Porthcawl, Bridgend

'Every year my late father would dress up as a clown
and swim lengths in the sea on Christmas Day,
he was such a character. Now, in memory of him,
my sister and I do the same.' – Wendy

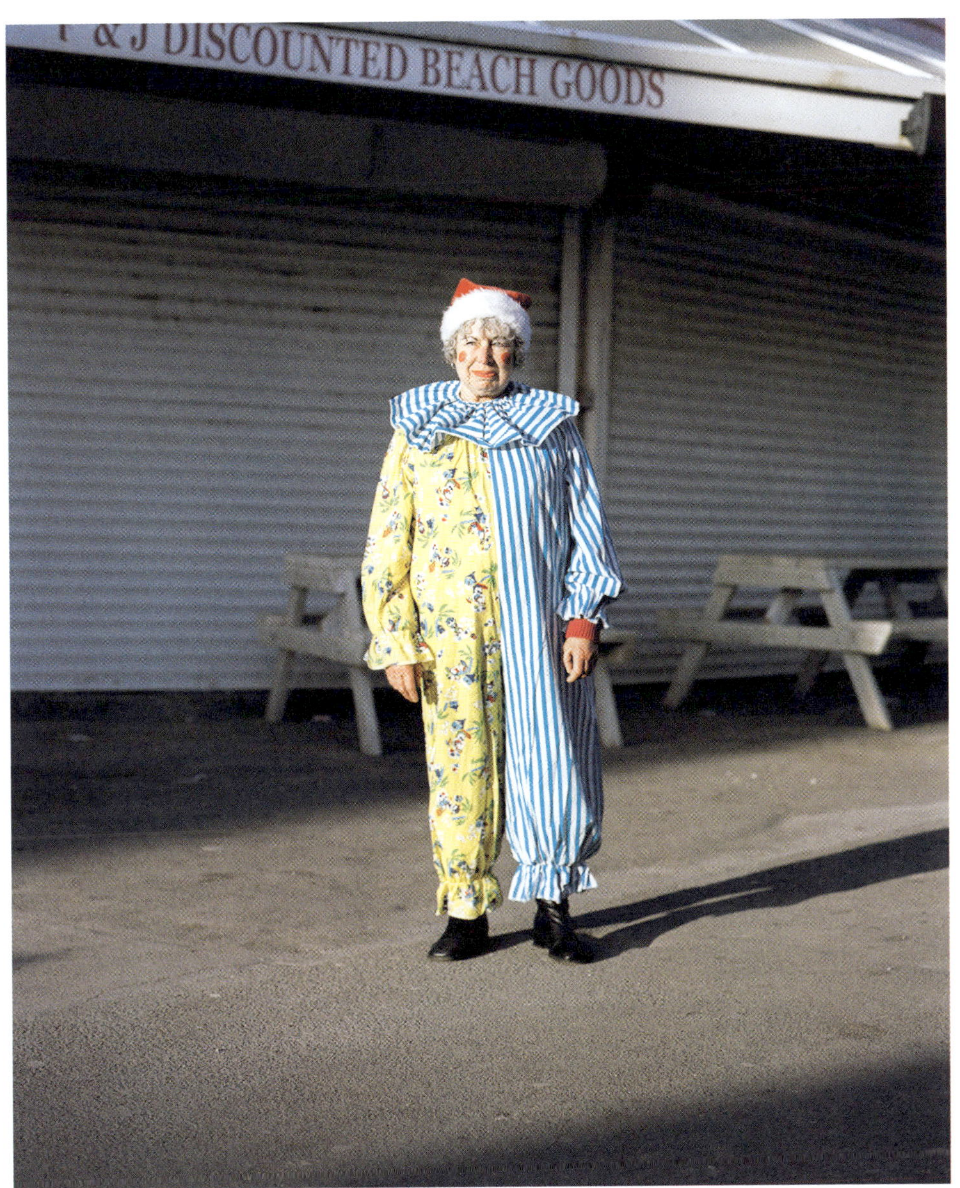
P & J DISCOUNTED BEACH GOODS

WE'RE BLACK, WE'RE QUEER, WE'RE HERE,
GET USED TO IT!
by Fran Gomez de Villaboa
London

'If you are supporting BLM, it needs to be for
ALL Black lives – I am talking for my trans brothers
and sisters. They have been dismissed. They are
being killed daily. Everyone deserves to have the same
voice and to live. No one deserves to die because
of the way they look.' – Aaron Porter (*pictured*)

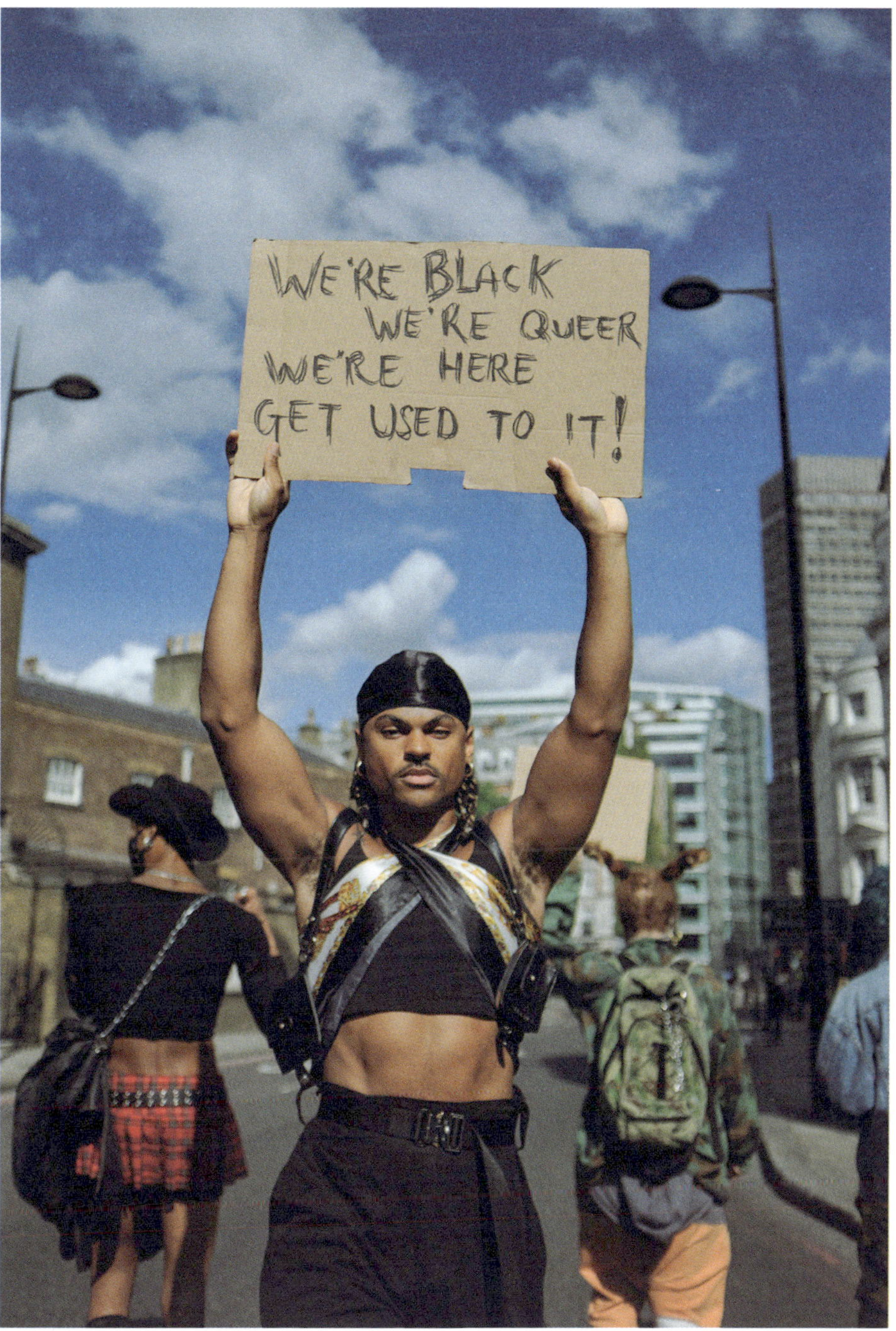
WE'RE BLACK
WE'RE QUEER
WE'RE HERE
GET USED TO IT!

HS2 PROTESTER
by Liam Prior
Jones' Hill Wood, Buckinghamshire

This protester had set up camp in Jones' Hill Wood,
along the planned HS2 route, to try and protect it from
being felled. Jones' Hill was the wood that inspired
Roald Dahl to write *Fantastic Mr Fox*, one of my
favourite childhood books. Sadly, the wood
no longer exists; it was cut down a few
weeks after I took this portrait.

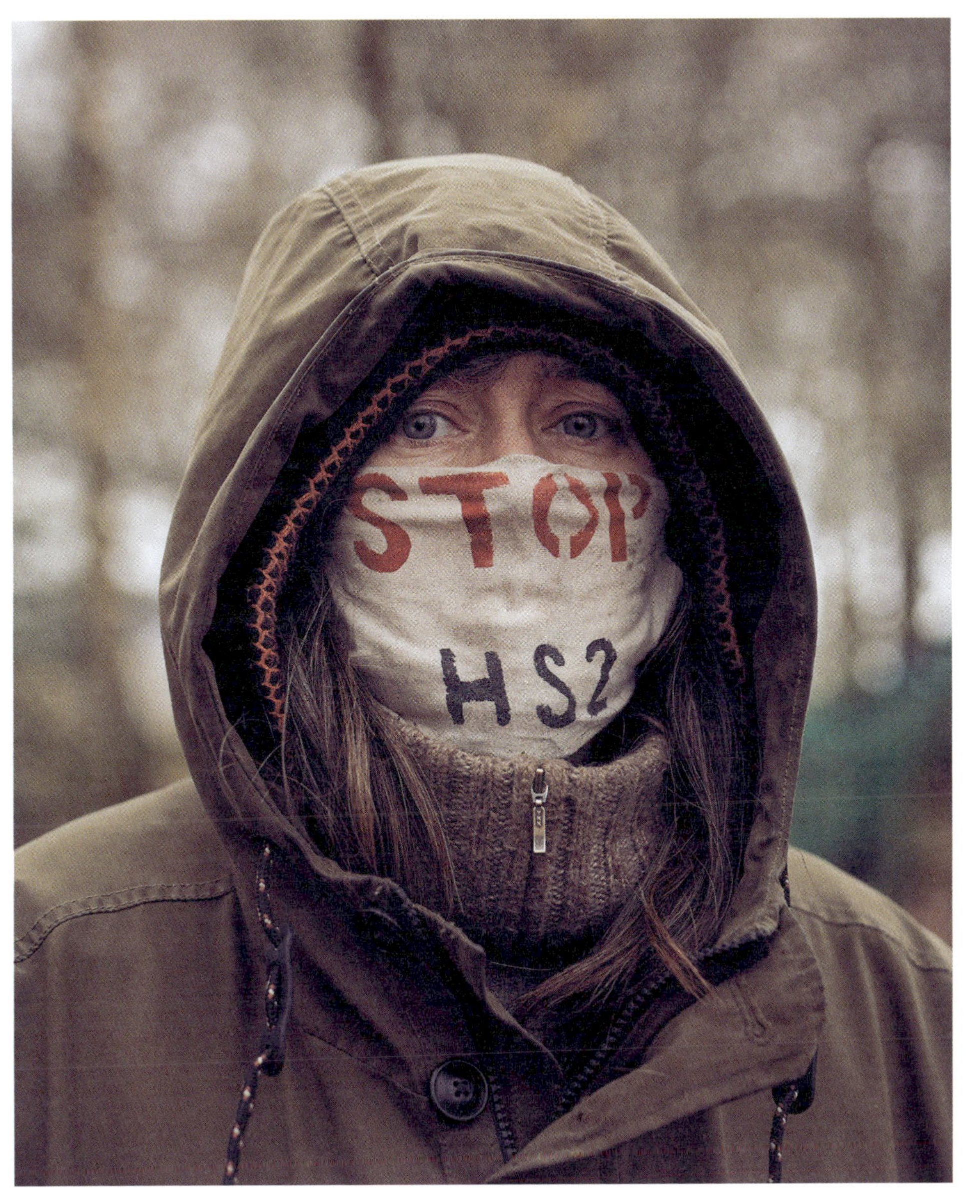
STOP
HS2

RUGILE
by Sarah M. Lee
London

I was cycling home from a job near Primrose Hill
and it was such a beautiful dusk that I decided to
wheel my bike up the hill and admire the view.
I noticed Rugile enjoying a drink with some friends
near the summit. I was drawn by the group's carefree,
open demeanour – that unique energy of young women
drinking wine from paper cups on a warm evening,
with London literally laid out at their feet.

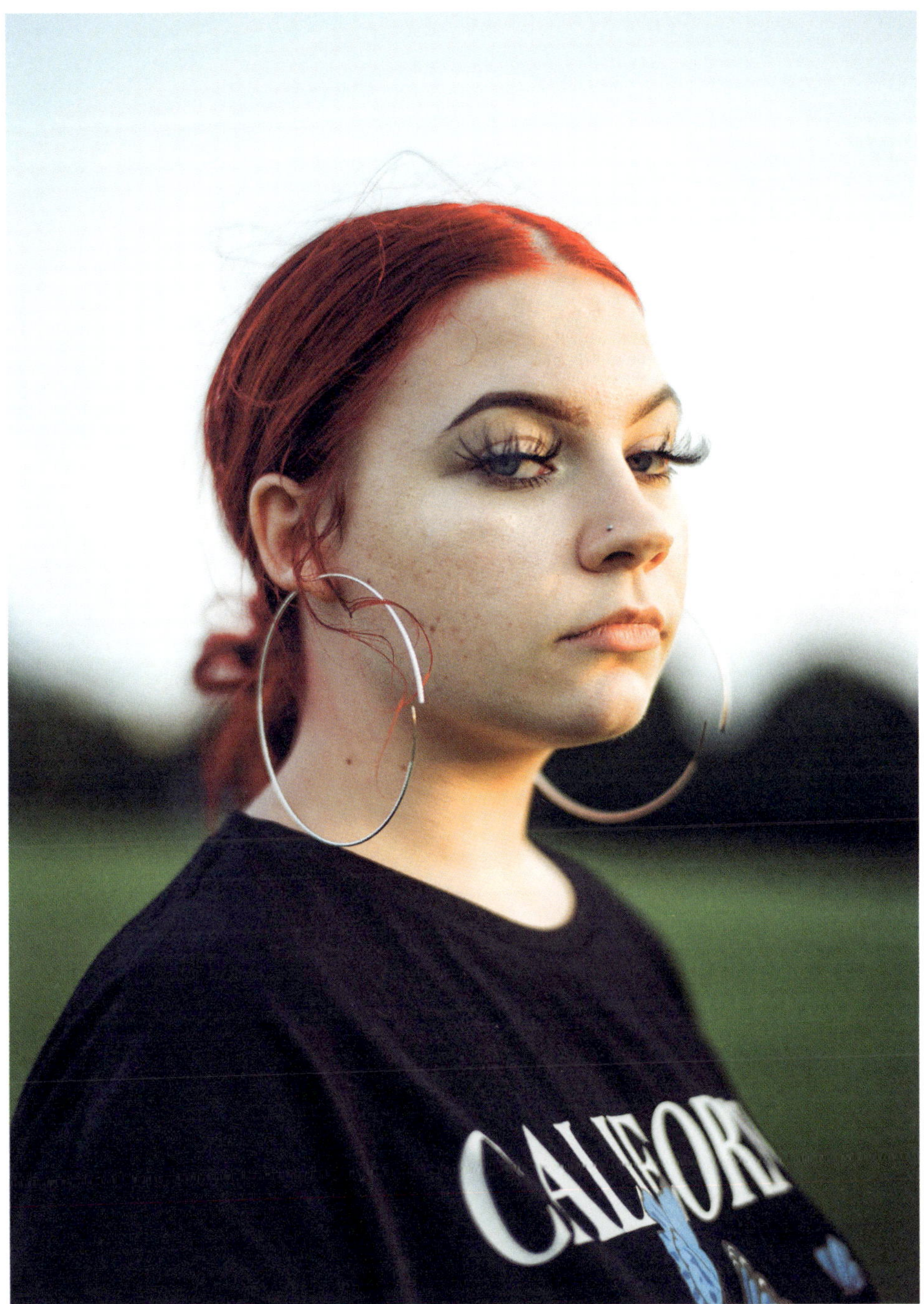
CALIFOR

VENUS
by Fran Gomez de Villaboa
London

Morgana (*pictured*) is a freelance photographer
who did a work placement with me four years ago;
since then we have formed a strong connection.
Recently, she asked me to take some nude portraits
of her. This picture was inspired by Morgana's
heritage; her mother is a well-known medium
in Portugal and witchcraft is something
Morgana is very proud of.

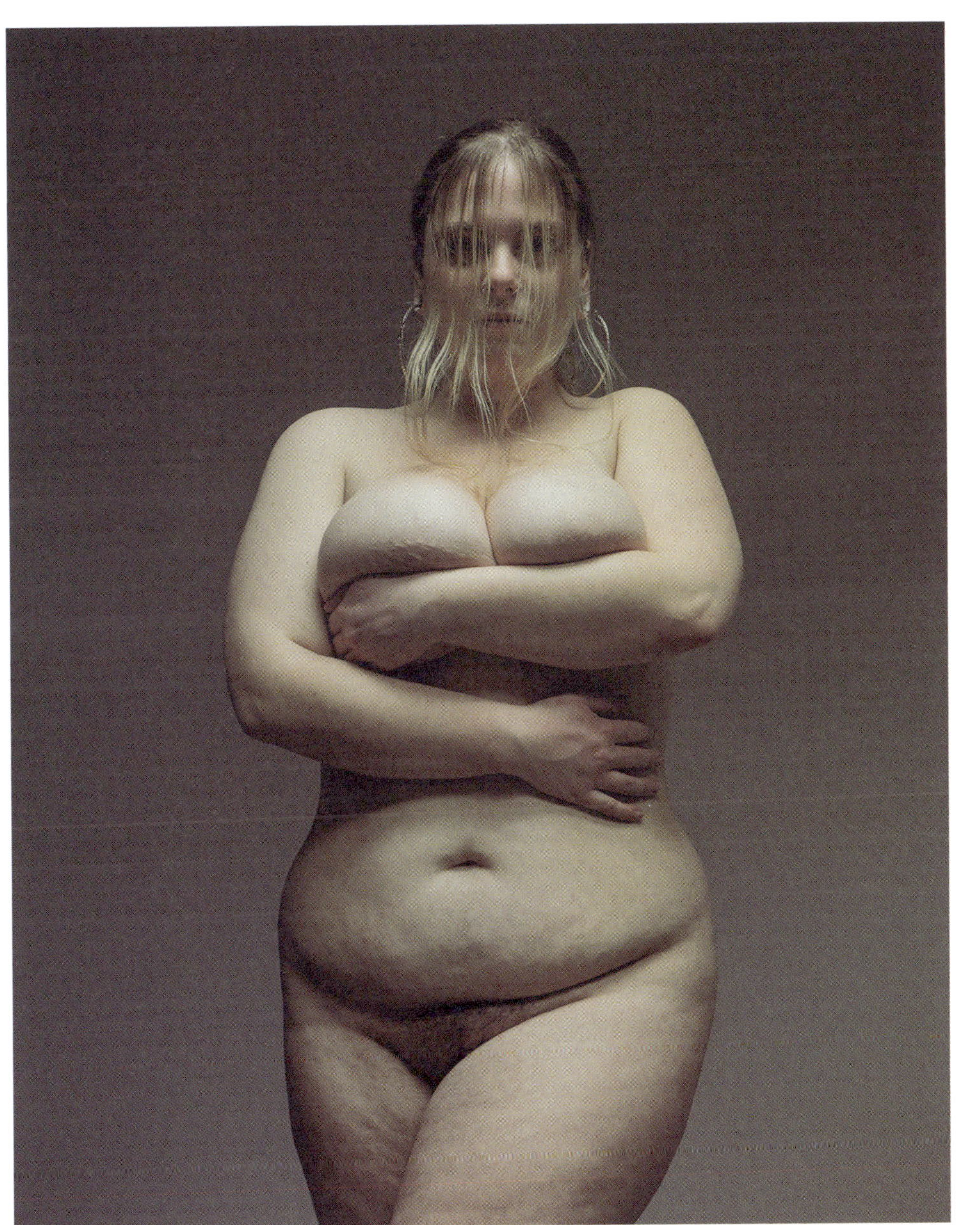

BARBS, TOTTENHAM
by Leon Foggitt
London

Barbs is a London-based drag queen. I photographed
her for a feature in *Suitcase* magazine about the
feelings of peril and liberation drag performers
can experience while travelling to shows. Barbs told
me, 'Sometimes people shout "yaaass" across the
street, other times I get heckled. What they don't seem
to realise is that a girl can bite back – and usually
a lot harder. Making that journey helps create
visibility for people like me. It gives hope to the
many people who want to truly express themselves.'

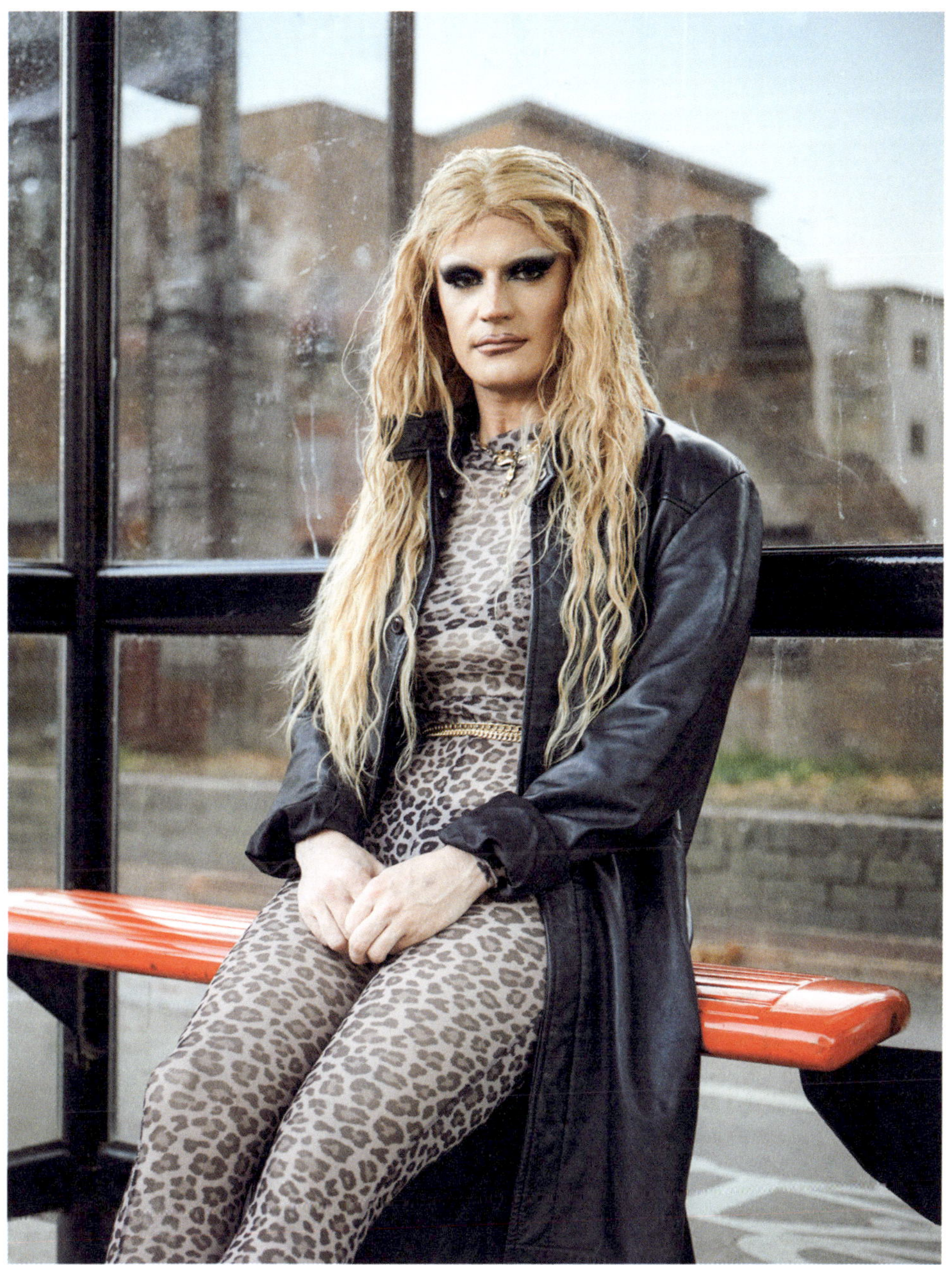

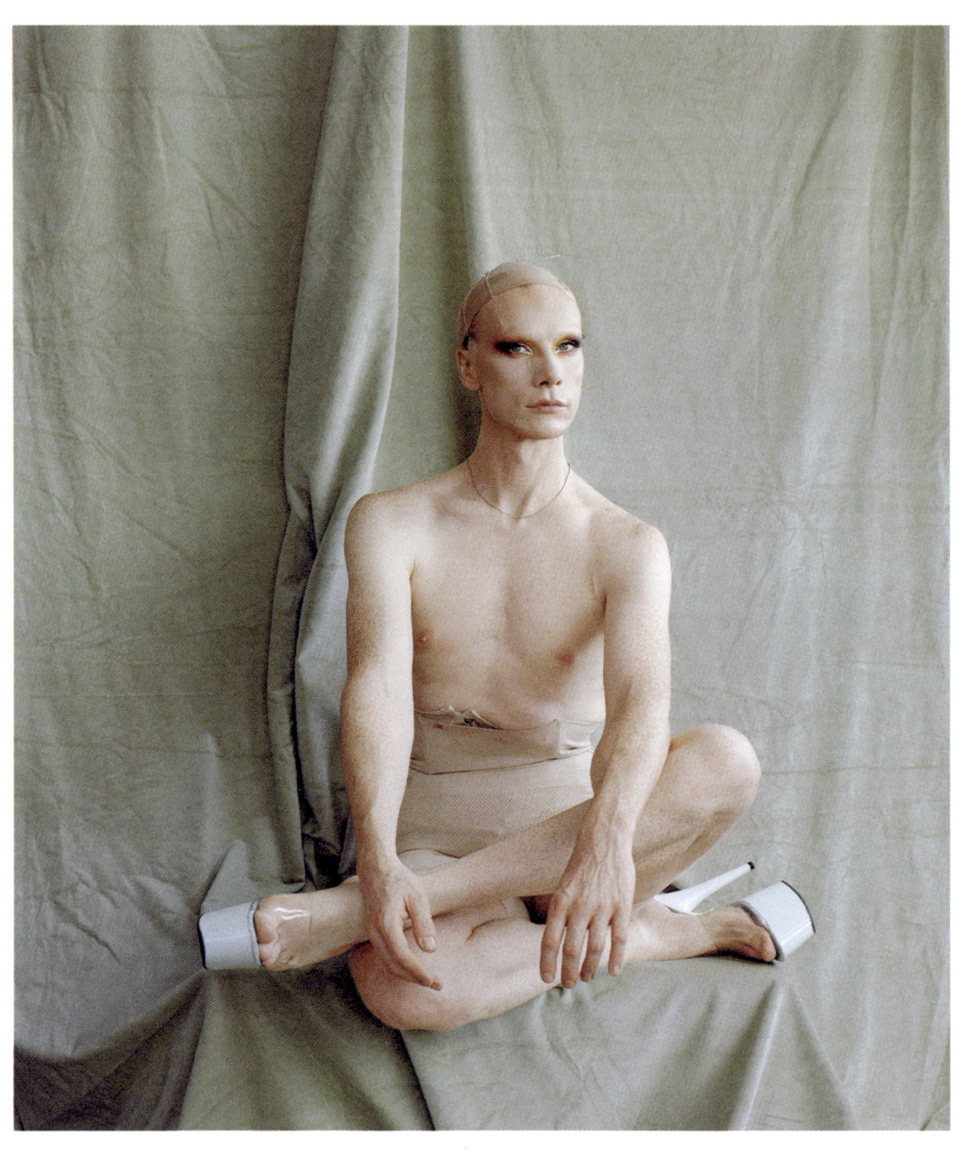

AIRY
by Anna Louise Brooks
London

130

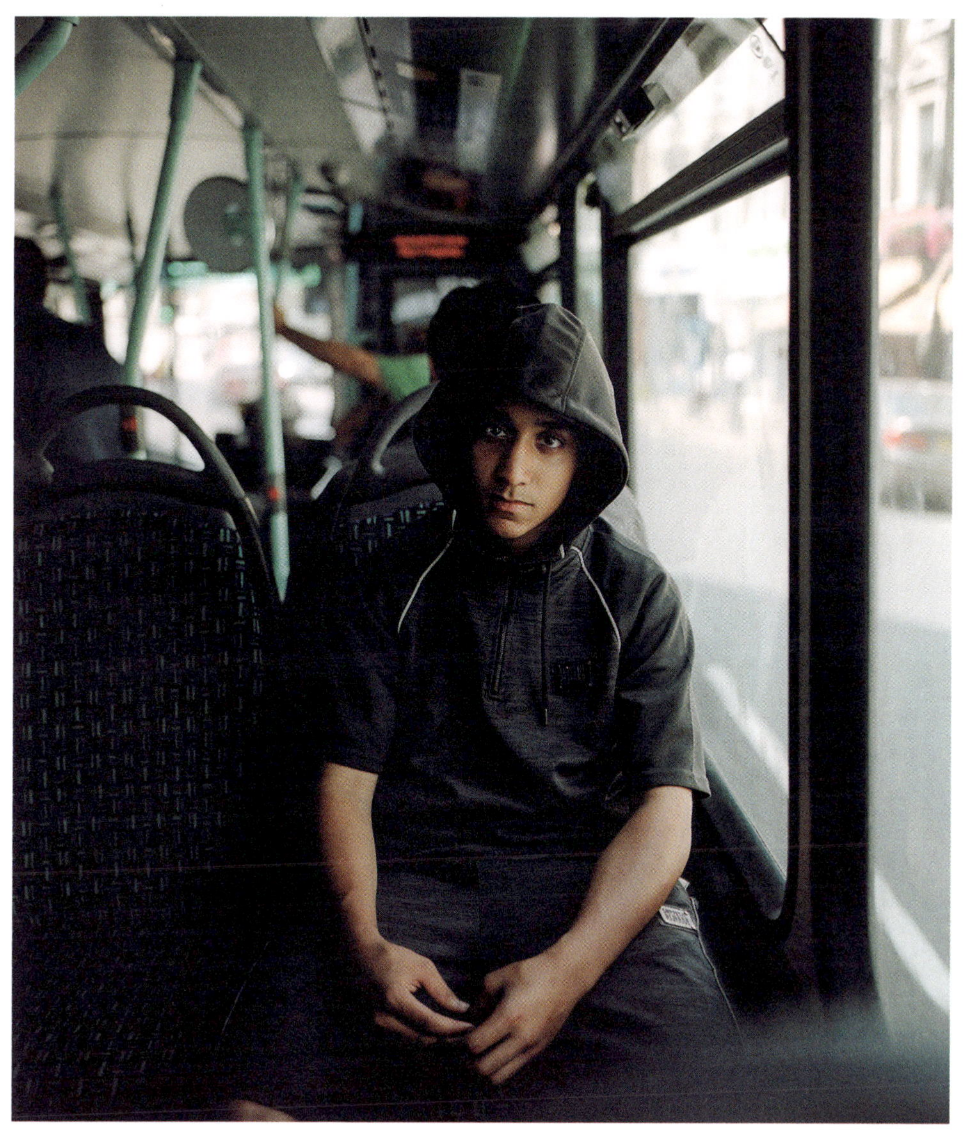

TALHA, 18 BUS TO SUDBURY
by Matt MacPake
London

ADRIAN LUKIS
by Michael Wharley
London

Adrian is a successful actor with hundreds of
stage and screen appearances to his name, but is
perhaps best known as dastardly Mr Wickham from
the BBC's timeless adaptation of *Pride and Prejudice*.
He had come to my studio to shoot light, bright,
promotional images for a new show, but when
I asked him to sit for five minutes at the end
so we could shoot a more painterly portrait, he
couldn't help delivering a roguish twinkle.
Some roles, you never leave behind.

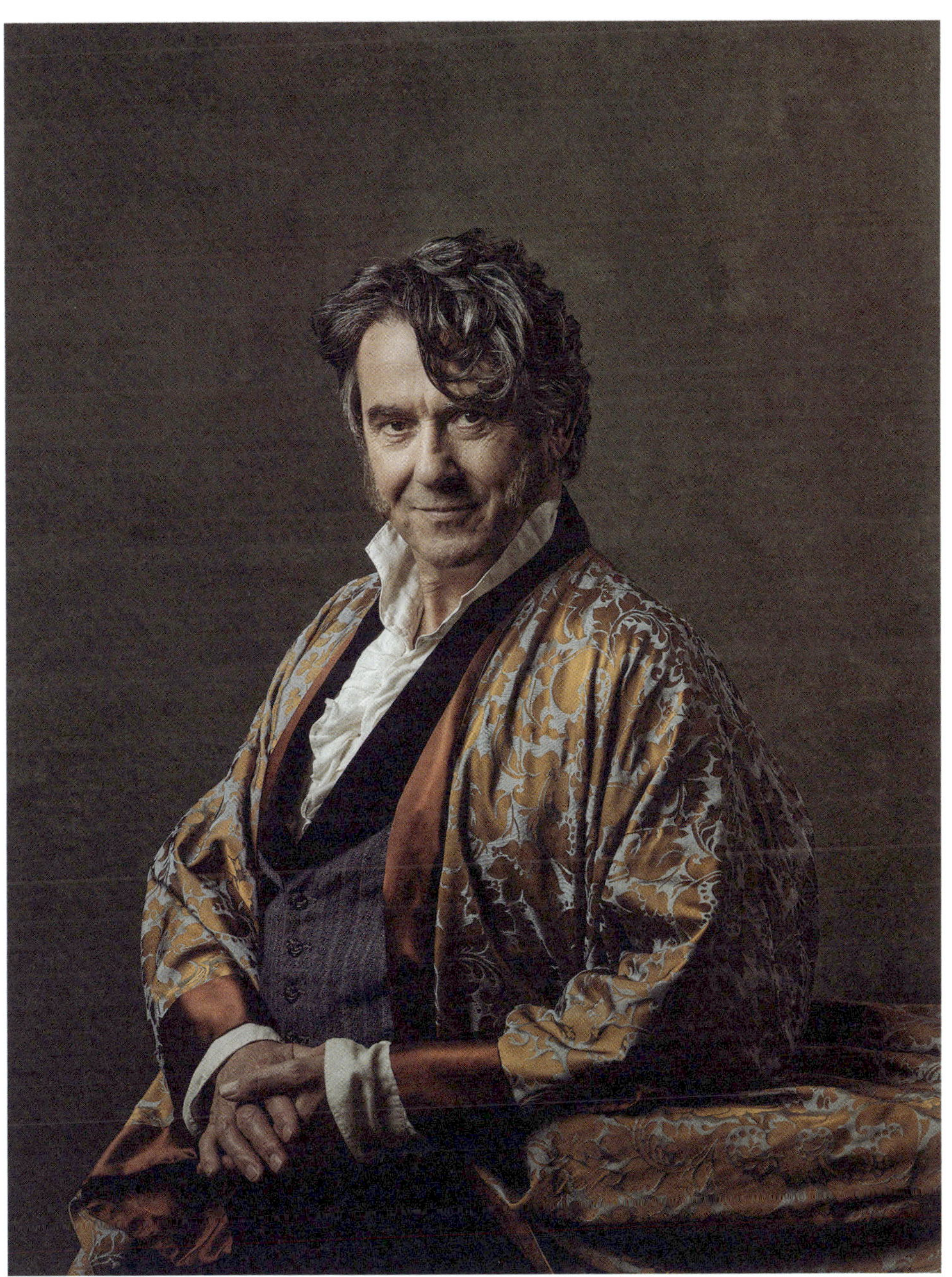

AMIR
by Mark Taylor
Newcastle upon Tyne

I noticed Amir and his impressive beard as he
walked past me with a bag of shopping in each hand.
I asked if I could take his photo and he kindly agreed.
It was a very quick portrait, as Amir's shopping
was heavy and he wanted to get home.

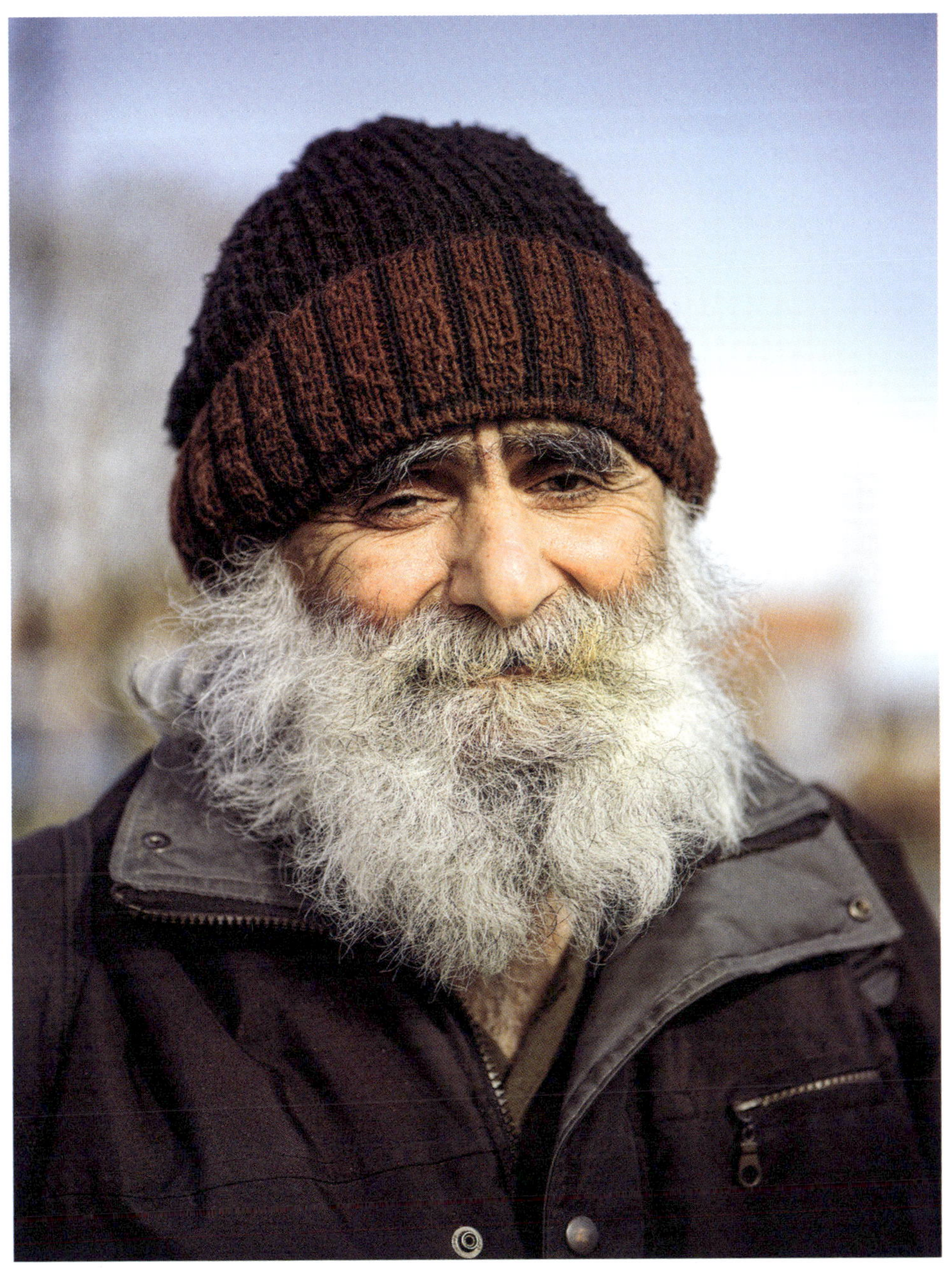

UNTITLED
by Marley Starskey Butler
Birmingham

This is my friend Danni Ebanks-Ingram + Zaz.
They are a producer, curator and artist. We spent
this morning chatting, drinking tea together
and making photographs.

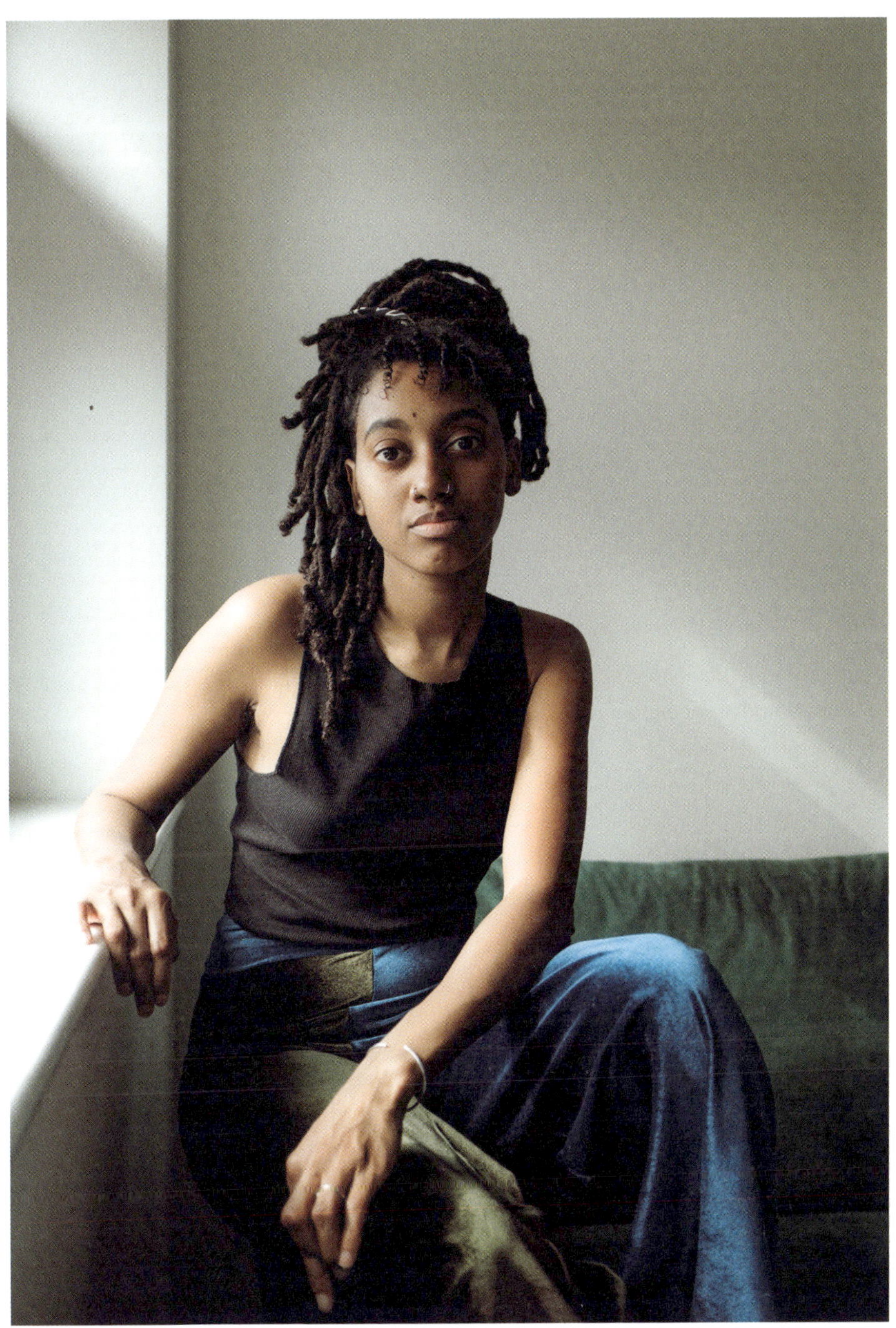

MOHAN
by James Deavin
Slough, Berkshire

Driving along the M4, I always notice the allotments
near Slough that back right onto the motorway.
I was working on a project about farming, so one day
decided to go and investigate. That's how I met
Mohan, who has had an allotment here ever since
he first moved to Slough from Delhi; he grows many
of the fruits and vegetables he used to eat in India.
He welcomed me with great hospitality, and sent me
home with armfuls of homegrown veg.

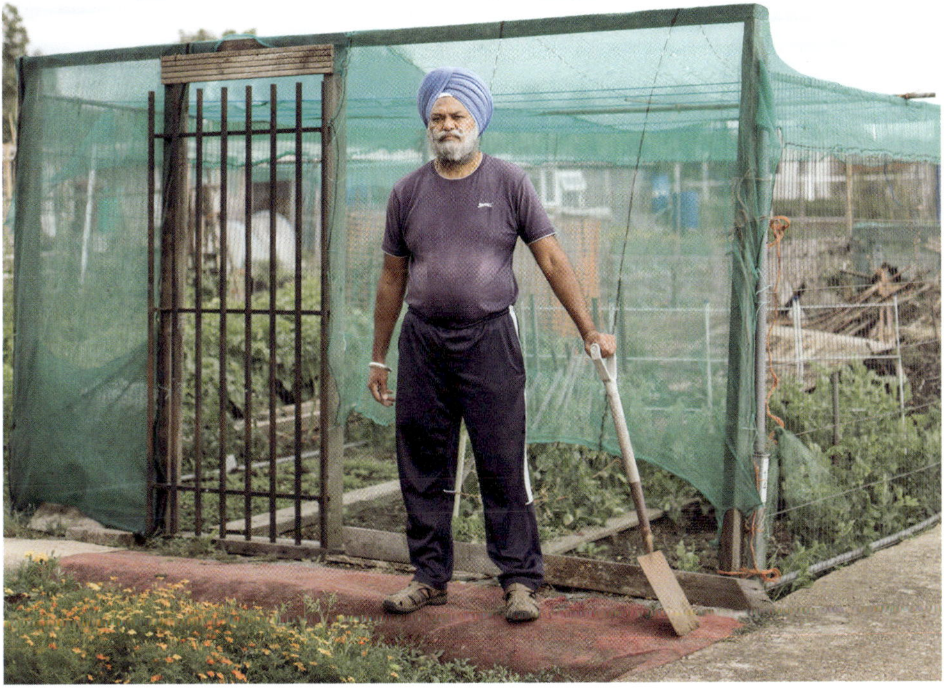

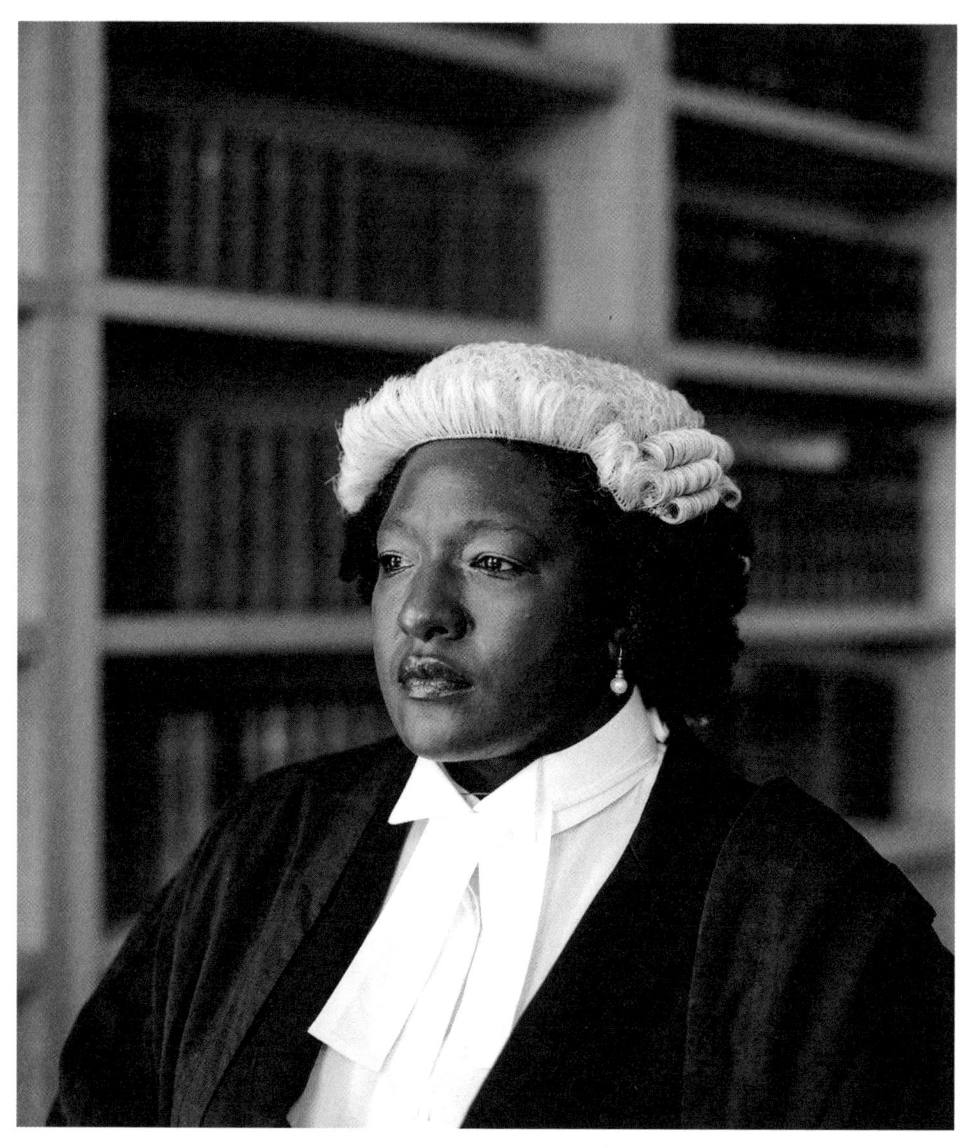

KAREN
by Myah Jeffers
Nottingham

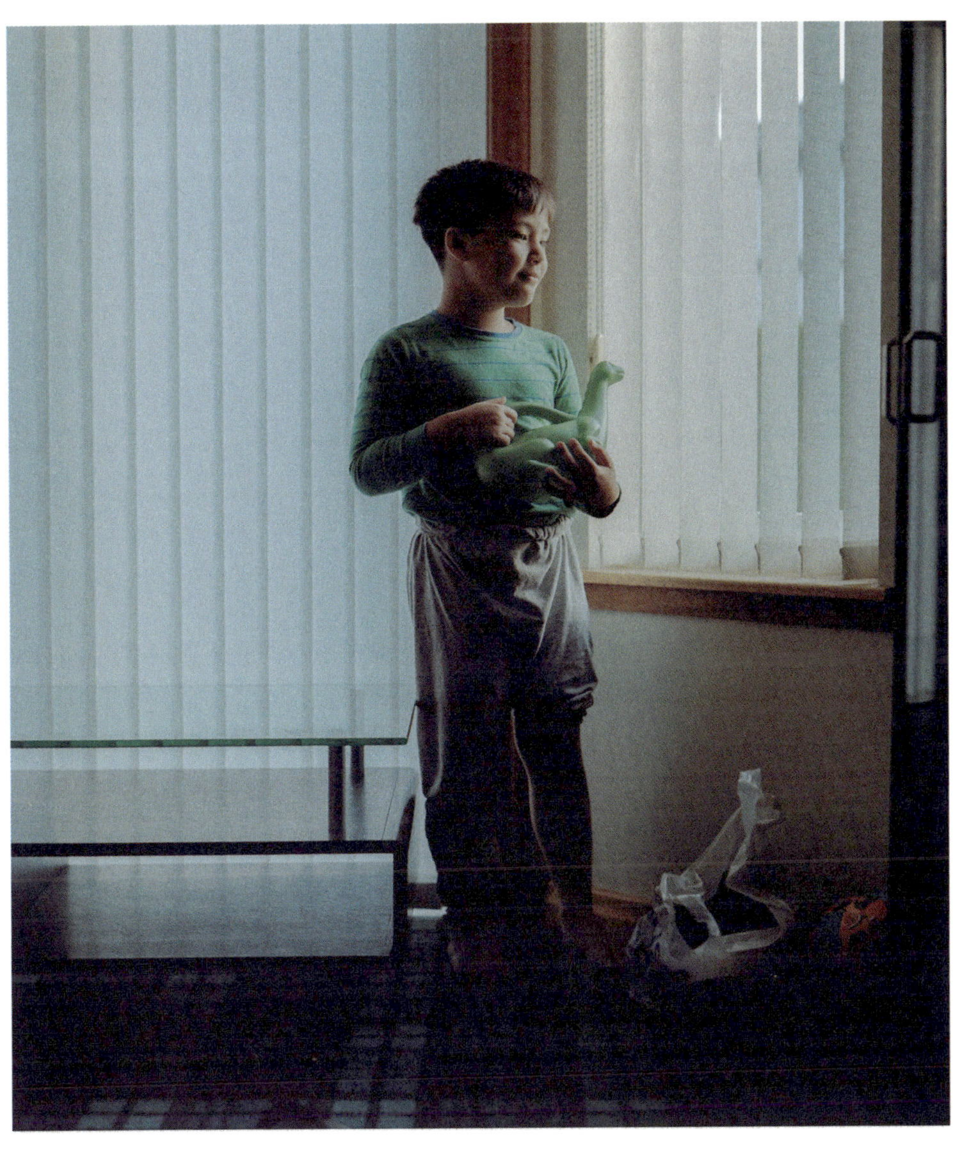

JAYDEN CHAN
by Timothy Chan
Perth, Perth and Kinross

141

DESTINY, 17,
CRYSTAL PALACE GARDENS
by Harry Rose
London

Destiny is a climate change activist. She is one
of the co-founders of Choked Up, a youth
organisation run by Black and brown teenagers
that raises awareness of the toxic levels of pollution
in London, and lobbies MPs for a new clean air deal.
She is currently studying English Literature, French
and Philosophy at A-Level, with the ambition to
study French and Philosophy at Oxford University.

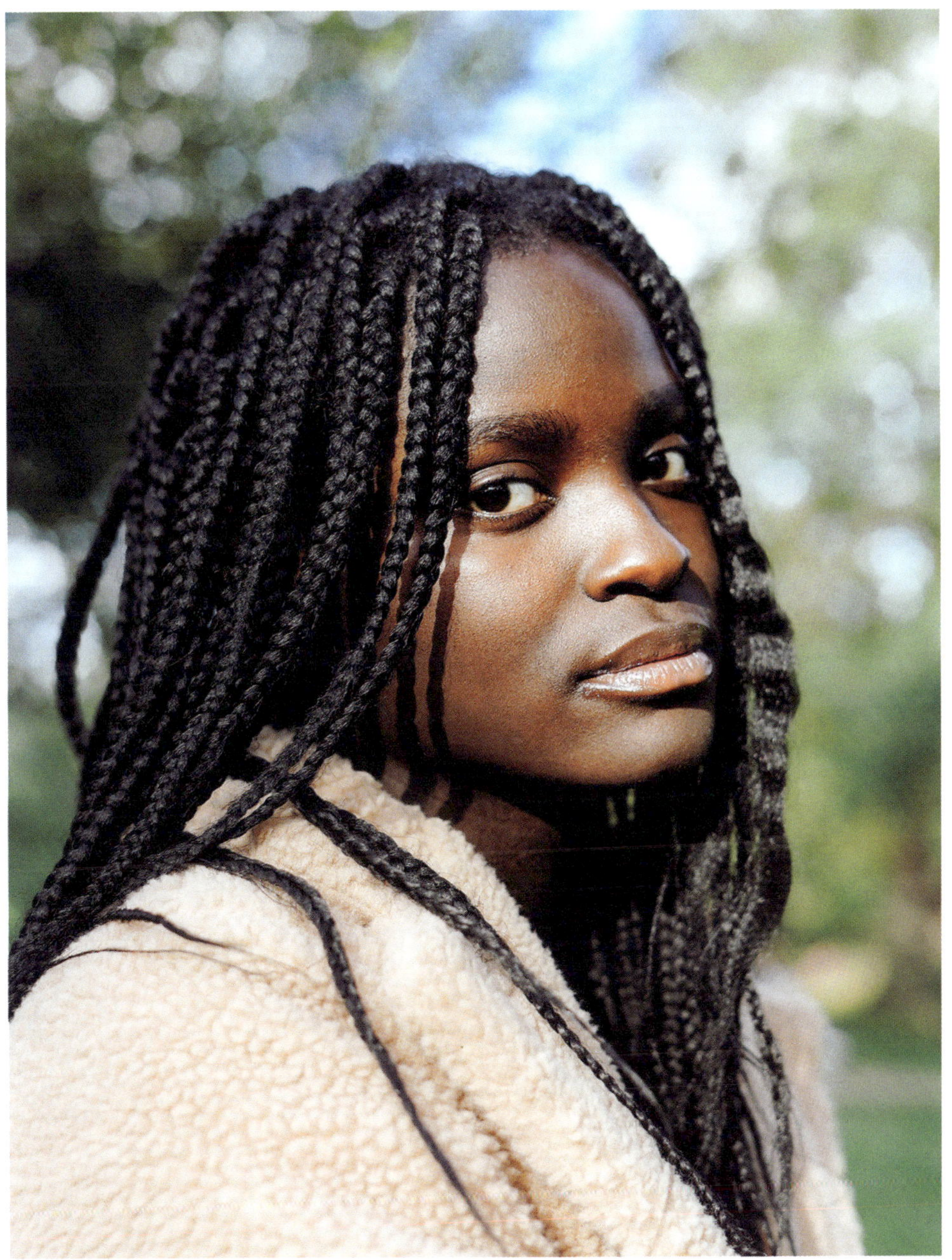

HOPE
by Ross Cooke
Manchester

I was commissioned to photograph the footballer
and campaigner Marcus Rashford in his back garden.
This portrait of him was taken off the cuff on my film
camera, while Marcus waited patiently between takes;
he was in his own world but still looked so strong
and hopeful. I thought his expression captured
perfectly what a shining light he has been
for underprivileged children.

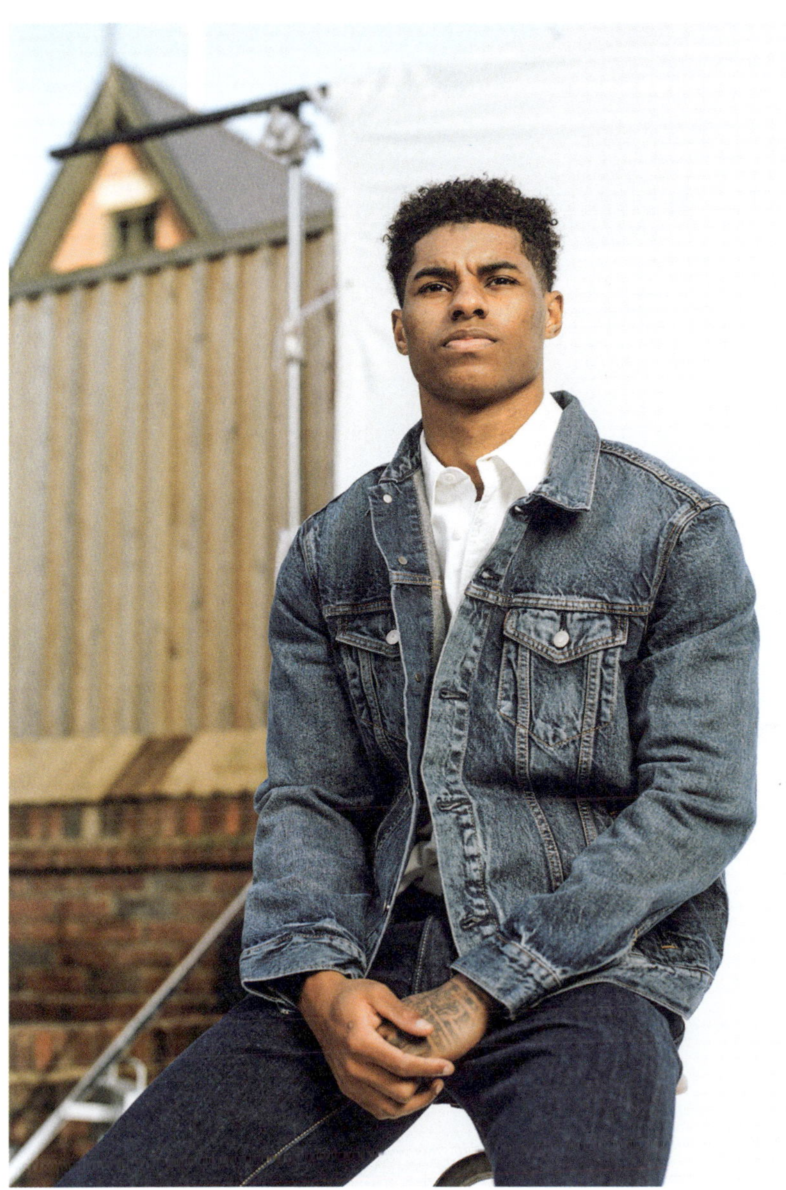

JAYSON
by Harry Rose
Brighton, East Sussex

Jayson, a painter and decorator, identifies
as a gay man. I photographed him as part of my
series about openly queer people who have a different
relationship with masculinity, and we spoke about
his background working in typically all-male and
over-masculine environments like building sites.

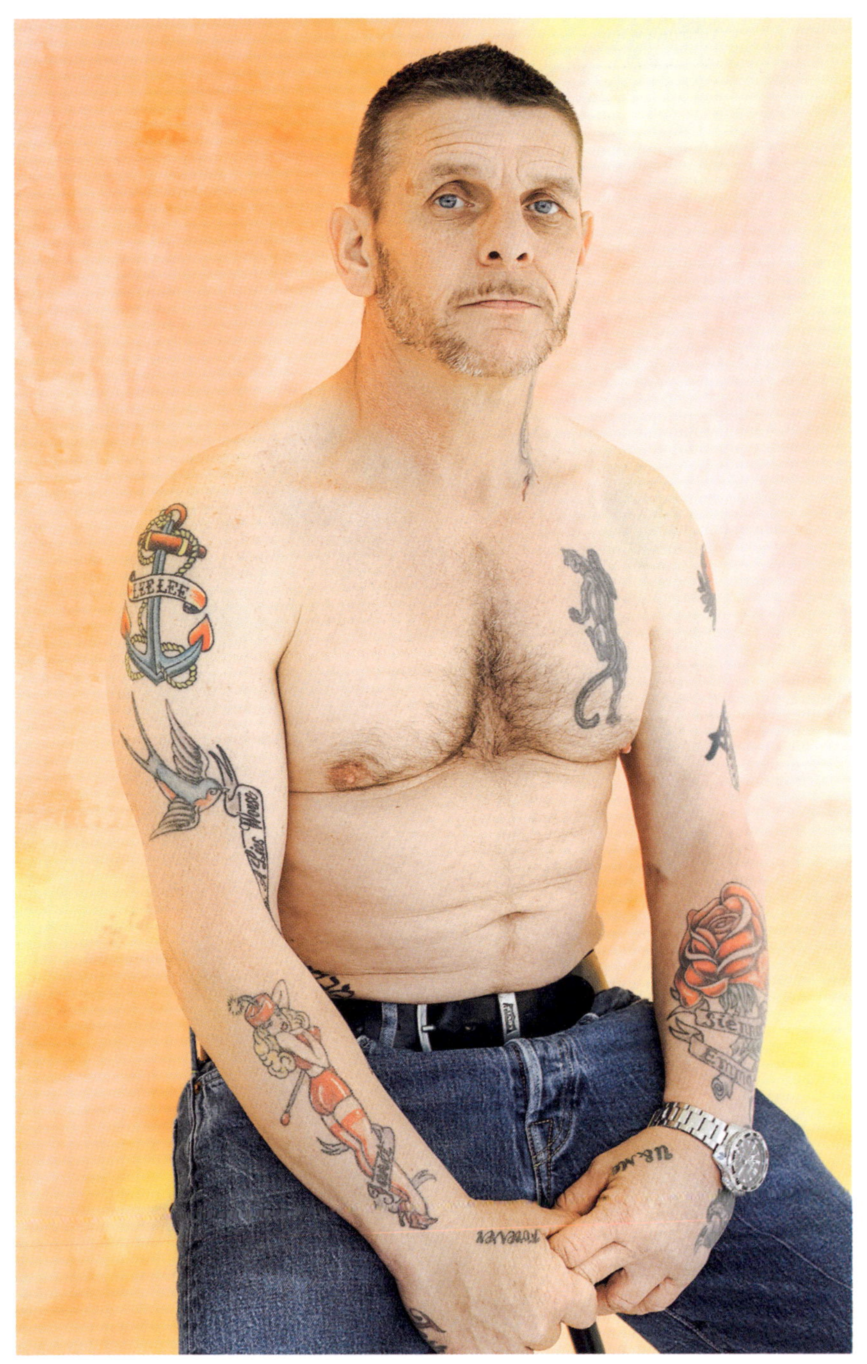

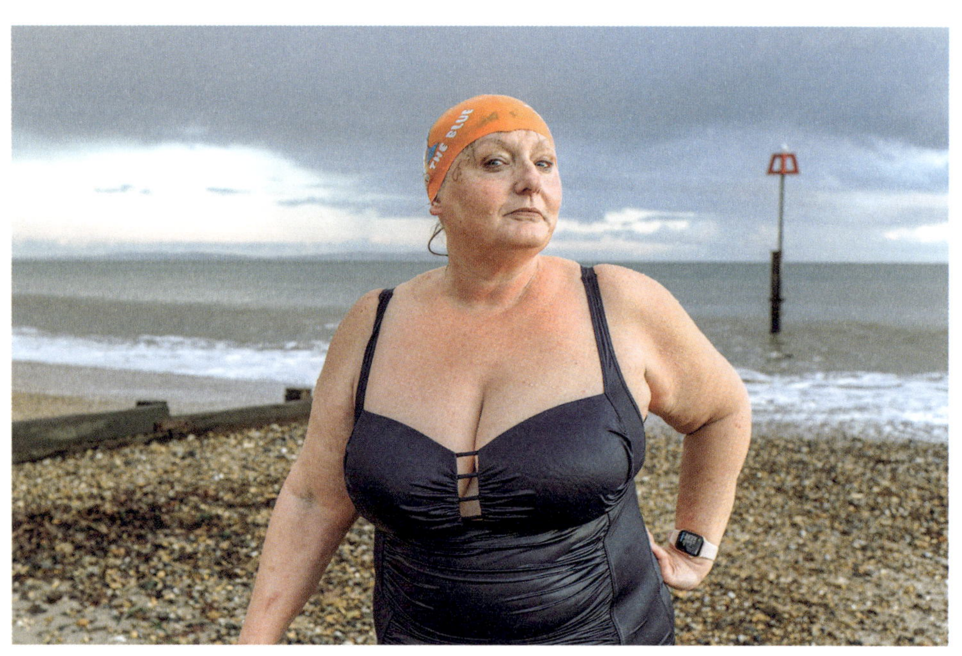

JENNY
by Steve Reeves
Avon Beach, Dorset

I was walking my dog along the beach on a freezing
winter's day when I spotted Jenny striding out of the sea.
I always carry my camera with me, and she kindly let me
take this shot. Jenny told me she took up 'all year round'
swimming in 2014, after her dad passed away. She'd spent
many years caring for him, and after his death found
that she had more time to pursue new interests.

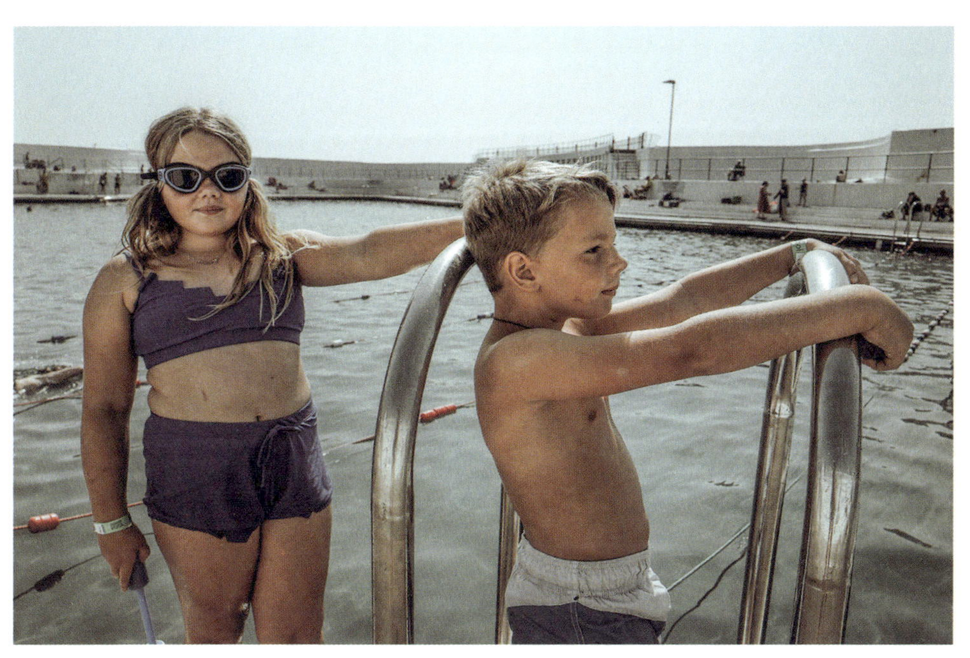

ENGLAND'S LITTLE TREASURES
by Lucy Mohr
Penzance, Cornwall

While on our camping holiday in Cornwall, my children
and I visited Jubilee Pool in Penzance, which first opened in
1935. Being there felt timeless, like an experience that
has been enjoyed long before us and will hopefully
be enjoyed long after us.

REVÉE WALCOTT-NOLAN FOCUSES
ON HER OLYMPIC JOURNEY
by Nigel Bramley
London

Revée Walcott-Nolan is an athlete who I have
photographed a number of times at athletics track
races. In 2020, track events were few and far between
and athletes had to race wherever they could. With the
Tokyo Olympics delayed, there was an opportunity
for athletes to have an extra year to prepare. At this
race in September 2020, Revée ran a huge PB
that kickstarted her Olympic journey. Here she is
on the start line, lit only by the track floodlights.

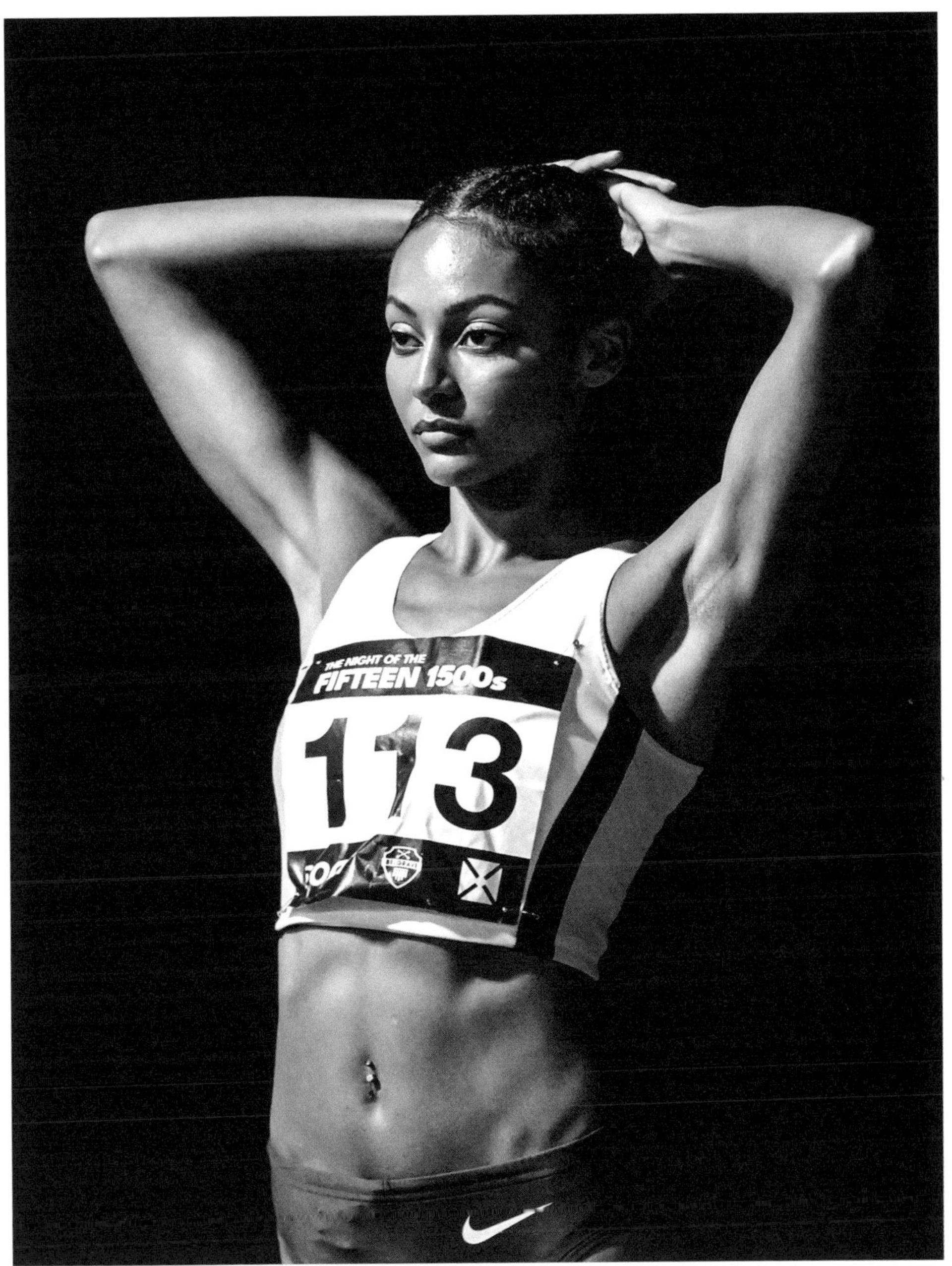

THE NIGHT OF THE
FIFTEEN 1500s
113

AMBER
by Sujata Setia
Aston, Oxfordshire

Amber is a recent graduate and a new mother.
Her daughter was born weighing almost 13 pounds,
making her the second heaviest baby born in the UK.
Amber told me, 'My belly had become so big, doctors
thought I was going to have twins. My stomach
muscles completely split, they said it was the worst
damage to stomach muscles they had ever seen.
I have scars. I will wear my scars like jewels on
my body and my soul. I celebrate my scars.'

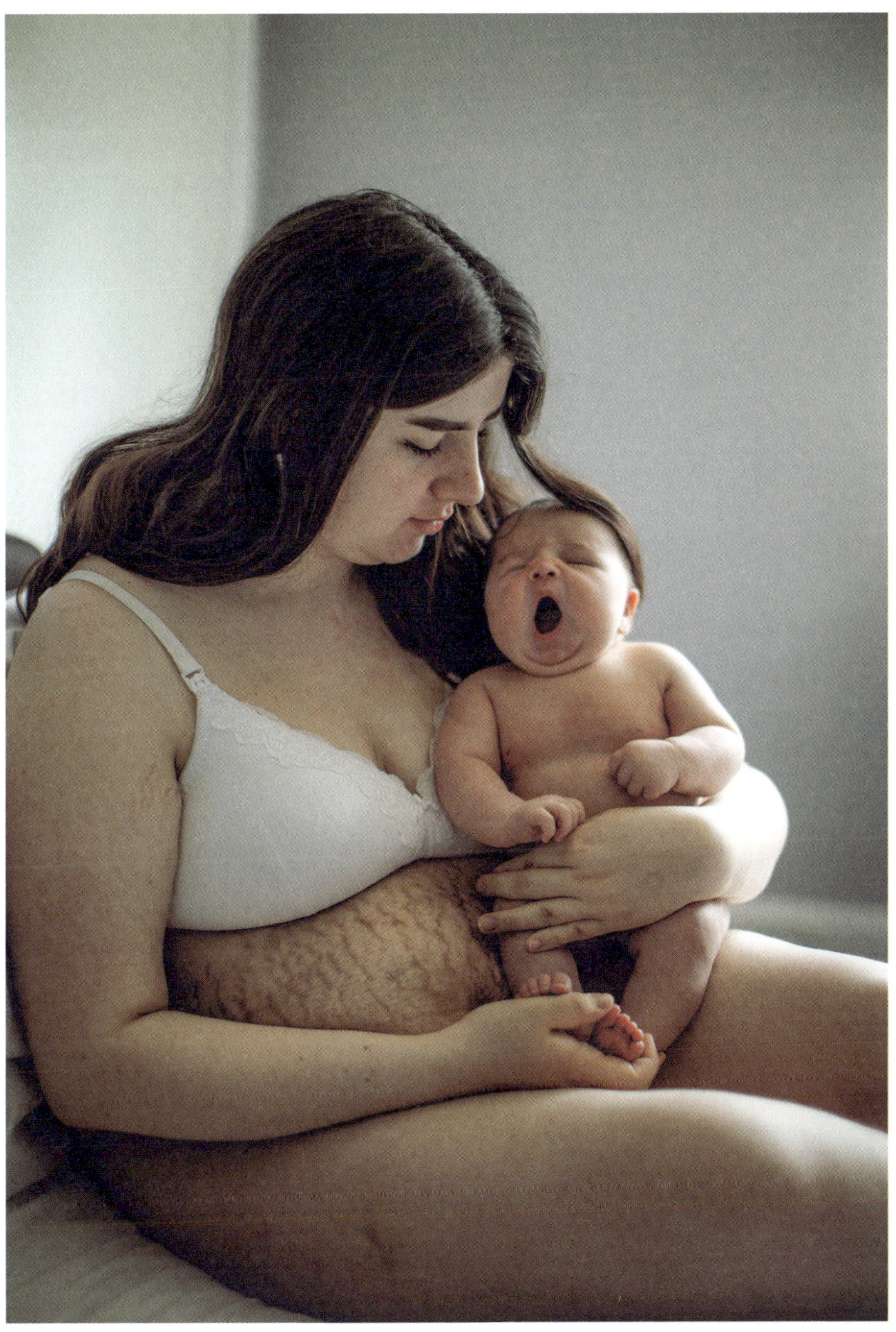

IN HER MOTHER'S BED
by Hannah Norton
Derby

My younger sister Katie developed OCD in
March 2020, and our mother had a mastectomy
five days before England went into a national
lockdown. The combination of these events created
a perfect storm and the pandemic has been an
incredibly challenging time for both of them.
They have shown a huge amount of strength
and resilience and I am so proud and so lucky
to have them. Watching my sister experience
OCD has made me aware of how narrow
our understanding of it is.

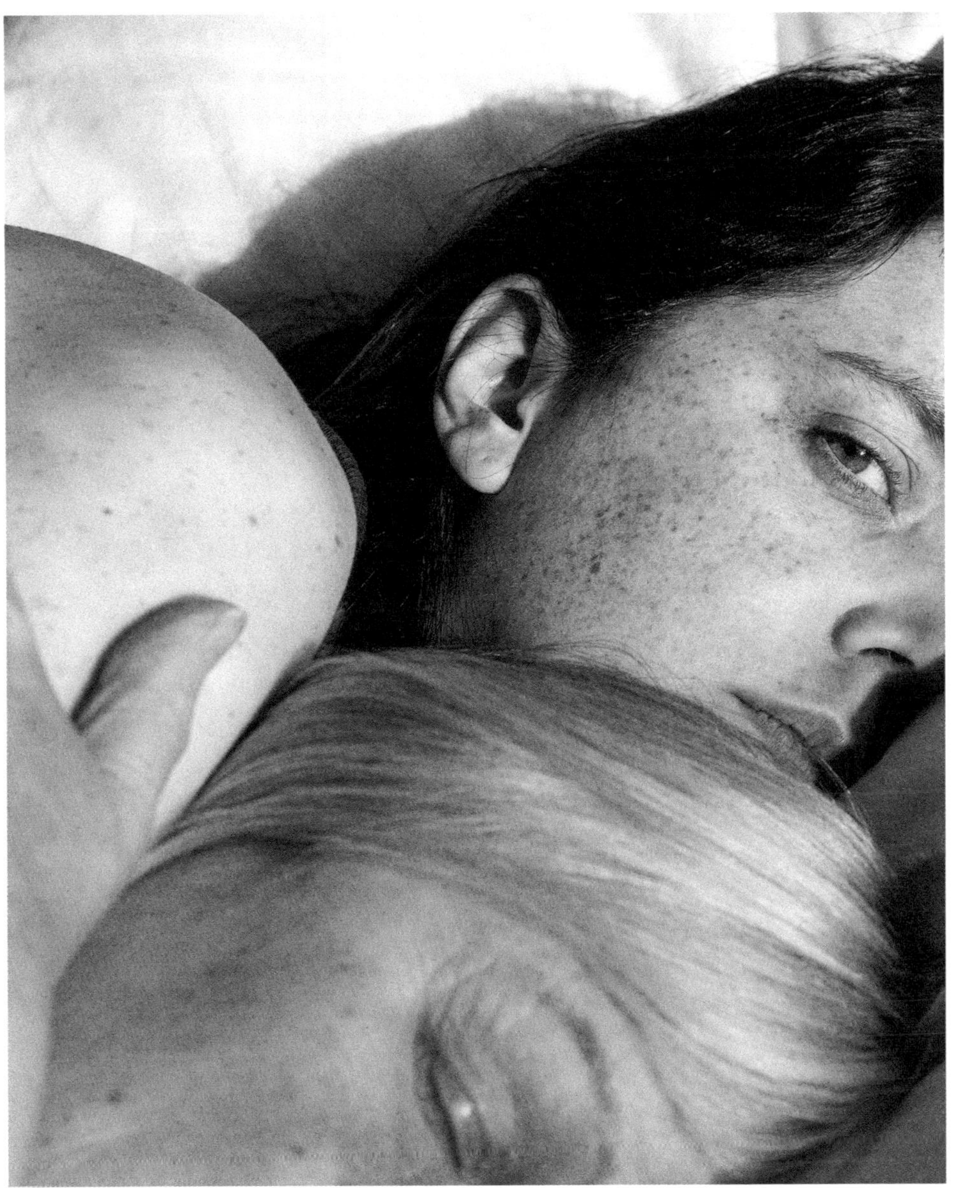

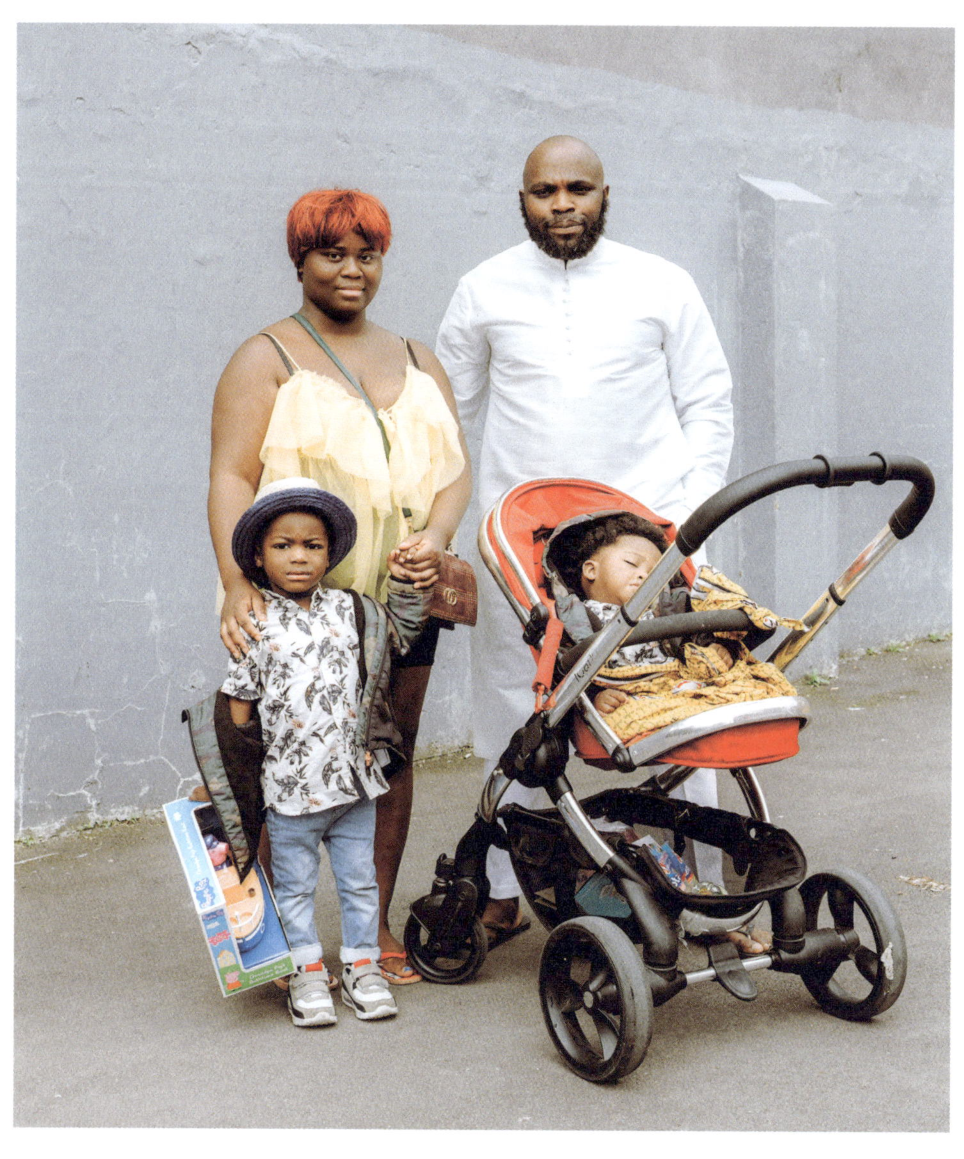

ERNEST, SINITA AND THEIR FAMILY
by Joshua Atkins
Chatham, Kent

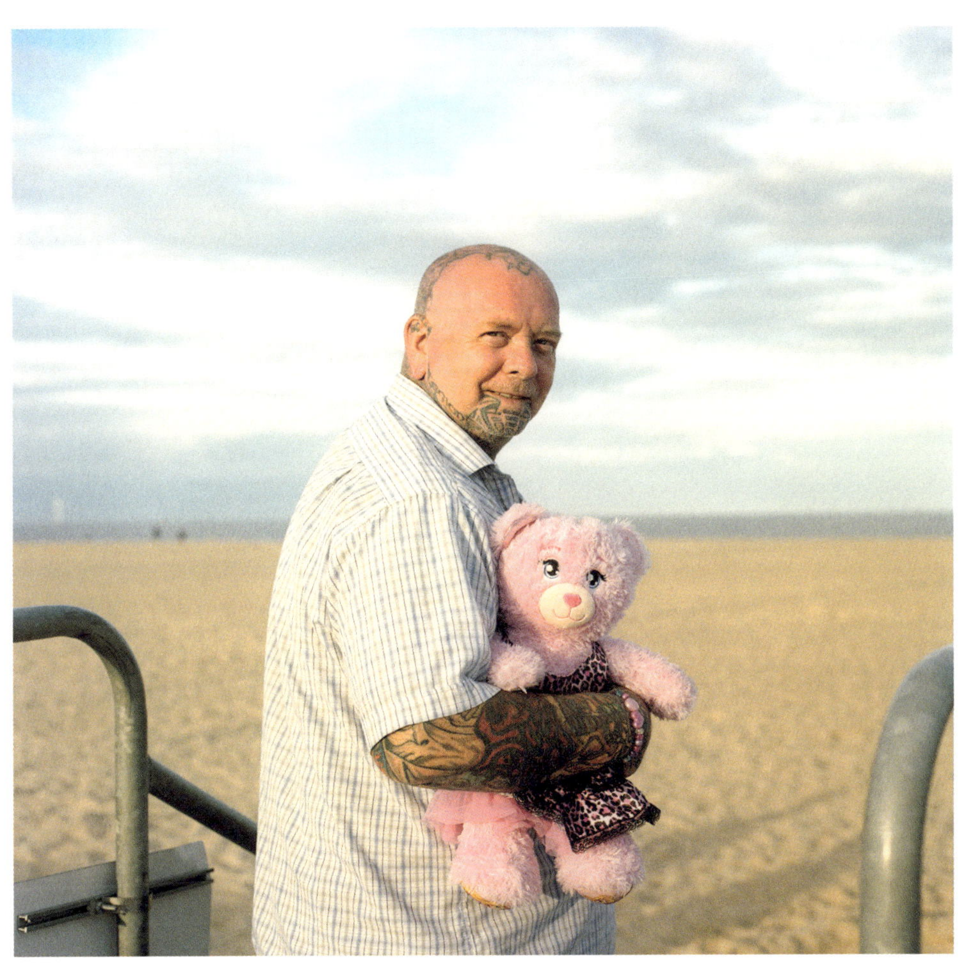

KEVIN
by Rhiannon Adam
Great Yarmouth, Norfolk

I saw Kevin carrying his granddaughter's teddy down to the
beach one morning. When I approached and asked to
take his picture, his wife laughed so much she almost cried.

LADY IN DIOR
by Brock Stanley
London

I was shopping in Tesco when I noticed this woman
walking by outside. I was in awe. I ran out of the shop
and asked to take her portrait. She was immediately
completely at ease with being photographed, looking
just above the line of the camera as if she'd done it
a thousand times before. Perhaps she had.

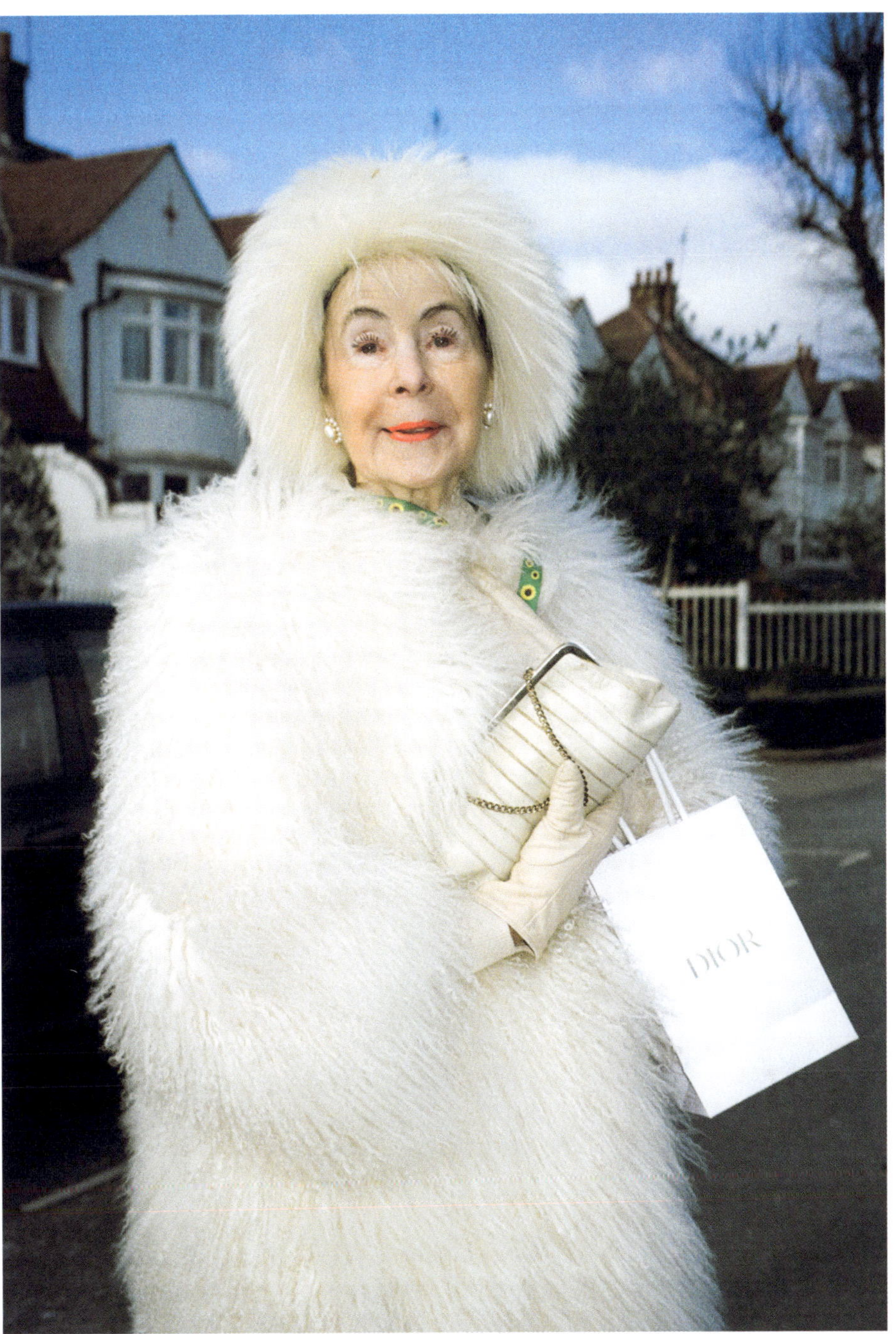

DIOR

THE FRENCHMAN
by Danny Jackson
London

Florent (*pictured*) organises a monthly 'Colour Walk'
in east London, where creative people who love colour
and dressing-up can meet, walk and talk.

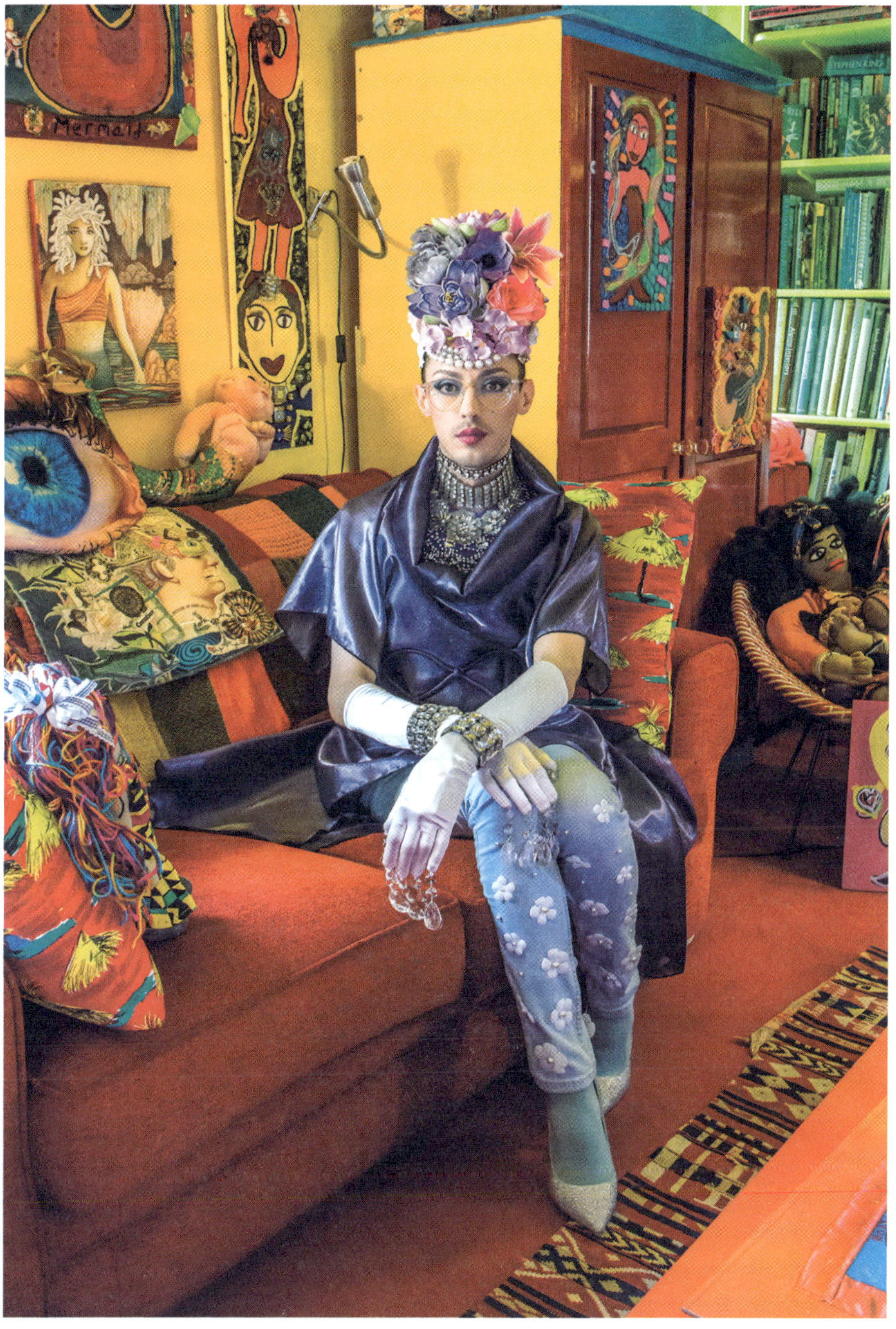

WONDER BOY
by Marksteen Adamson
Cheltenham, Gloucestershire

This is George, my youngest son. He chose this outfit for his project on 'How Social Expectations of Masculine Attractiveness Have Restricted Male Expression Through Fashion'. George means the world to me, and more importantly he has taught me a lot about the new world we now live in.

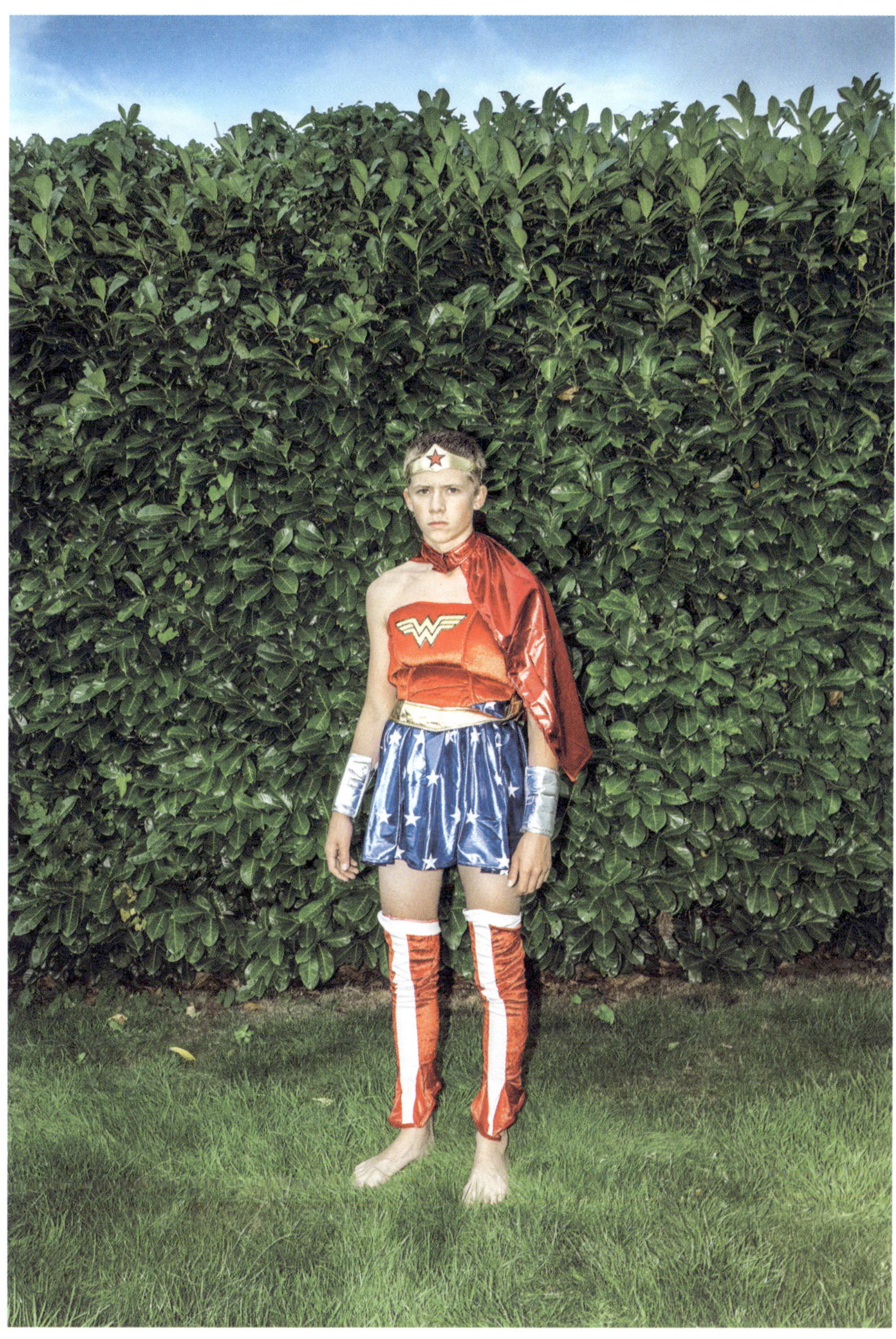

TROOPER AINUSON, HOUSEHOLD CAVALRY
by Rory Lewis
London

Trooper Ainuson (*pictured*) of the Blues and Royals
ranks among the elite of the British Army responsible
for guarding the Queen. Each day, a squadron from
either the Blues and Royals or the Life Guards
regiments rides down to take over guard duties from
each other at Horse Guards Parade, an event
known as 'Changing the Guard'.

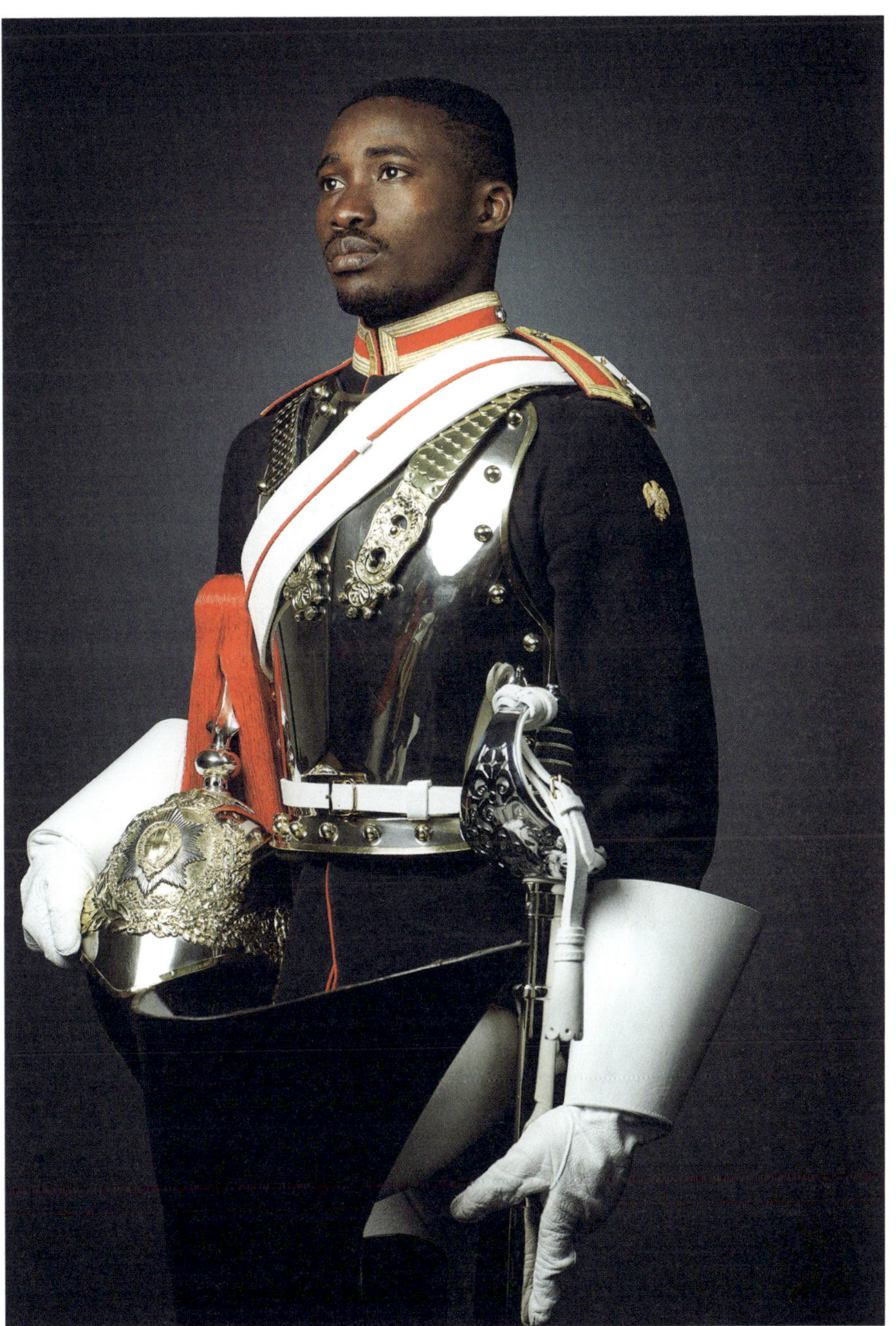

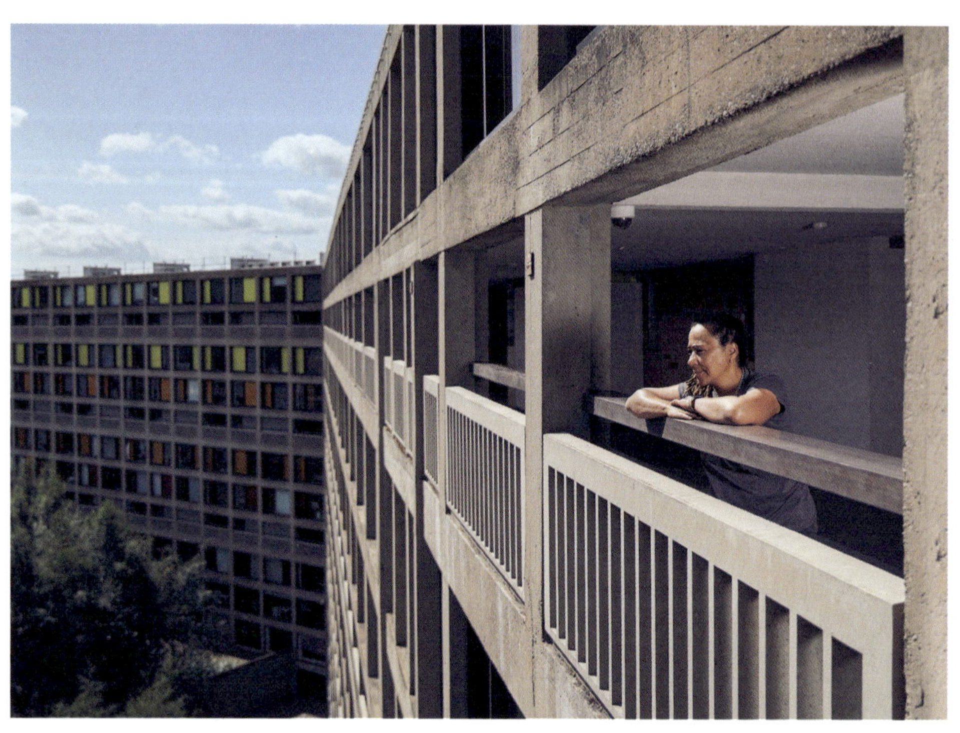

JOANNE
by Leigh Anderson
Sheffield, South Yorkshire

Joanne Marsden has lived almost her entire life
on the iconic Park Hill estate, one of the UK's largest
surviving examples of post-war Brutalist architecture.
Joanne was born in the back bedroom of her nan's flat
in 1965, four years after the estate was opened.

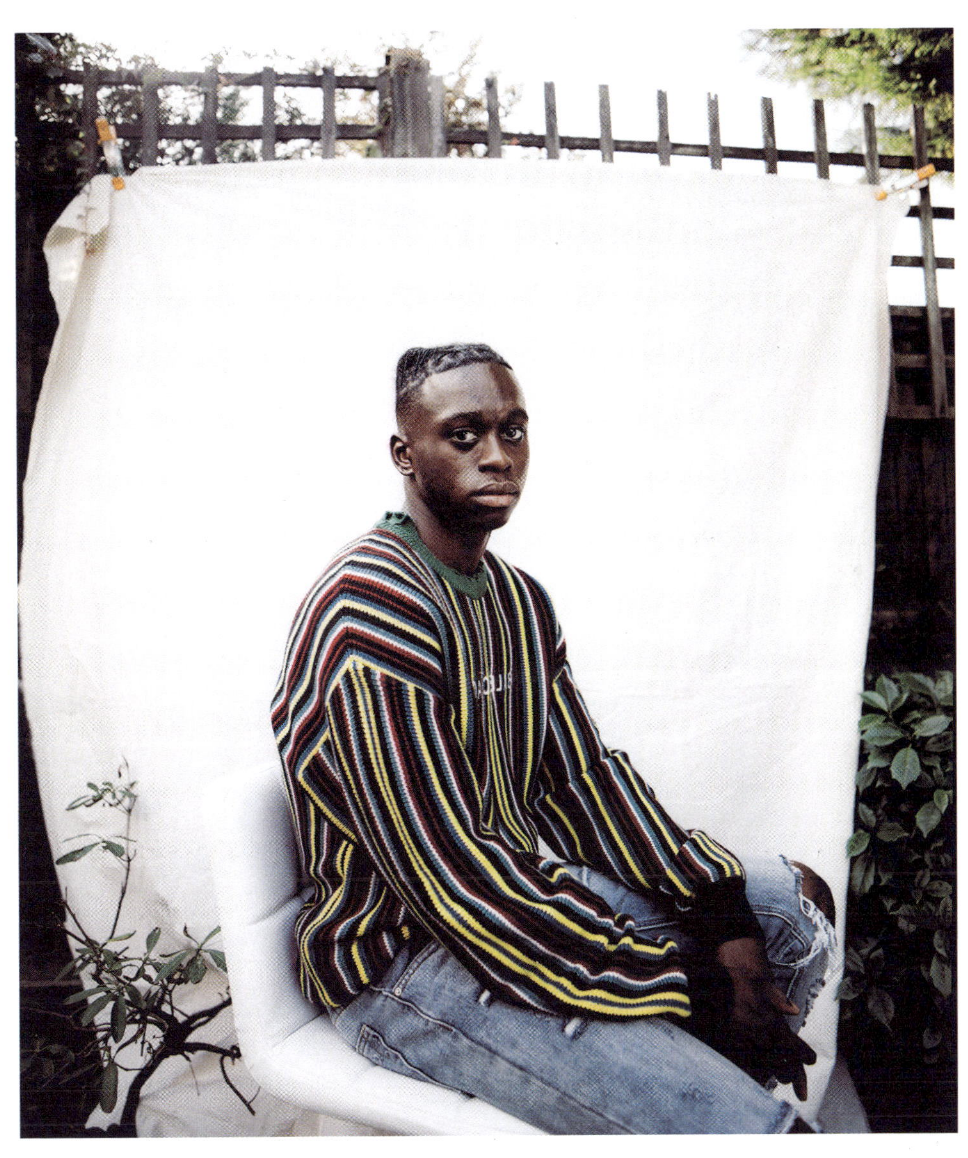

AARON WAN-BISSAKA
by Filmawi Efrem
London

JOSEY, CLOUD FARM CAMPSITE
by Robert Darch
Oare, Devon

Josey works for the National Trust in North Devon.
I have been working with the Trust on a longterm
commission to record the effects of ash dieback,
a fungal disease that affects ash trees. Many UK
landowners are having to fell their diseased ash trees,
and it is predicted that ash dieback will have killed
90 percent of all ash trees in the UK within ten to
15 years. Dieback is caused by an airborne fungus
that infects the whole tree, suffocating it.

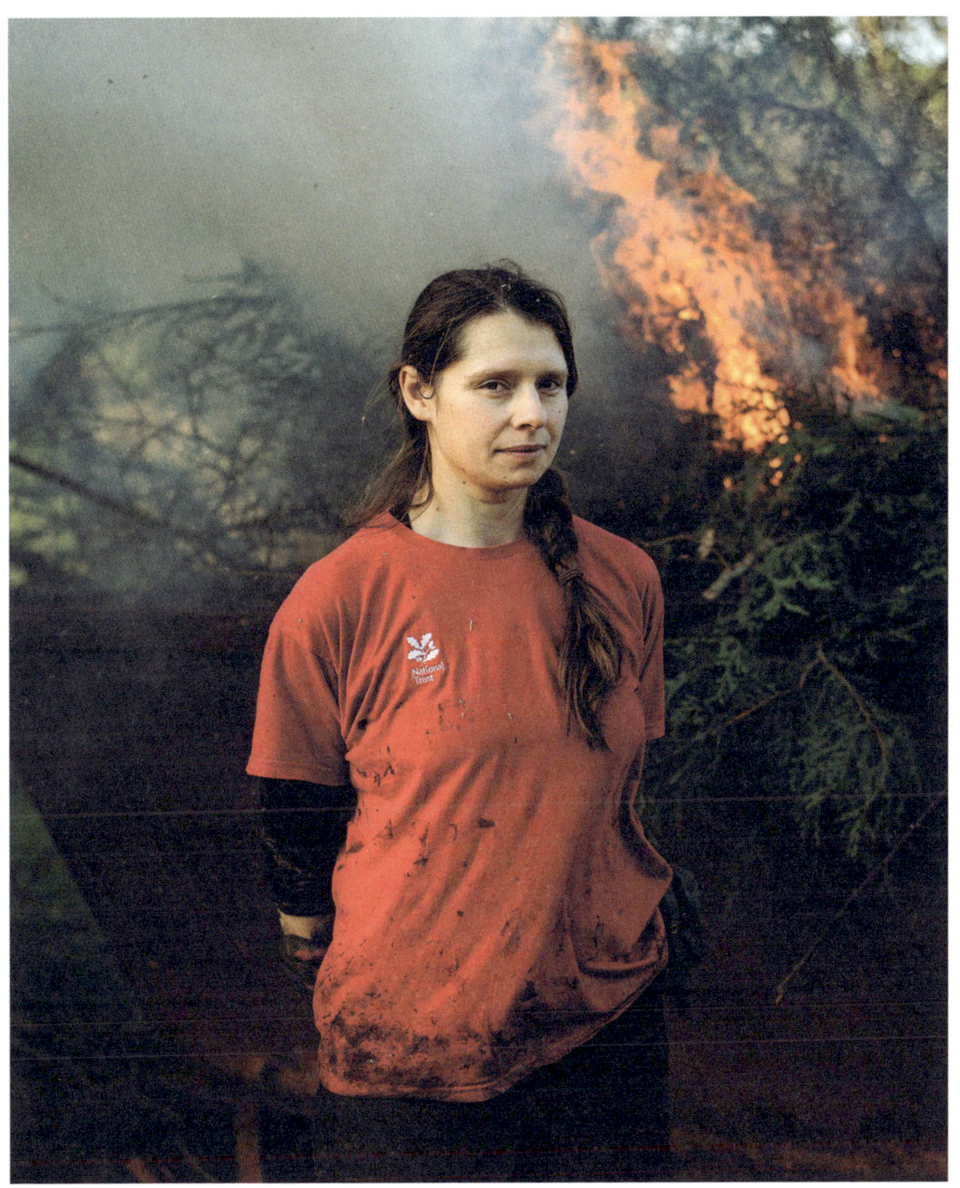

REBECCA HAZLEWOOD
by Jon Nicholls
Black Country, West Midlands / Nova Scotia, Canada

I took this portrait of the actor Rebecca Hazlewood
via Zoom during the pandemic, while both of us
were isolating – me in Canada, her in the UK. Where
Rebecca lives in the Midlands is close to where
I grew up. I was yearning to be back home so taking
photographs via Zoom was a way to experience
a sort of virtual visit, no masks required.
Even though I was in Canada, I still consider
this image to be of the UK.

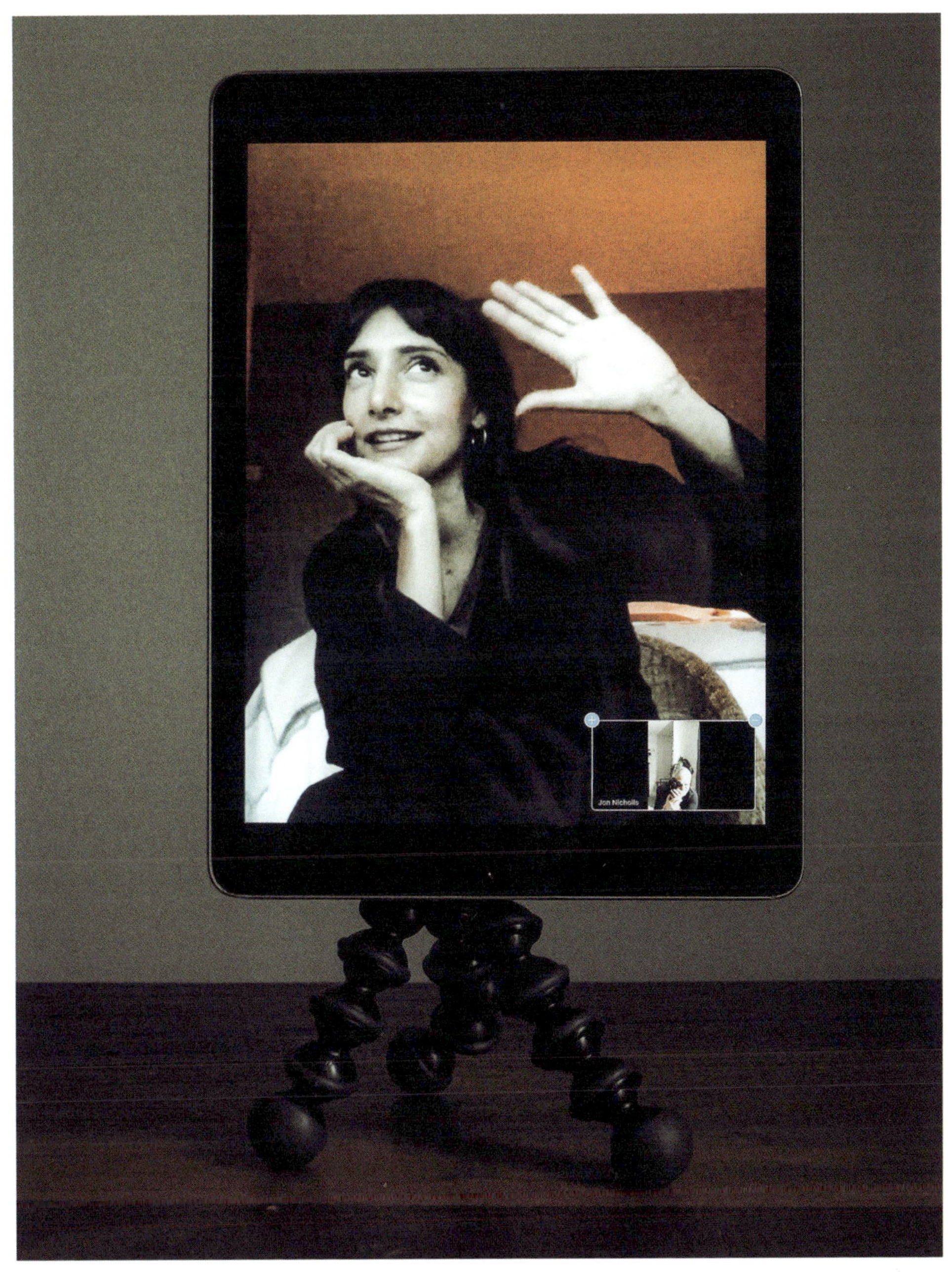

Jon Nicholls

A QUIET MOMENT
by Harry Deadman
London

I met Louie (*pictured*) while shooting a fashion film.
There was a quiet moment on set, in between takes,
and Louie just looked so comfortably still sitting there
as the camera and lighting were being adjusted
around him that I asked if I could take his portrait.

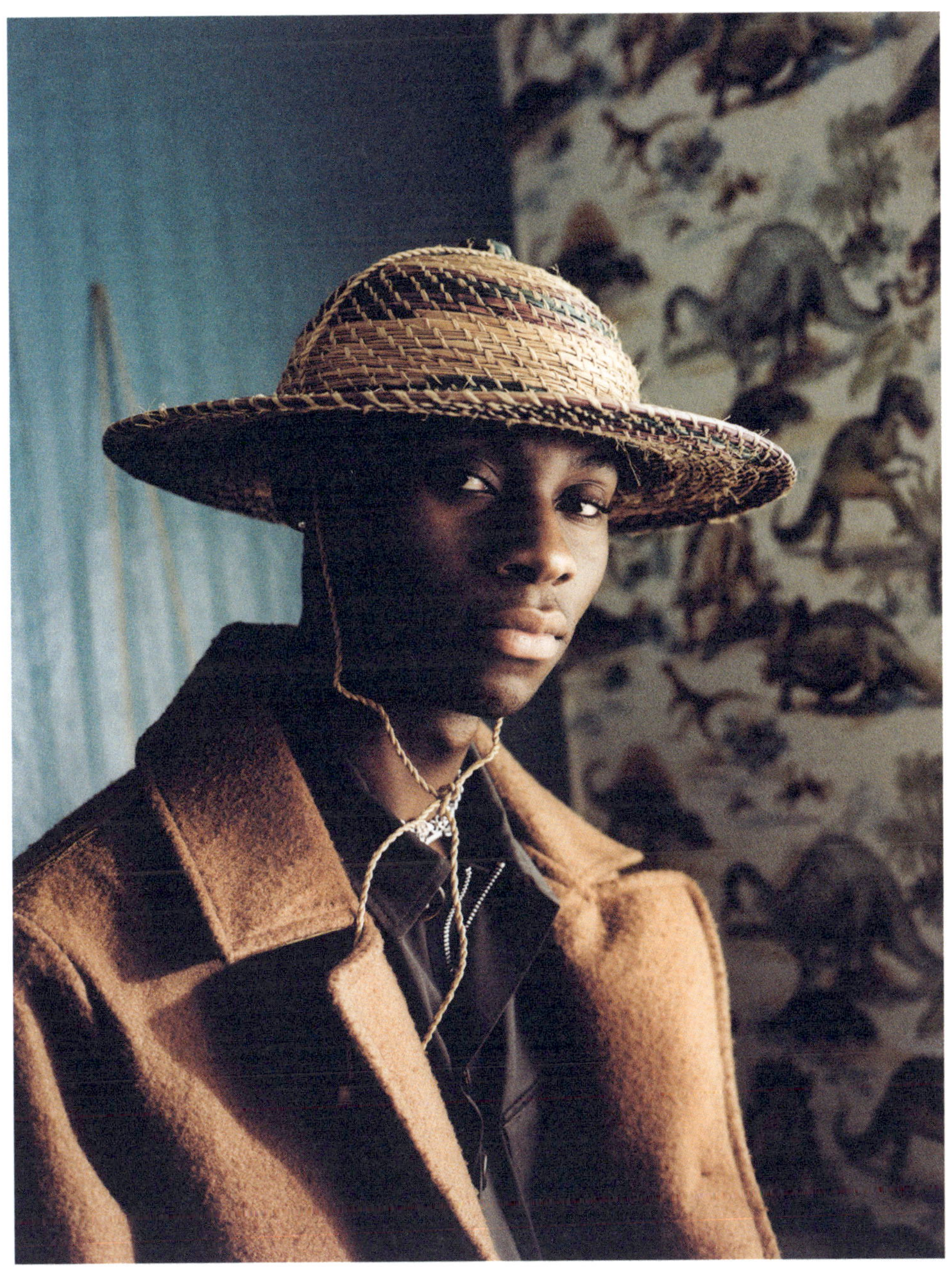

JACK
by Harry George Hall
London

'When I was 16, I had elective surgery to amputate
my leg above the knee because of a condition that was
becoming progressively worse. Before my amputation,
I considered myself as disabled. I have a theory that
when you have an amputation, you are reborn.
Like a child, you need to start from scratch: learning
how to walk, balance and face the world with
confidence. The best way to practise this and develop
motor skills is through sport and exercise.' – Jack

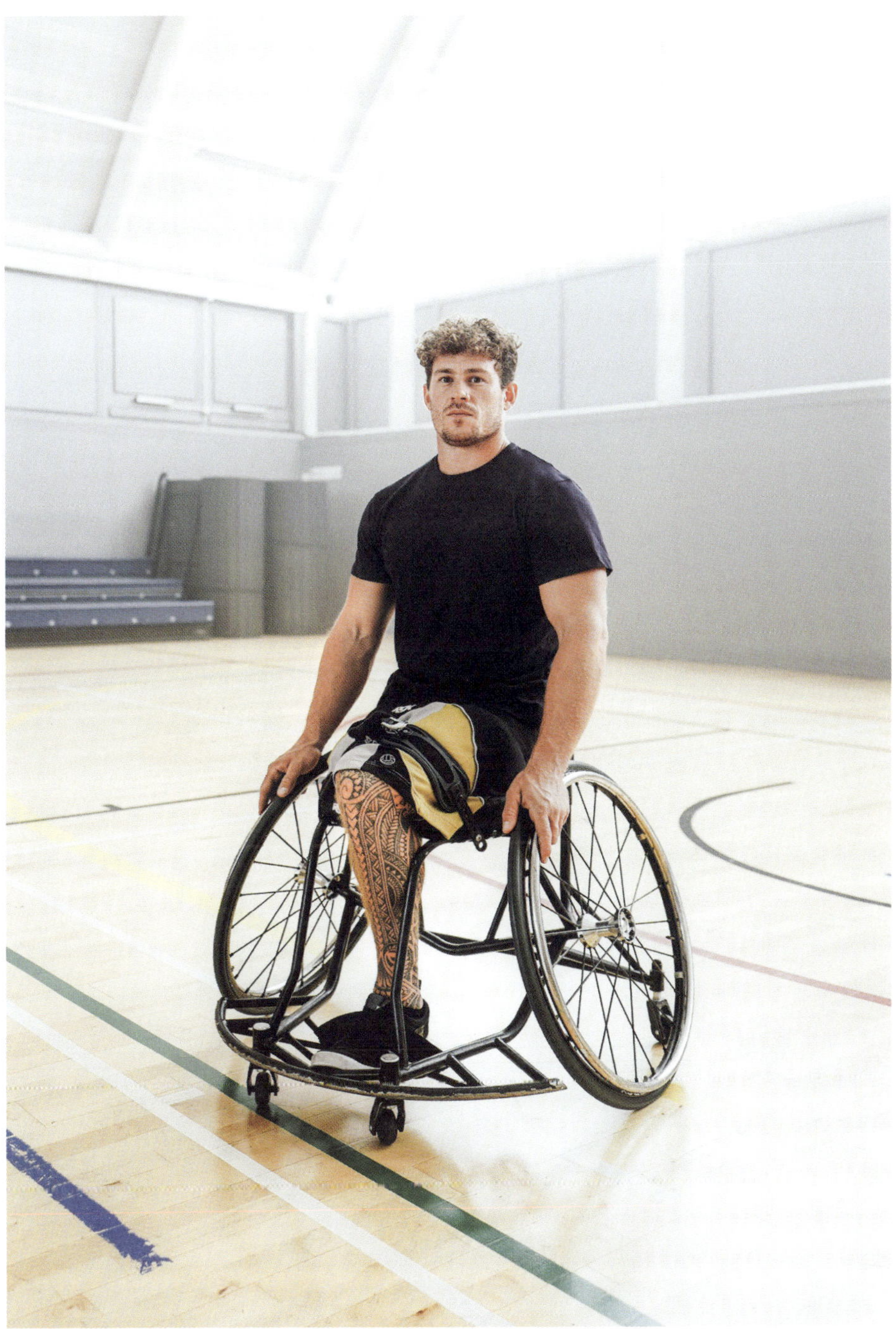

MOST WORSHIPFUL CHRISTINE CHAPMAN
by Caitlin Chescoe
London

Christine Chapman is the Grand Master of
the Honourable Fraternity of Ancient Freemasons,
now known as 'Freemasonry for Women' – a fraternity
for women, organised by women. She told me,
'We think that Freemasonry empowers women, we
think it gives you self-confidence and makes
you believe in yourself.'

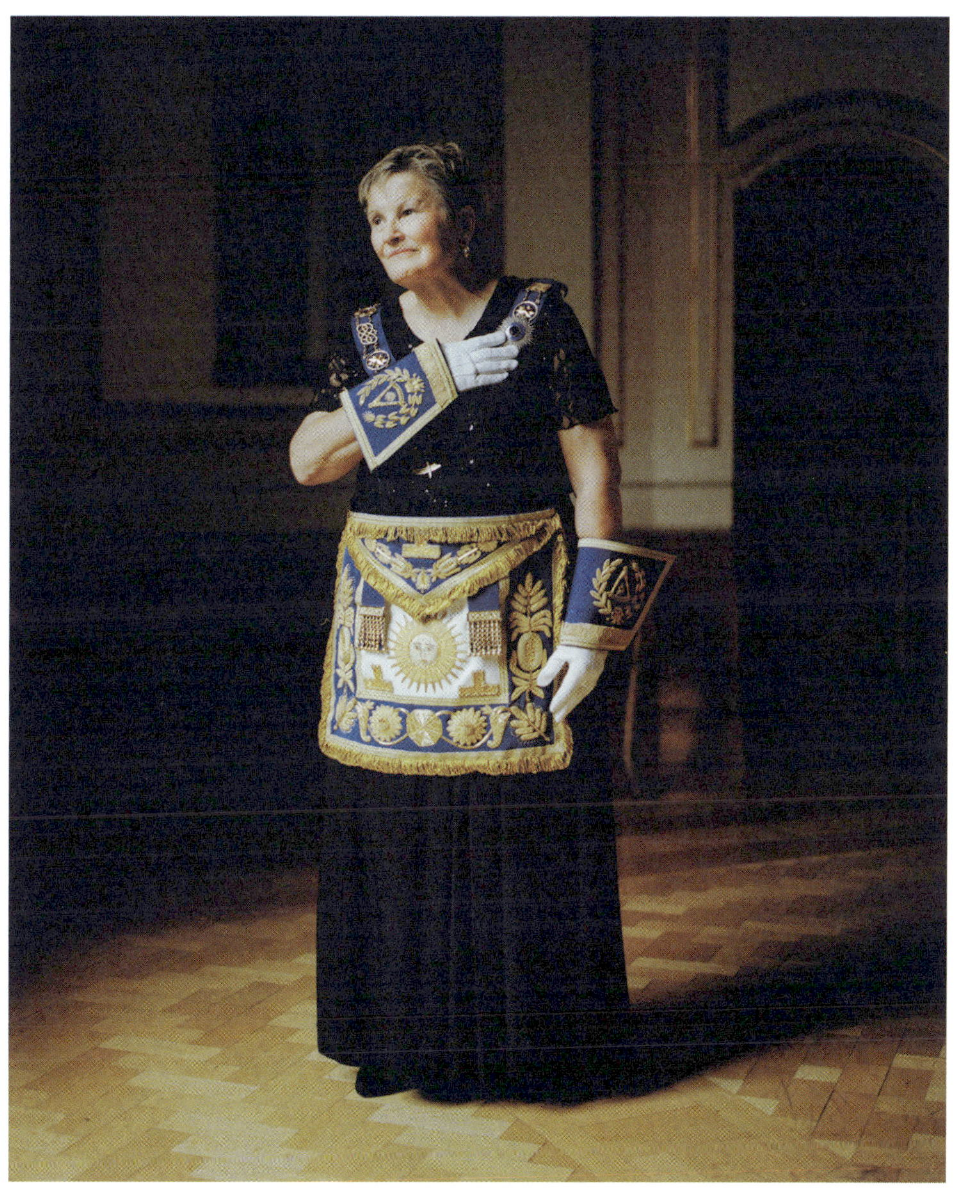

KACIE AND JAMI
by Samuel Hicks
London

I met Kacie and Jami roller skating in a car park
in Vauxhall. Before lockdown hit, I'd often see groups
of roller skaters having a great time together, dancing
on their skates – they reminded me of the late-1980s
rave scene in London. When lockdown lifted,
I started meeting up with some of these skaters.
I've discovered that skating brings all sorts of people
together, there's a real community; they call it
the 'skate family'.

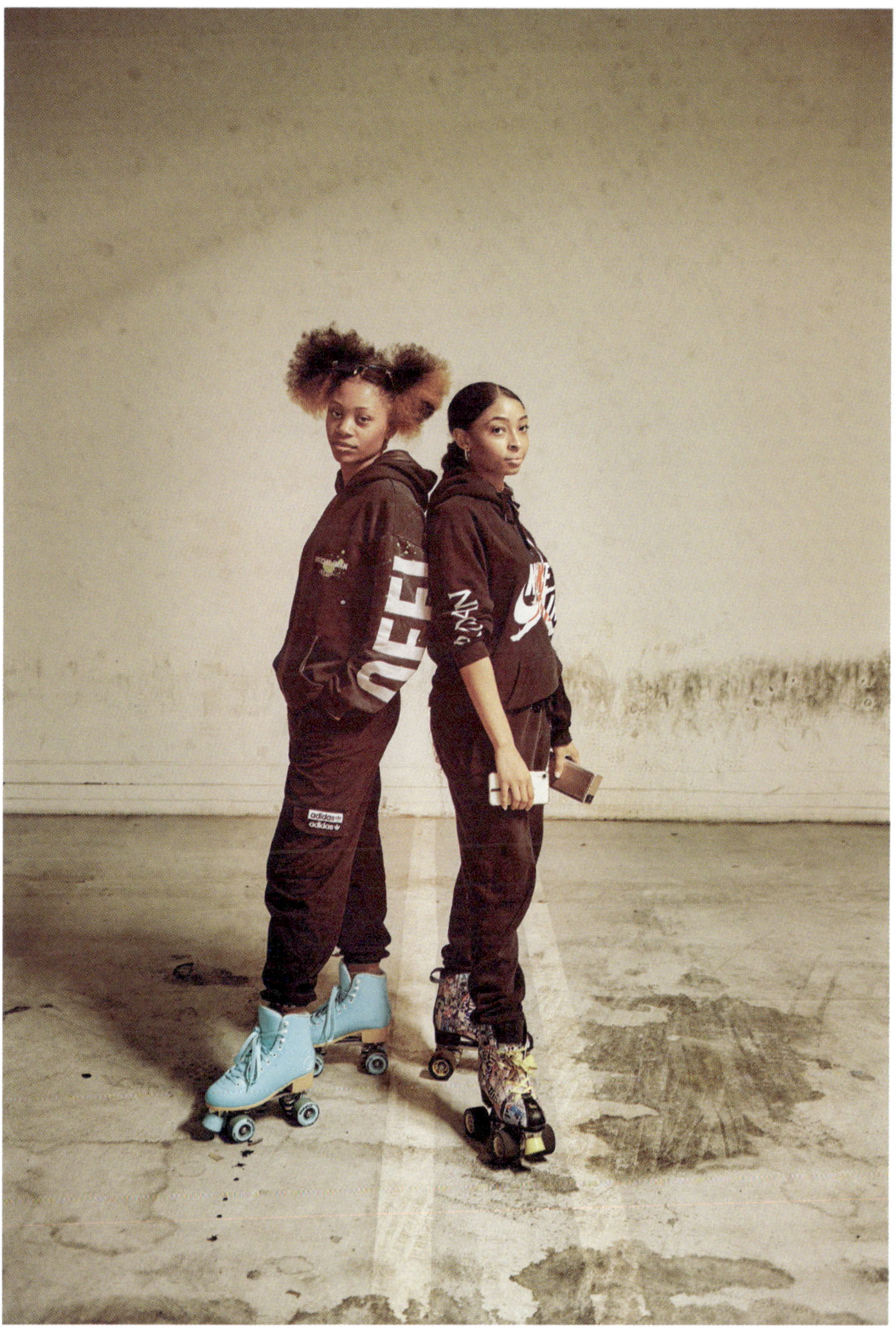

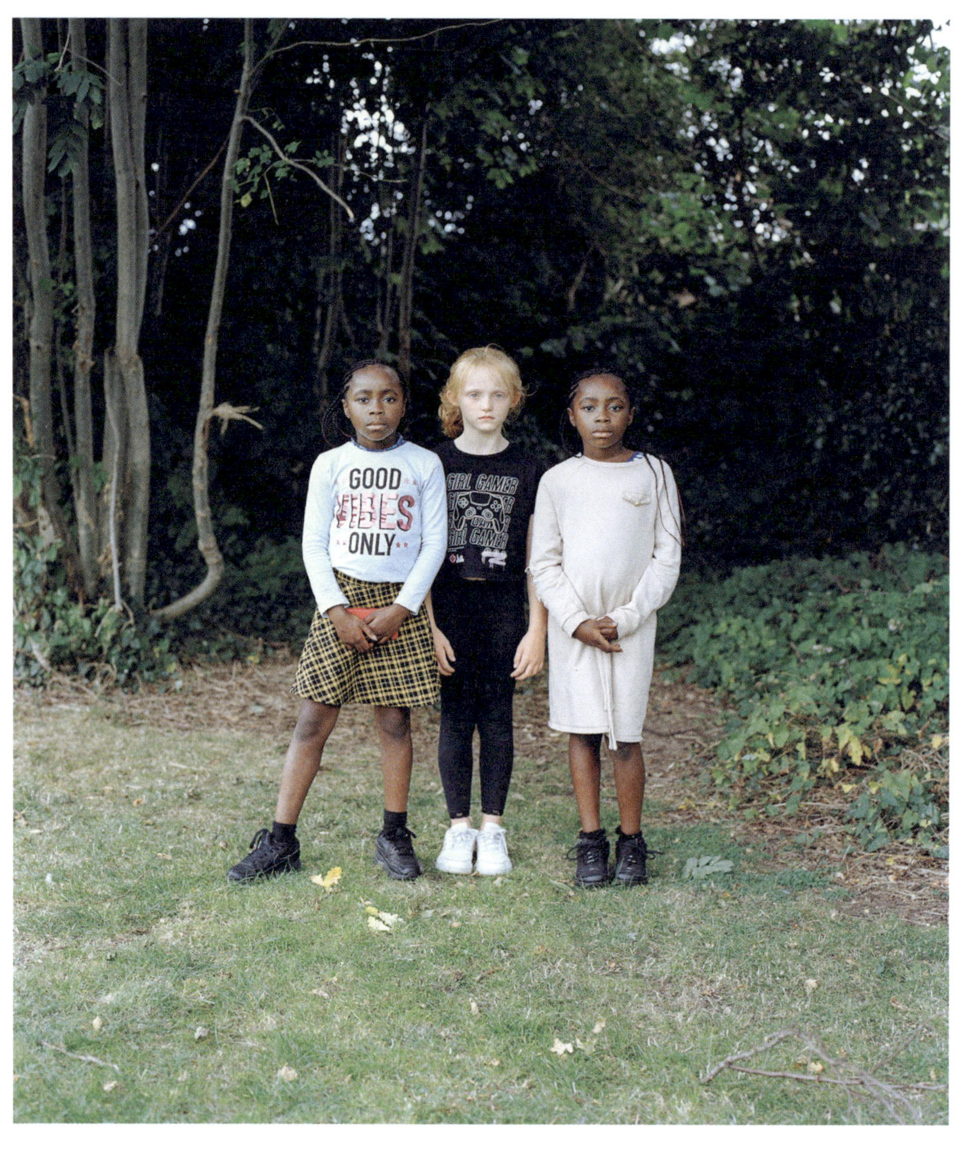

MONET, AMY AND VENICE
by Curtis Hughes
Cardiff

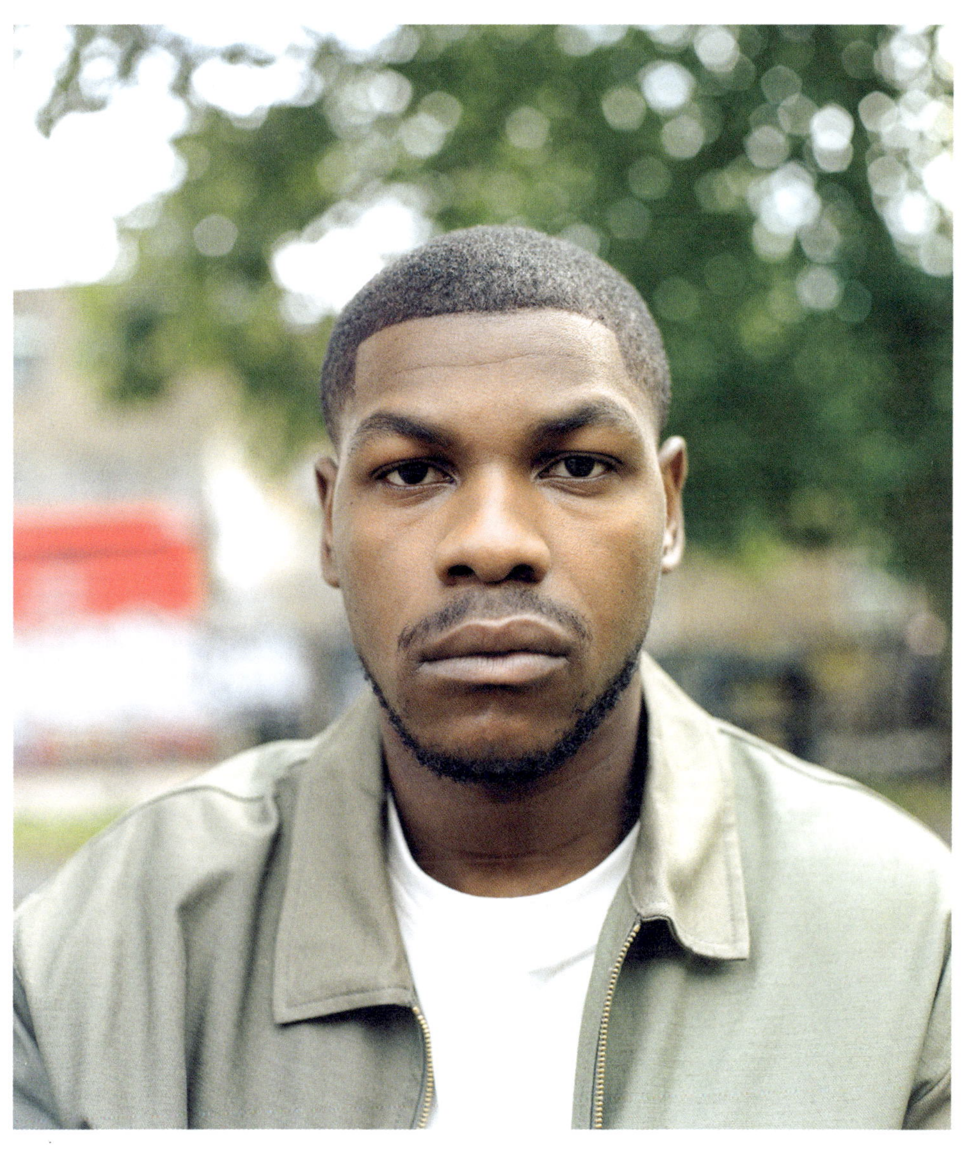

JOHN BOYEGA
by Jonangelo Molinari
London

JOSSY
by Alfie White
London

I was on the 197 bus to Peckham when I saw
some kids doing wheelies on their bikes in an estate
car park. Without thinking, I pressed the button, got
off, and asked if I could take some photos.

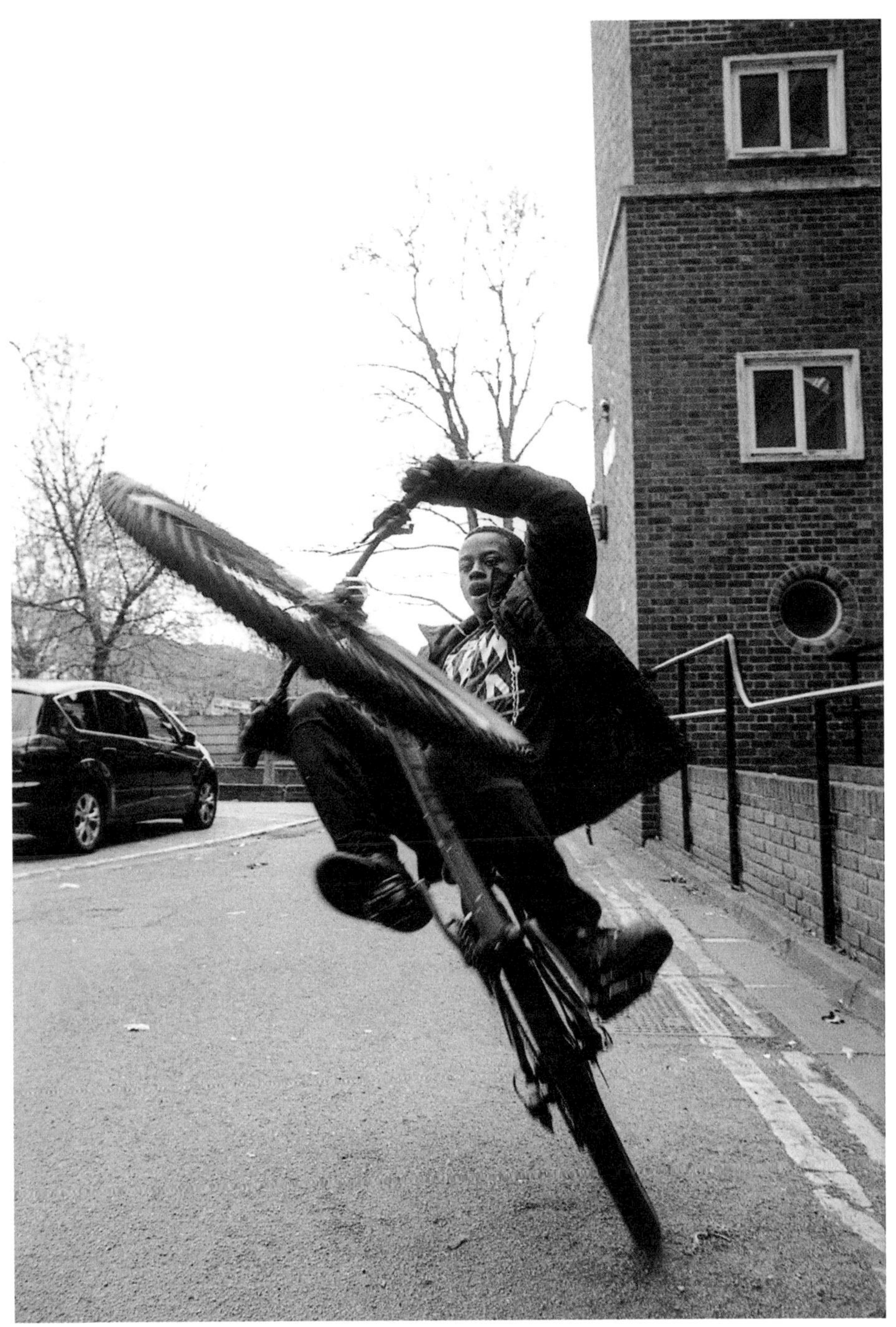

SAM AND JAMES' WEDDING RENEWAL
by Natalia Poniatowska
Glasgow

While studying at the Glasgow School of Art,
I supported myself by working as an events
photographer. My tutors told me that I shouldn't be
working as a commercial photographer if I was an
artist, as it would have a significant impact on my art.
And it did. This image I took of a little girl looking
for some freedom to play at a wedding renewal proved
to me that I should never switch off my fine art
approach, wherever I'm working.

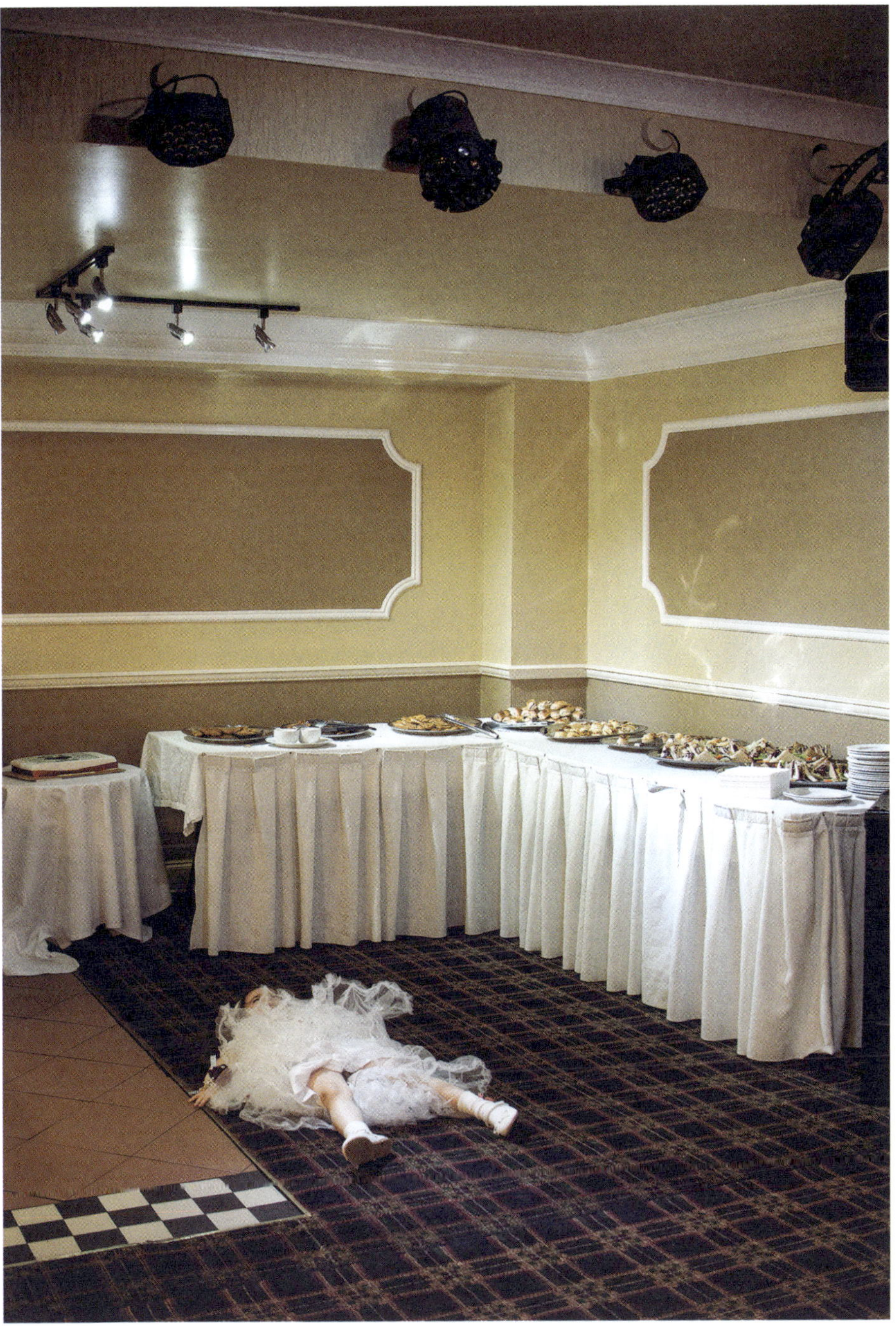

BELDINA ODENYO ONASSIS
by Simon Murphy
Glasgow

Beldina was a Scottish musician, poet and writer
of Kenyan descent who went by the stage name
'Heir of the Cursed'. She was on the cusp of great
things when she sadly passed away in November 2021.
I took this portrait of her in May; I had been trying
to get hold of her for a while, but we never quite got
the shoot arranged. I bumped into her one Sunday
and we agreed, this had to be the day. She had a
strikingly beautiful, strong and defiant gaze.
Rest in power, Beldina.

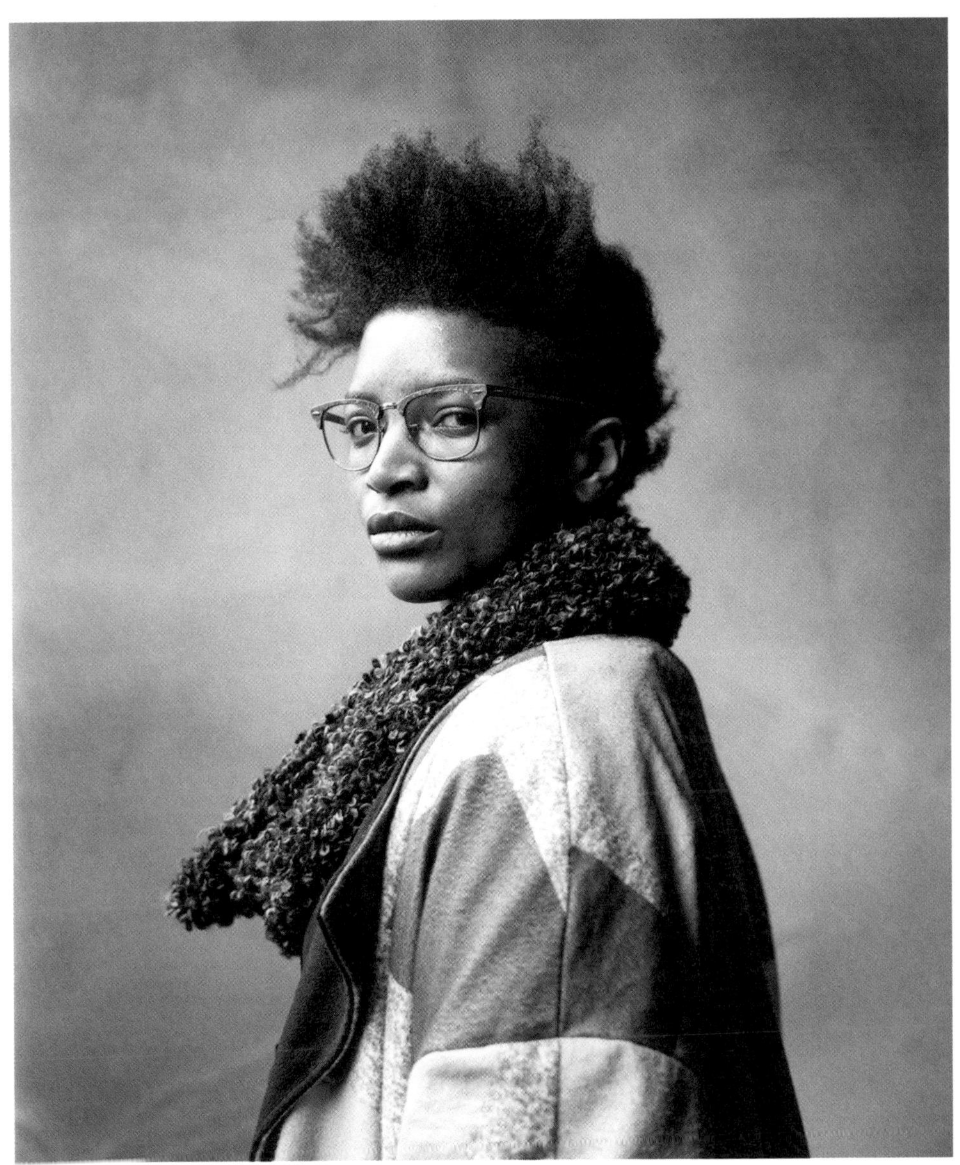

CHANEEN AND OCEAN
by Imogen Freeland
London

My first introduction to Chaneen was through social
media, where I found her openly sharing her maternal
journey. As a new mum myself, her honesty and
transparency felt like a breath of fresh air. I arranged
to photograph Chaneen, and when I arrived at
her house we instantly connected. I took pictures while
she juggled breastfeeding, sometimes feeding both
her daughters at once. This image captures
a moment between Chaneen and her youngest,
Ocean, while her older daughter Jasmine
bounced around us on the bed.

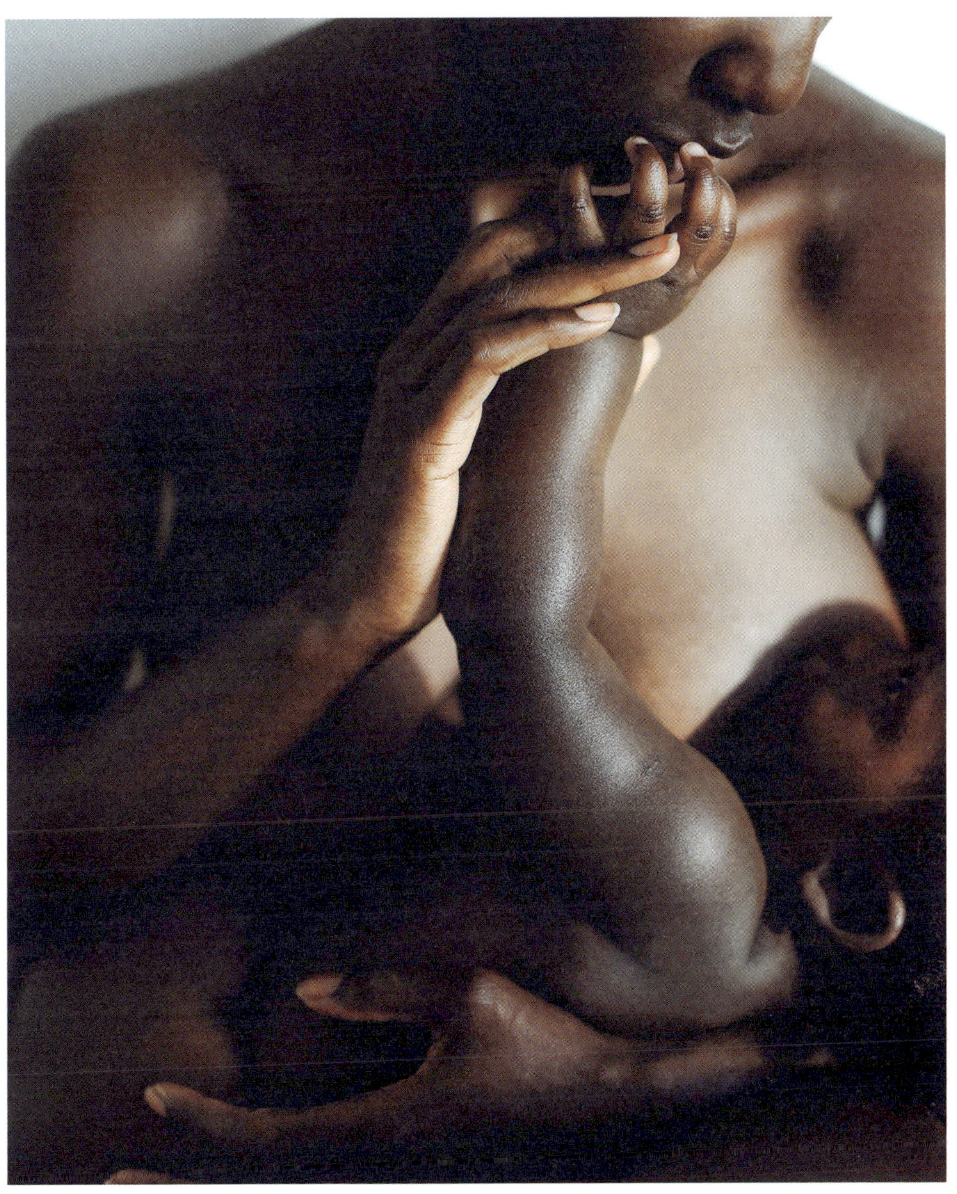

KEVIN
by Tero Puha
London

Kevin is a proud gay man who was diagnosed
with HIV in 1992. He is a poet and art collector, and
an old friend of mine. We met 20 years ago,
and I always thought I would love to photograph
him, so when we recently reconnected on
Facebook I suggested a shoot.

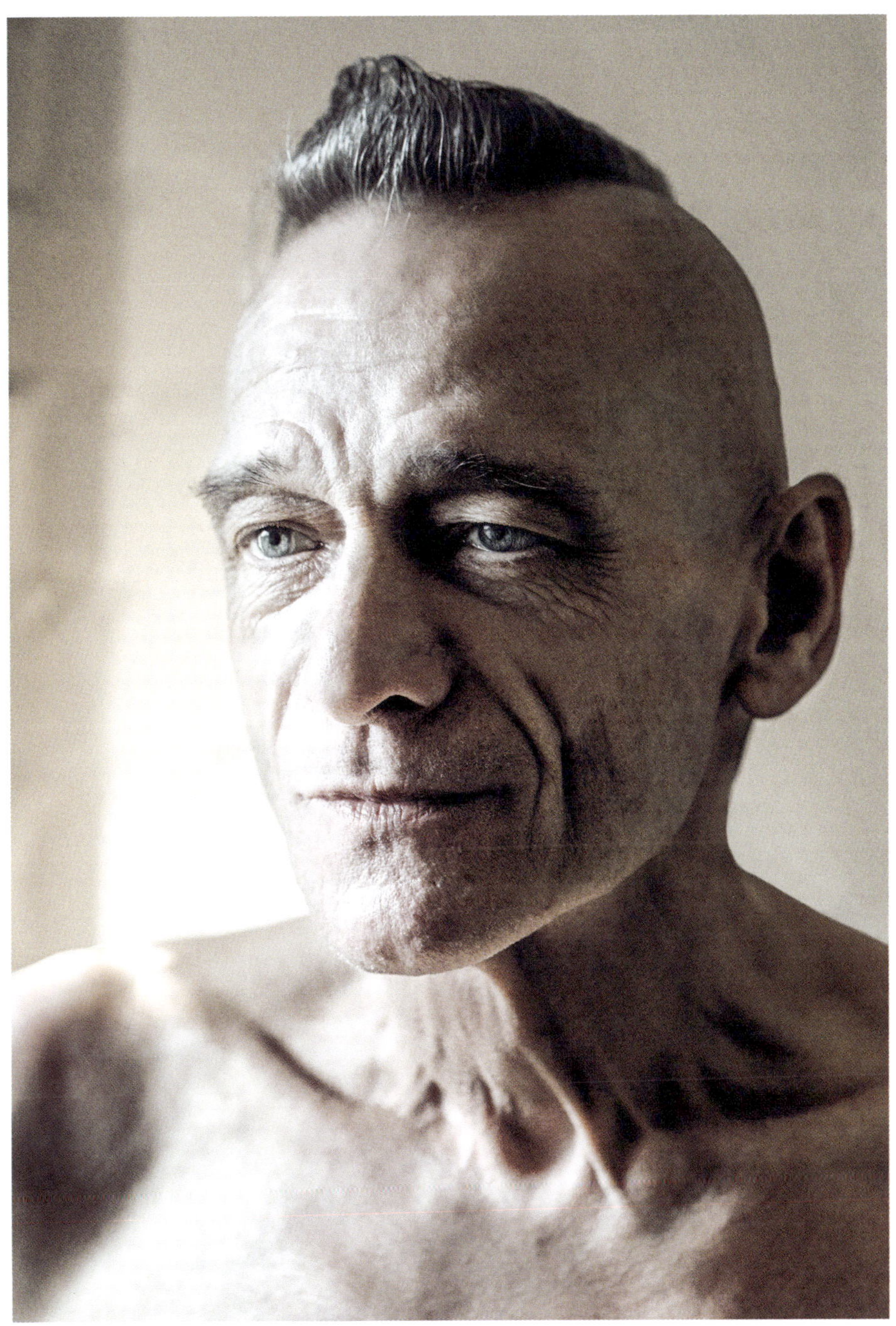

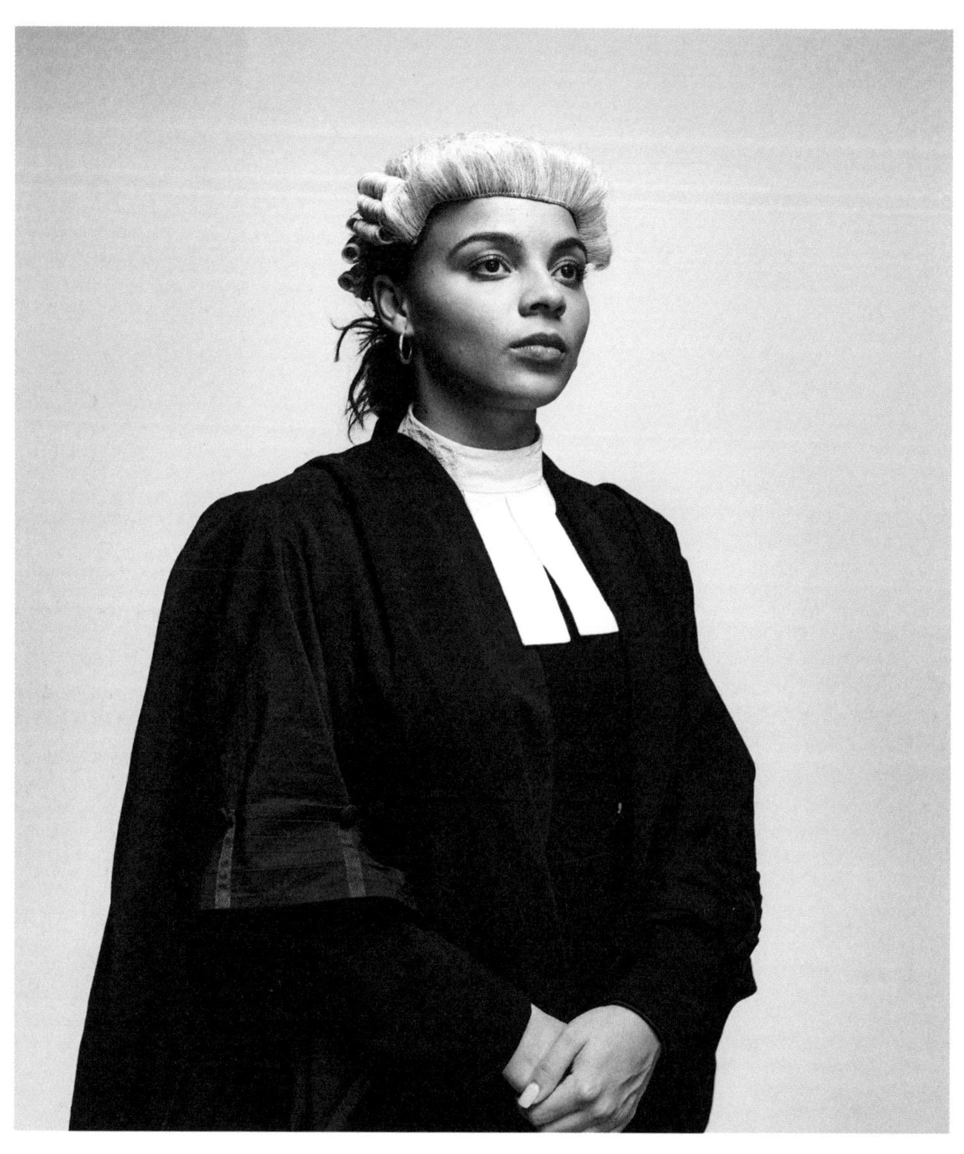

ALEXANDRA WILSON
by Jake Green
London

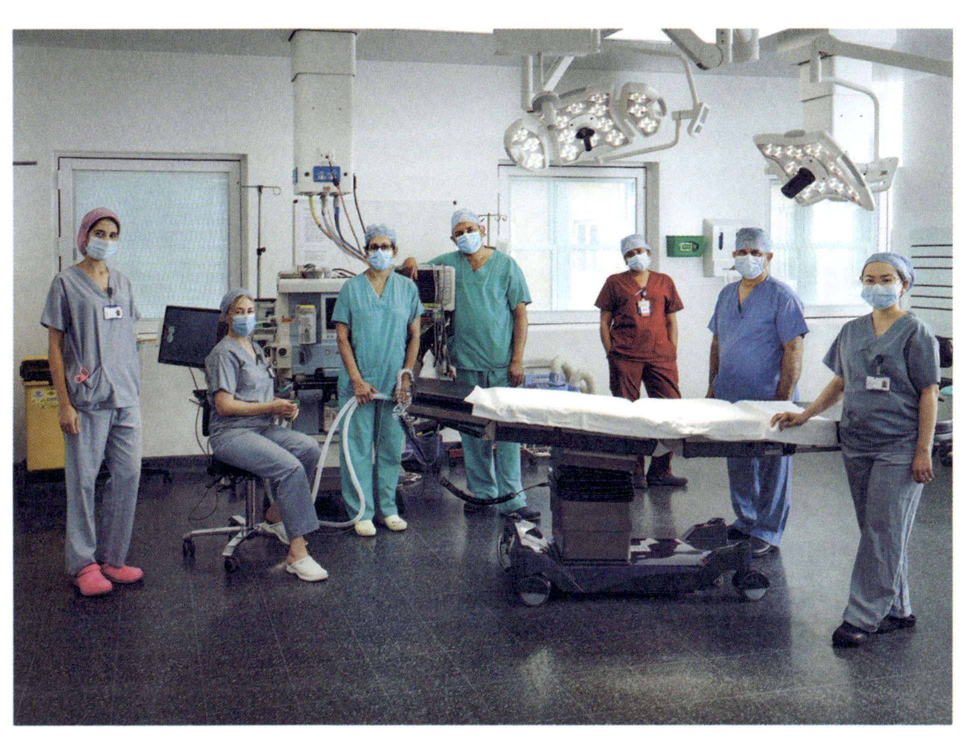

BARNET HOSPITAL ICU
by Frederic Aranda
London

At the end of the first wave of Covid, the *Guardian*
asked me to photograph the ICU staff at Barnet Hospital.
I was taken aback by how friendly everyone was.
You got the feeling that they had been through some
terrible times together and had seen it all.

STRENGTH
by Sander Vos
London

This is my friend Joe. I took this picture of him shortly
after he completed a virtual bike ride of 840 miles
'from London to St. Tropez' during the first lockdown.
Having never even touched an exercise bike before,
he managed to raise £30,000 to pay for medical
treatment for one of his dear friends who is suffering
from cancer. His journey didn't go unnoticed
and he was named the Pride of London
Fundraiser of the Year.

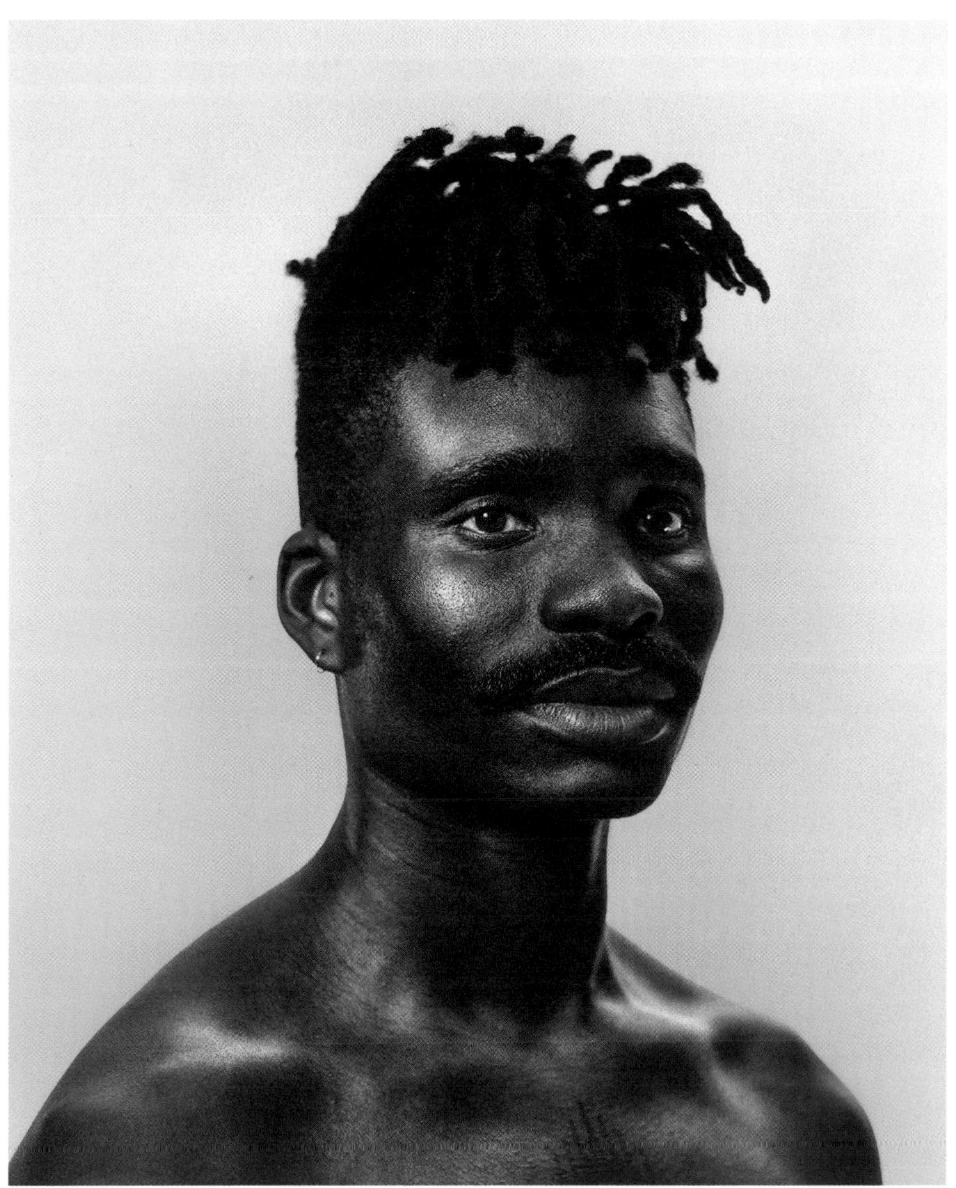

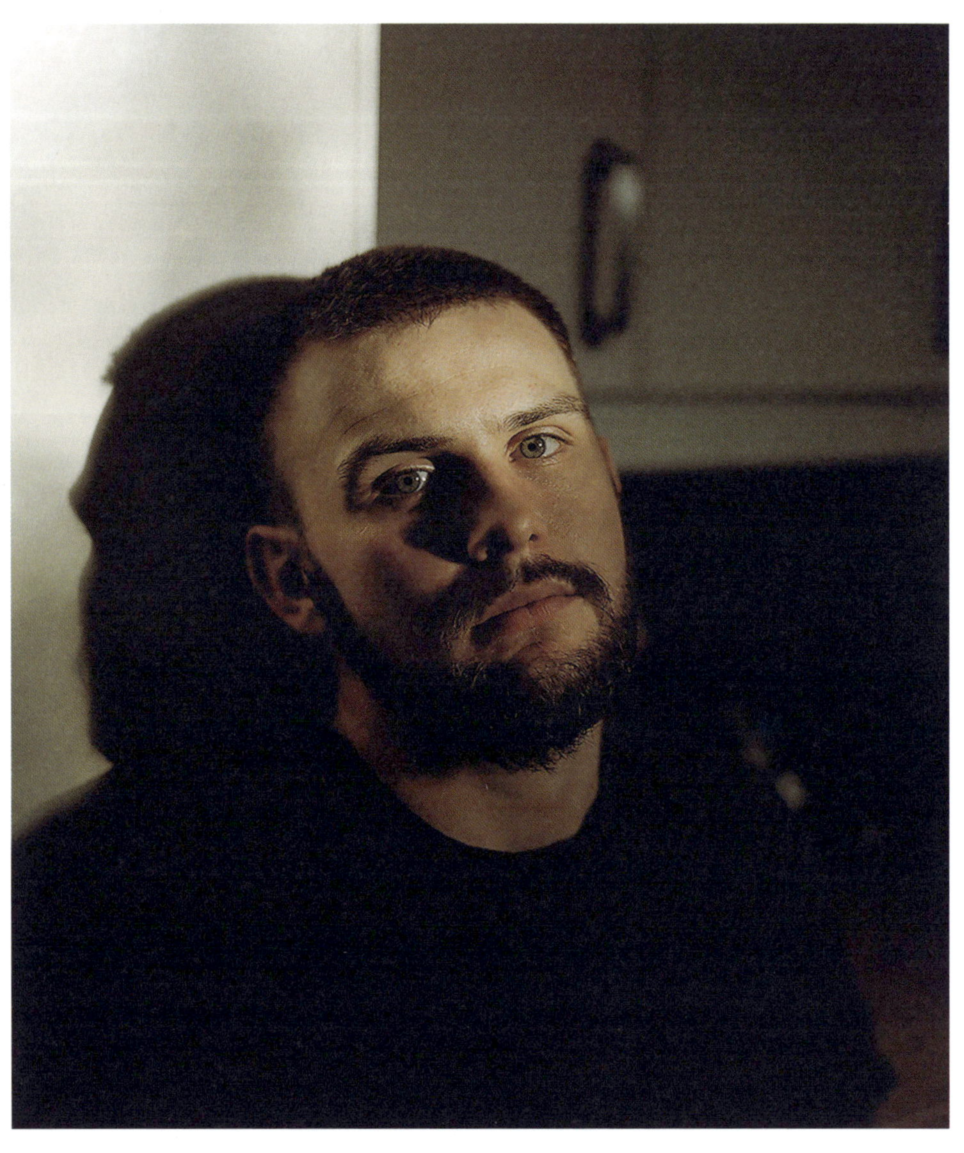

WILL
by Ellie Jenkins
Plymouth, Devon

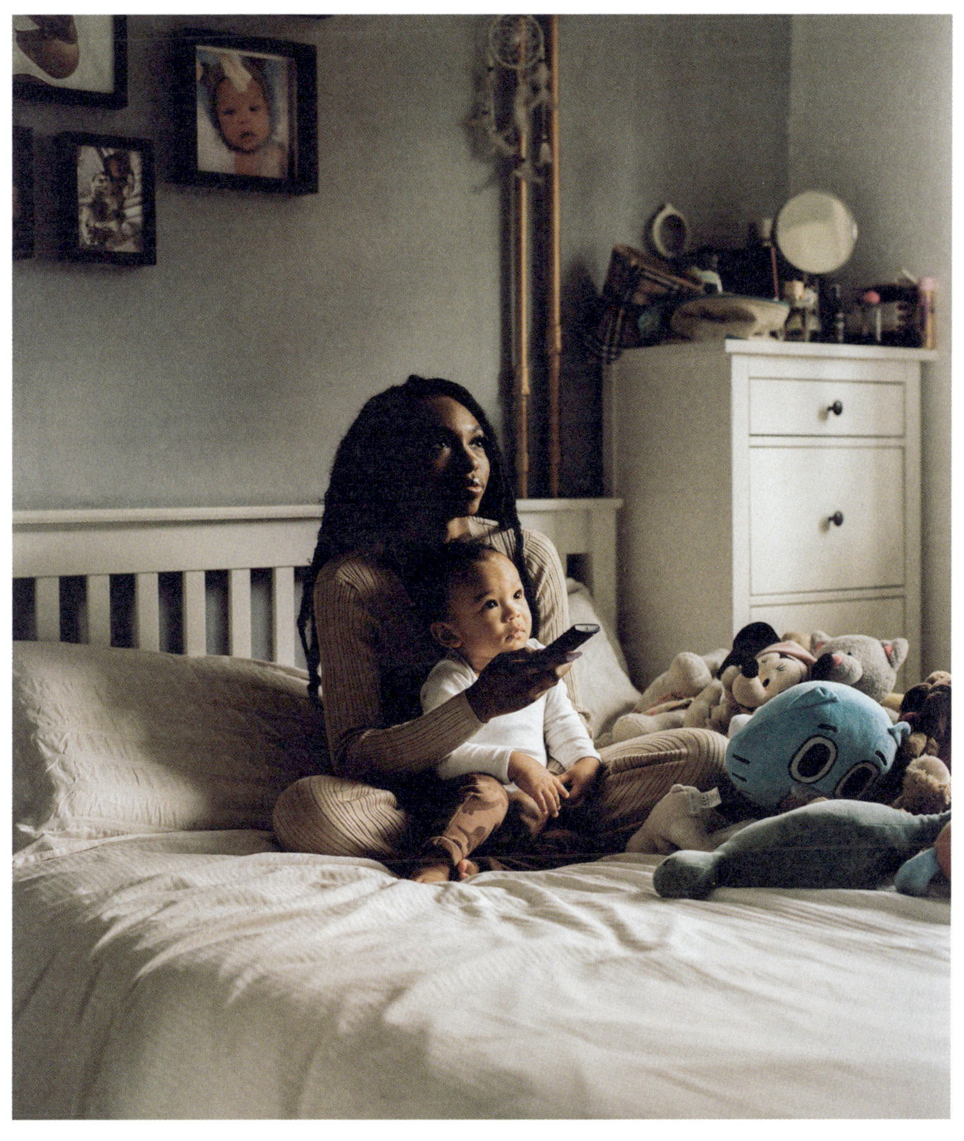

ALEXIS AND KENZO AT HOME
by Christopher Bethell
London

SUMMER DAYS IN FULL SWING
by Iko-Ojo Mercy Haruna
Gravesend, Kent

I took this photo of my son and daughter and
their friends playing together on the first day they
had all seen each other in over a year, since
the pandemic began.

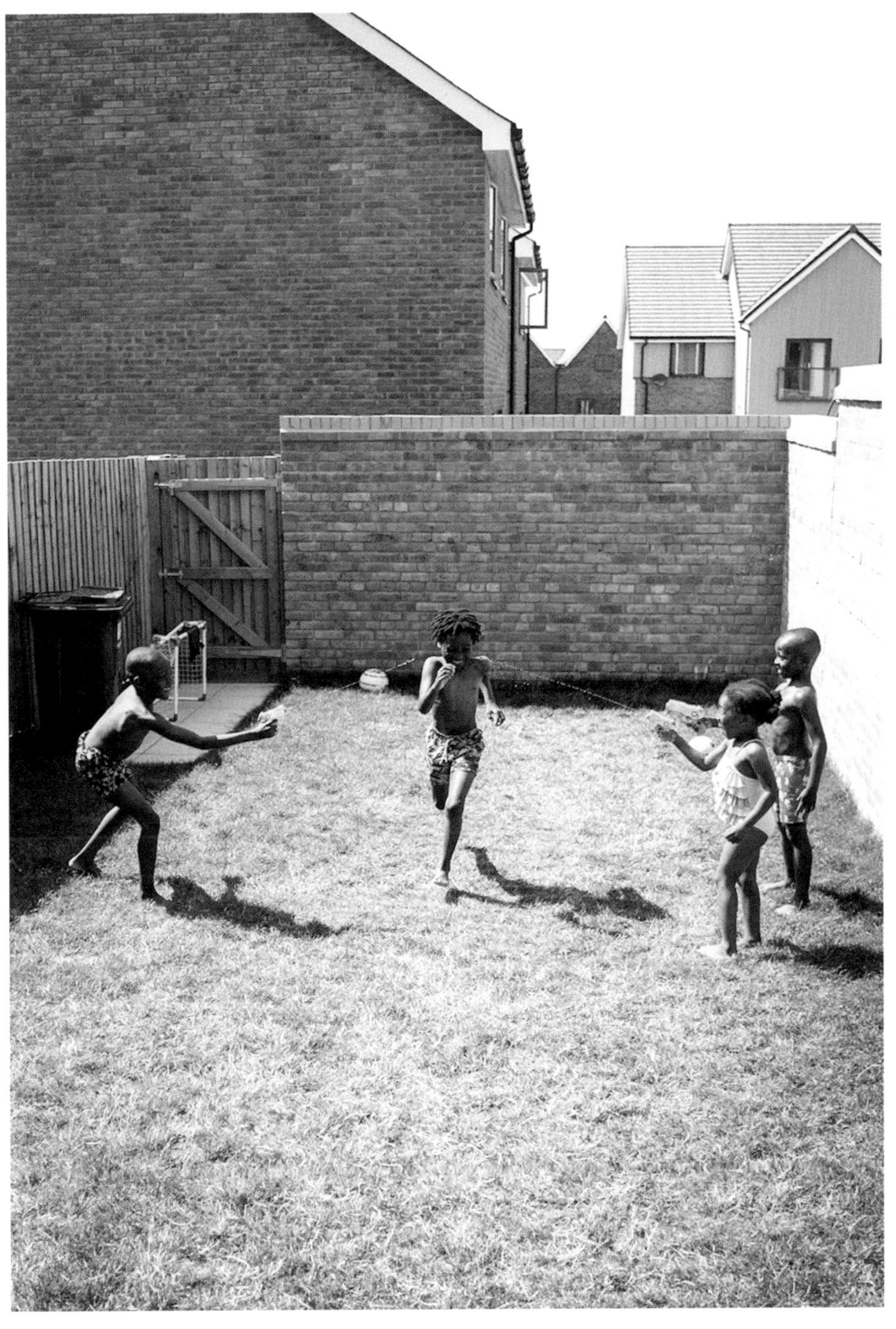

EDDIE
by Lewis King
Camborne, Cornwall

I met my boyfriend Eddie online during the
second lockdown. We have now been together for
five months and he has become my main muse,
constantly pushing me to create more work.
He has taught me true love.

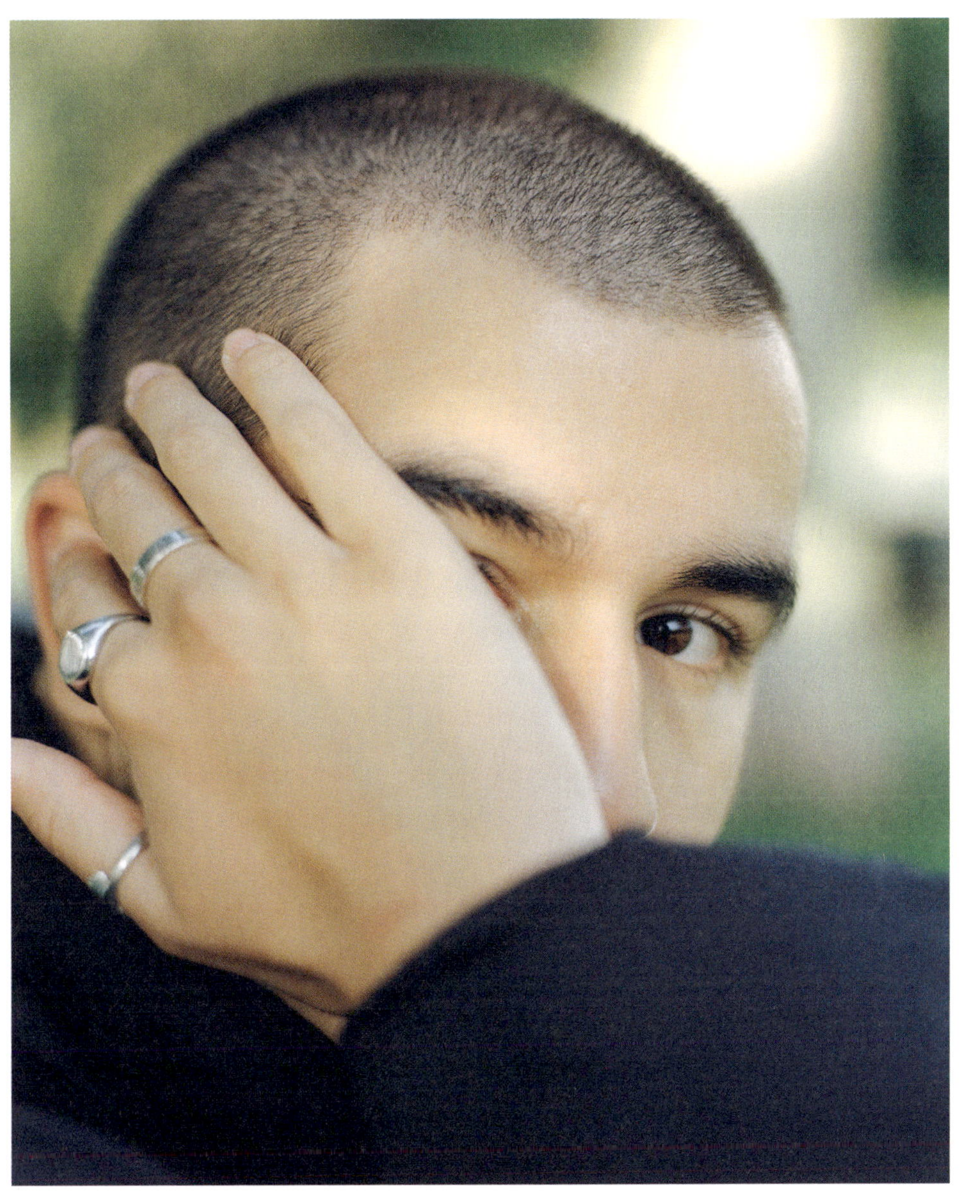

JOANNE AND MARCUS
by Megan Eagles
London

Joanne is a plus-size model with albinism.
I met Joanne and her son Marcus while working on
a project about mothers and babies. Joanne had
Marcus a week after I had my own baby, in the same
hospital, and we bonded over new motherhood.

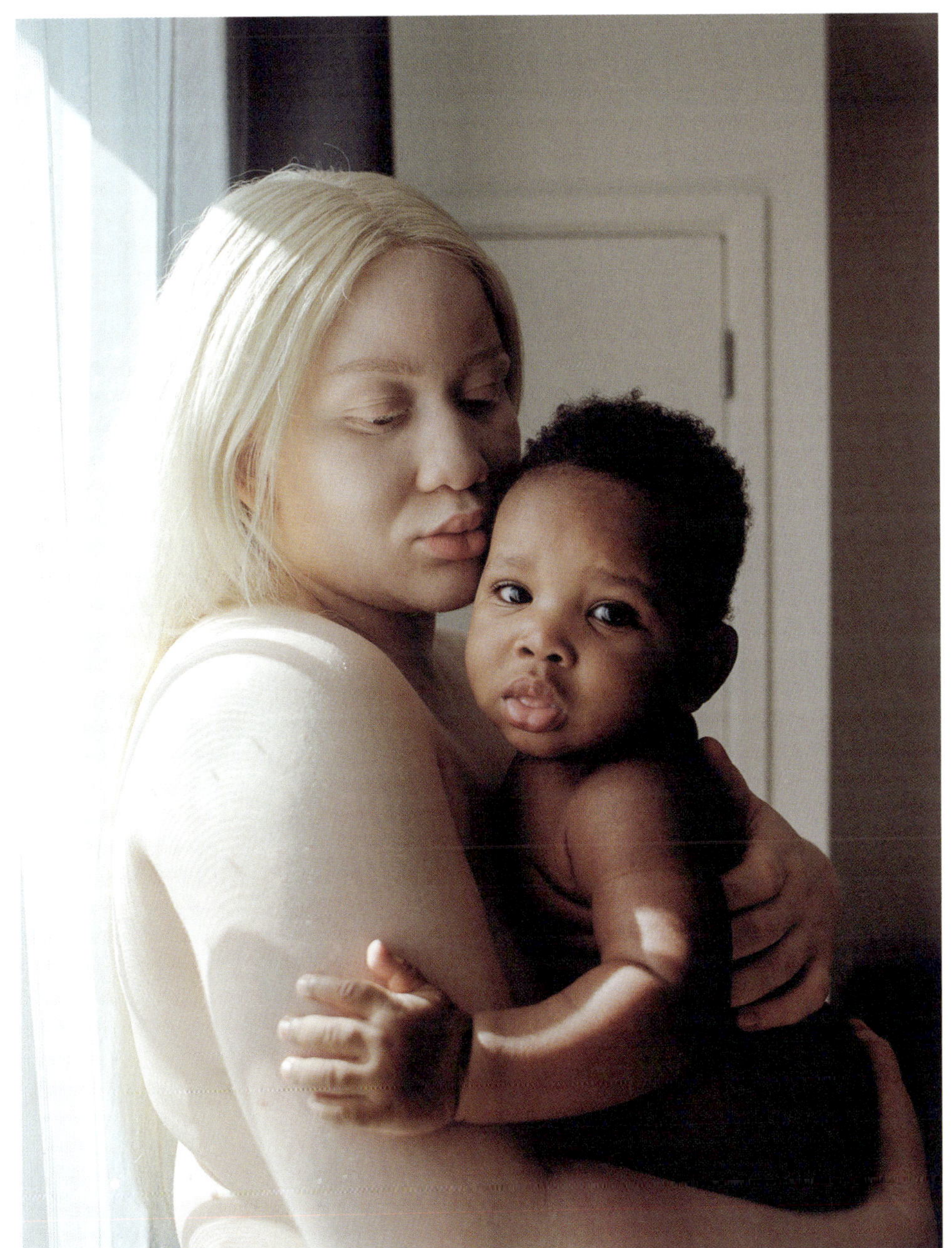

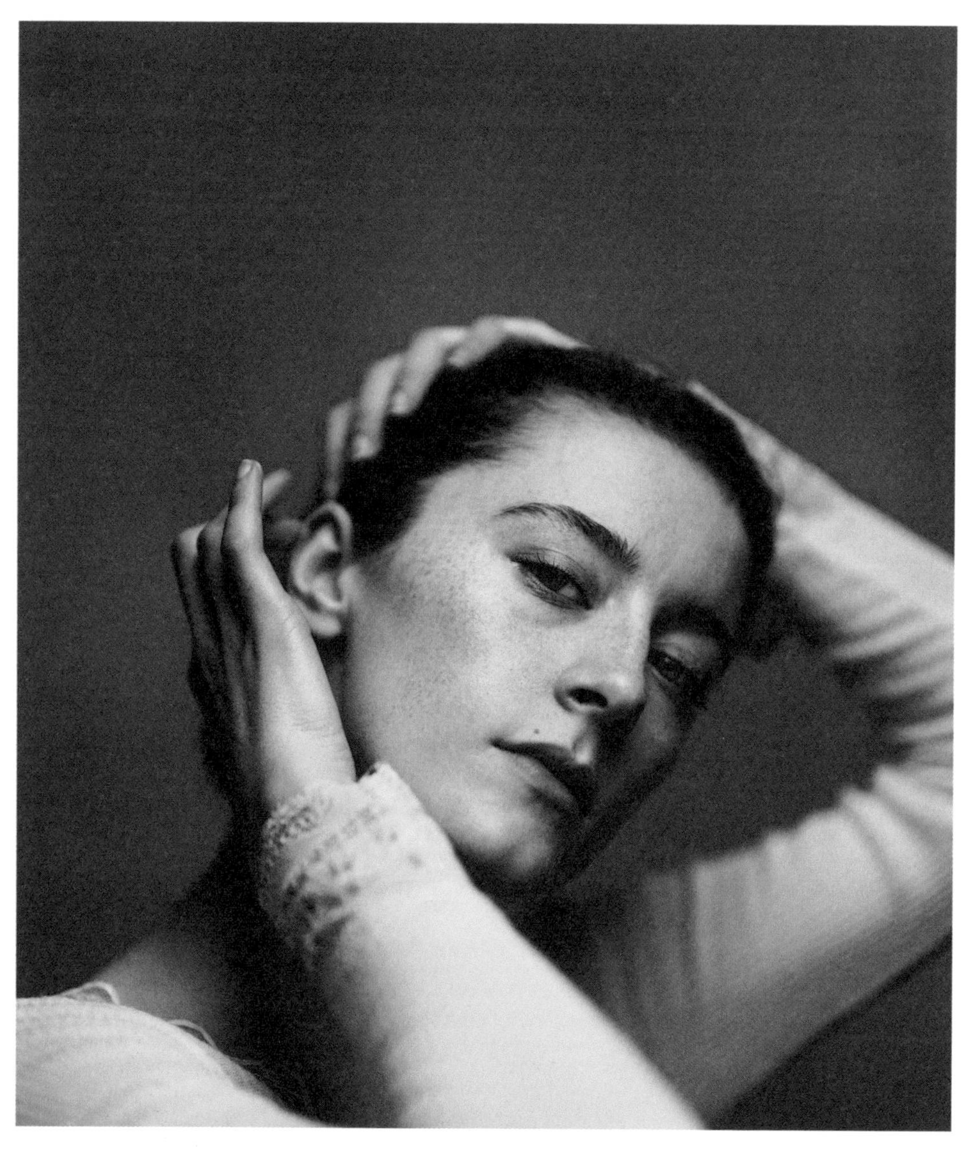

GRACE COOPER MILTON
by Phil Sharp
London

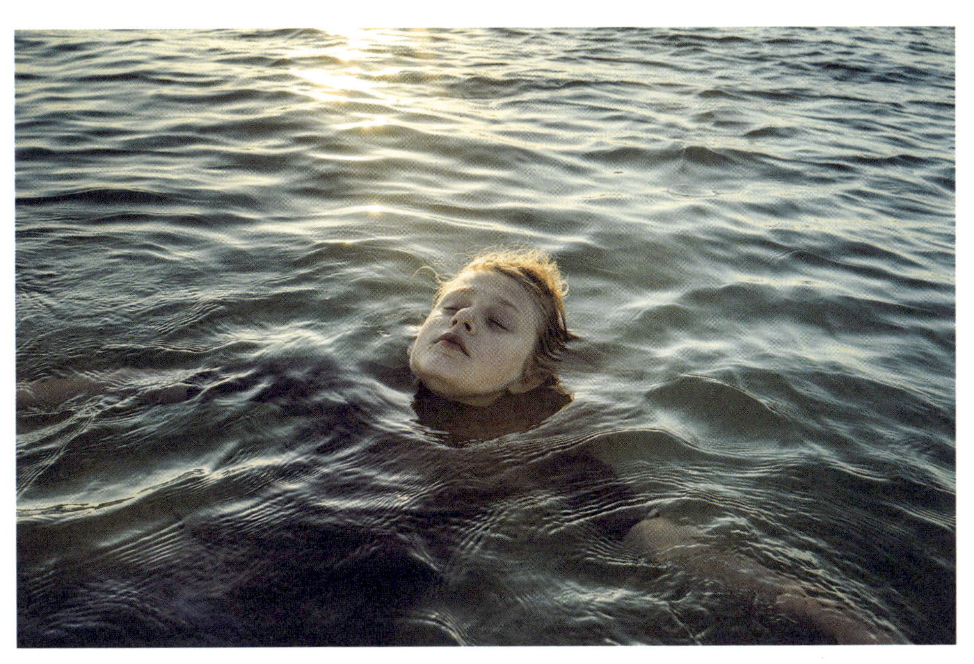

SASHA AT 10
by Antonina Mamzenko
Bracklesham Bay, West Sussex

During both summers of the pandemic, my 10-year-old
son Sasha and I found calm and serenity amongst
the chaos of the world by spending as much
time as possible in the sea.

BENNY AND TIZER
by Will Creswick
Seaton Carew, County Durham

I spotted Benny and his horse Tizer in the water,
and was eager to ask what they were doing. He told
me that this was a regular practice in order to clean
the horse's hooves and build riding confidence.
Benny has kept horses his whole life.

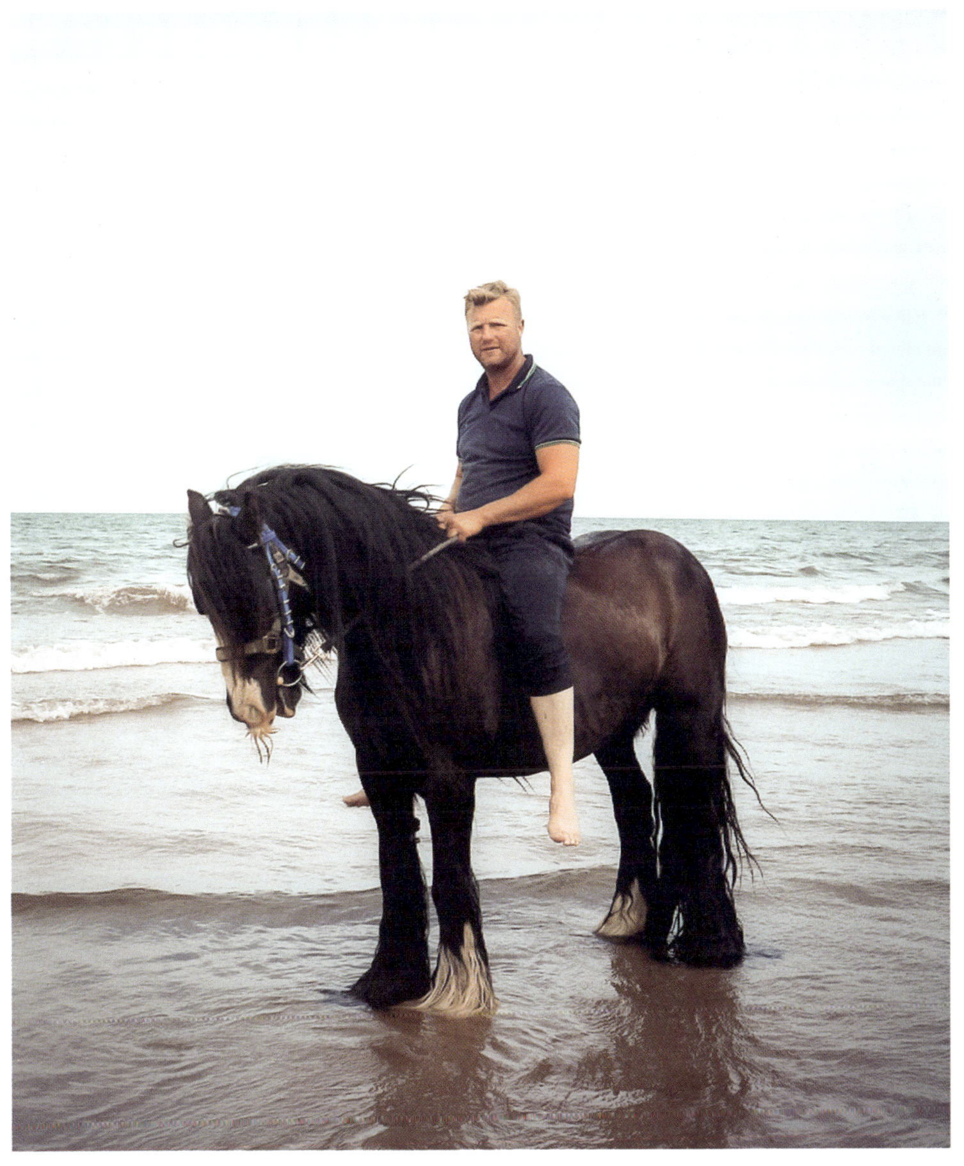

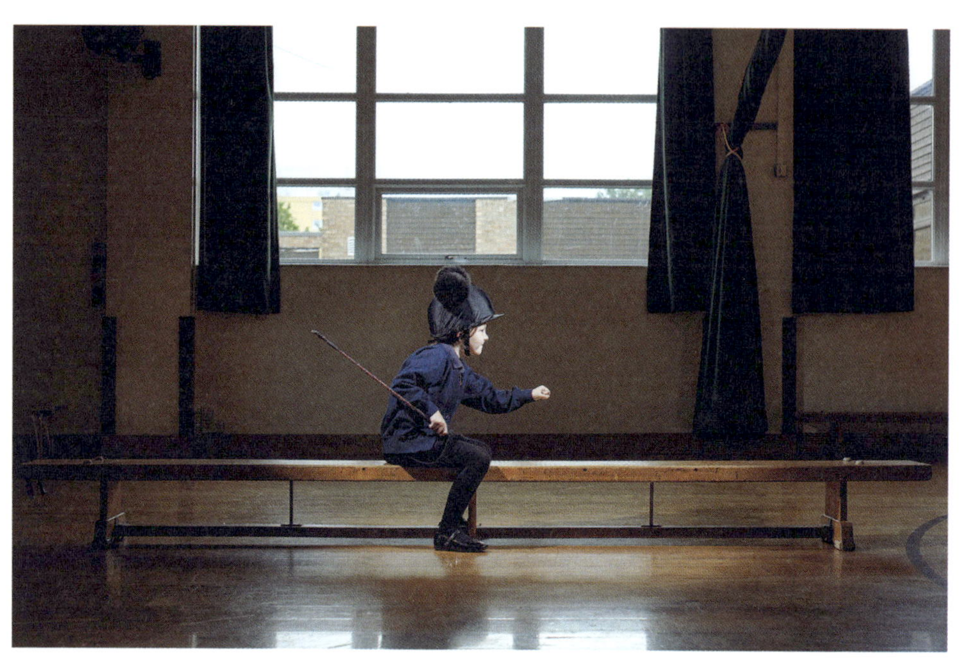

TALLIAH AND HORSES AND PONIES
by Jamie Bubb
Doncaster, South Yorkshire

Talliah is obsessed with horse riding, and spends most
weekends and some evenings after school at the stables.
We arranged a school photoshoot and she brought
her riding hat and crop along for the image so we
hunted around for something horse-like. Here,
she is showing me what a jockey does.

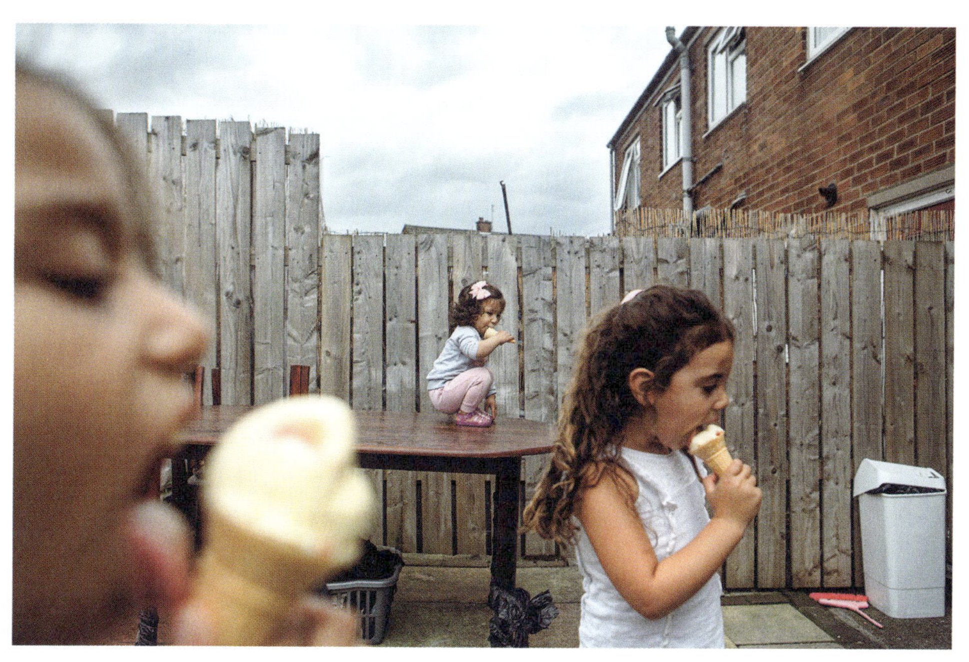

HANAN, RAYAN AND NADIA
by Rich Wiles
Driffield, East Yorkshire

Hanan (*left*) and her family arrived in the UK in 2017,
having been forcibly displaced from their home in
Syria five years before. Hanan's younger sister,
Rayan (*centre*) was born shortly after they arrived.
My eldest daughter Nadia (*right*) was born in Palestine
to a Palestinian mother and a British father.
These three girls are all growing up somewhere
in between cultures, languages and homes.

SECOND PLACE
by Leif Sebastian
Great Gransden, Cambridgeshire

Looking to get out of London, I attended
the Gransden agricultural show. This boy had
won second prize in the Young Sheep Handler
competition. It was amazing to see how seriously
all the kids took it. They were quite shy with all
the attention (as were the sheep).

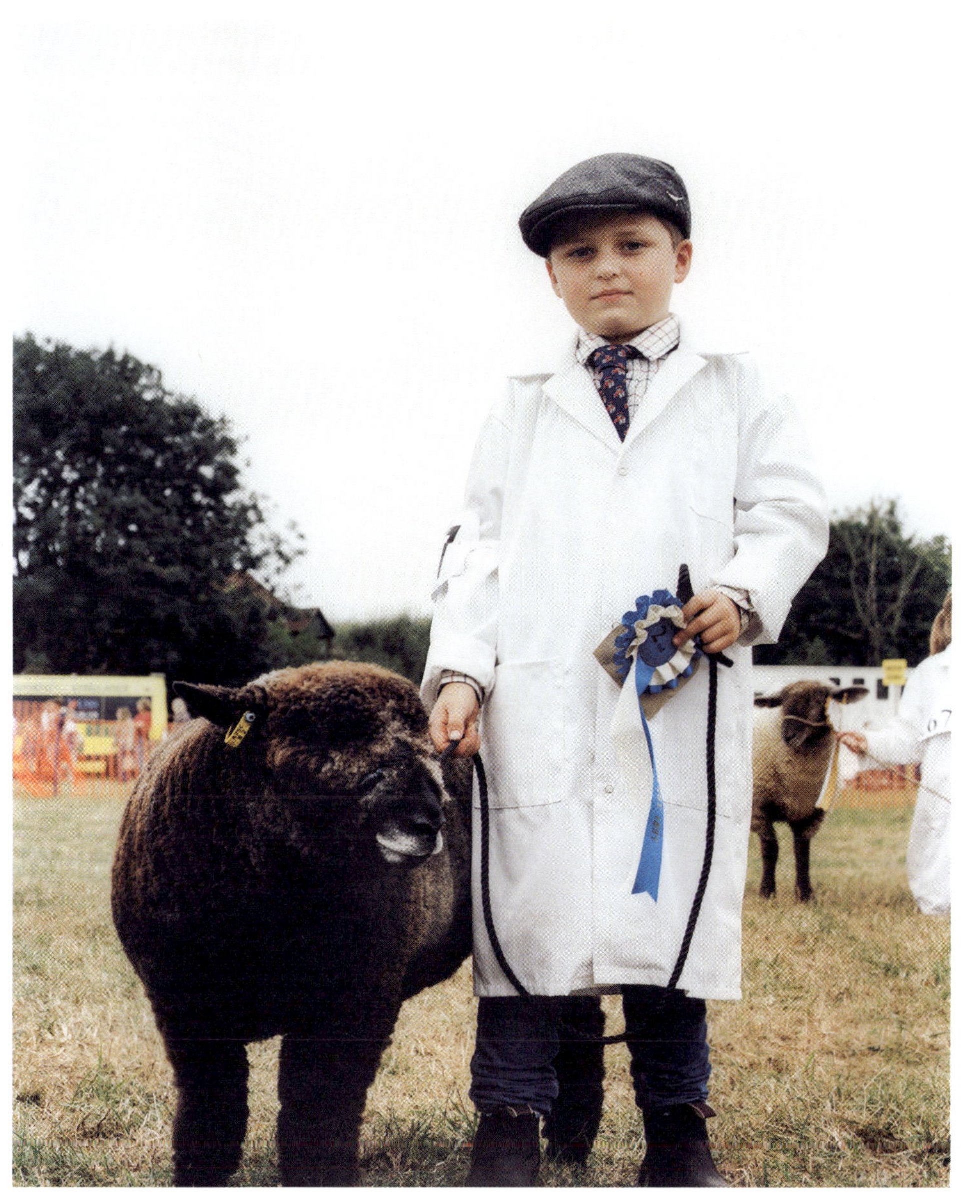

THE DORSET GROVE
by Michael Farra
Knowlton, Dorset

Dennis (*left*) is the Bard of a congregation of
animist druids living in Dorset. He, his wife Rita and
their fellow druids follow the religious practices
and traditions that were commonplace in pre-Christian
Europe. Here, Dennis and Rita are wearing outfits
designed to emulate two of the gods they follow:
the Horned God and Mother Nature.

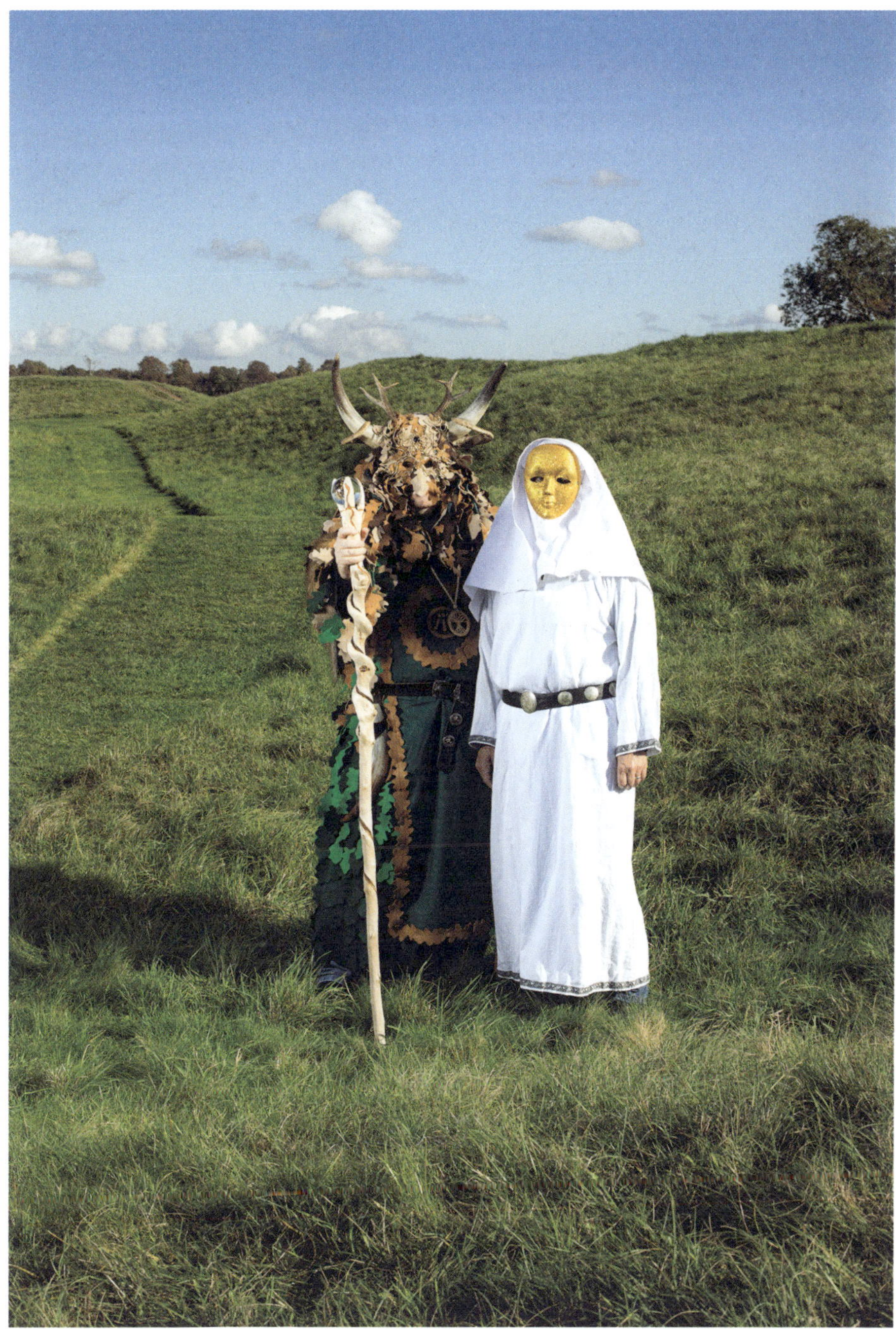

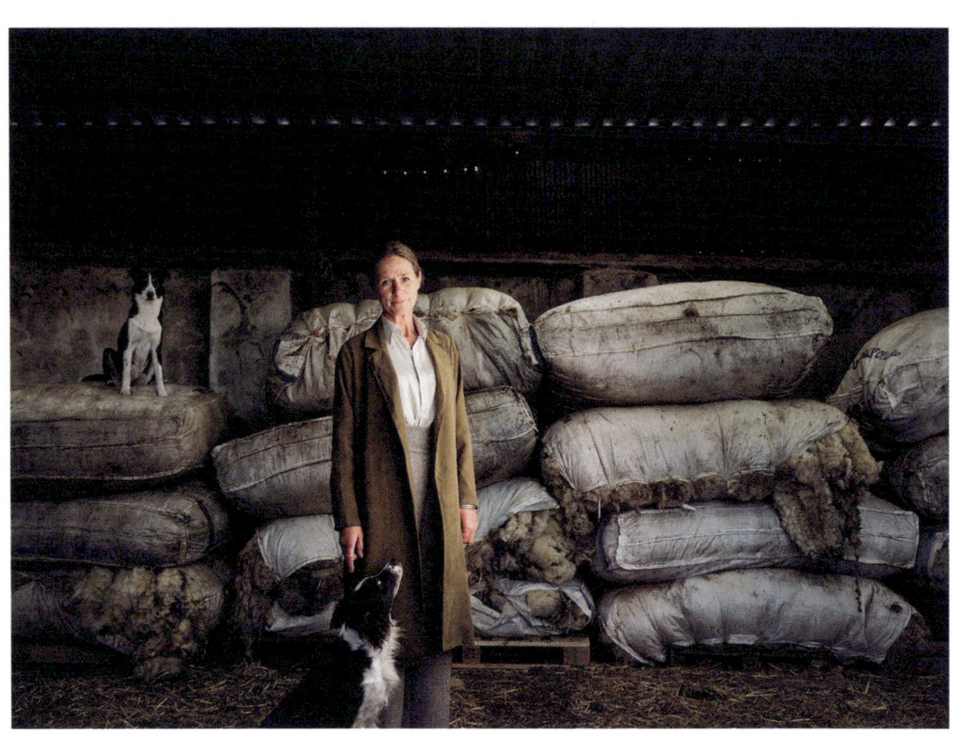

CHARLOTTE
by Cris Barnett
Lindale, Cumbria

Charlotte is a sheep farmer who makes the most
beautiful clothing from her flock's wool. Her family have
farmed sheep in the Lake District for hundreds of years,
and she wanted to keep up this cultural tradition
while building a sustainable business.

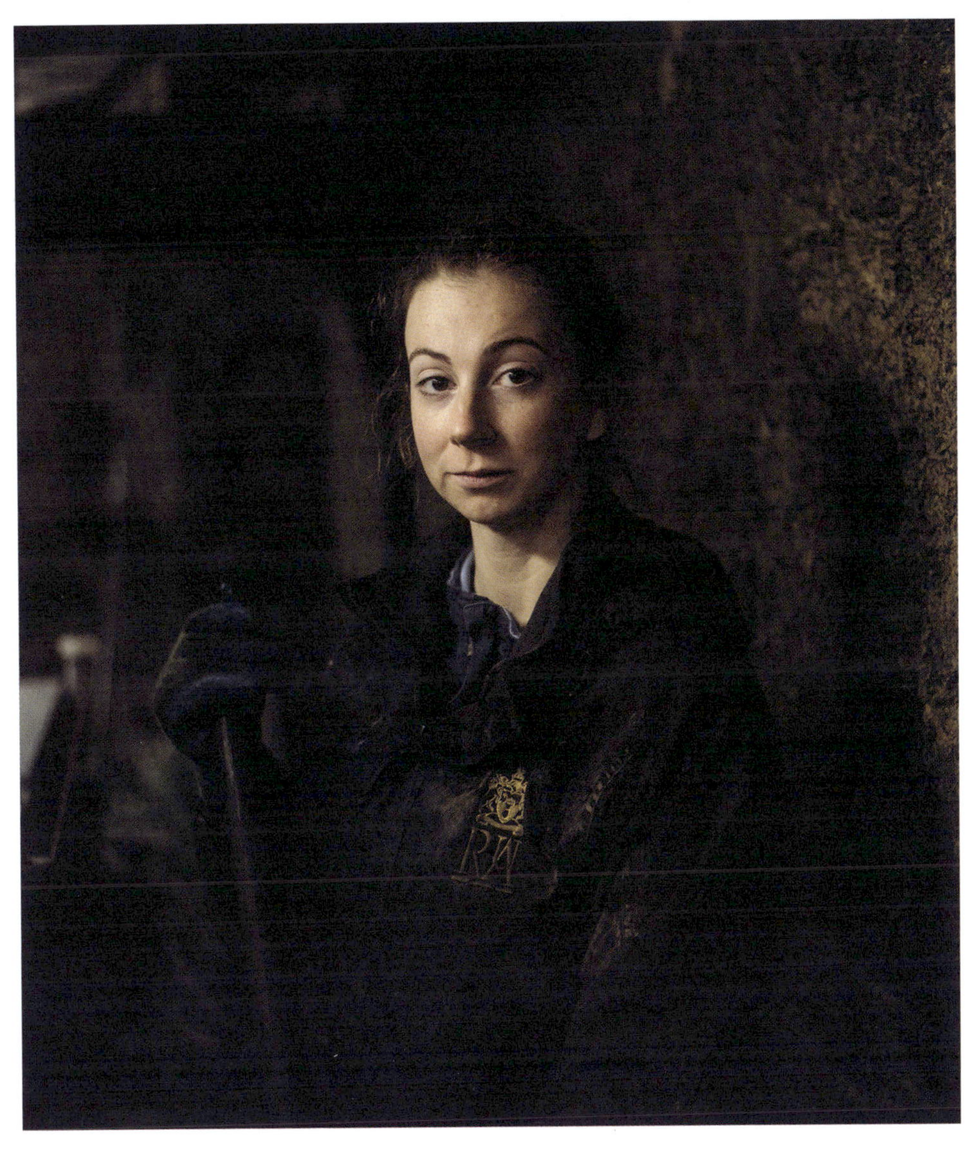

ELLIE BY THE CIDER PRESS
by Robert Darch
Exeter, Devon

JAMES CORBIN
by Paul Scala
London

James is a model who I met while shooting an
editorial fashion series. He was such a nice guy, and
very passionate about promoting different body types
in editorial and fashion photography. I think he
looks incredibly beautiful in this image.

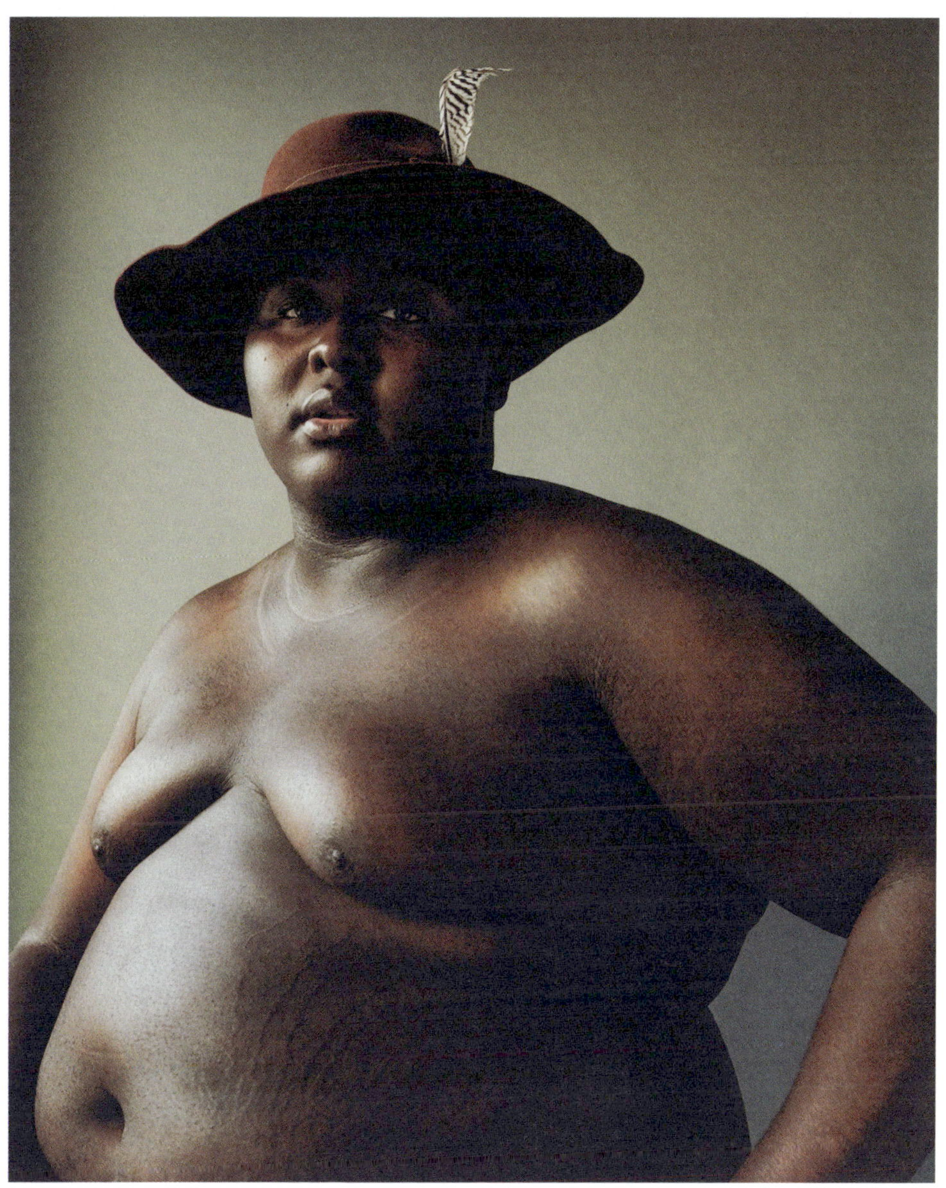

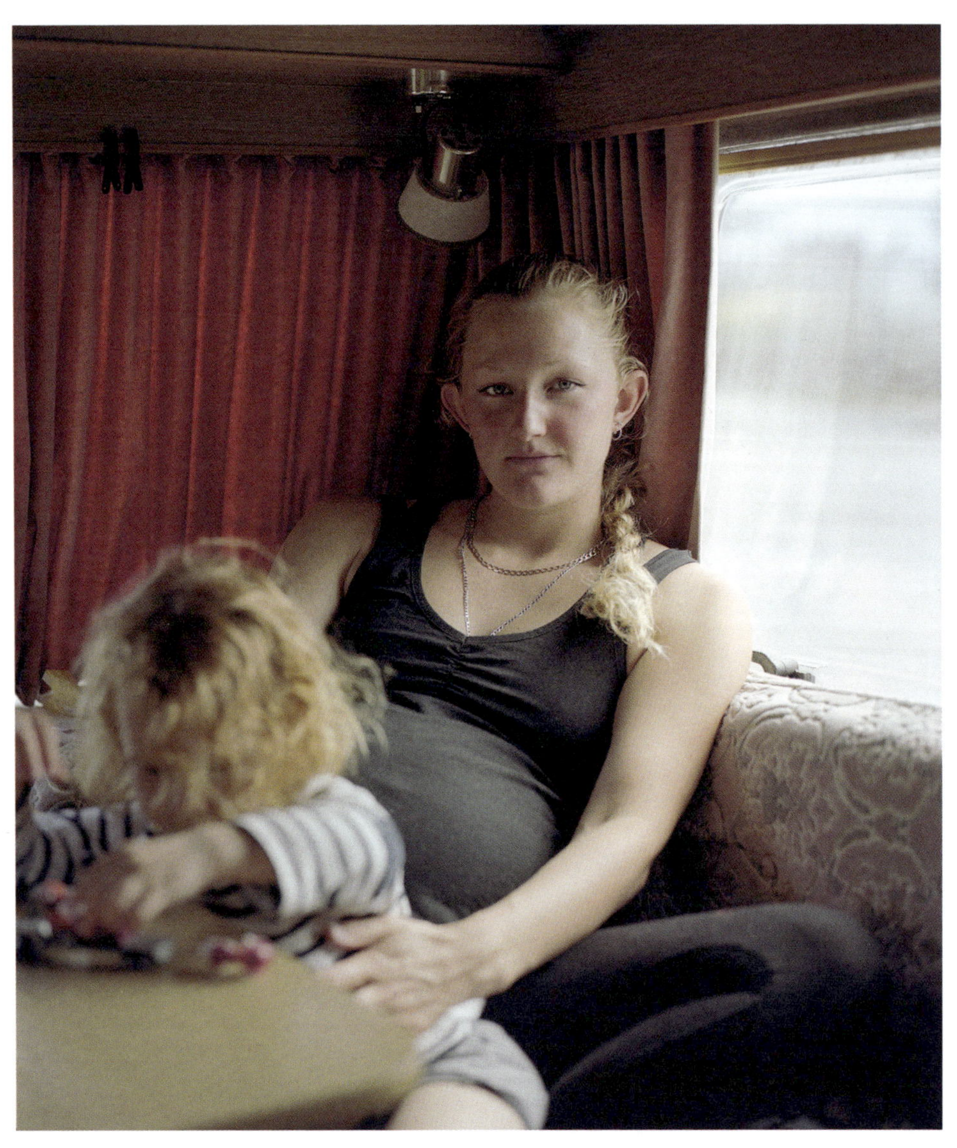

AMBER, GUNNE AND BUMP AT HOME
IN THEIR CARAVAN
by Becky Tyrrell
Penzance, Cornwall

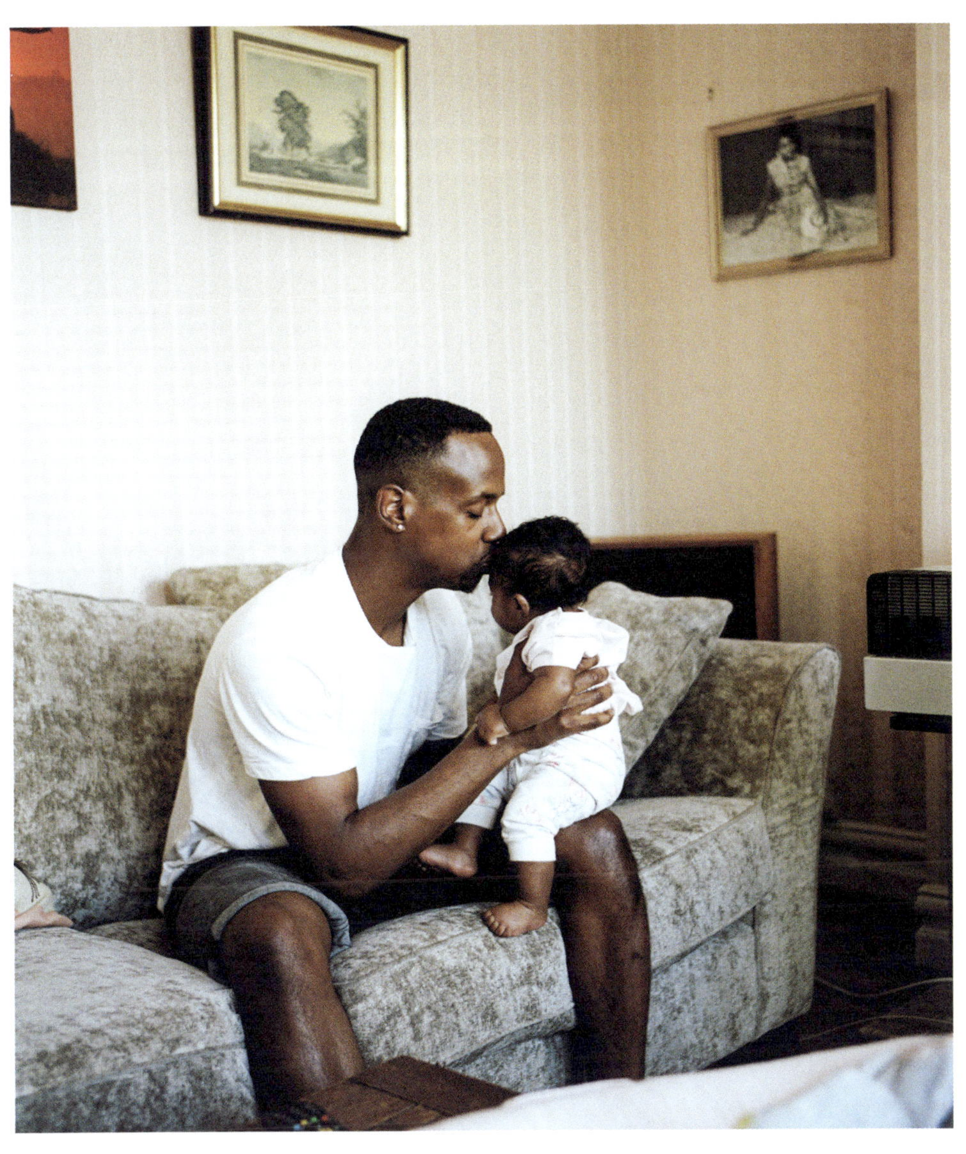

KADEEM & LA'NYAH-ROSE
by Renee Maria Osubu
London

219

KIM, SEEDS OF HOPE
by Joanne Coates
Middlesbrough, North Yorkshire

Kim runs Streets Ahead, a charity based in the
Gresham area of Middlesbrough – one of the most
deprived places in the UK – that supports local
residents in all sorts of ways. I photographed her
as part of my series about the hidden heroes
whose acts of kindness have really made
a difference to their communities.

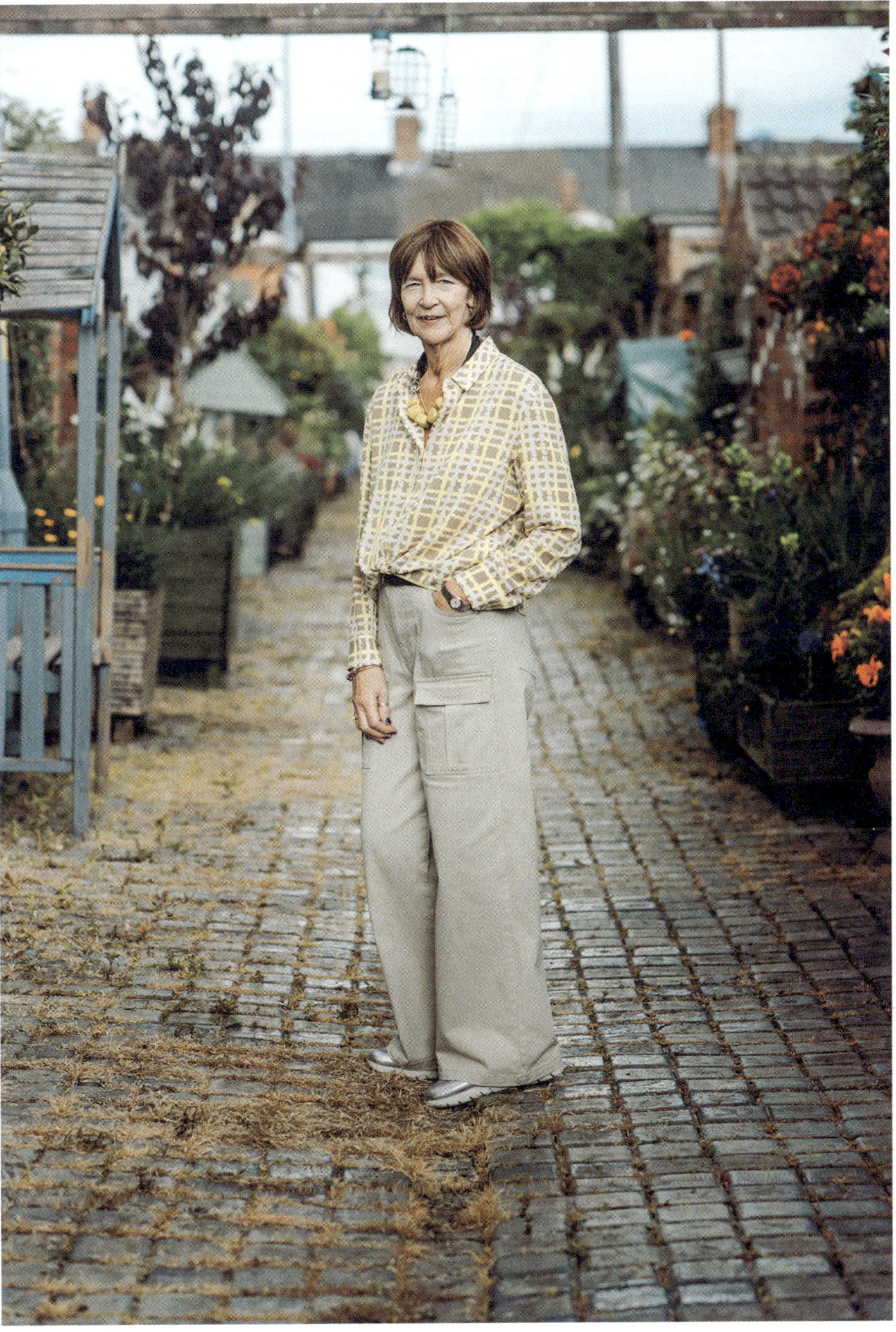

JORDAN
by Benjamin Brooks
London

Jordan is a carer for the elderly in south east London.
She told me about her experience as a frontline
worker during the pandemic: 'People would see my
uniform in public and very obviously make it a
big deal to move away from me or cross the road,
as if I was dirty. It made me feel as though I was
doing something wrong. I would try to hide
my carer's uniform with a jacket, or take it off
in between clients.'

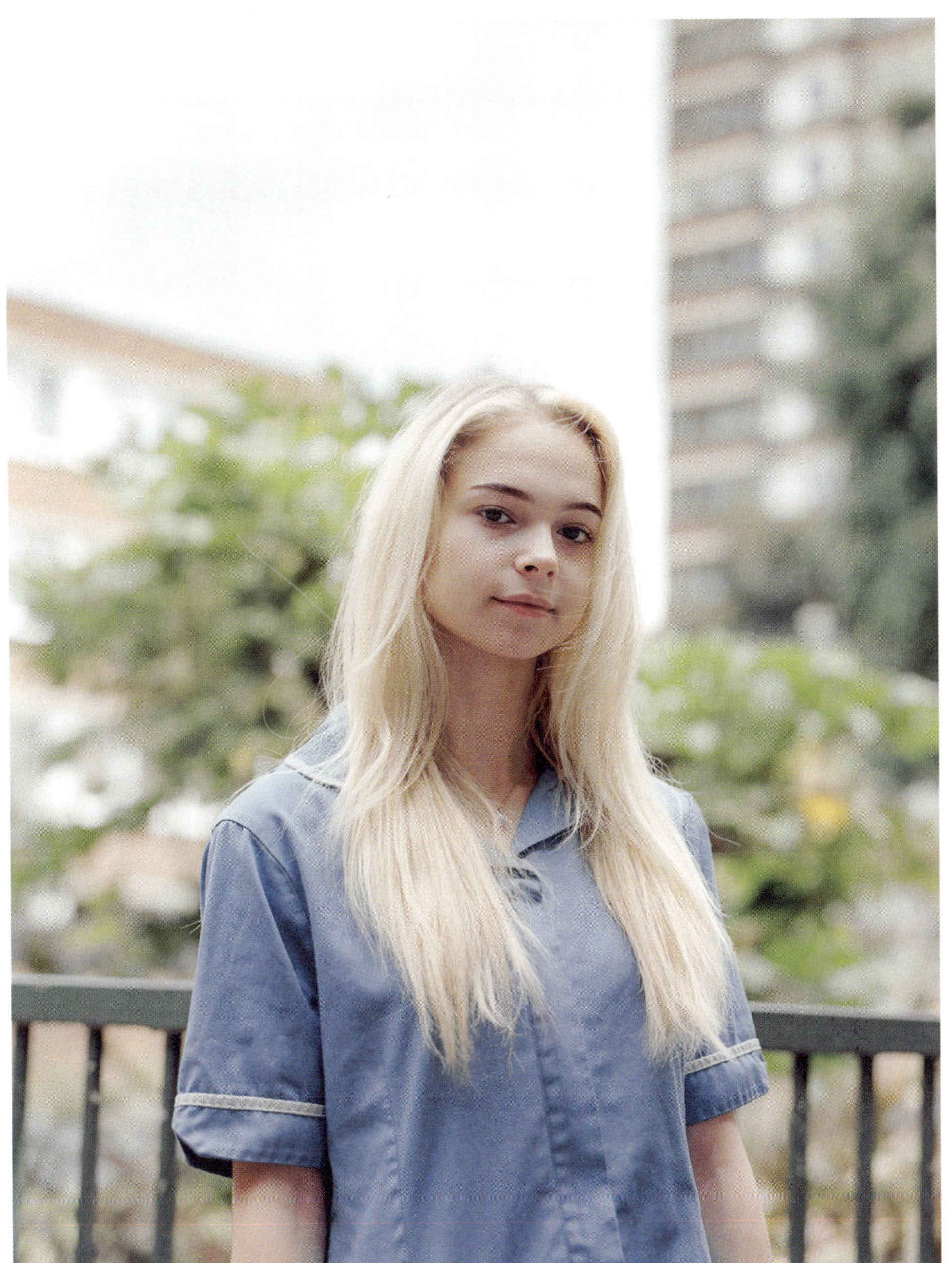

WAY BACK HOME
by Udochukwu Emeka-Okafor
Egham, Surrey

Farhia (*left*) and Asma are sisters. Farhia and I met
at the Miss Universe Great Britain pageant in 2019.
We were only roommates for a day, but we
have become lasting friends.

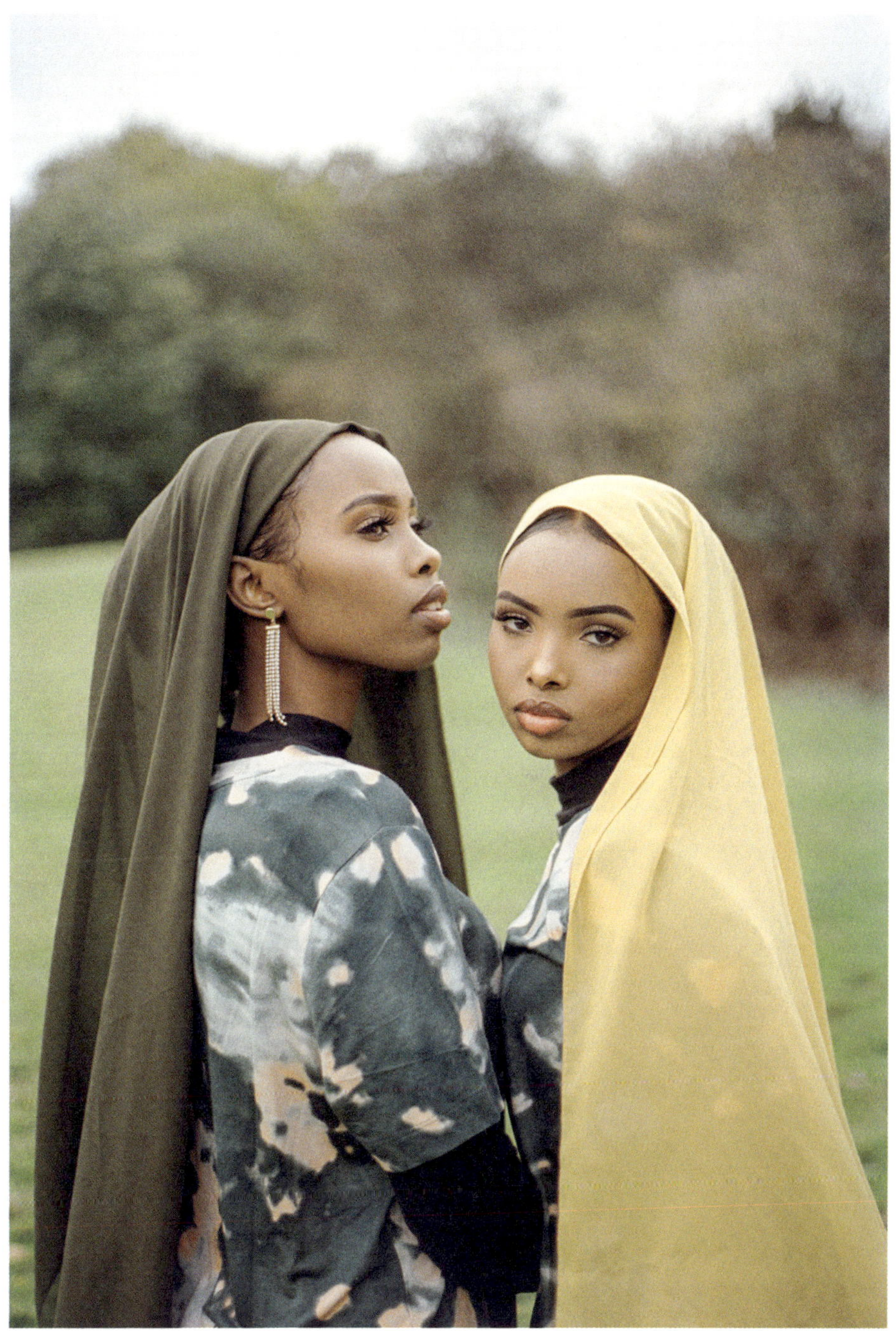

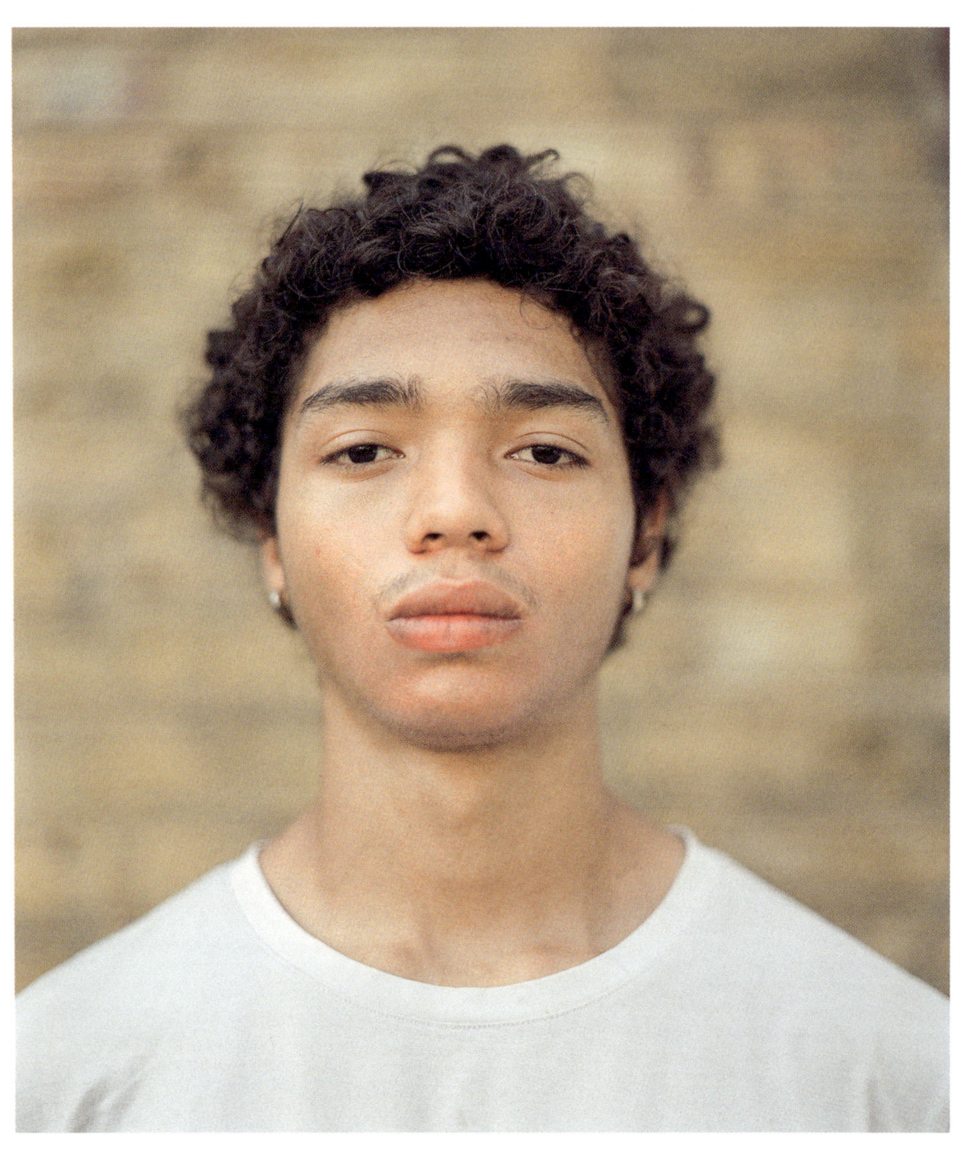

MATEO
by Sukhy Hullait
London

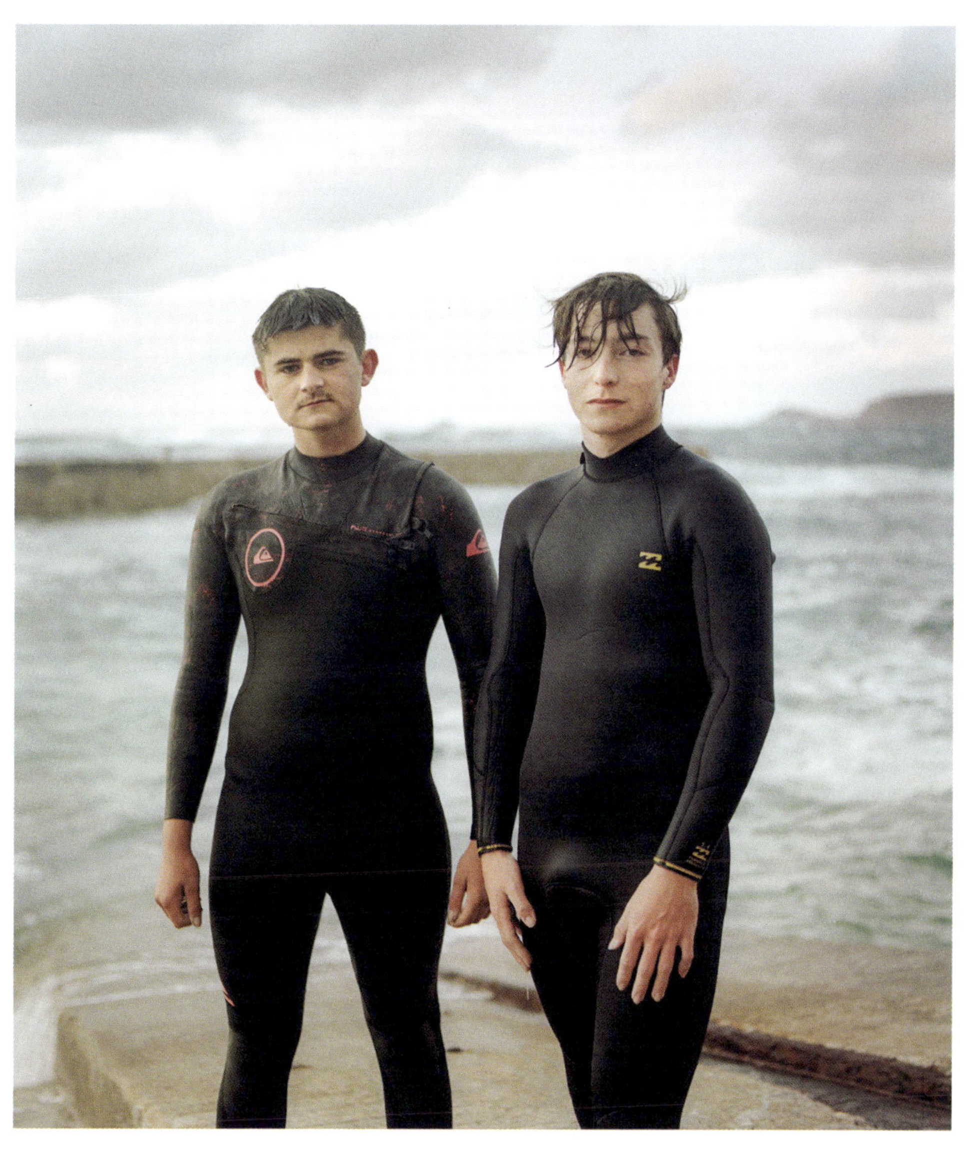

ZACHARY AND ALBERT
by Rhiannon Adam
Sennen, Cornwall

AIRSOFT PLAYER, INVICTA
BATTLEFIELD
by Danny Burrows
Tonbridge, Kent

Airsoft is a martial sport in which teams of
players complete a day of tasks and objectives,
known as 'skirmishes', armed with pellet-firing guns
and dressed in combat uniforms. It's often described
as a physical version of video gaming. I have been
working on a photo project that aims to discover
who these self-imagined warriors are, and why
they choose to play war in their leisure time.

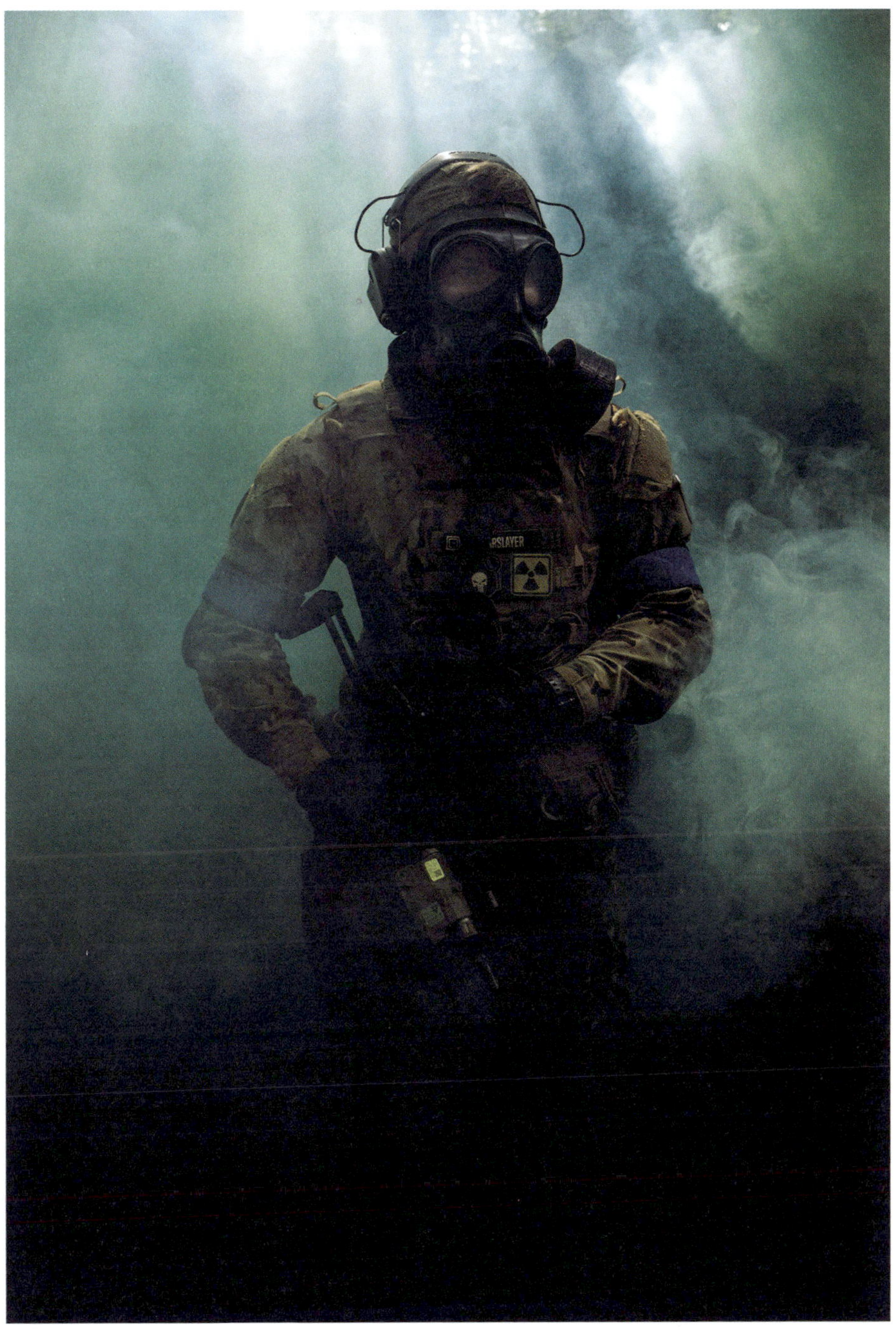

EDINBURGH PARK RESIDENCY
WORKFORCE, PORTRAIT ONE
by Andy Mather
Edinburgh

I took this photo shortly before the first Covid
lockdown, as part of my residency documenting
the development of Edinburgh Park. My aim was to
highlight some of the people responsible for making
the buildings we often use without thinking of how
they were built. Ian (*pictured*), known as 'Spook',
is a groundworker on the site – he prepares the ground
for construction. He said, 'If the task is challenging,
be like a stamp and stick to it till you get there.'

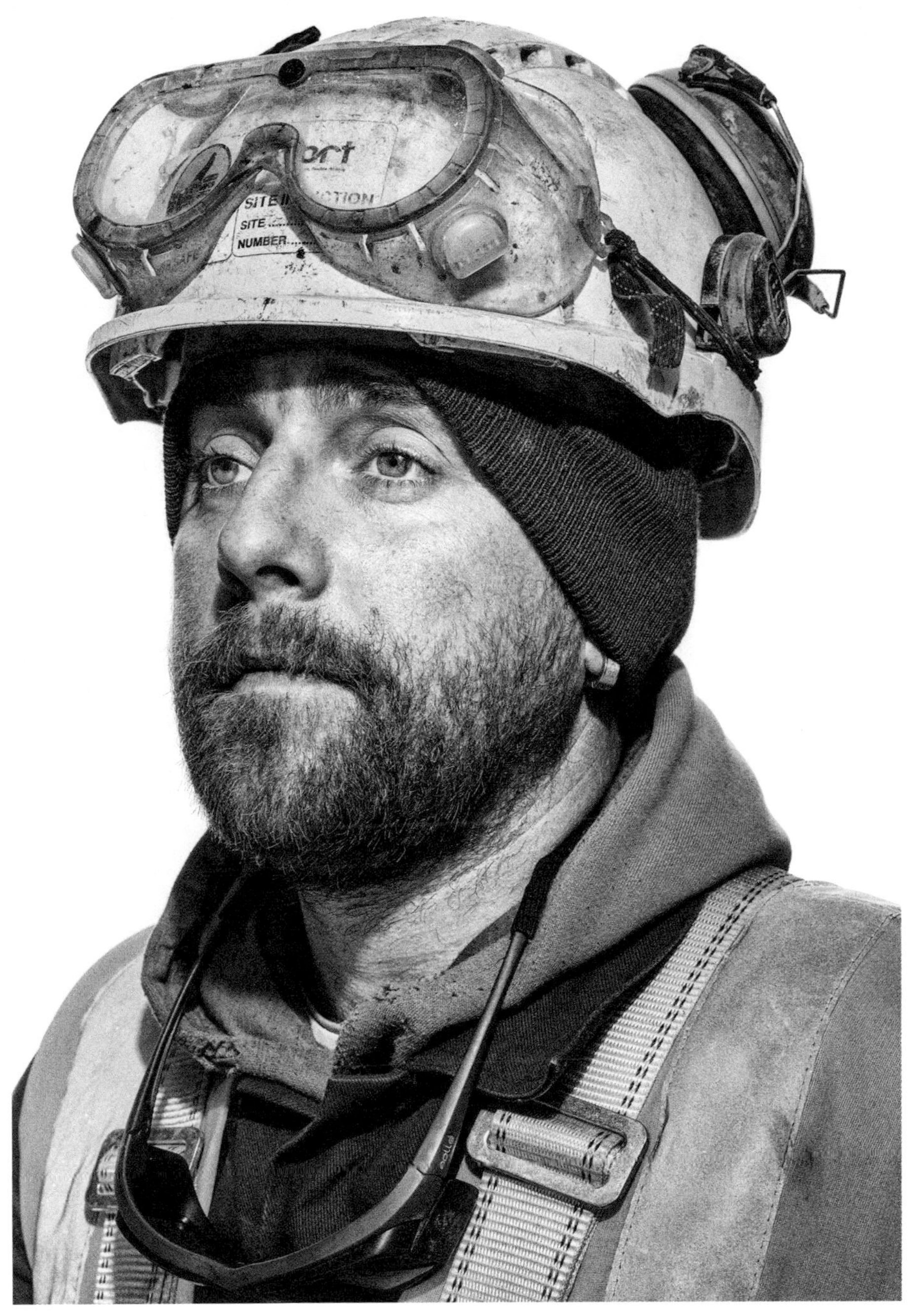

DELROY, VOLUNTEER BEEKEEPER
by Anne-Marie Briscombe
London

Delroy volunteers at Bee Urban in Kennington Park,
a social enterprise that provides a space to learn about
beekeeping, organic gardening and sustainable living.
He told me, 'You get lost here, transfixed, it's good
for the mind and soul.' Delroy is very passionate about
bees, and wants to become a Master Beekeeper.

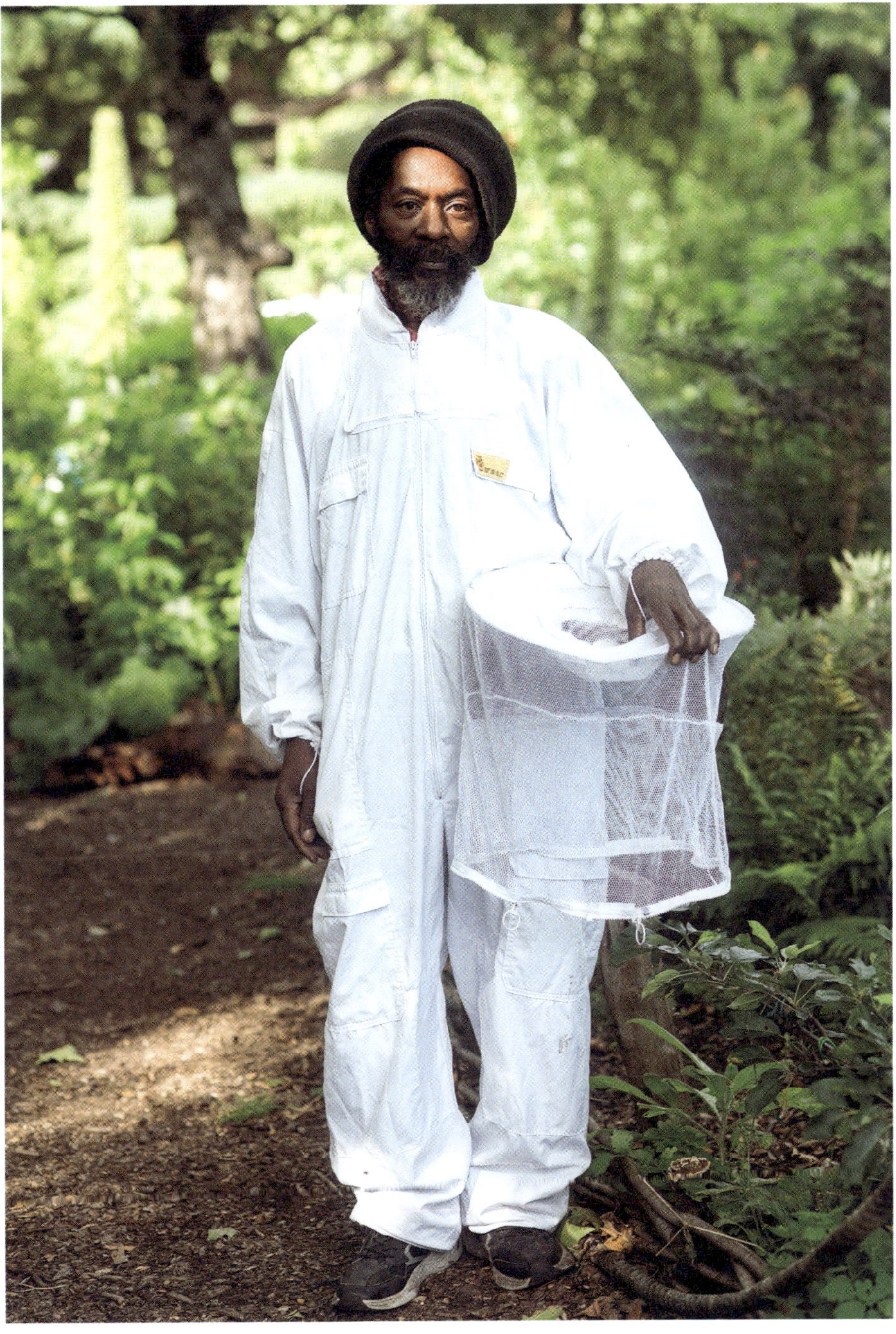

MUSTAPHA
by Rich Wiles
Driffield, East Yorkshire

Mustapha and his family arrived in the UK in 2017,
having been forcibly displaced from their home in
Syria, and our families have since become close friends.
I took this photo of him in January 2021, just as
the third national lockdown began. Having not
been at school from March to September 2020,
Mustapha was disappointed to find time
with his friends halted once more.

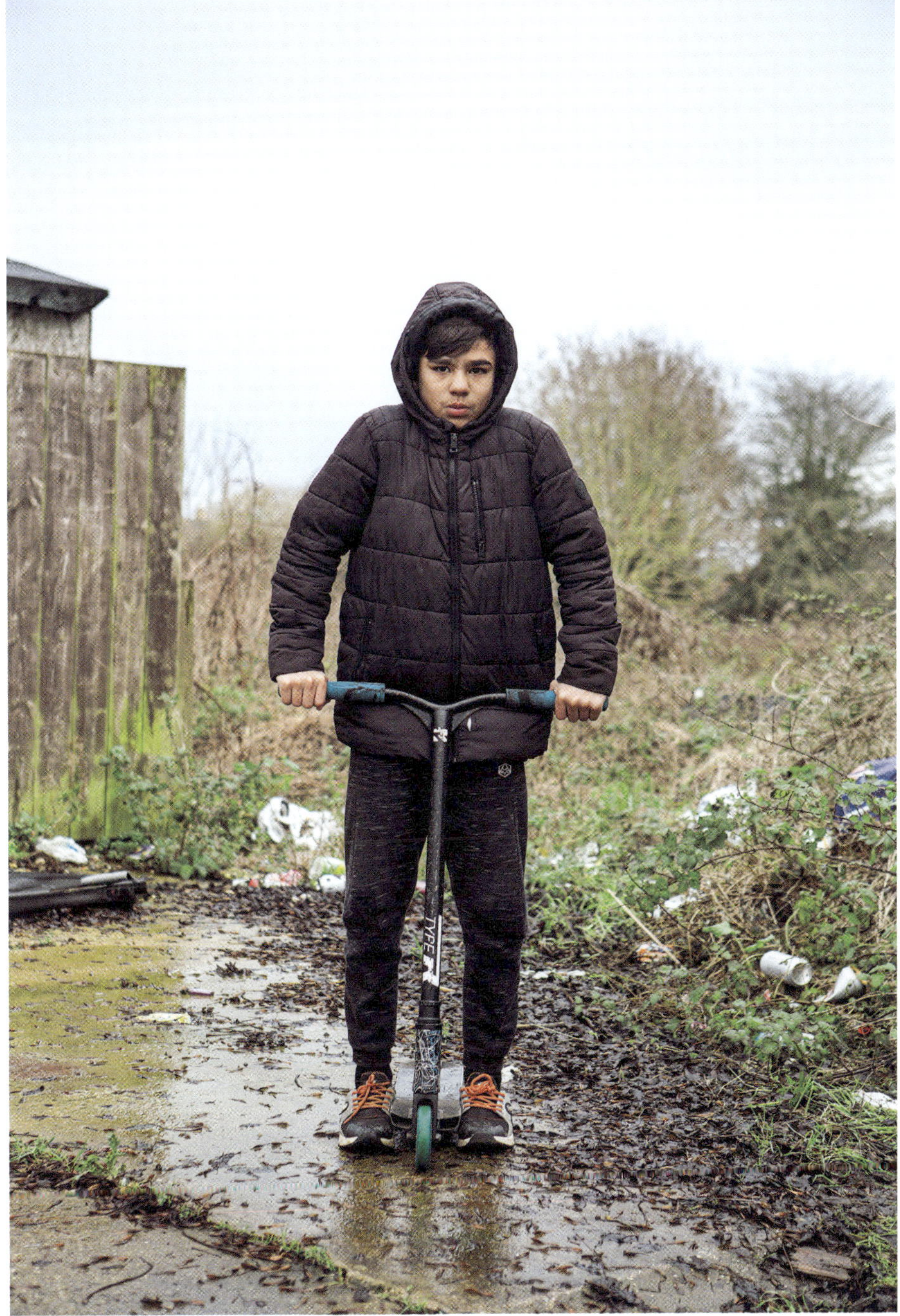

TEA FOR TWO
by Will Creswick
Cresswell, Northumberland

I was out walking along the coast near Cresswell
when bad weather led me inland in search of refuge.
I found this café, but it turned out to be closed. Before
turning away, I peered through to the patio and
spotted this couple in the otherwise empty seating area.
They smiled as I approached, and were happy
for me to take a photo. It all struck me as
very quintessentially British.

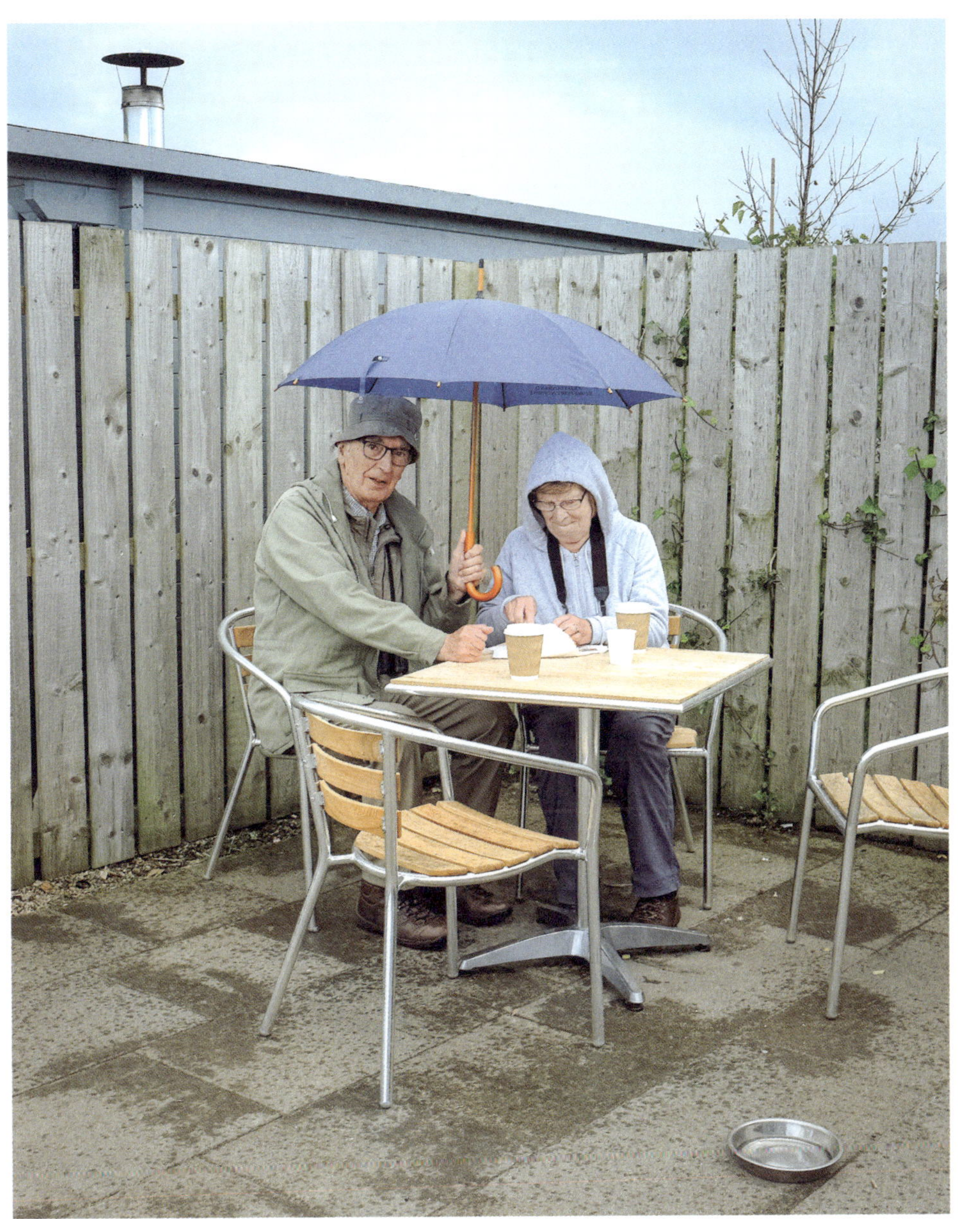

CECELIA AND HUGO
by Jon Attenborough
Swadlincote, South Derbyshire

I took this photo during my first visit to meet
my girlfriend's father and his partner, Cecelia.
Hugo, Cecelia's dog, is so beloved that he
features on all of their mugs.

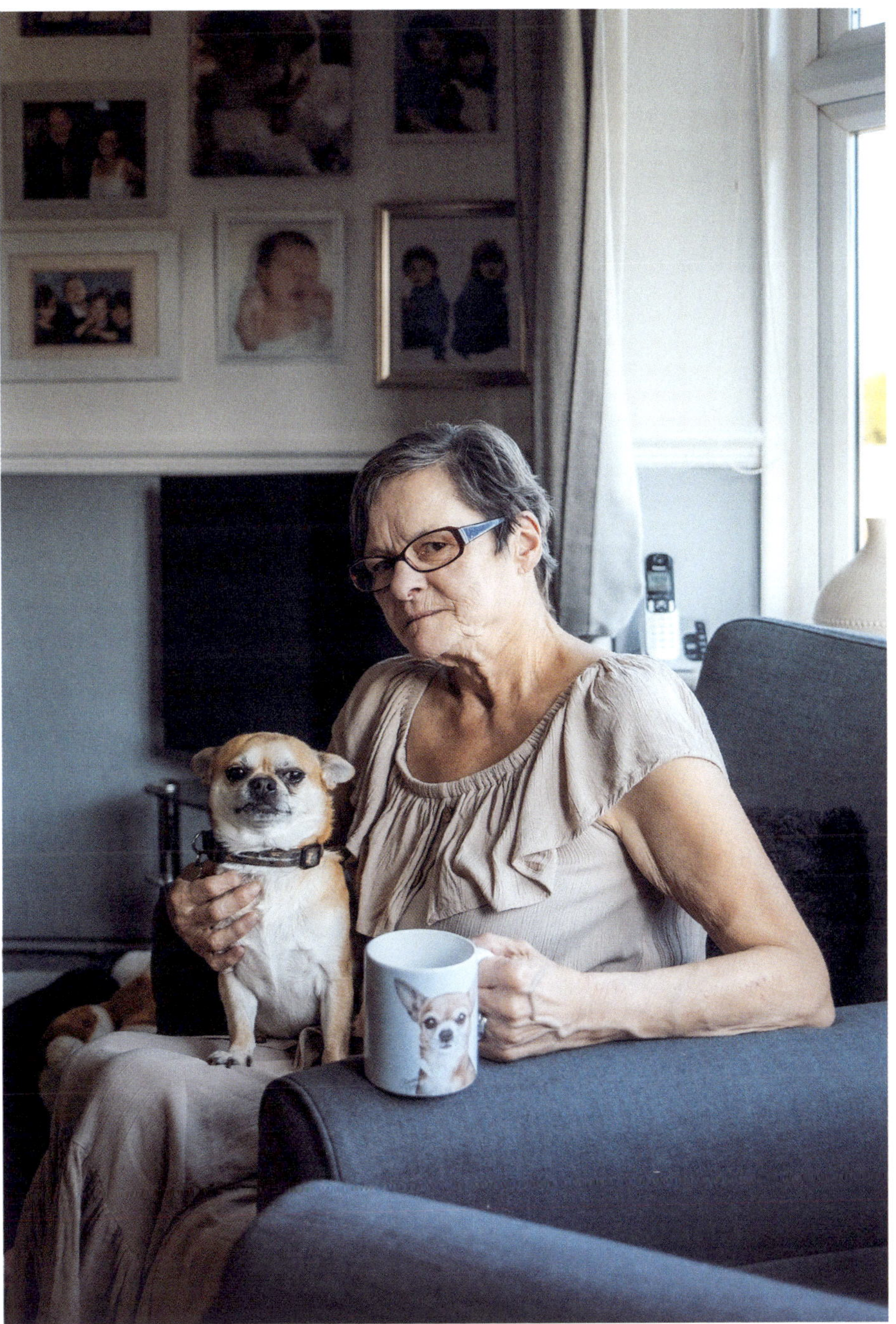

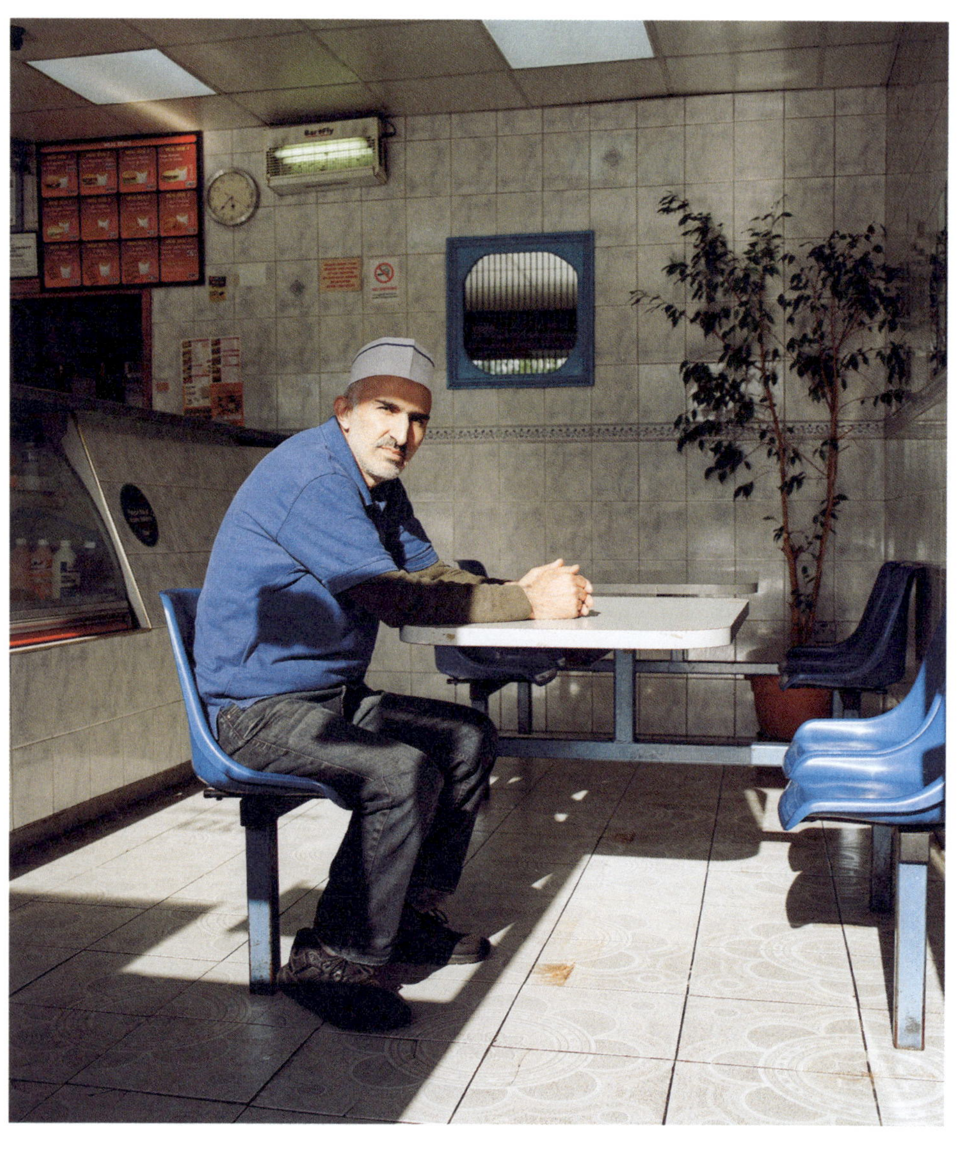

LOCAL KEBABBY
by Nico Froehlich
London

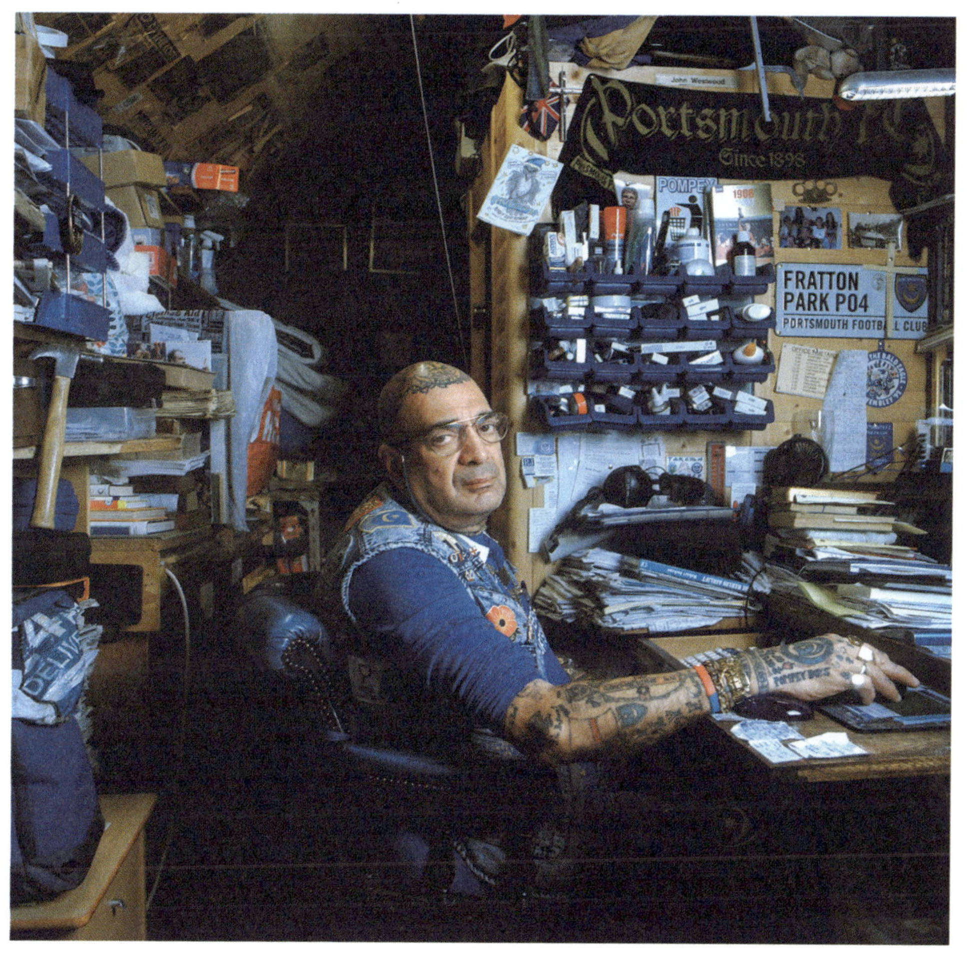

JOHN PORTSMOUTH FOOTBALL CLUB
WESTWOOD SAT AT HIS DESK
by Callum O'Keefe
Petersfield, Hampshire

John is one of Portsmouth Football Club's most famous
supporters; he changed his name by deed poll in 1989.
When he's not watching football, John runs an
antiquarian bookshop.

RESILIENCE
by Gabrielle Motola
London

During the summer of 2021, I went to stay
with some friends in the East End while recovering
from depression. One day, the neighbourhood had
a street party and I saw Corey (*pictured*) playing
by himself while the adults drank and talked.
I had seen him before, and had heard that both of his
grandparents had passed away from Covid. They were
extremely close and it had been really hard for him and
his mother. Yet there they were, not long afterwards,
mixing with the neighbourhood and facing life.

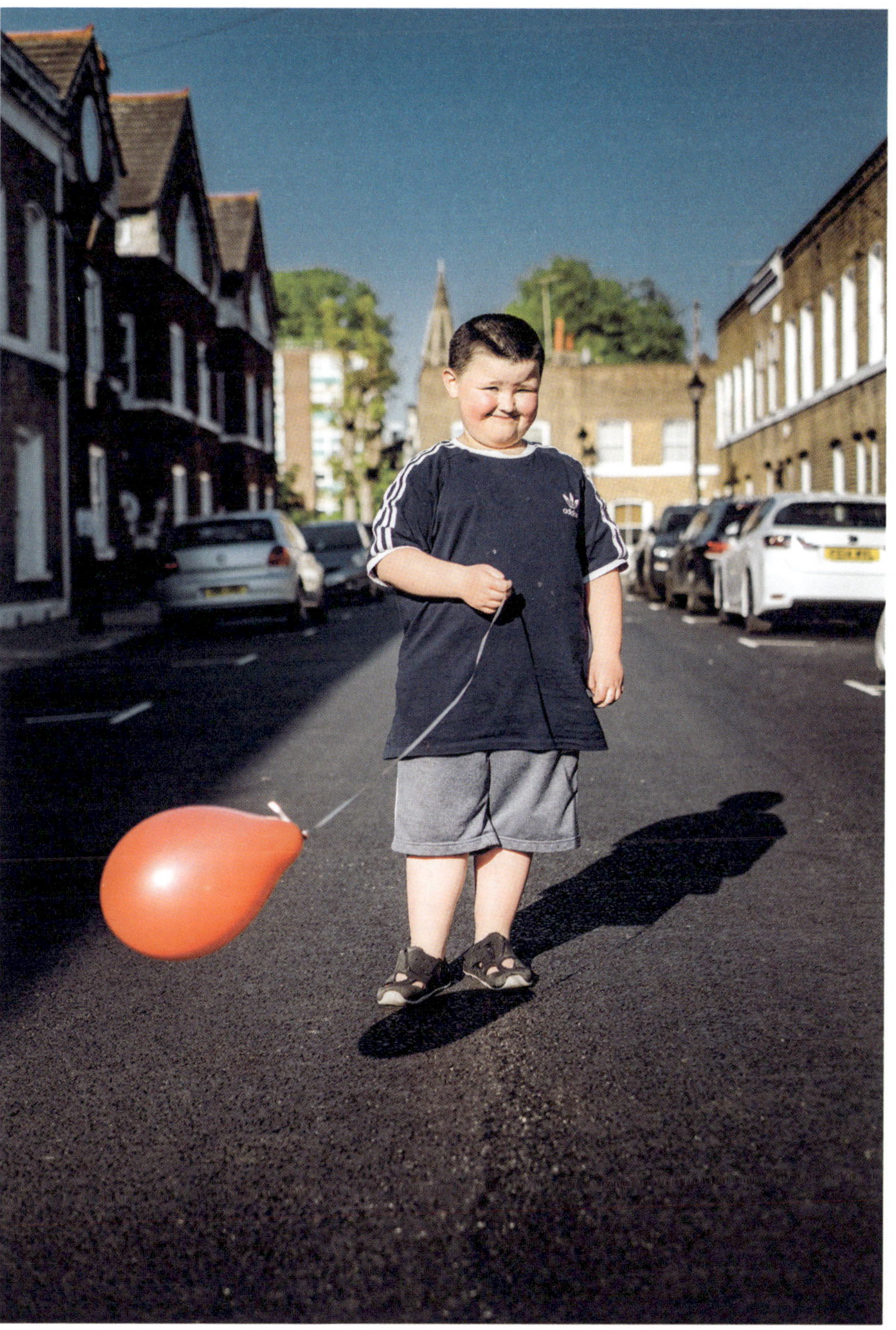

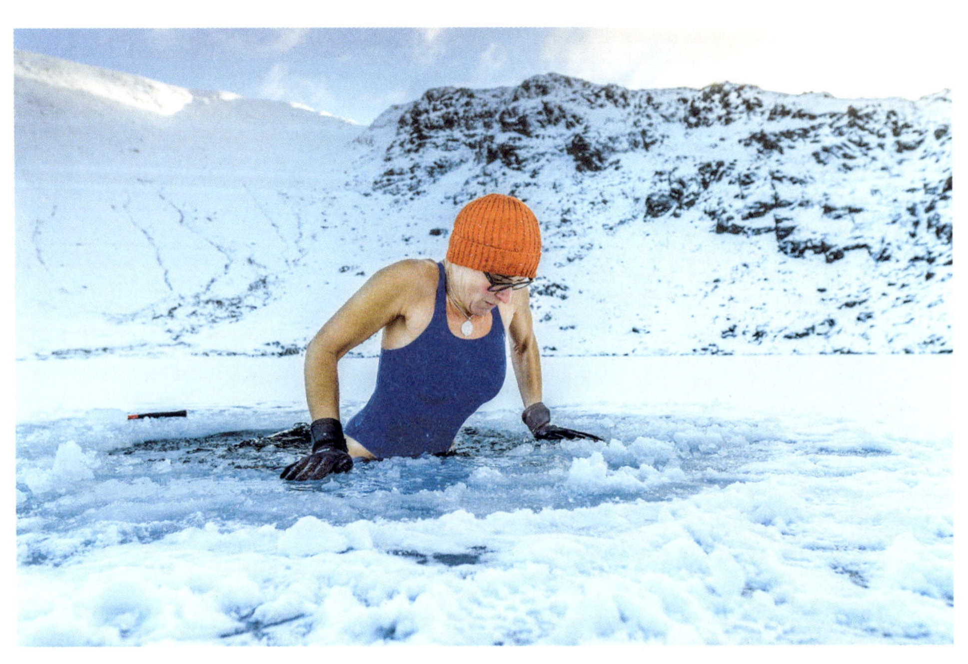

ZERO°
by Scott M. Salt
Mardale, Cumbria

In January 2021, a nationwide group of wild swimmers pledged to swim every day of the month to raise money for the homeless charity Crisis. My friend Gilly was one of the 28 swimmers who took part, and collectively they raised £60,000. All of the swimmers 'skin swim' without wetsuits. It was the coldest January in over a decade.

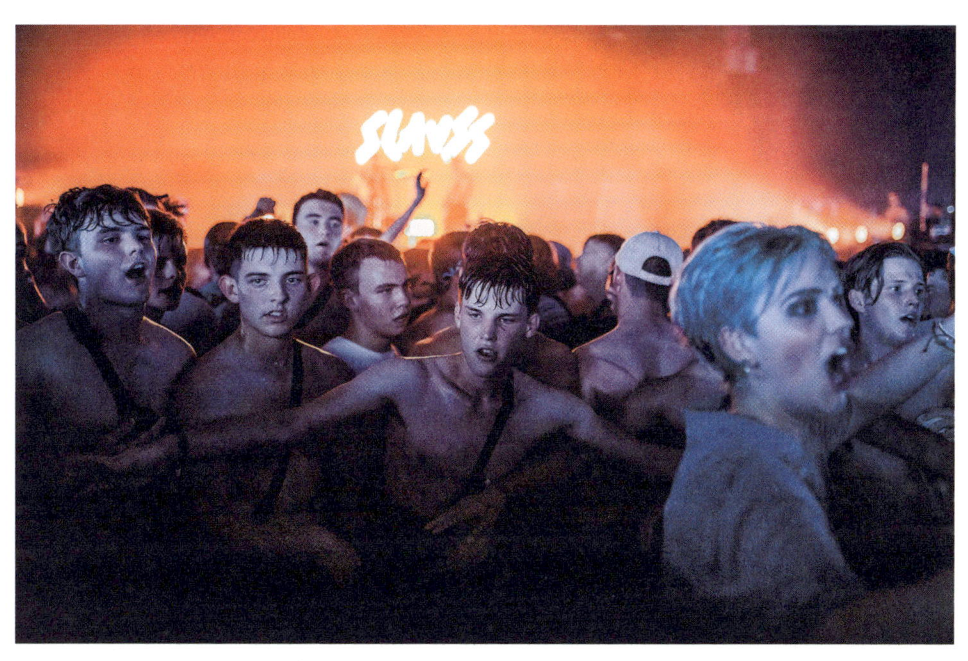

LOVE AND MOSH PITS
by Francis Augusto
Steventon, Oxfordshire

This photo was taken in the middle of the mosh pit
at Truck Festival. All around me, people were
freely expressing their joy together.

GRASSROOTS FOOTBALL
by Lee Coventry-Walsh
London

I took this photo of my eldest son, Remy, on one
of the many Saturday mornings I've spent on Hackney
Marshes watching him play football. To me,
grassroots football is such a Great British institution:
the training, the cold mornings spent standing
pitch-side. Throw a packet of Walkers into the mix,
and you couldn't get more British.

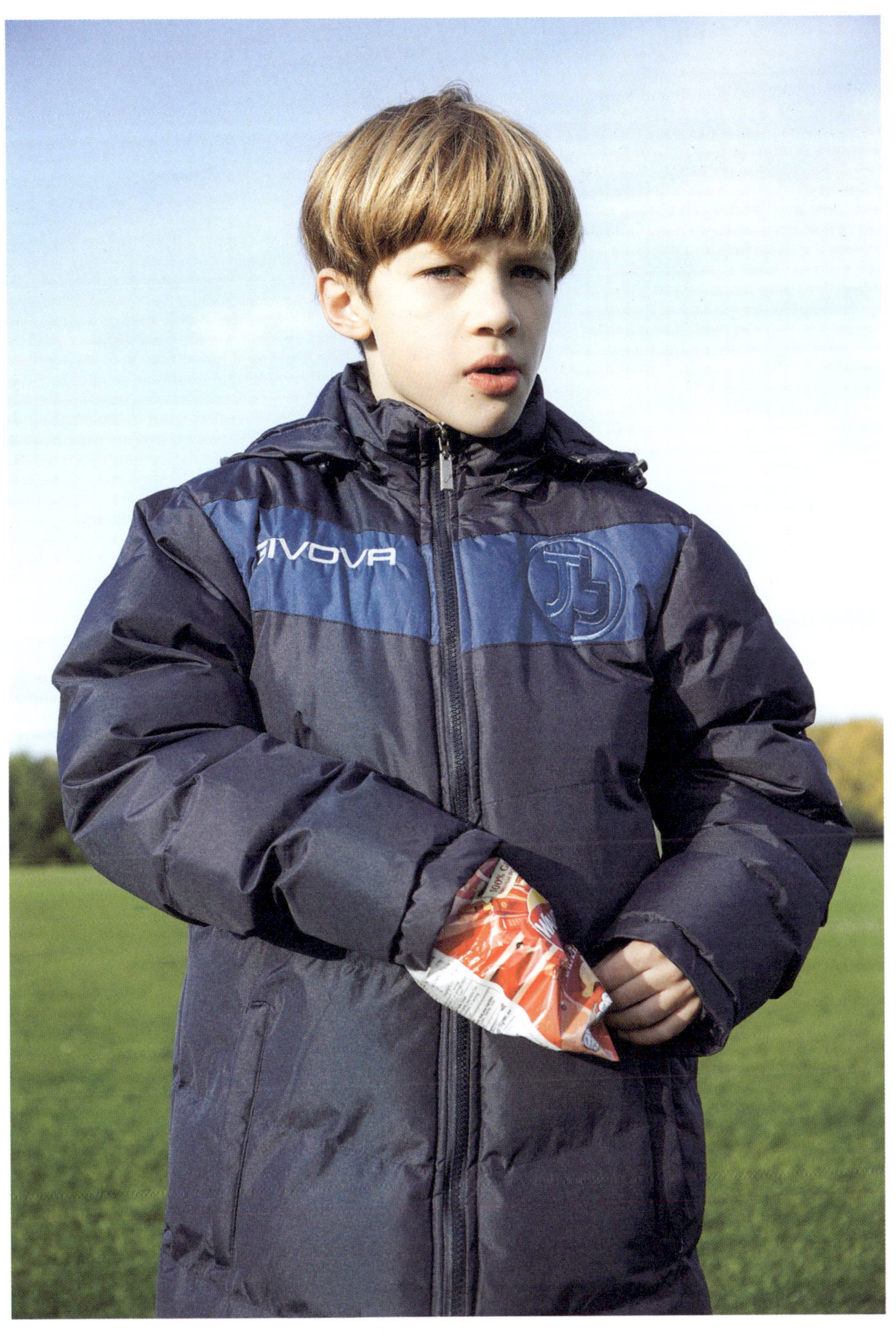

TAEKWONDO – HANNAH
by Lisa Doyle
Bournemouth, Dorset

Hannah has practiced Taekwondo since she
was young. I photographed her as part of my project
highlighting the strength and determination of women
in sport, who are often sexualised, objectified and
discriminated against. Sport is for everyone.

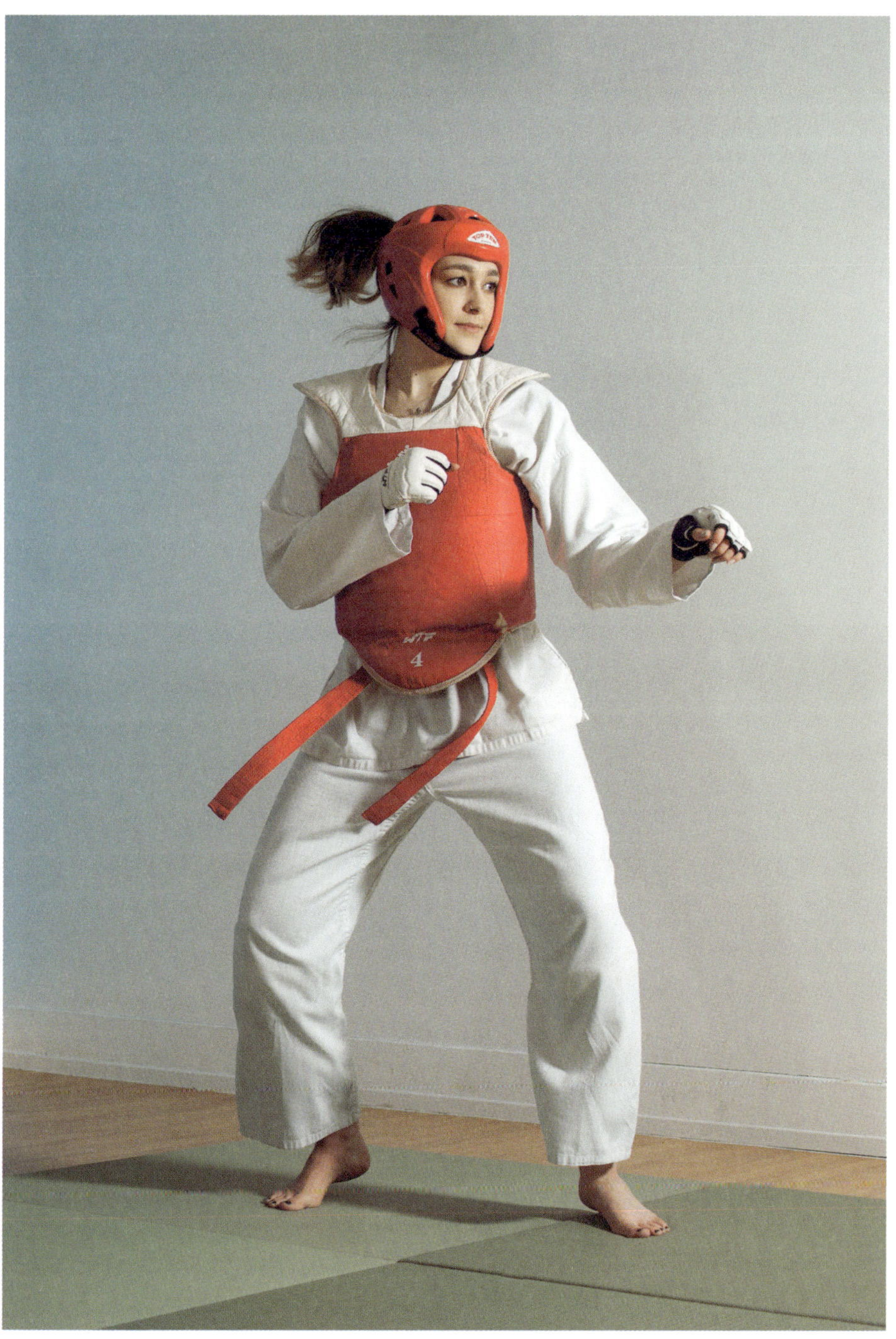

ELLA THE INVENTOR
by Jon Attenborough
Winchester, Hampshire

This is Ella, my niece; she means the world to me.
I may be a little biased but Ella is an exceptionally
creative and resourceful girl with a huge imagination.
She enjoys making her own toys, and fashioned
these eye-catching sunglasses from repurposed Quality
Street wrappers and an old piece of cardboard.

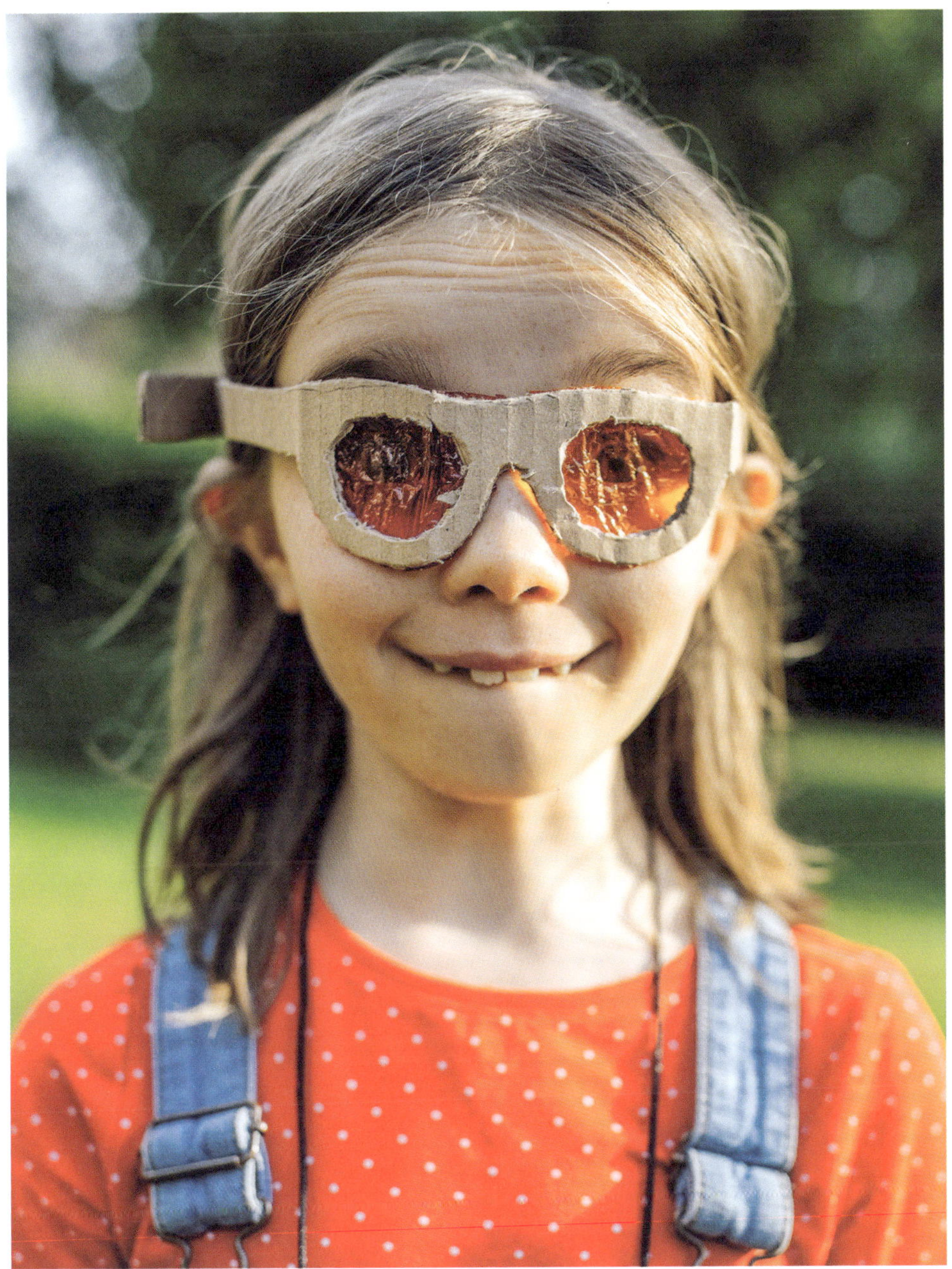

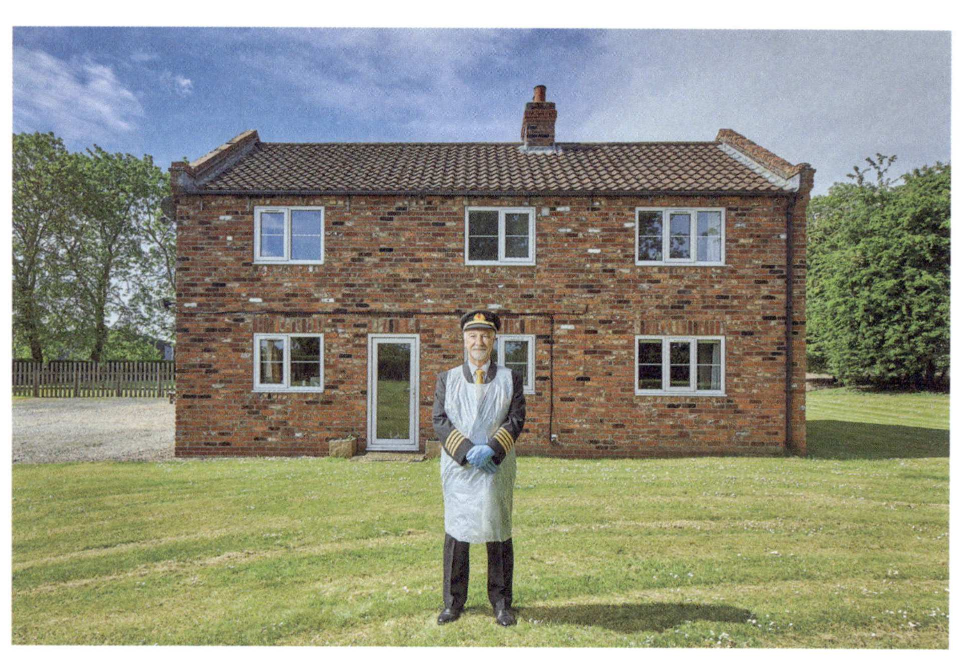

ALAN, VACCINATION VOLUNTEER
by Matt Davis
Rufforth, North Yorkshire

Alan Wrigley, a 69-year-old former commercial pilot,
now volunteers as a vaccinator with St John Ambulance.
He and many other selfless volunteers are helping us all
slowly get back to normal. Alan was part of the team that
built the Eurofox two-seater glider. He also plays
the saxophone and speaks Spanish.

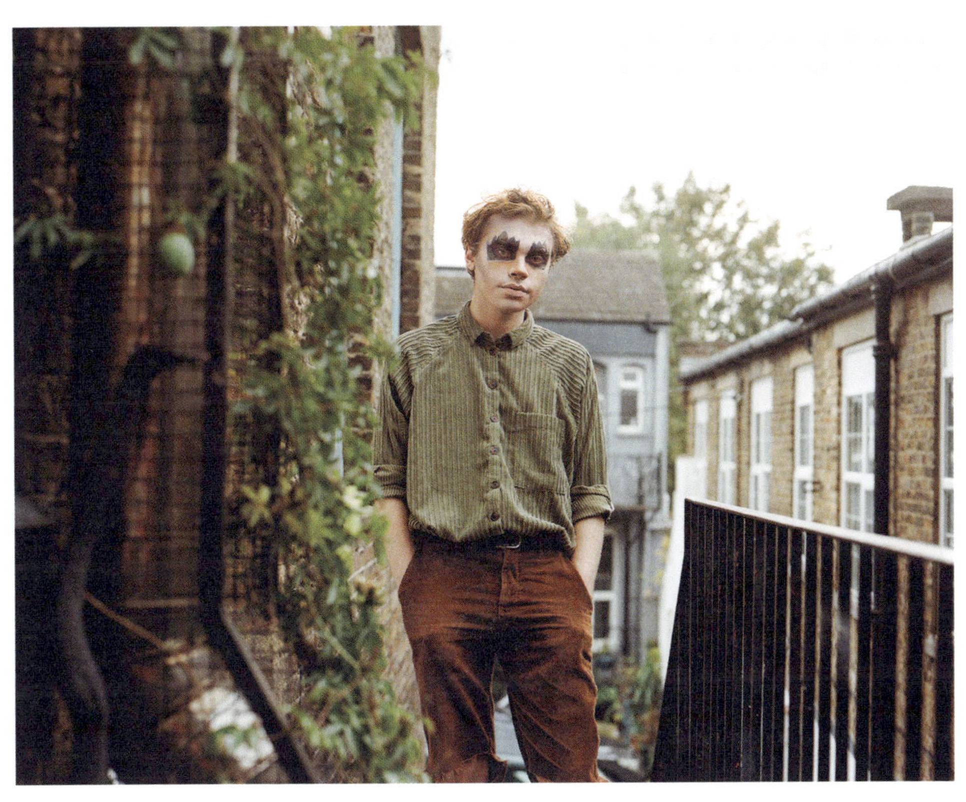

MID-BEAT
by Hollie Brook
London

This is Cameron Turner, a drag performer based in
London. I took this photo in a quiet moment as Cameron
was putting on the make-up of their drag persona, Morag
Equinox. When Cameron saw it, they joked that
they 'looked like a Metallica fan'.

ANNA
by Leigh Anderson
Sheffield, South Yorkshire

I have been working on a project about the vibrant,
diverse community of Park Hill estate in Sheffield.
I was setting up for a portrait there, waiting for
my subject to arrive, when Anna and her boyfriend
walked past, on their way to KFC. We got chatting
about the project, and she agreed to have her
photo taken. She told me she'd only just moved
there from Wigan, to study Fine Art.

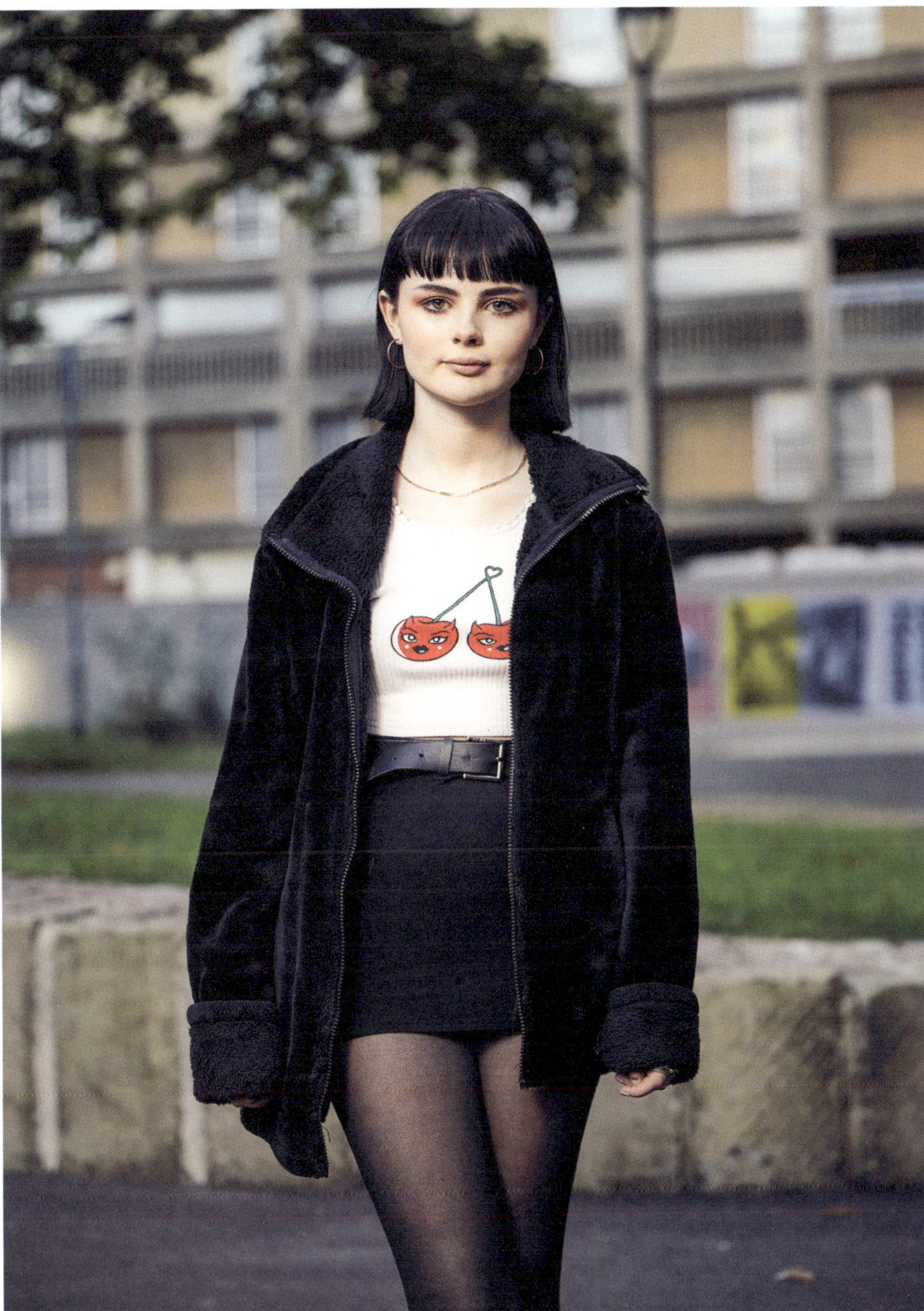

PROUD TO BE WHO I AM
by Yuen Ching (Hesther) Ng
London

I spotted this girl wrapped in a Palestinian flag on a
bus. She was looking through the window and smiled
at my camera in the brief second that the bus
stopped at a traffic light.

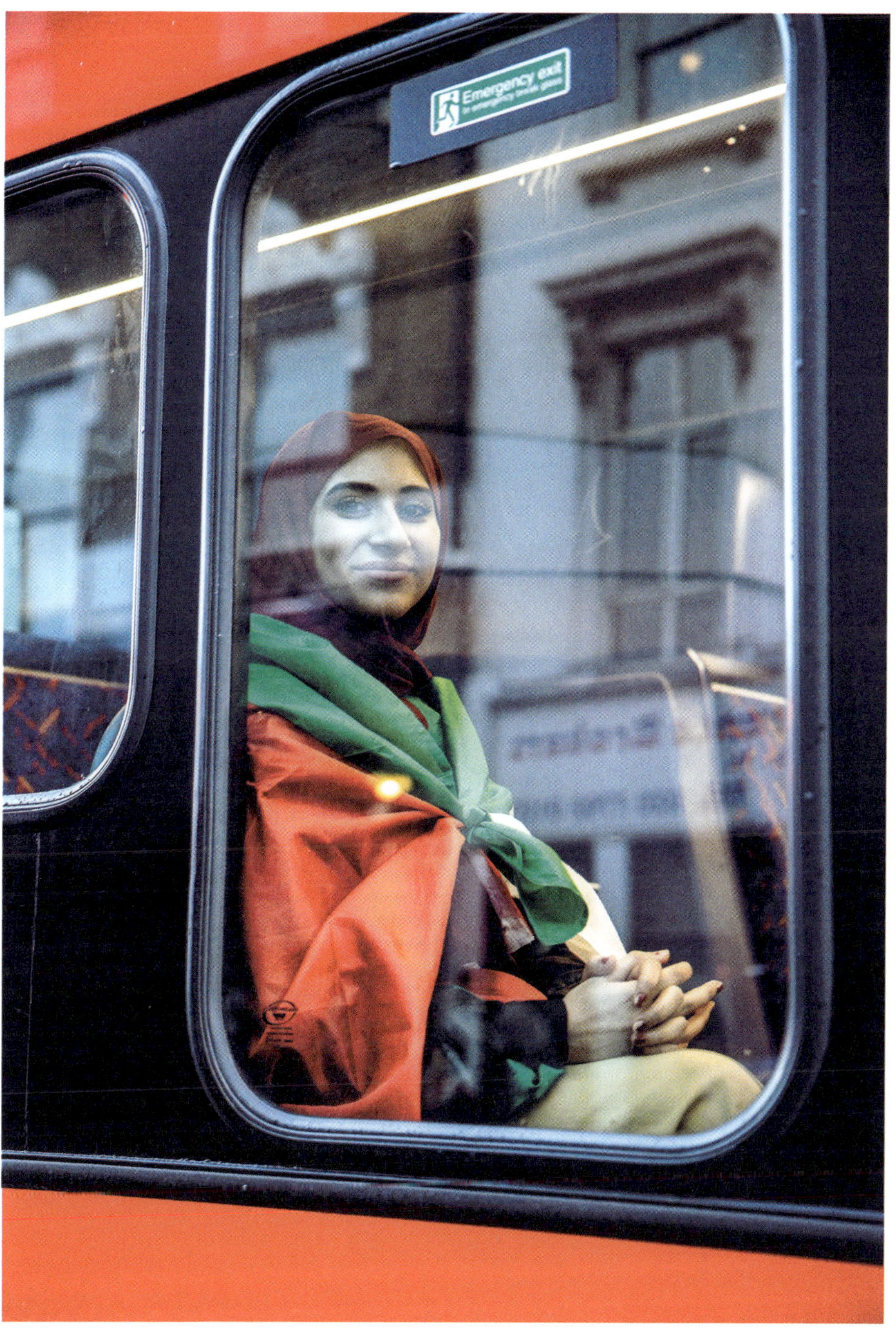
Emergency exit

AMIR BACCHUS-MARQUIS
by Roland Ramanan
London

Amir is a skate teacher and model, and a role model
in the London roller skating community. Having
previously interviewed Amir and read about him,
I wanted to take his portrait in his own home.
Amir raises awareness of the community benefits
of roller skating and the importance of
creating public space for skating.

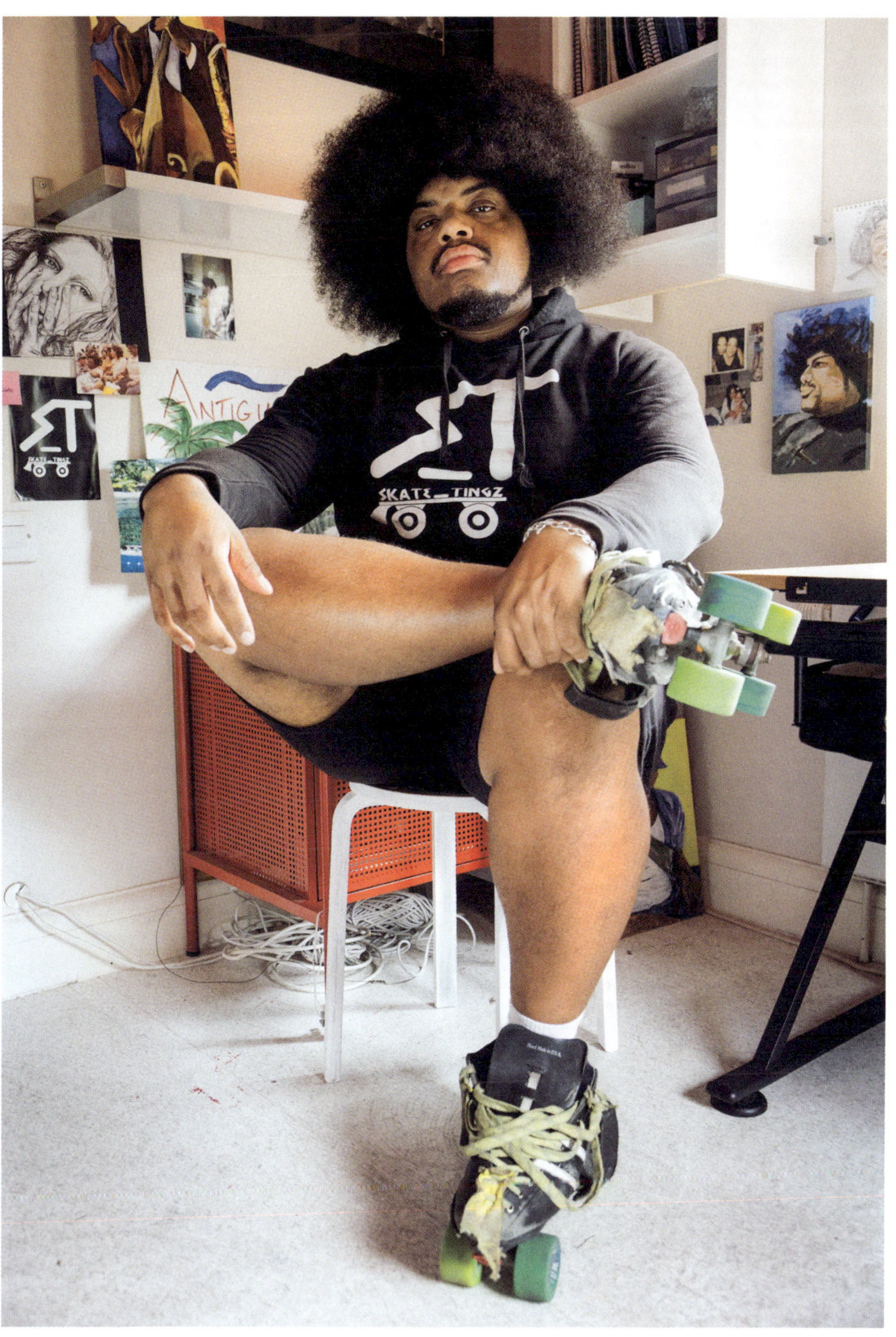

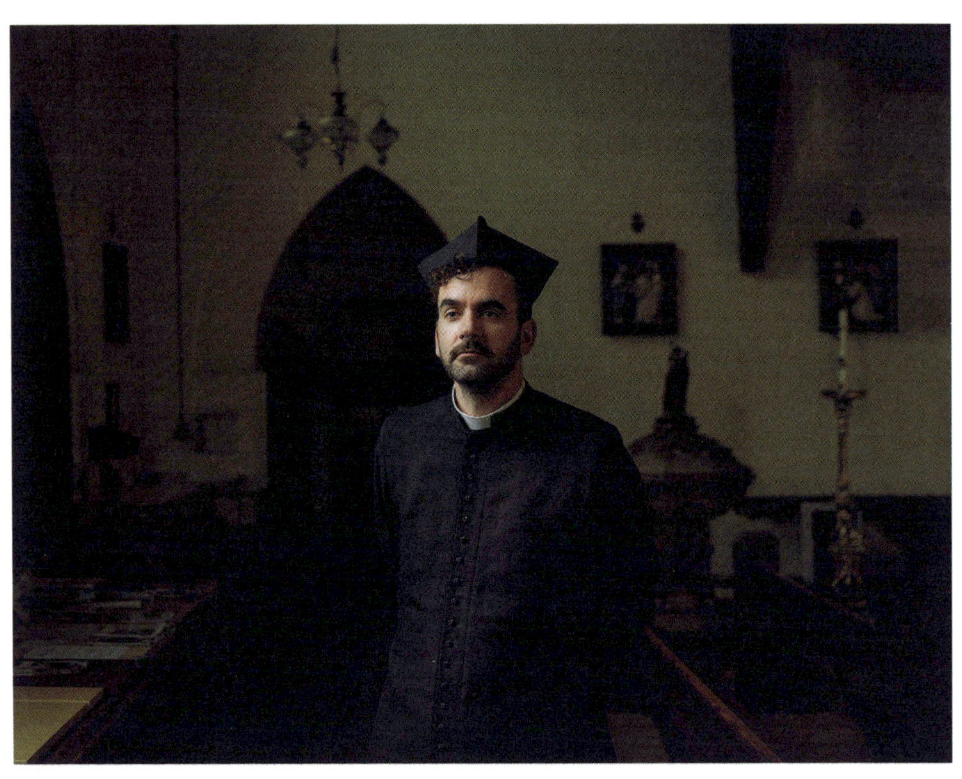

ANTHONY MURLEY
by Hugh Fox
Brighton, East Sussex

Anthony Murley is the vicar of the Church of the
Annunciation in Brighton. On the day I took this photo,
he had just found out a very close priest friend had passed
away that morning. I suggested we reschedule the shoot,
but he wanted to go ahead – though he decided to wear
traditional robes rather than his usual bright attire.

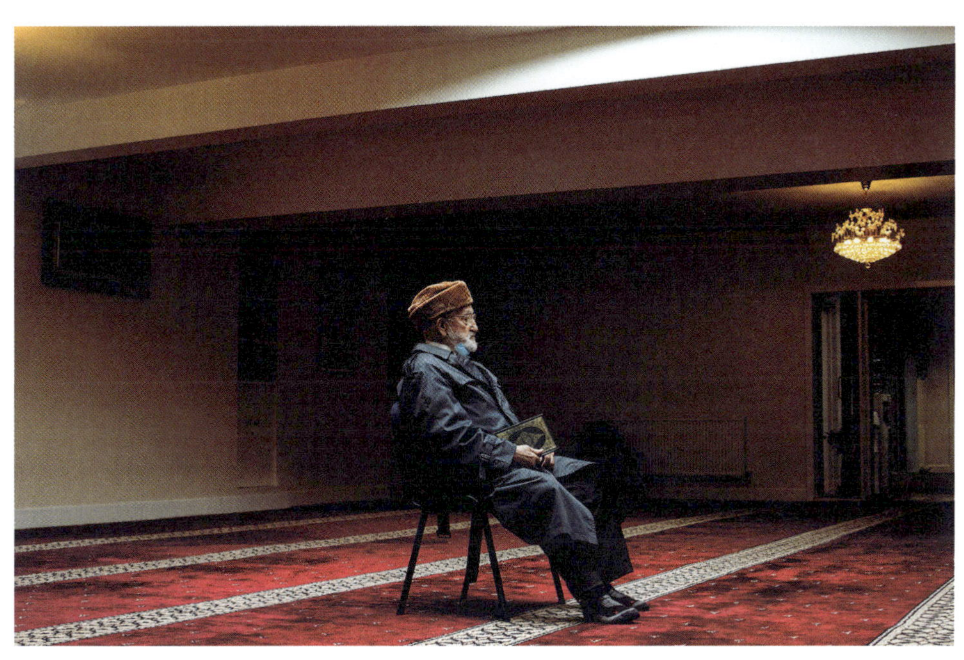

THE CALL TO WORSHIP
by Michael Farra
Bournemouth, Dorset

I took this photo during the second lockdown inside
Bournemouth Central Mosque. The Imam of the Mosque
told me that this man, who is in his early 90s, made the trip
on foot so that he could still carry out his daily worship.

BENJAMIN ZEPHANIAH
by Adam Docker
London

I was filming a big advertising campaign with lots
of sports personalities, when I noticed the poet, writer
and performer Benjamin Zephaniah in the café area.
He was using the same venue to film a documentary
about the Windrush Generation, and was speaking
to a footballer about it. I introduced myself and asked
if I could take his photo; he just had that 'something'
about him. I don't know what it was: charisma,
soul, personality, an extra layer of humanity?
Something special.

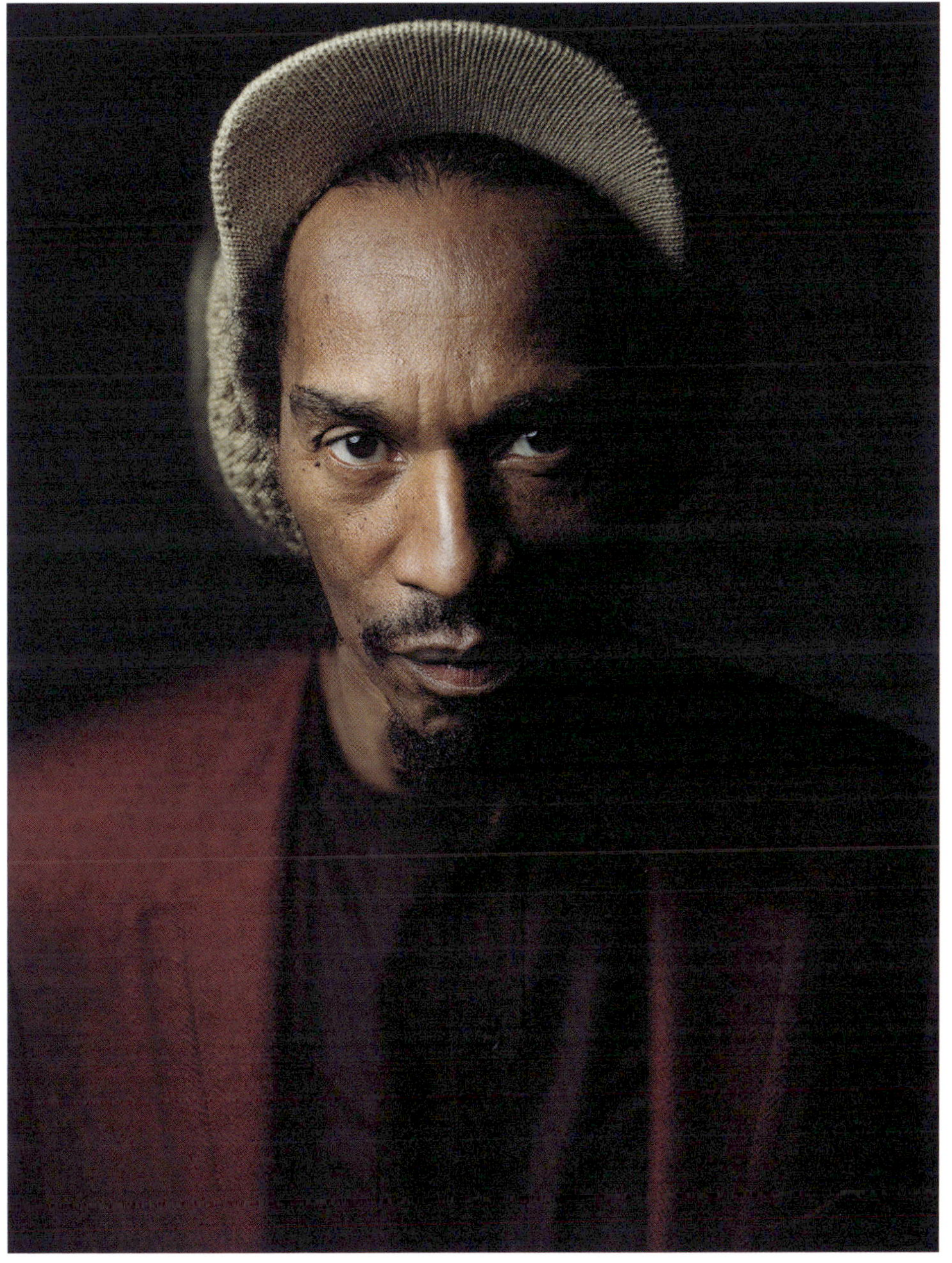

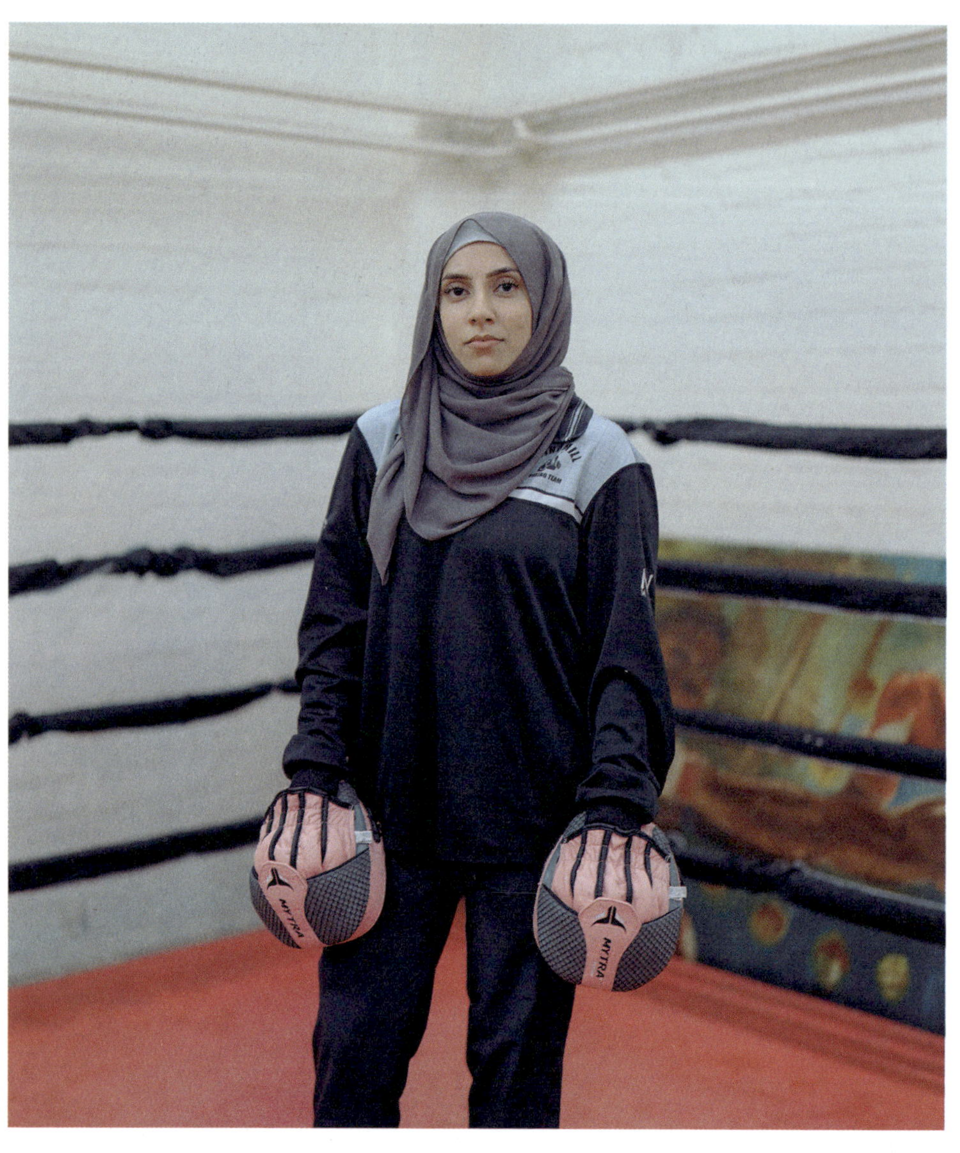

HASEEBAH, FIRST HIJABI BOXING COACH
by James Bannister
Birmingham

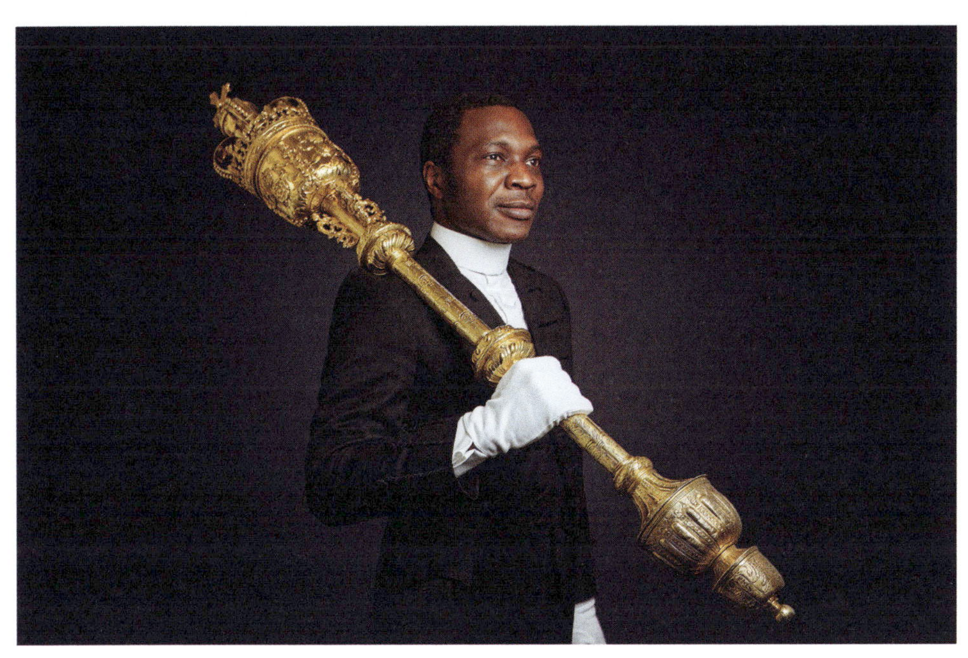

UGBANA OYET, SERJEANT AT ARMS
by Rory Lewis
London

The office of Serjeant at Arms dates back to 1415, during
the reign of Henry V, when the first Serjeant was appointed
to carry out the orders of the House of Commons. Ugbana
Oyet is the first British African person to occupy the role.

ALBERT
by Ming de Nasty
Birmingham

'Growing up in South Africa with the dangers of being
gay and all that, I sort of hid a lot of my sexuality,
which comes with a whole lot of other problems.
It was a brutal time to live, I was arrested many times
for being gay, for lewdness. Anyone that's gay will
know about cruising and being arrested while you're
cruising, anyway that was part of the journey.' – Albert

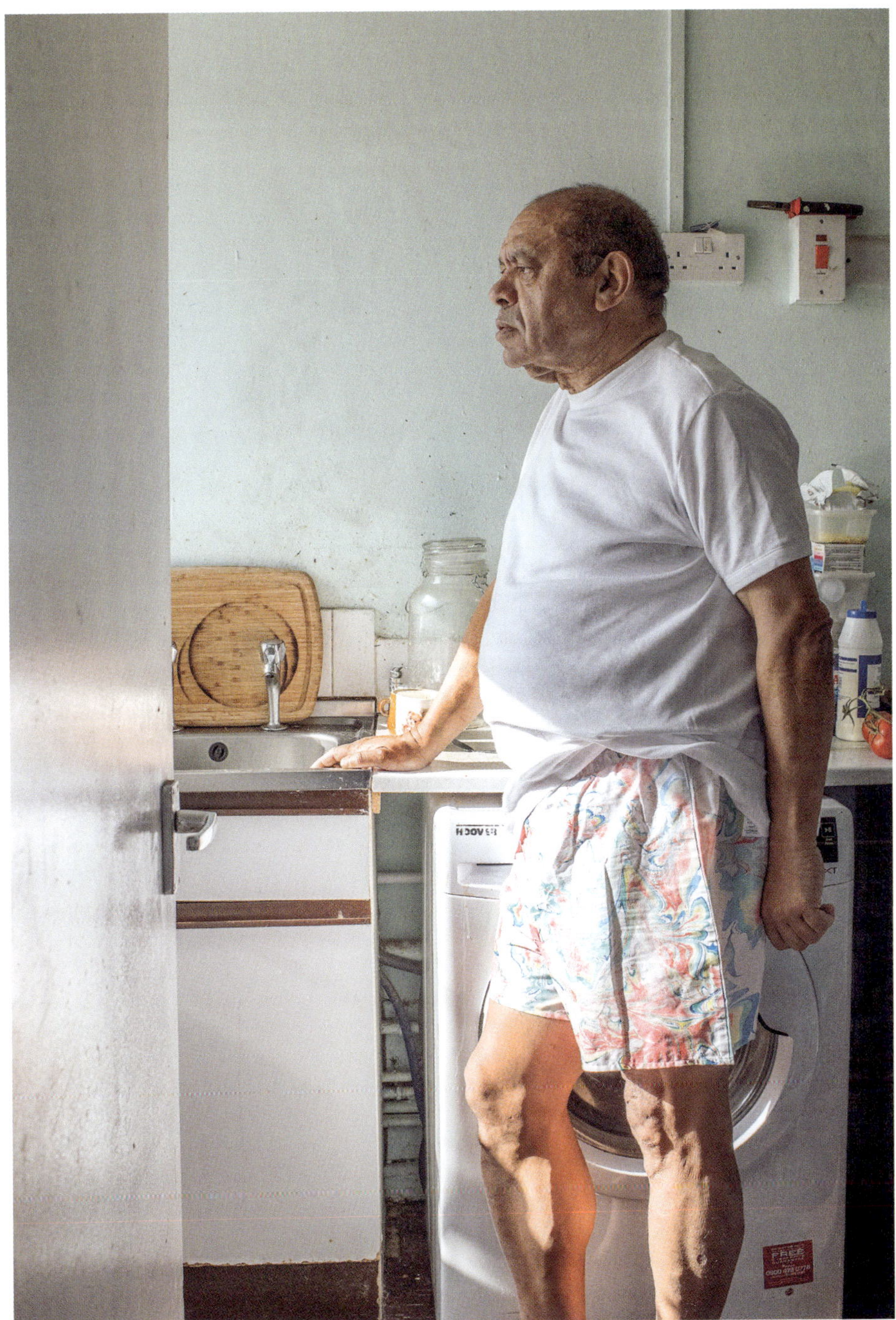

ROGER
by Jon Attenborough
London

Just before the second wave of Covid hit in the
winter of 2020, I was commissioned by *The Sunday
Times Magazine* to photograph frontline NHS workers
at University College Hospital. This photo shows
Roger Esmeralda, deputy matron on the critical
care ward, reflecting on the heartbreaking, gruelling
work that he and his colleagues had endured.

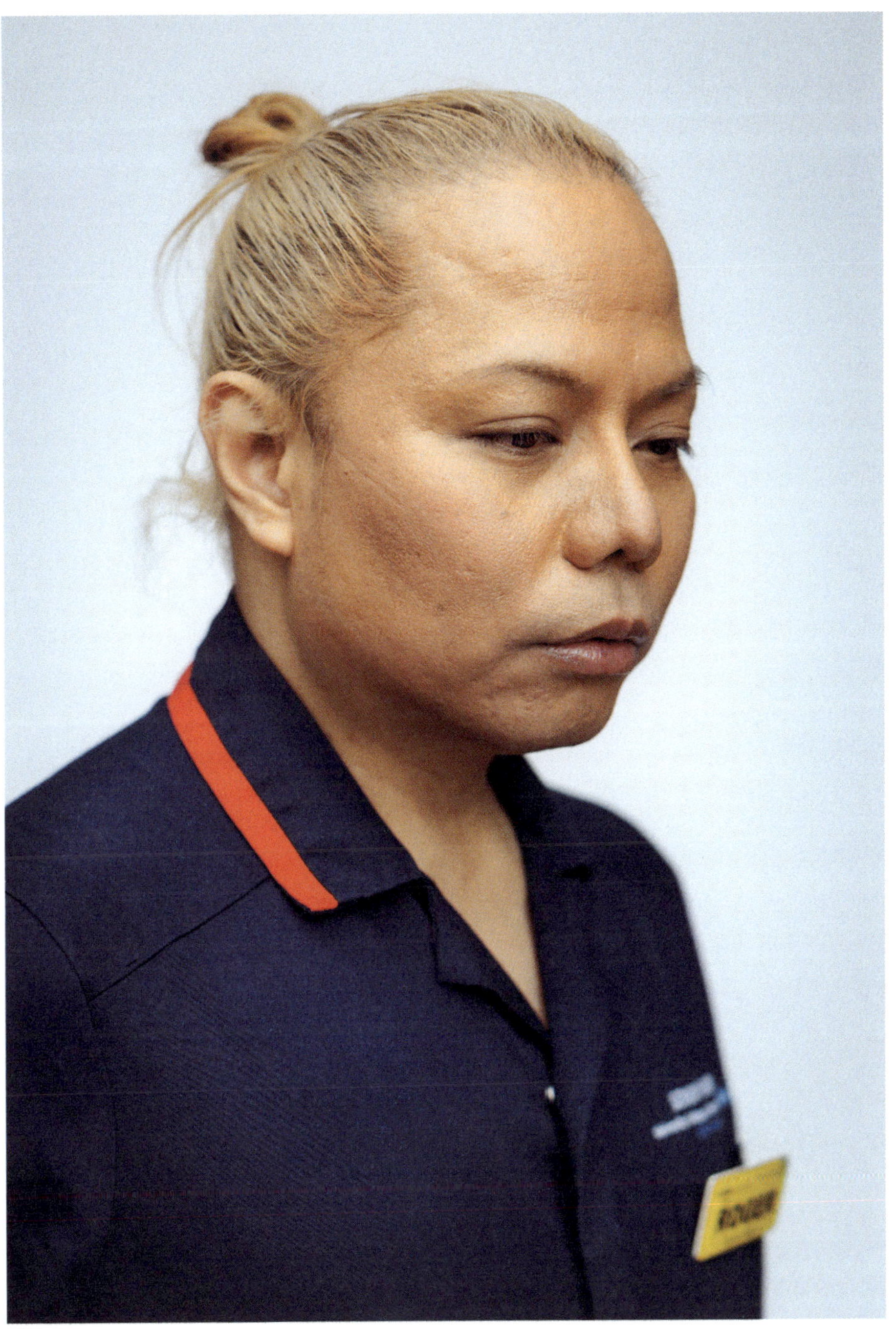

SIMON – ALL DRESSED UP AND
NOWHERE TO GO
by Joe Short
Ayelsbury, Buckinghamshire

Simon Shirley usually works as a toastmaster,
but during the pandemic he turned to gardening.
'On a couple's wedding day, I'm like their personal
butler, it's so intense that when it ends, it feels like
saying goodbye to a new best friend. In lockdown,
I've expanded my garden design business. Many
of my clients are elderly, so I've also kept them
company or brought groceries.' – Simon

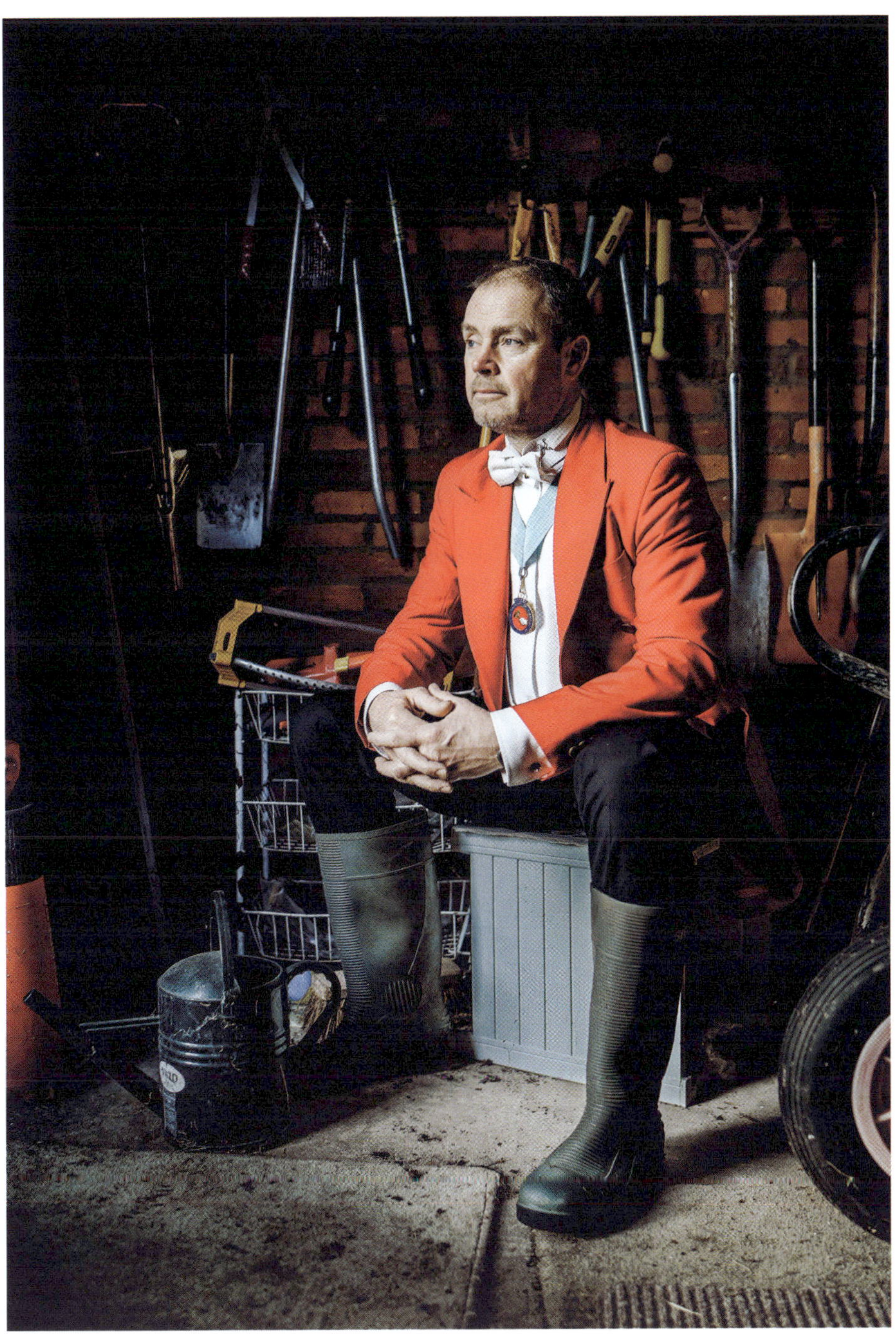

MUM READING THE QURAN
by Khuram Mirza
West Bromwich, West Midlands

My mum often reads the Quran before bed with just
a lamp on. I never want to disturb her, but this time
I managed to sneak in and take a few pictures. It was
during lockdown, when we were all shielding
because Mum is immunocompromised.

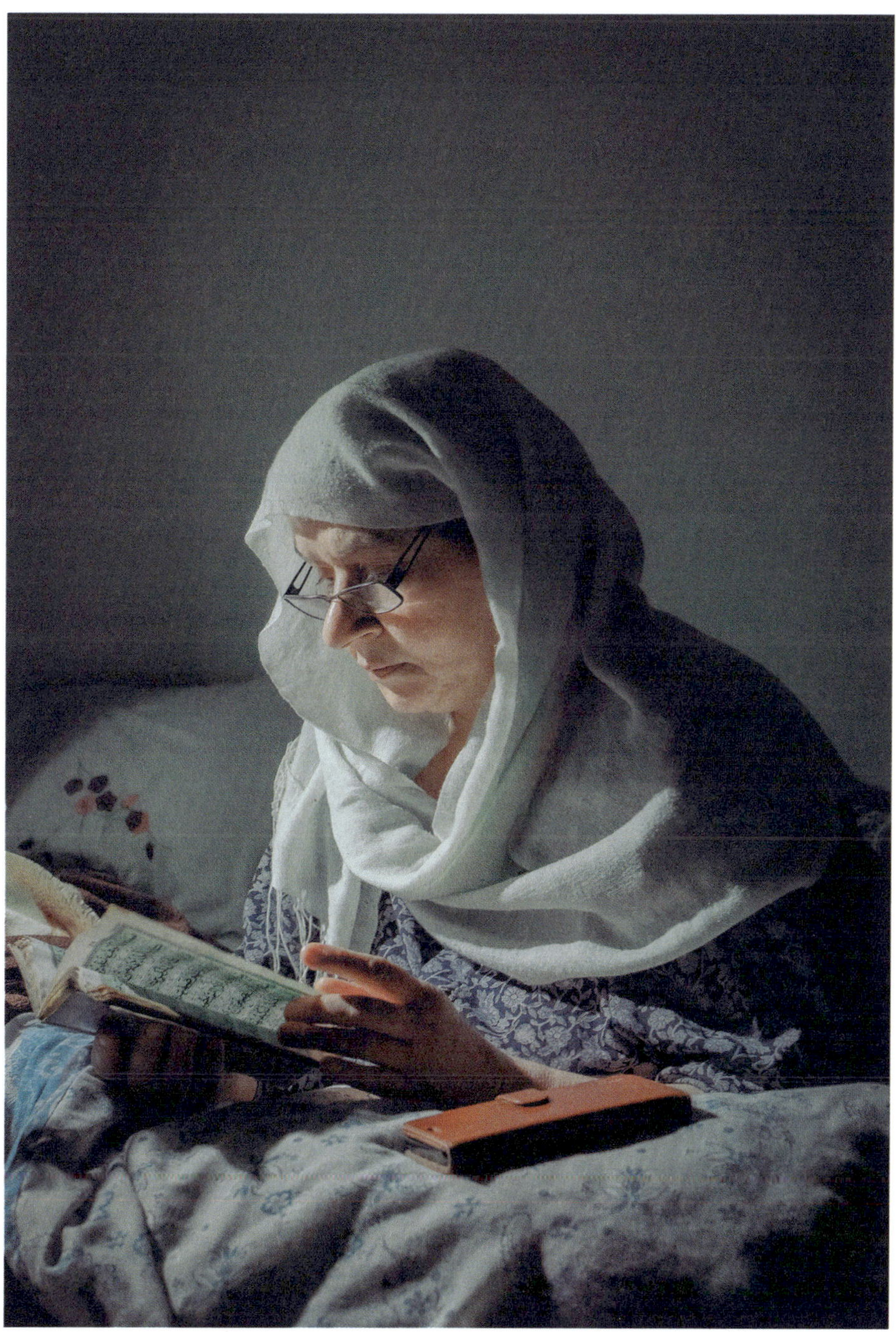

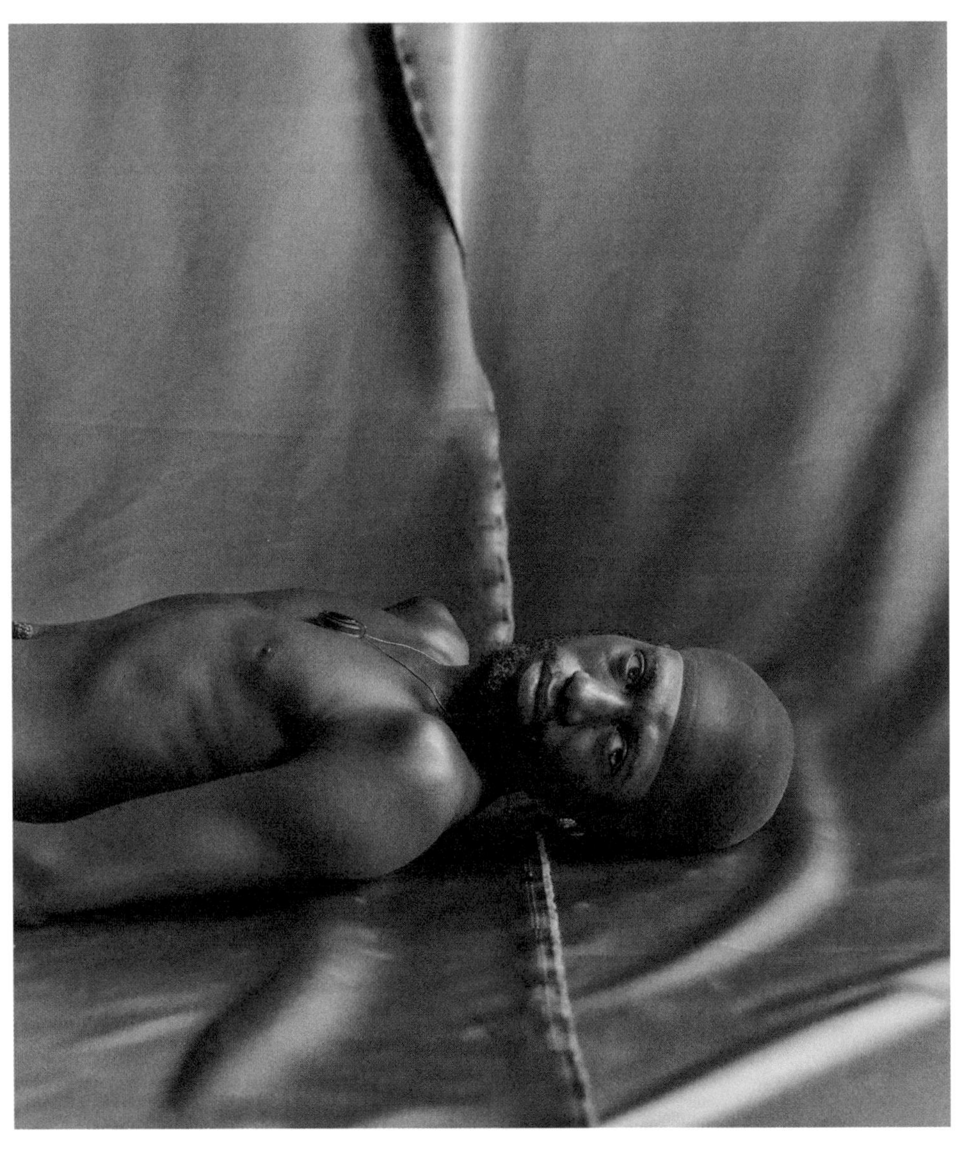

SEYON AMOSU
by Fran Gomez de Villaboa
London

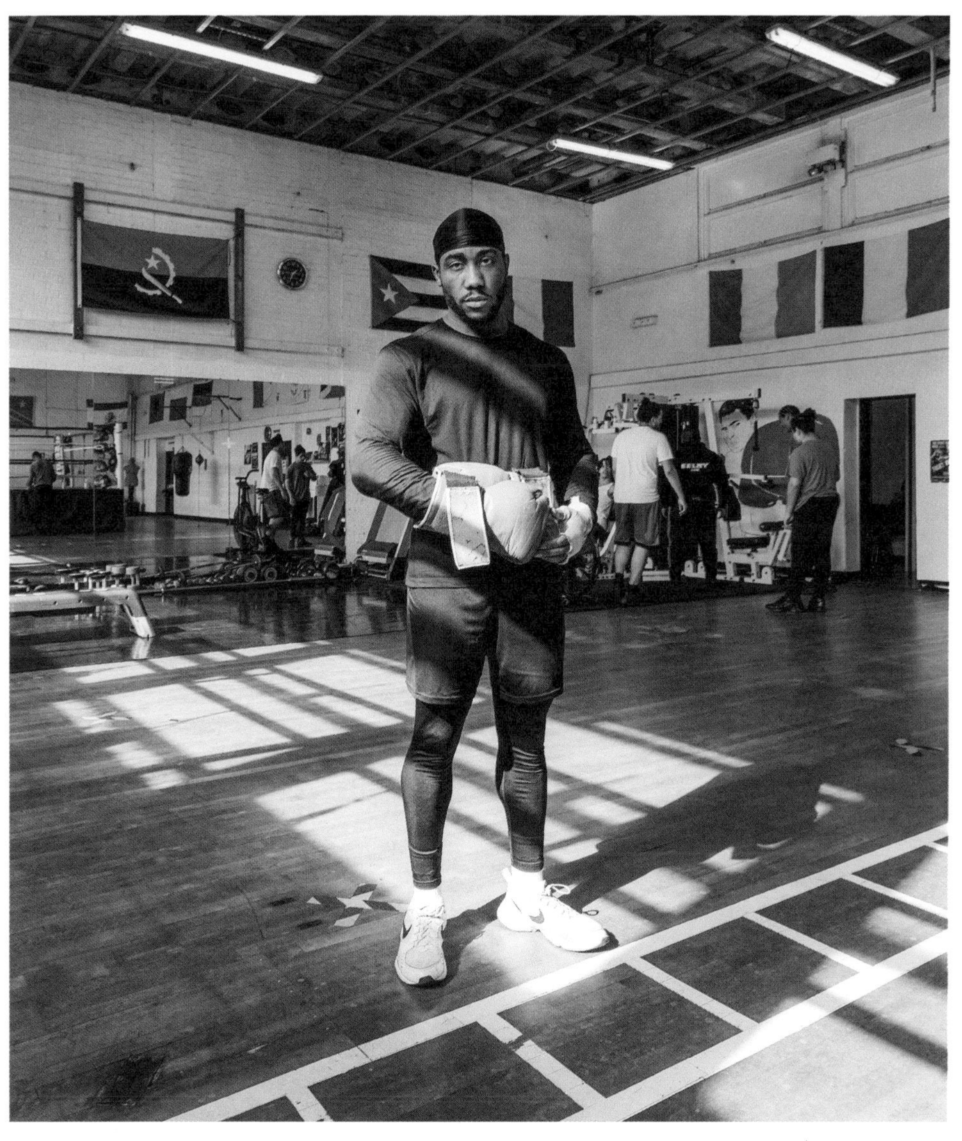

JORDAN
by Renee Maria Osubu
London

PORTRAIT OF TINA
by Marie Smith
London

'I can't remember a time without mental health
issues. Bulimia as a teen, post-natal depression in
motherhood. It never ends, it just evolves.
Your child holds a mirror up to you and you
see yourself through their eyes.' – Tina

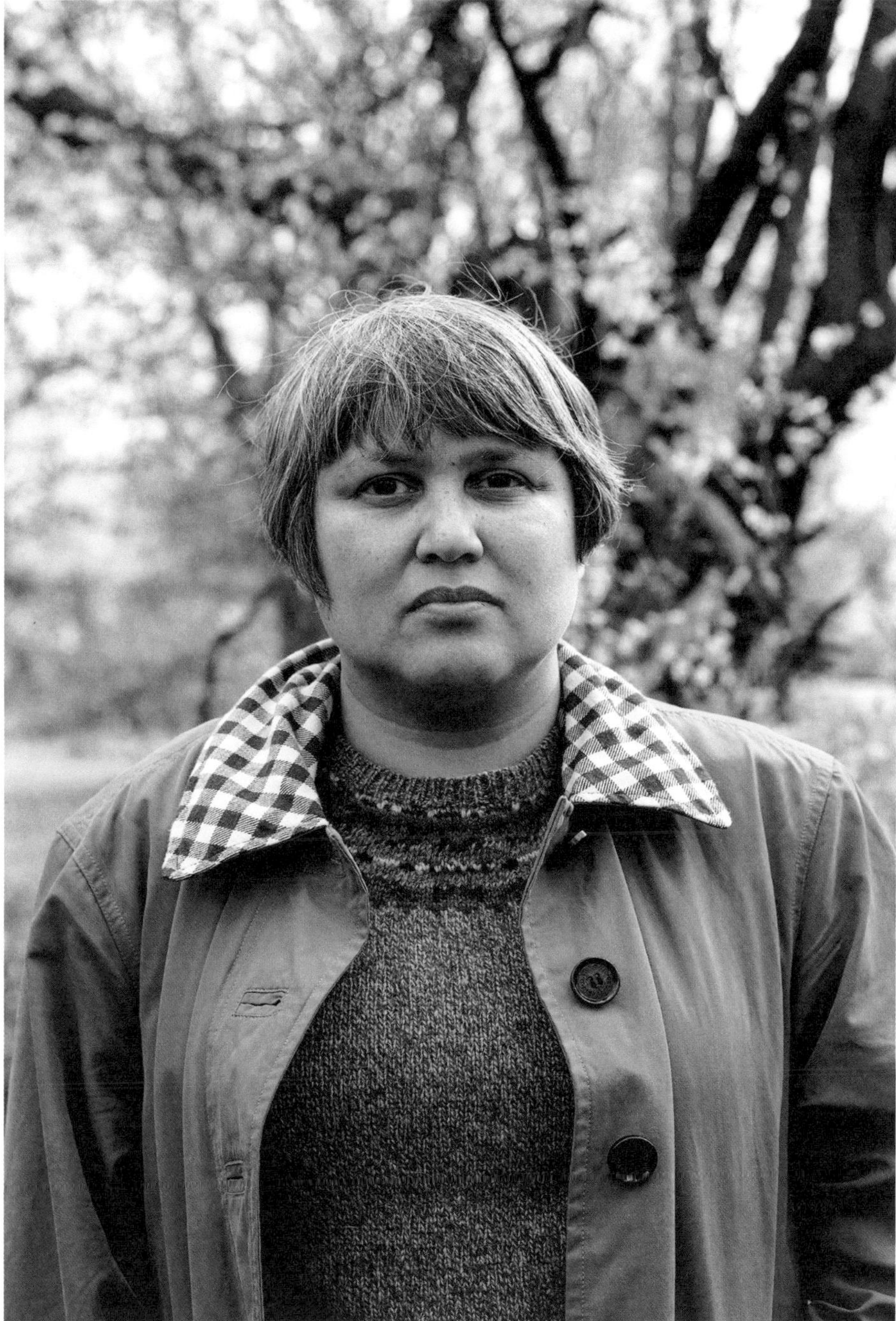

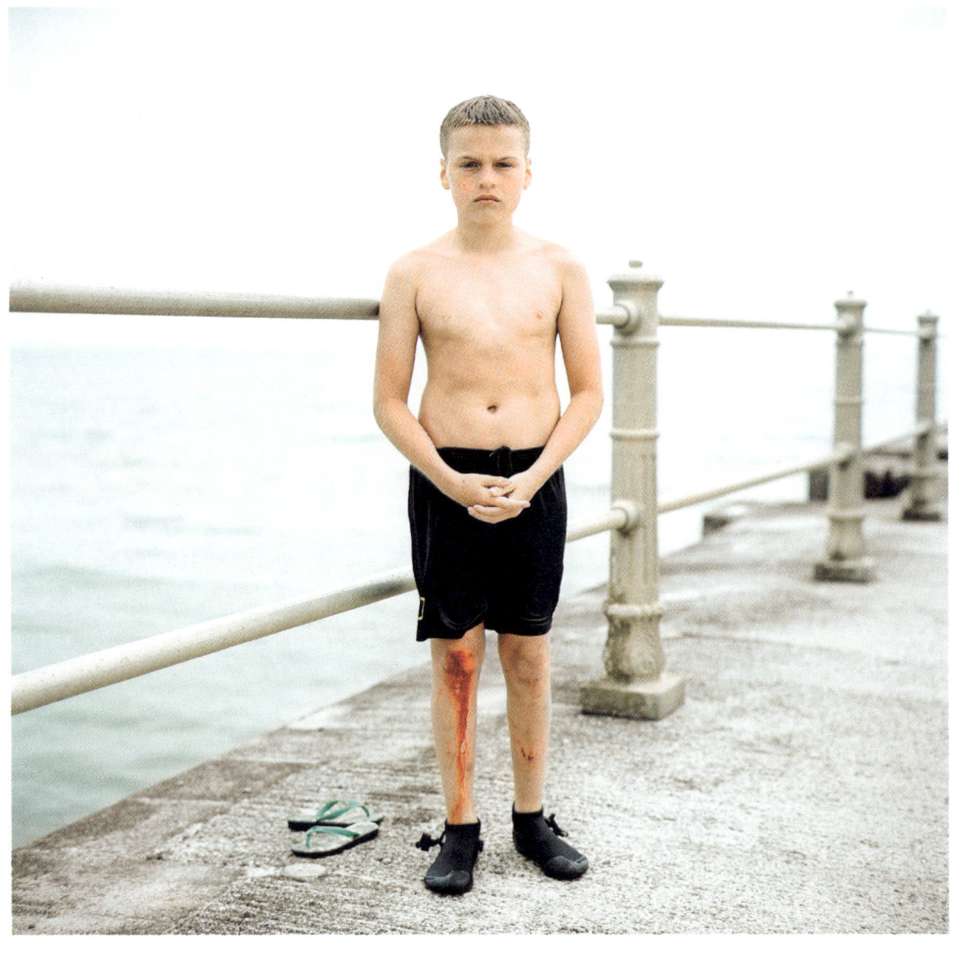

MAX
by Andreas Bleckmann
Hastings, East Sussex

I spotted Max at the harbour arm; he had scraped his
knee on the rocks. After he reassured me he was okay,
I asked to take his portrait.

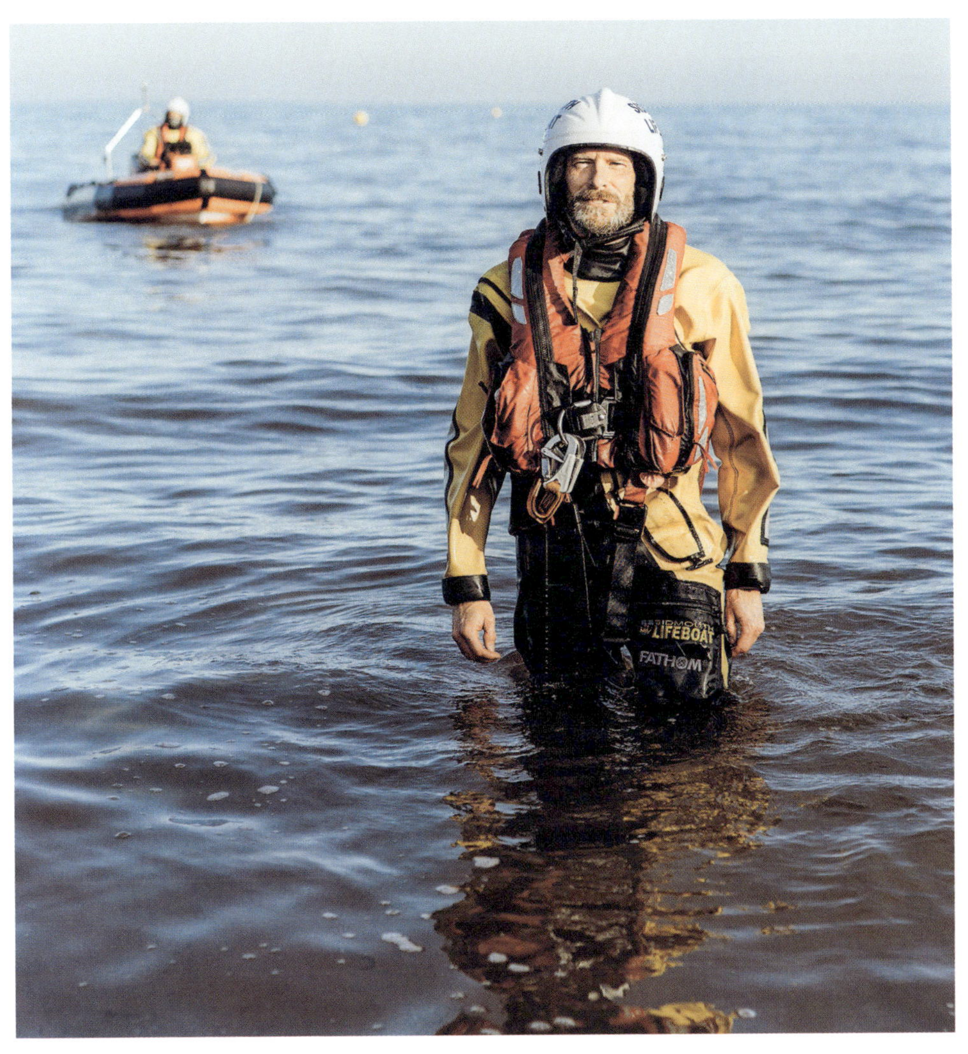

PORTRAIT OF A LIFEBOAT VOLUNTEER
by Sarah Hall
Sidmouth, Devon

Ian, a father of three, has been volunteering
with Sidmouth Lifeboats for seven years.

DREAMS OF A WALK BY THE RIVER
WITH THE LADIES
by Leigh Alner
Maidenhead, Berkshire

Mum contracted Covid at the start of the pandemic;
she went from being an independent, strong-willed free
spirit to being confined to hospital and care-home
beds for a year and a half, with two forms of
encephalitis (brain damage) along with a host of other
issues. Mum sadly passed away on 3rd November 2021.
I made a photography series to try to help me with
our family's struggles and her pain, I had never done
one before. In retrospect it was one of the hardest
things I have done, it still haunts me.

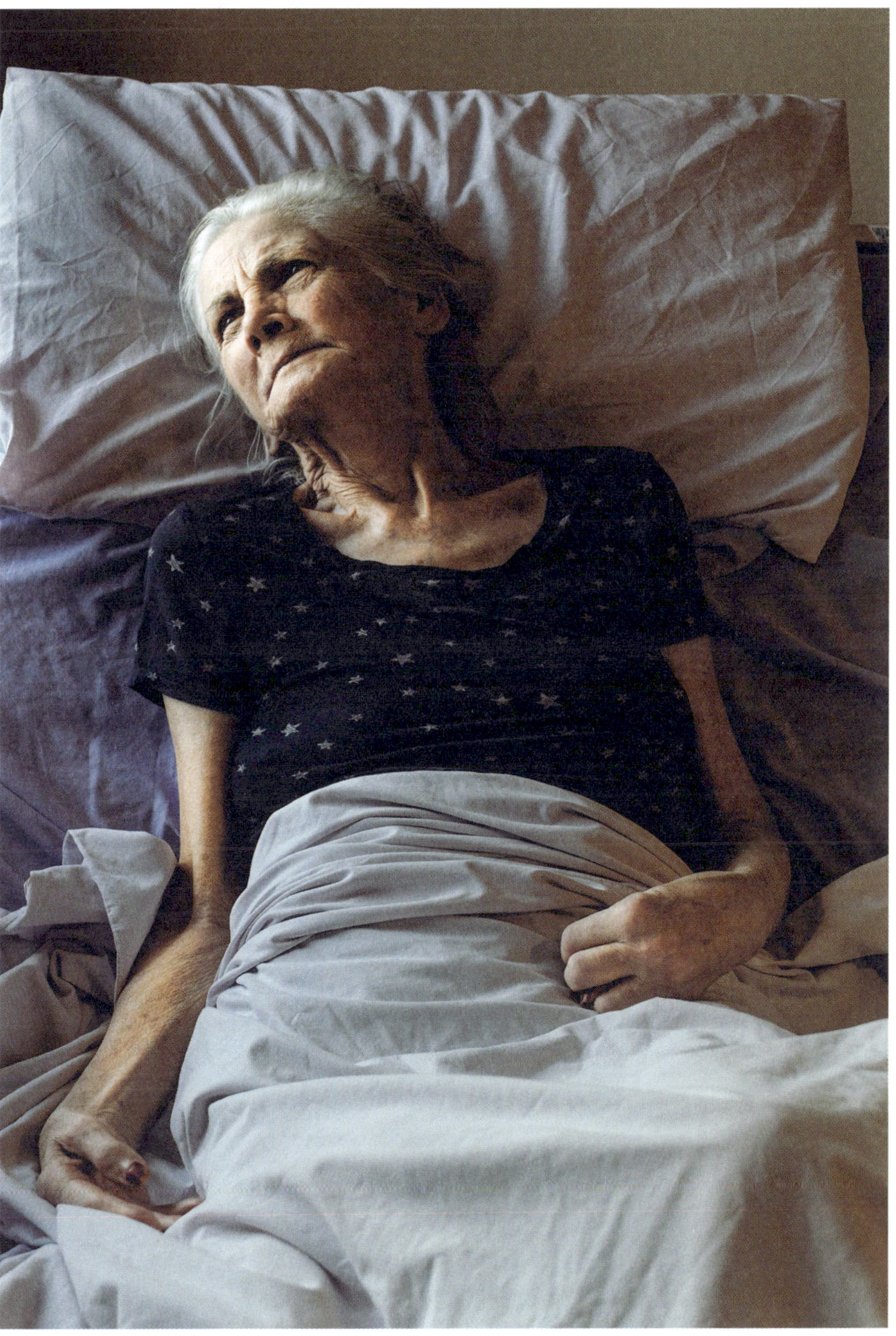

MICHAEL, 11 DAYS POST-SURGERY
by Gwen Riley Jones
Stockport, Greater Manchester

This is my husband, Michael, he means everything
to me. I took this photo just after he got home
from hospital following open heart surgery, in the
middle of the pandemic. When our daughter was eight
months old, we found out that there was something
wrong with Michael's heart. It took two and a half
years for us to finally get the surgery; the surgeon told
us that two of his other patients had died waiting for
similar surgery due to a lack of hospital beds,
and that was before Covid-19.

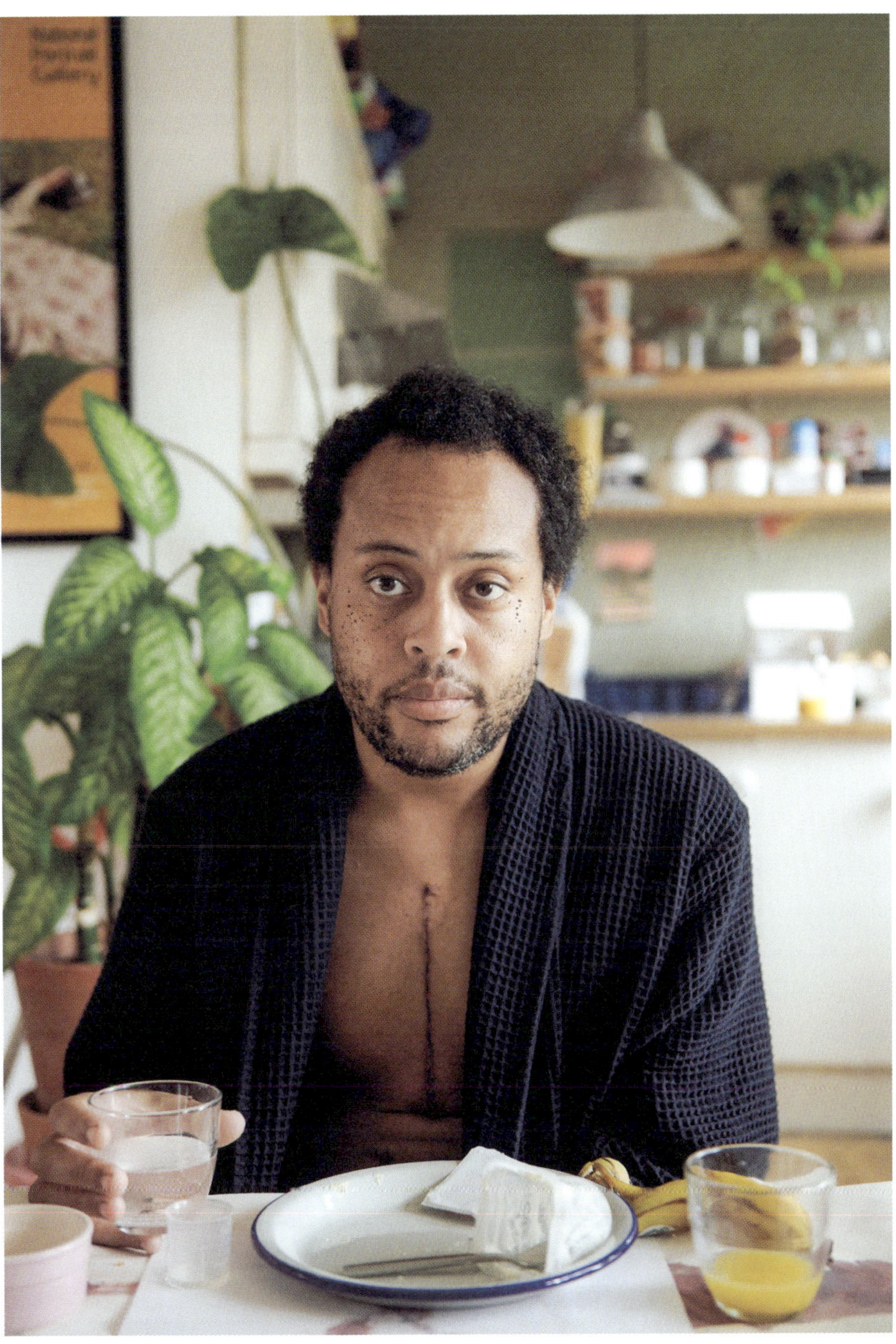

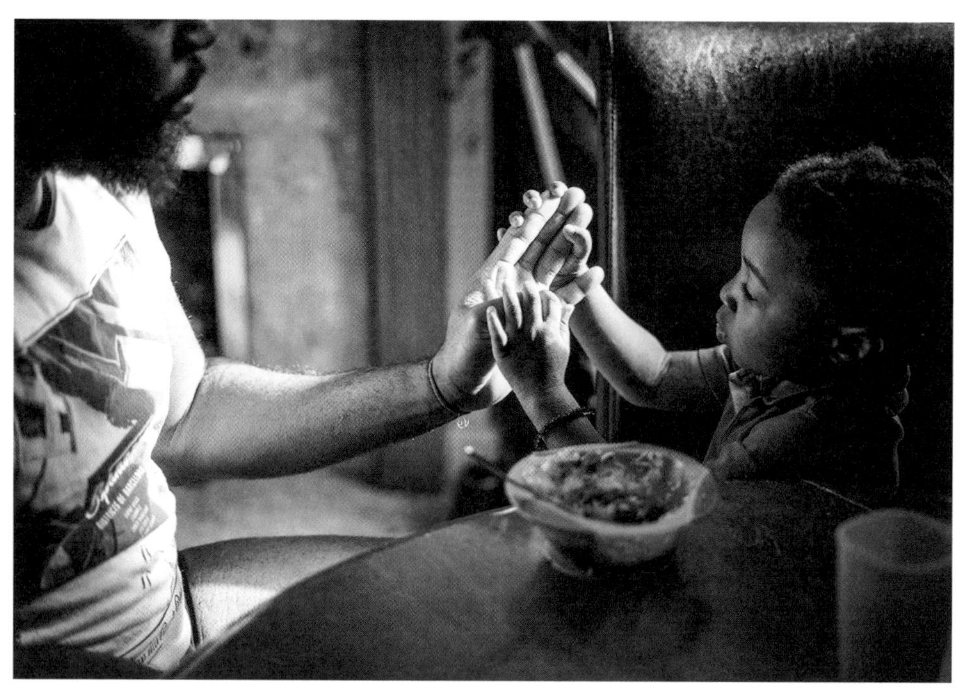

A PLAYFUL INTERLUDE BETWEEN
SPOONS OF RICE AND STEW
by Iko-Ojo Mercy Haruna
Rochester, Kent

I have been working on a personal project documenting my
British-Nigerian family in and around our home in Kent.
Inspired by photographs I would have loved to see of
my own childhood, these images capture our connection
as a family – the fleeting, unposed moments of life between
the big milestones we're used to recording. This is my
daughter, playing with her dad over lunch.

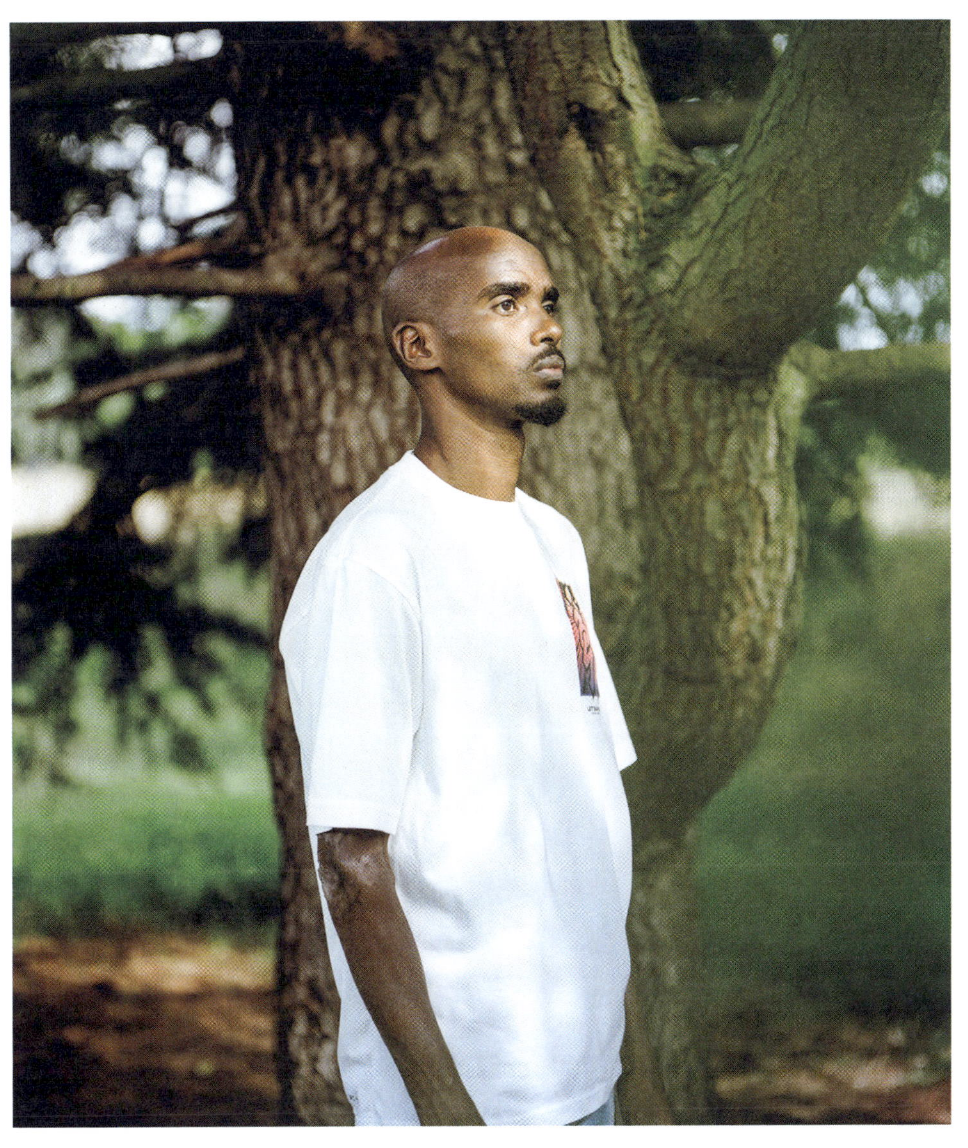

MOHAMED
by Neil Raja
London

URI WINTERSTEIN, HOLOCAUST SURVIVOR
by Jillian Edelstein
London

Uri Winterstein was born in Bratislava, Slovakia,
in 1943. At one month old, he was given to
a Sudeten German woman who agreed to hide him,
but his parents and sister were sent to Theresienstadt
concentration camp. Remarkably they survived,
though nine other family members did not, and
Uri was reunited with his parents and sister after
the war. When his mother died in 1988, the family
found this Star of David among her possessions.
All Jews over the age of six had to wear one.

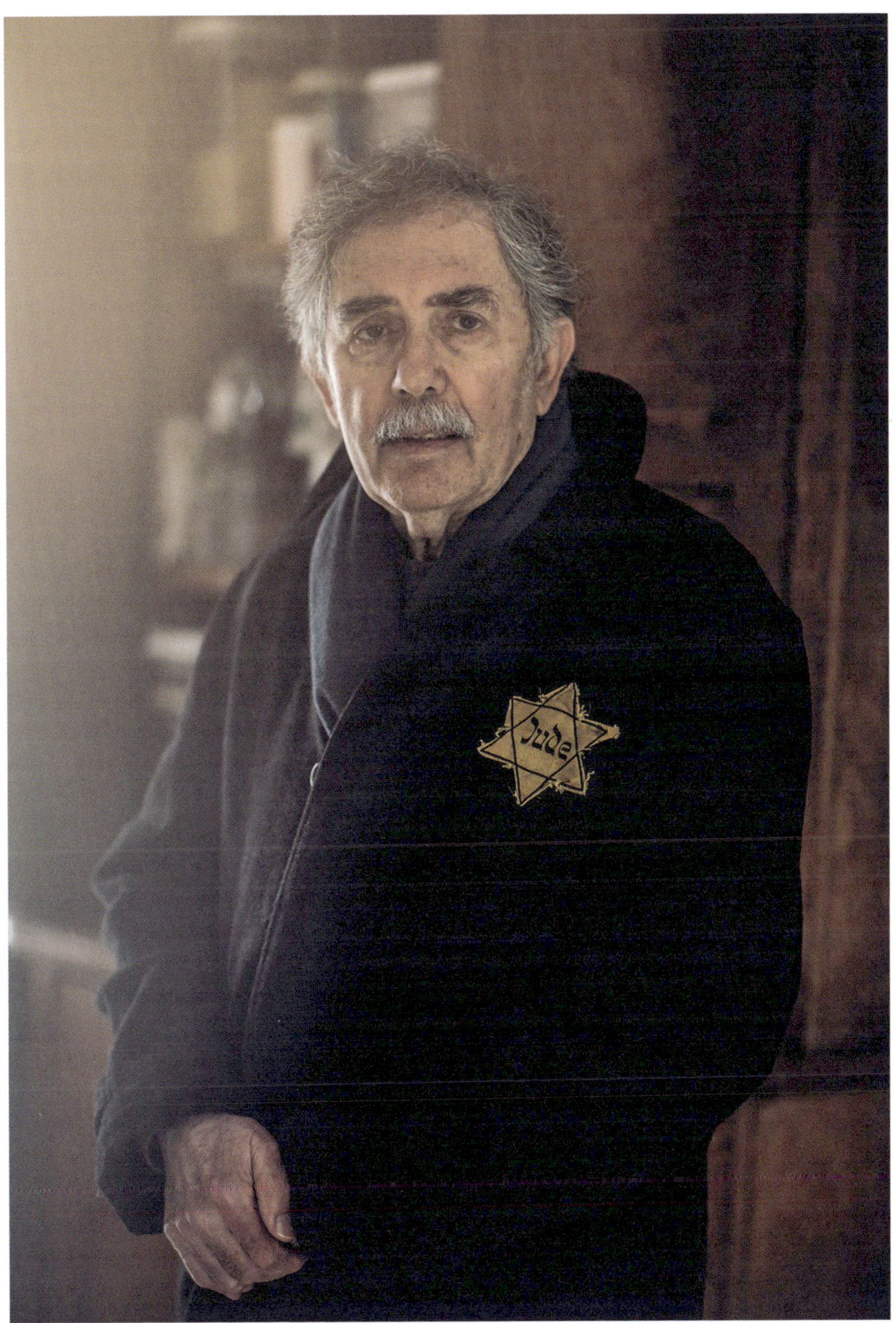

Jude

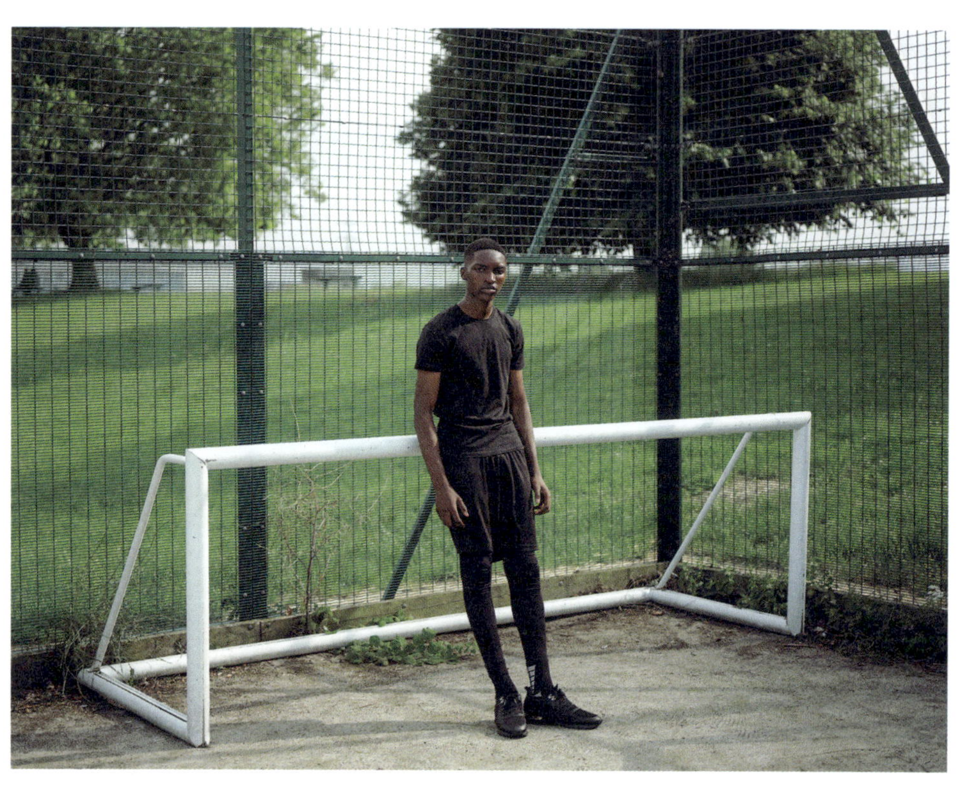

TUNJI
by Terry Graham
London

Tunji is a semi-professional footballer who plays
in the National League. He has recently been signed
by a model agency, but his main ambition is still
to have a career in football.

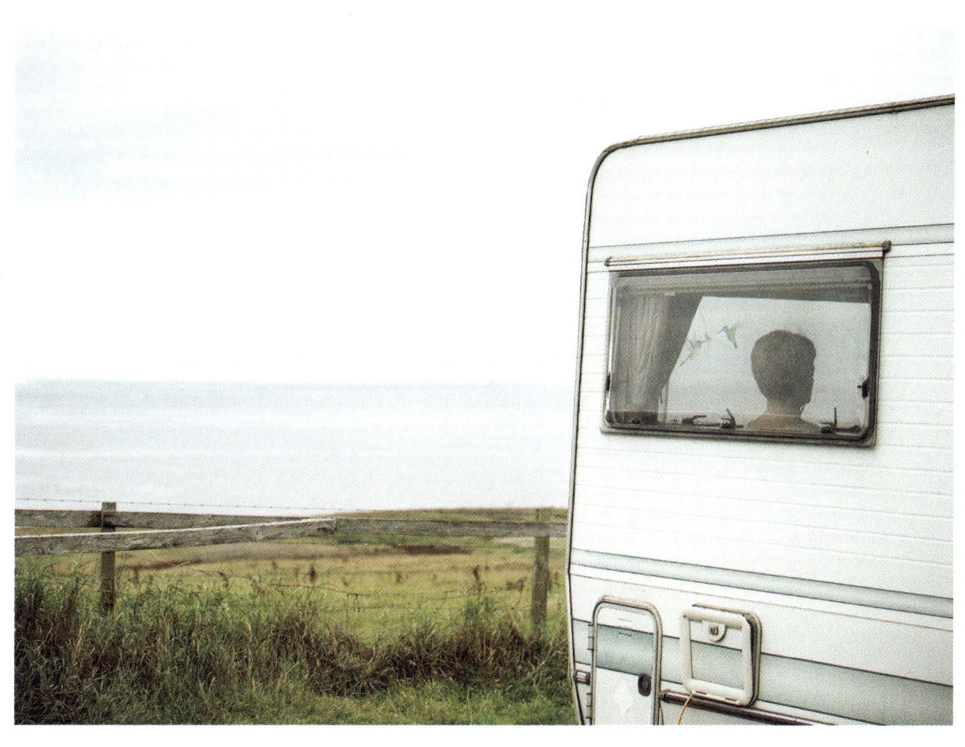

ORKNEY MORNING
by Julia Hawkins
South Ronaldsay, Orkney Islands

I got chatting to this woman a couple of times while
camping. I didn't catch her name, but she told me that
she was from Essex and had been travelling around
the UK in her campervan for several months. She said this
nomadic existence suited her; I took this picture
of her meditating one morning.

VIVIENNE WESTWOOD
by Andrew Quinn
London

I took this photo of Vivienne Westwood outside
the Arms Fair in London on 14th September 2021,
where she was protesting against the global sale
of weapons that many individuals and countries profit
from. Vivienne says that the world's problems, such
as climate change, are linked to 'the rotten financial
system' and that we must act now to change this.
I am in awe of Vivienne's relentless activism and her
constant ability to stand up for world issues.
She should be an inspiration to us all.

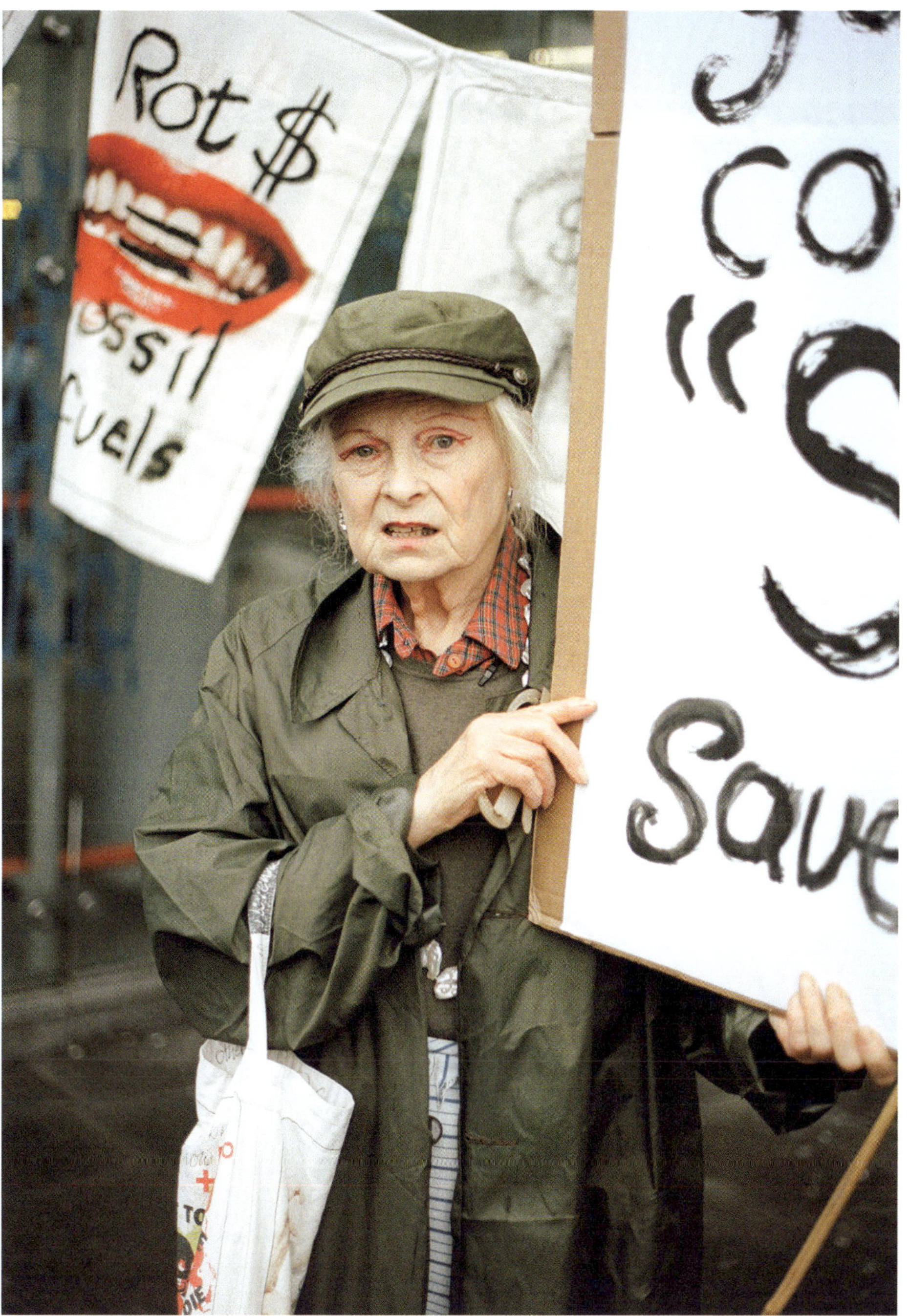
Rot $
ossil
Fuels
CO
S
Save

LITTLE BIG PHILOSOPHER
by Marley Starskey Butler
Liverpool

This was the first day I met Jonah; he is the
five-year-old son of some friends I hadn't seen in
around ten years. I arrived home to find him dressed
as a Neanderthal – his mother told me that he often
wakes up with an idea of something to dress up as,
and then it is down to her and his dad to make
an outfit from materials around the house.

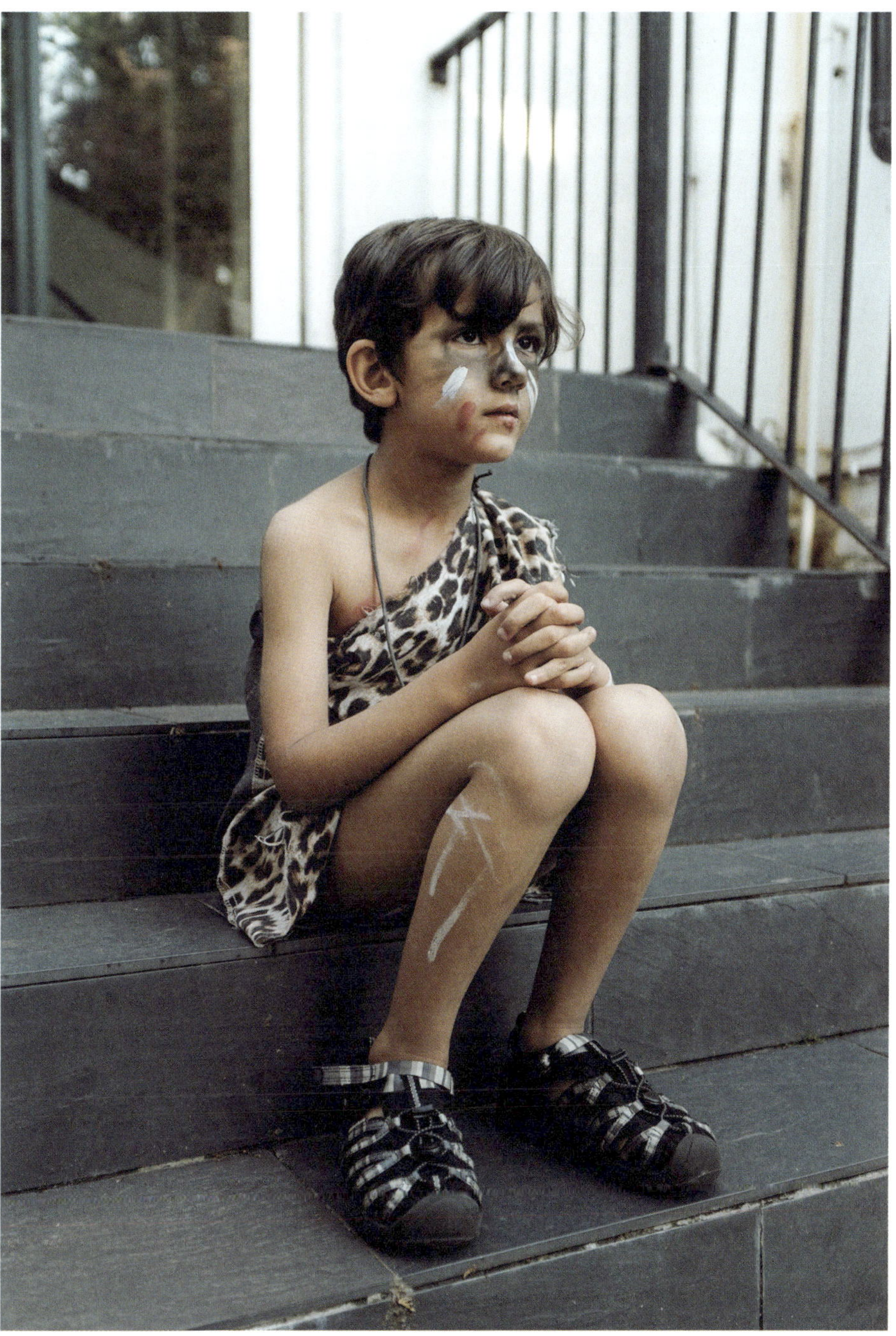

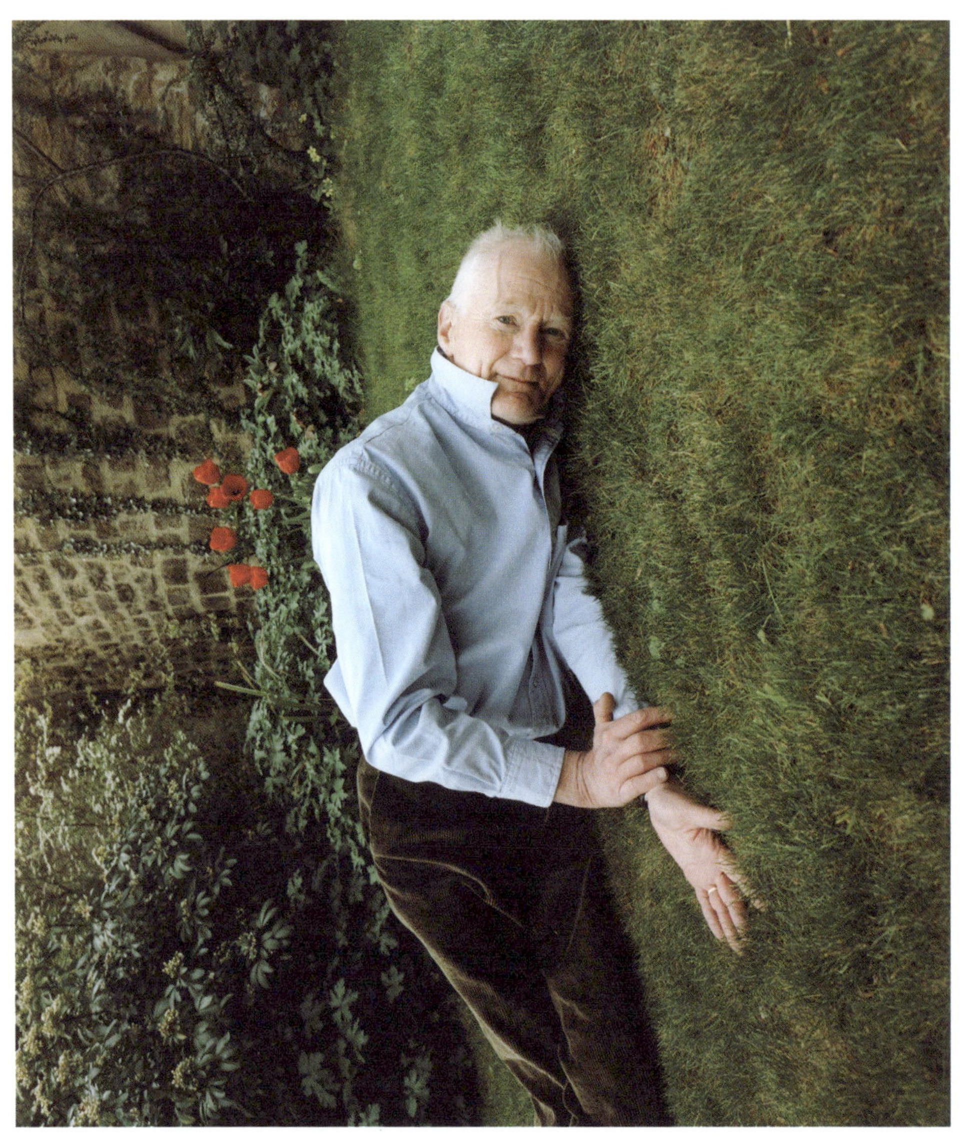

MUSICIAN PETER HAMMILL
by Max D'Orsogna
Bradford-on-Avon, Wiltshire

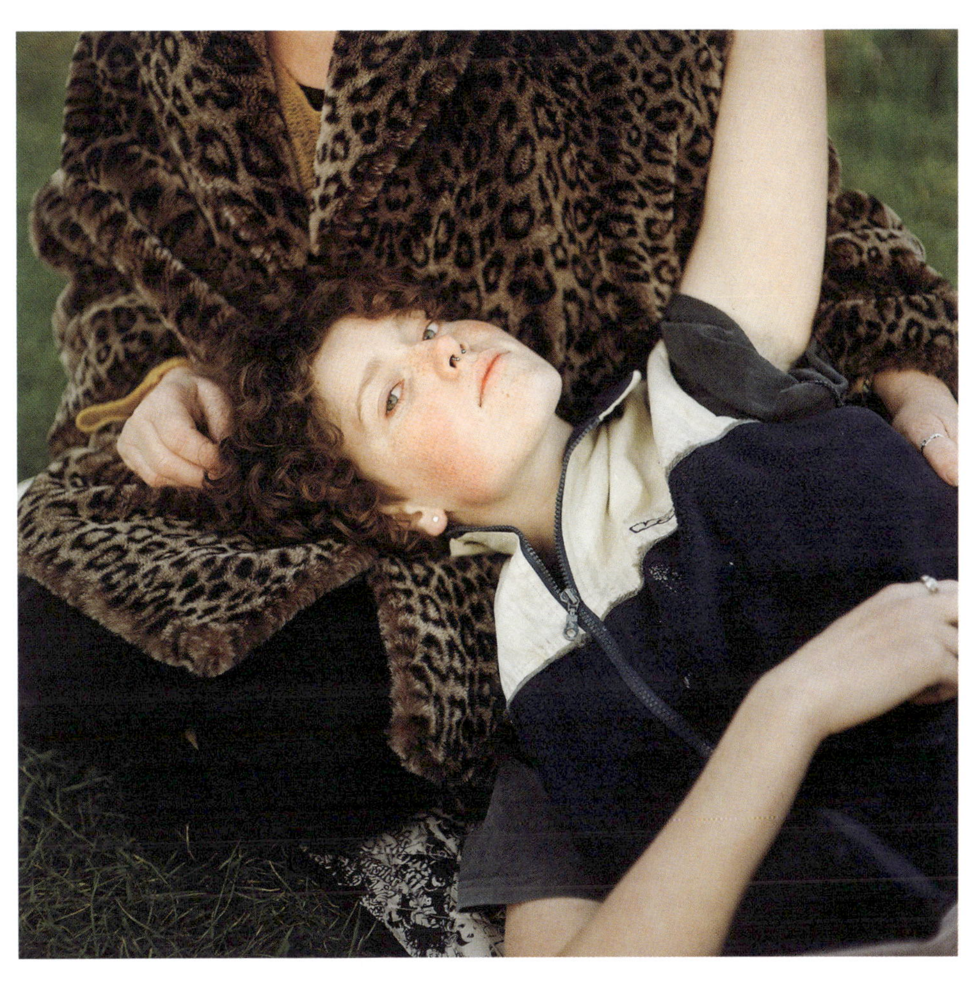

MARTHA
by Laura Pannack
Hastings, East Sussex

KYRA – THE FREEDOM
by Sane Seven
Liverpool

Kyra is a singer, a dancer, a performer, a model and
my friend. When I first met her she seemed shy,
but when she stood in front of the camera, I could tell
she was a true performer. Her beautiful skin patches
are created by vitiligo. They remind me of a starry sky,
predicting that she was born to be a star herself.

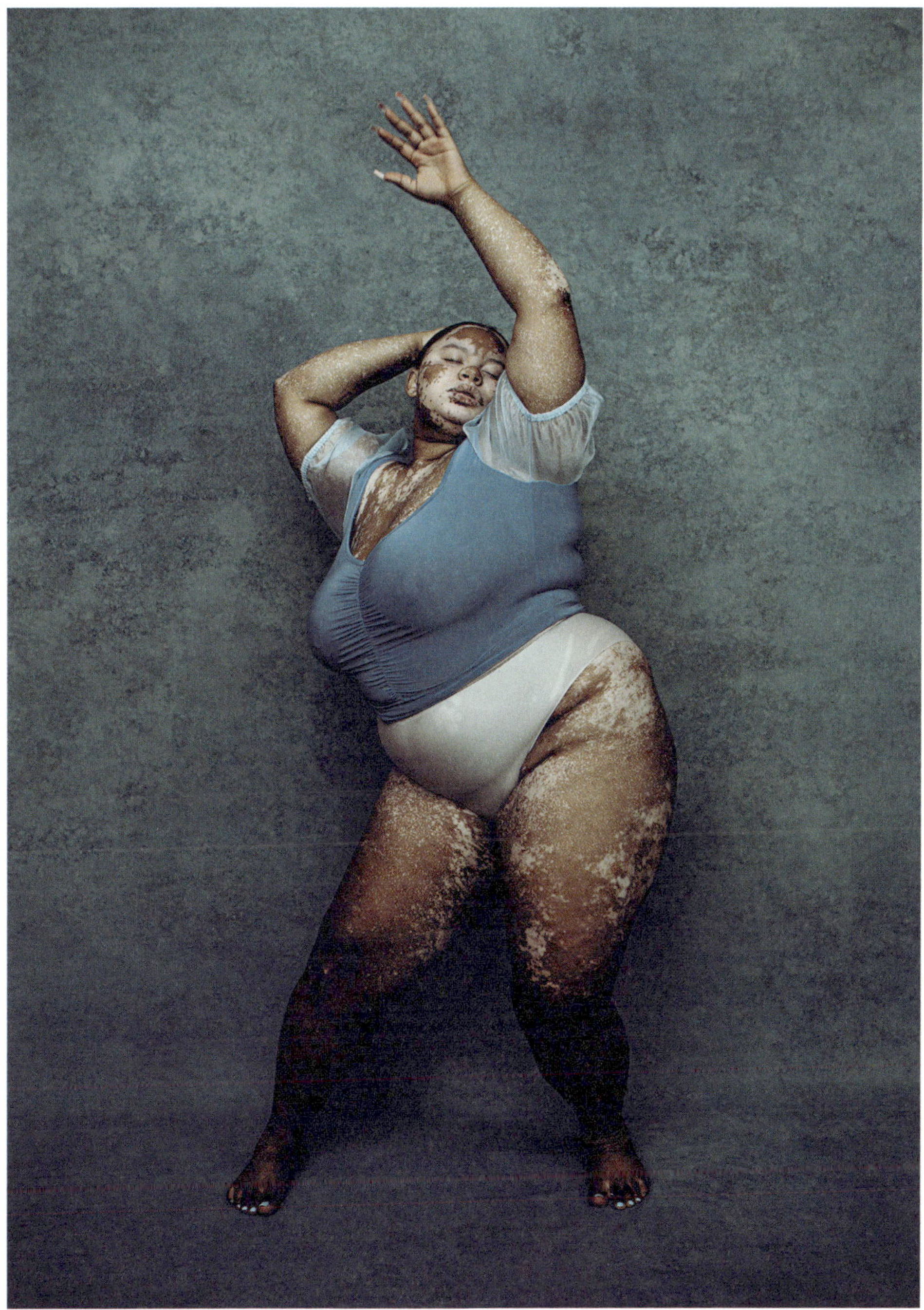

ADRIAN, STEPNEY GREEN, 2021
by Daniel Keys
London

I photographed my friend Adrian as part of a personal
project I am working on about the coincidental
nature of friendship. This project began due to Brexit;
I was afraid it would mean that many people would
leave the UK and I wanted to capture my current
relationships as moments in time. I set my camera
beside me as Adrian and I spoke about when he first
moved to London from Poland, and clicked the
shutter when it felt right.

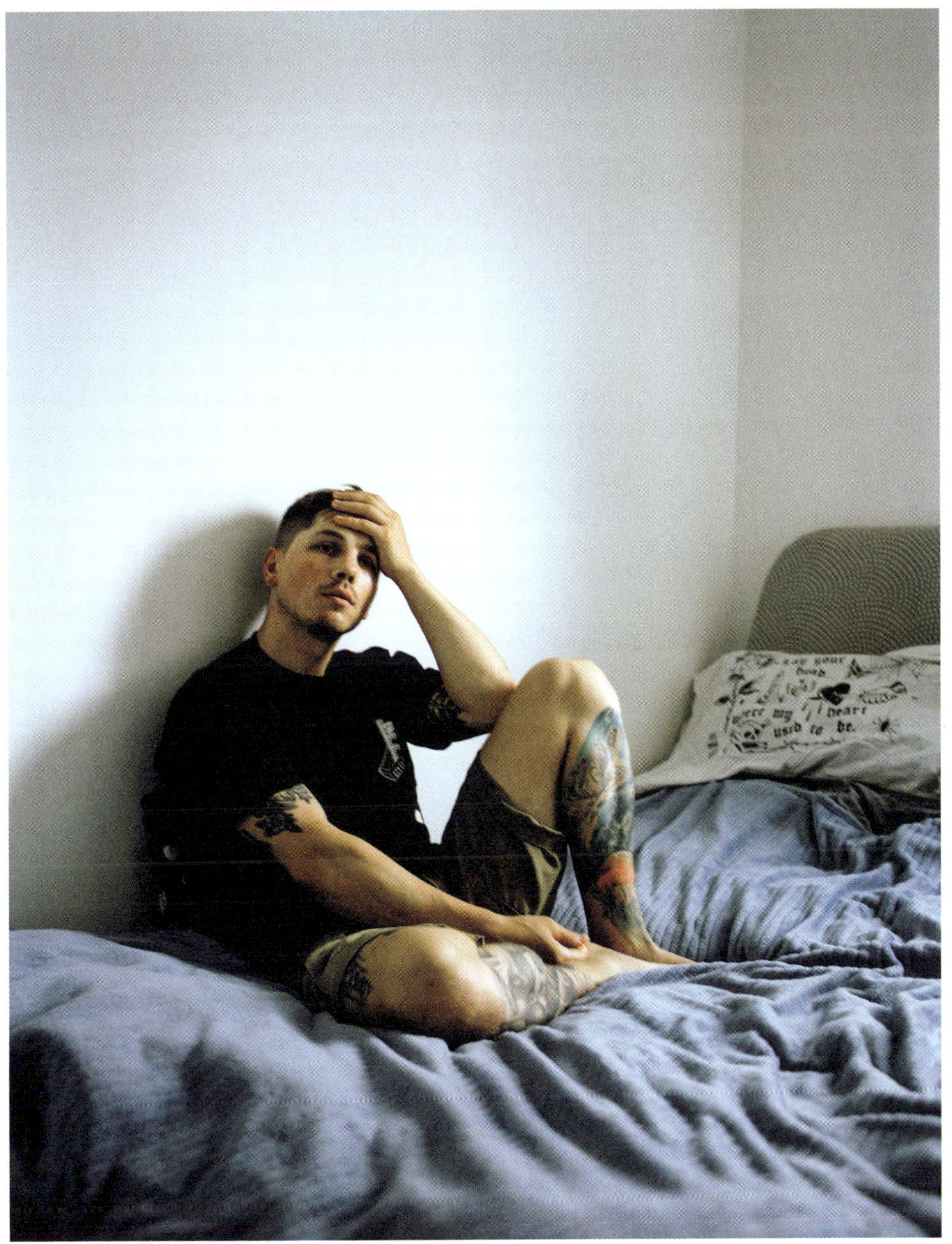

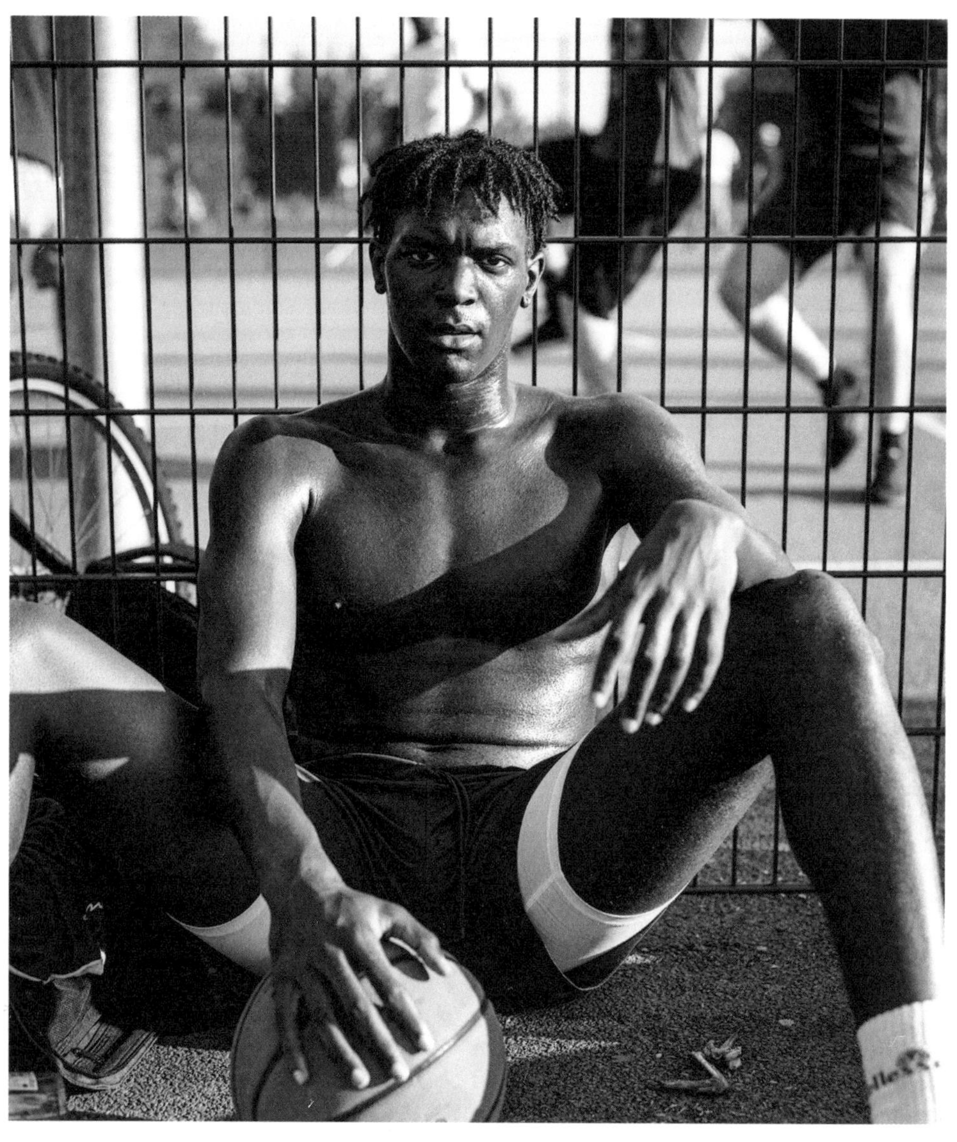

JAY T, FINSBURY PARK BASKETBALL COURTS
by Brunel Johnson
London

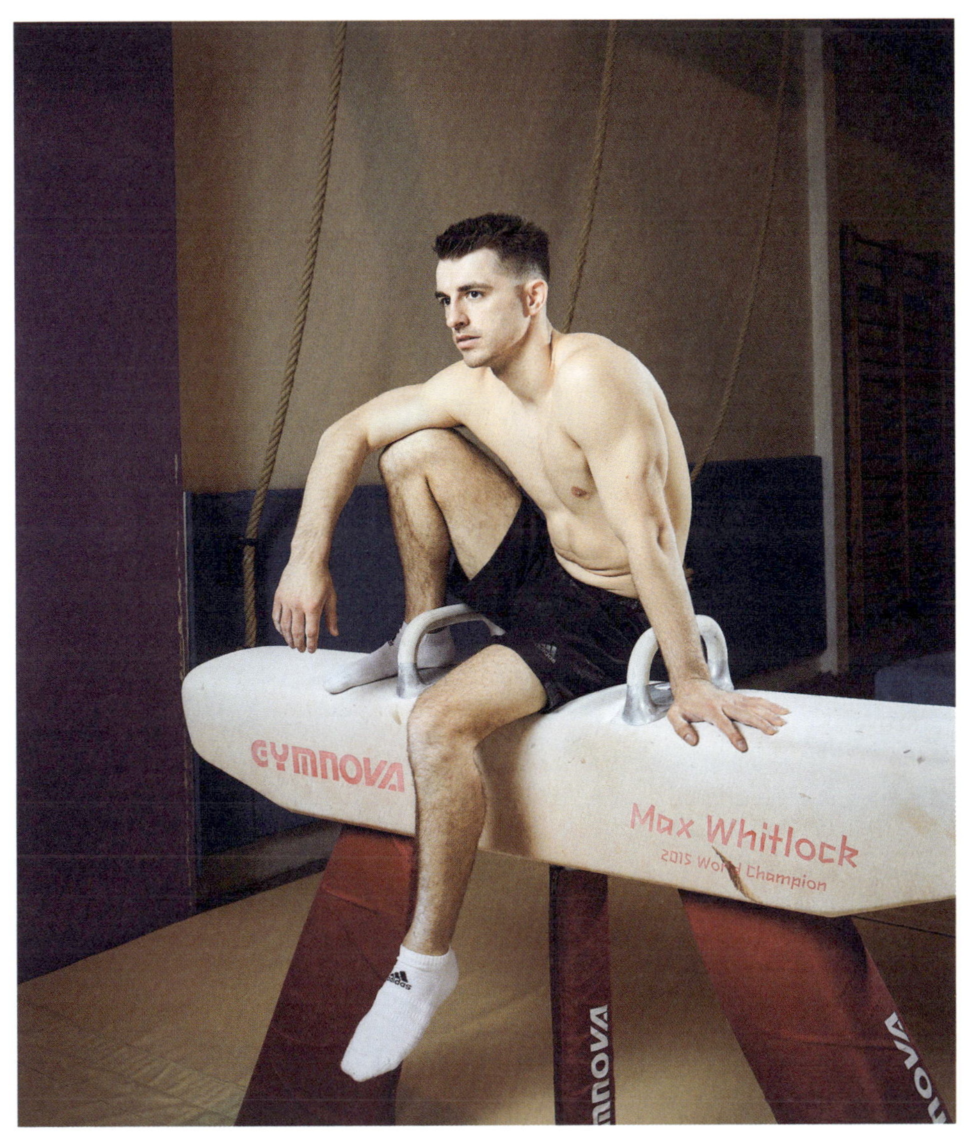

WAITING FOR TOKYO
by Jake Green
Basildon, Essex

PRETTY GIRL WITH AN UGLY BACK
by Ayesha Jones
Preston, Lancashire

When I was 13, a doctor told me that unless
I had spinal surgery I was going to grow up to be
'a pretty girl with an ugly back'. I was determined to
prove him wrong; I wanted to celebrate my difference
rather than be influenced by the doctor's ignorance.
A decade later, when the curve of my spine hit
100 degrees, I realised I had to let go of his words
and focus on what was right for me. I took this
self-portrait before I had surgery to express
my defiant self-acceptance.

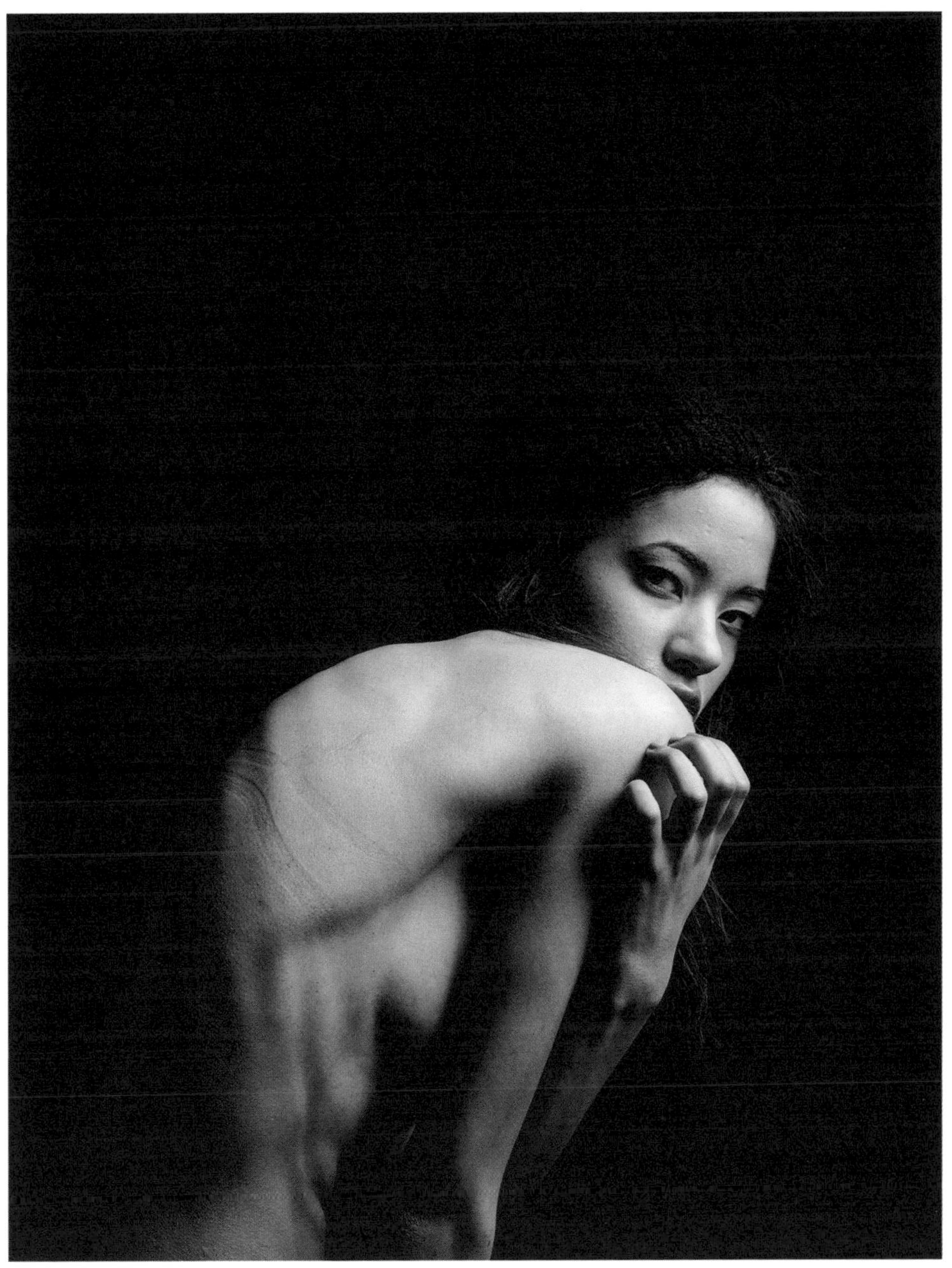

BADGE OF HONOUR
by Paul Wenham-Clarke
Newbury, Berkshire

Len, 88, is an ex-member of the parachute regiment
who is proud to have had the Covid vaccine. 'My year
of Covid to be quite honest has been absolute murder.
I have lived through the Blitz and in 1942 our home
in the East End of London was blown up and
I was evacuated to Hungerford in Berkshire,
so I know hard times.' – Len (*pictured*)

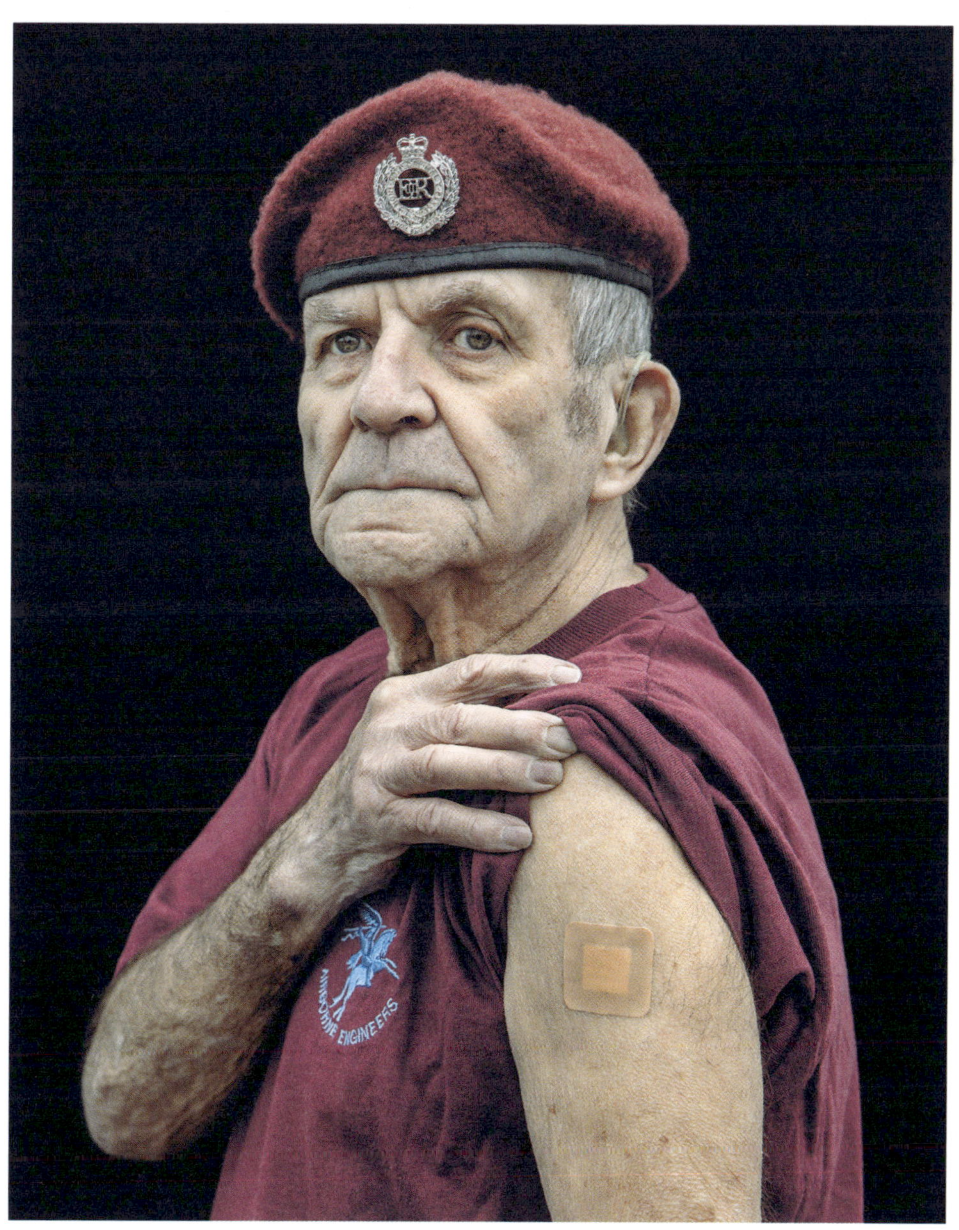

AIRBORNE ENGINEERS

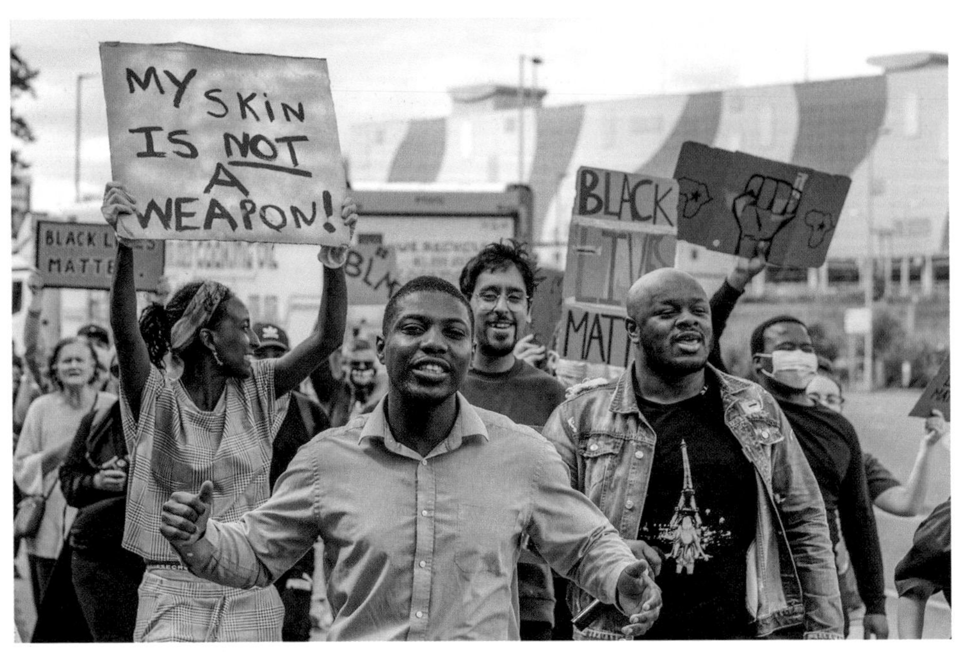

MY SKIN IS NOT A WEAPON
by Marc Davenant
Luton, Bedfordshire

Levi (*front*) is one of three young people who organised
a Black Lives Matter protest in Luton in 2020. Levi says,
'Being a Black male myself means that I have experienced
racism and discrimination. However, I am extremely proud
of where I come from due to educating myself on the
positive parts of Black history, which is what we should
as a community pass on to the next generation.'

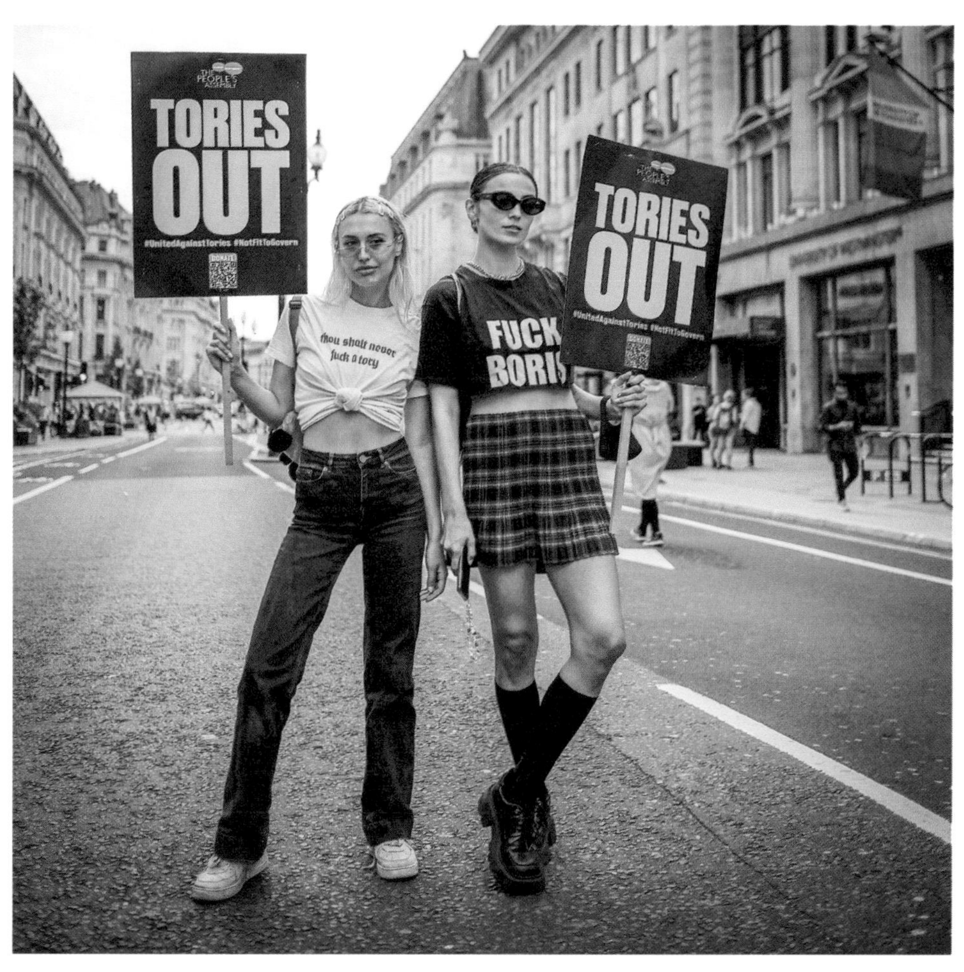

TORIES OUT
by Marc Davenant
London

These two women were attending the Kill the Bill protest
against expanded police powers. They came up to me
and asked me to take their photo.

STILL NOT ASKING FOR IT
by Joshua Windsor
London

I saw this activist at a protest in Parliament Square,
a couple of days after the vigil for Sarah Everard on
Clapham Common. Large crowds of protesters
had descended on parliament, outraged by the lack
of action in tackling systemic male violence.

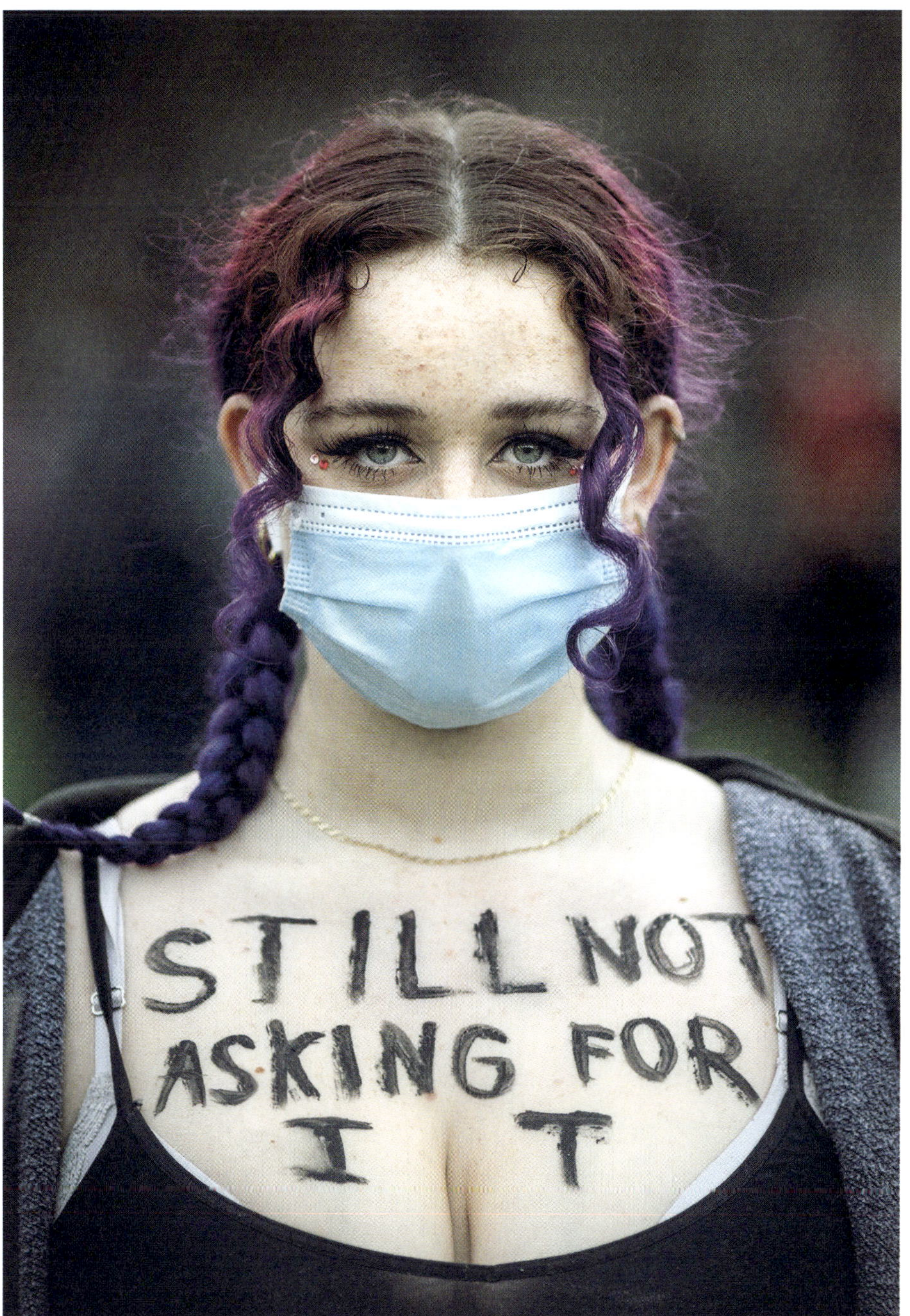

STILL NOT
ASKING FOR
I T

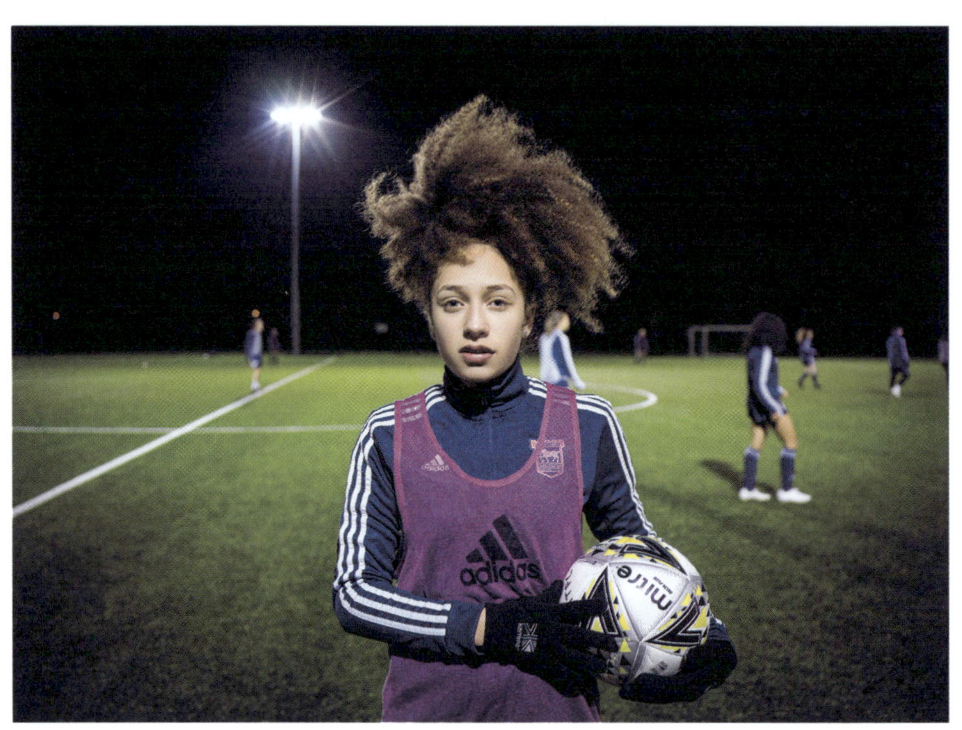

IPSWICH LADIES SOCCER PLAYER
by John Ferguson
Ipswich, Suffolk

Abbie Lafayette plays for Ipswich Town Ladies; I took her
portrait at a training session while covering the team's FA
Cup run. They had just got through to the next round
by beating a much higher-rank team, and were about
to face the current League champions, Manchester City.
Unfortunately they went on to lose 10–1, but
they live to fight another day.

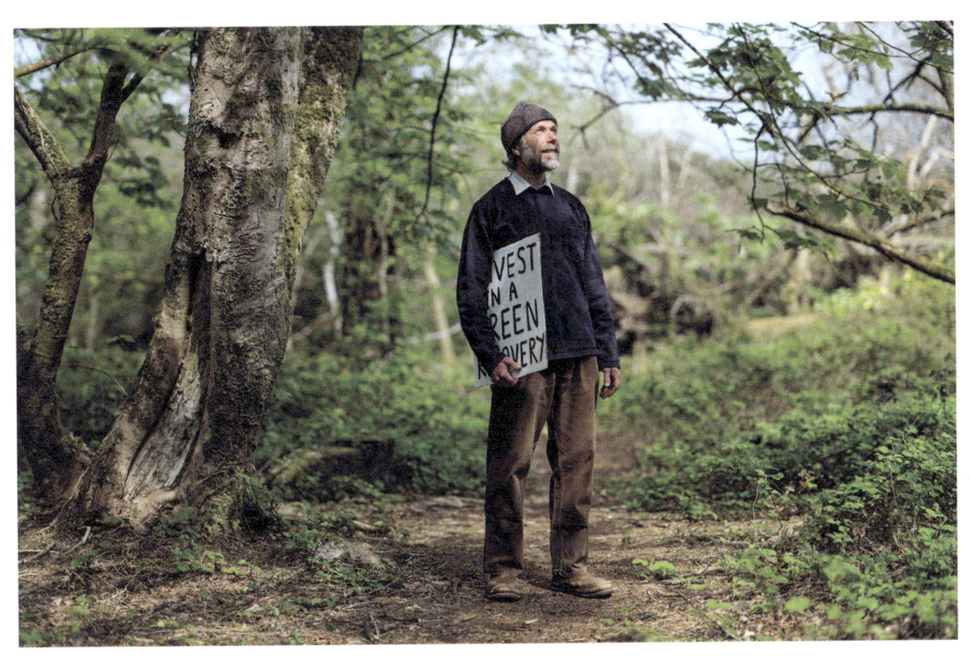

RUPERT, A CITIZEN OF LOVE AND RAGE
by Gavan Goulder
St Ives, Cornwall

Rupert is a retired doctor who now spends a great deal
of his time looking after a small area of woodland near his
home in St Ives; he is hoping to buy it to protect it from
developers. During the G7 summit, protesting was
only allowed at designated areas a long way from the
summit but a few people who already lived nearby
were able to protest a little closer.

BROTHERS
by Lee Coventry-Walsh
London

This is Reuben and his little brother, Jonah.
They both play for a local Hackney football club,
which my sons are also part of. Reuben is so
sweet with his little brother; they have such
a strong bond of love and connection.

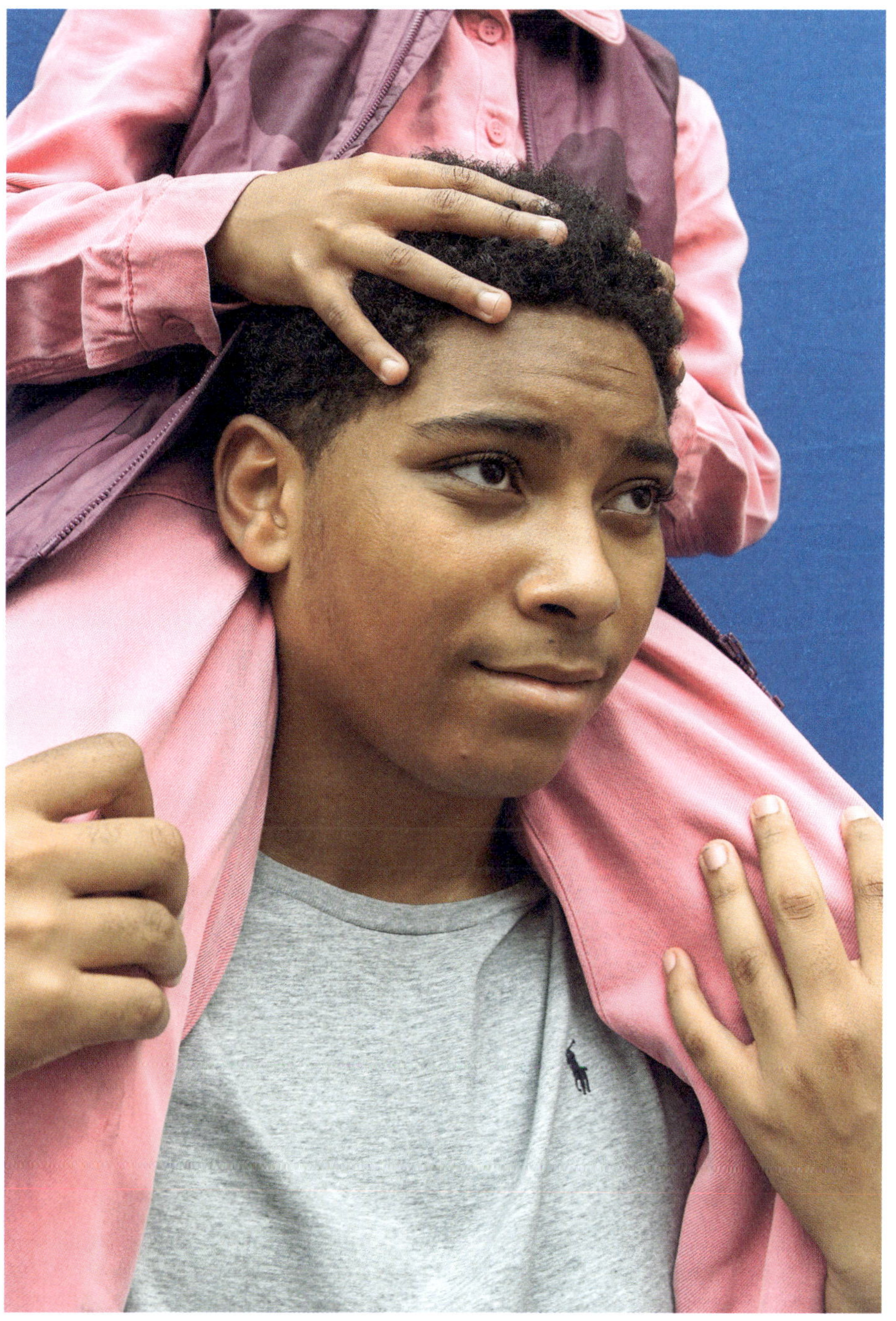

L'OREAL 316 PLUM
by Clynt Garnham
Bawdsey, Suffolk

My mother Jean (*pictured*) has coloured her own
hair since her mid-50s; she says that she's never going
grey, gracefully or otherwise. Now 83, she applies
her favourite brand and colour at six-week intervals –
or at the first sign of any grey hairs.

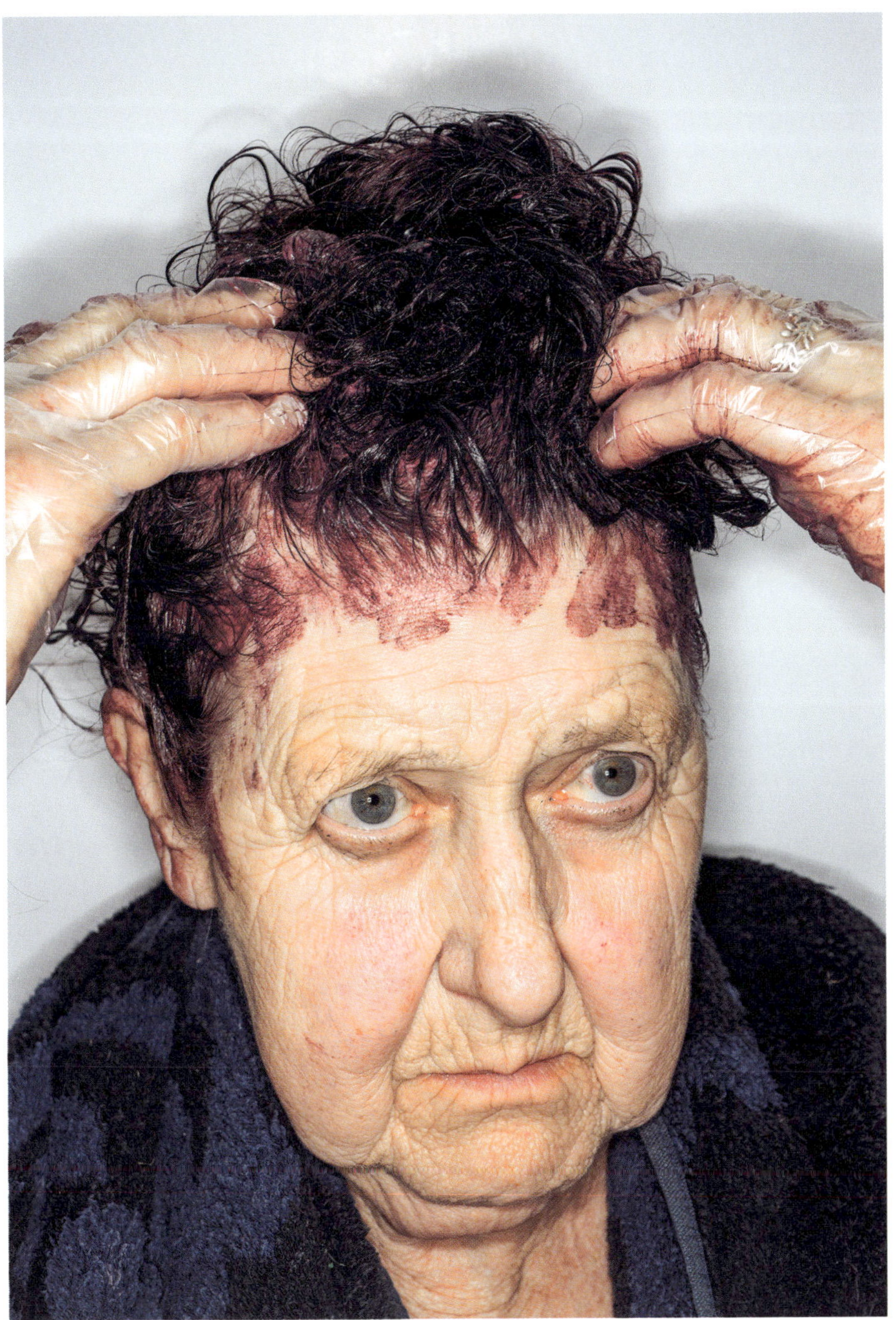

RUBY AGED 11
by Carolyn Mendelsohn
York

'I hope that in the future society is more open
about body image, because not everyone is like
what you see in the magazines, everyone is different,
and I really hope people can accept that more.
Everyone is perfect and unique in their own way.
My ambition is to be more self-confident when I am
older and to help other people be more confident
about themselves. My dream is probably to have
a decent job and two Pomeranians.' – Ruby

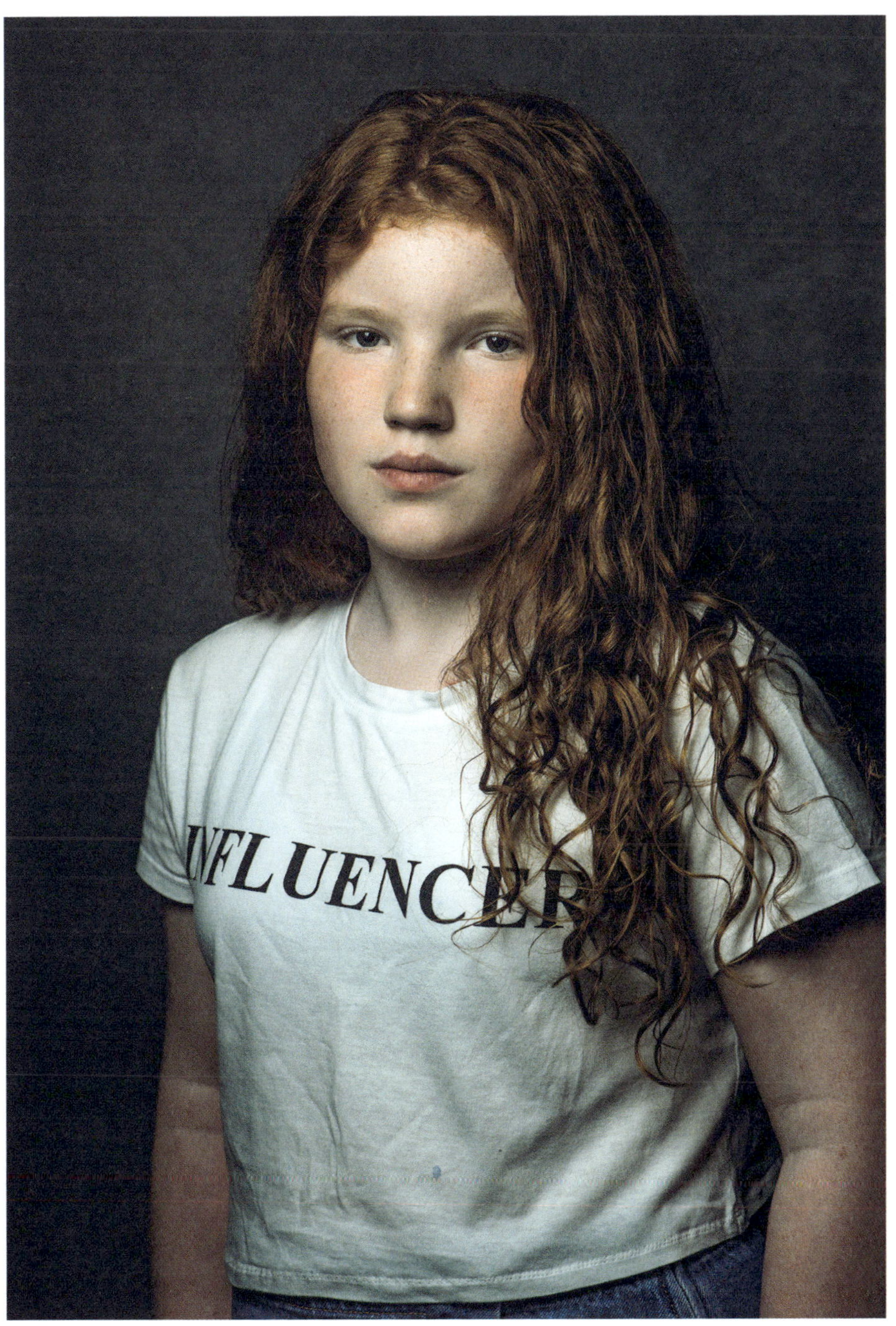
INFLUENCER

DR MAVI
by Jaskirt Boora
Birmingham

Dr Mavi was a frontline doctor at Heartlands Hospital
during the pandemic, on the medical emergencies
ward. He told me, 'At its worst our staffing
was so stretched we had doctors deployed in areas
of the hospital they hadn't practiced in for 15 or
20 years. We had a gynaecologist managing my
ward for a week. Medical students were stepping
up as doctors, consultants were working in different
specialities and there was no sense of hierarchy.
That completely went. And morale was so high.'

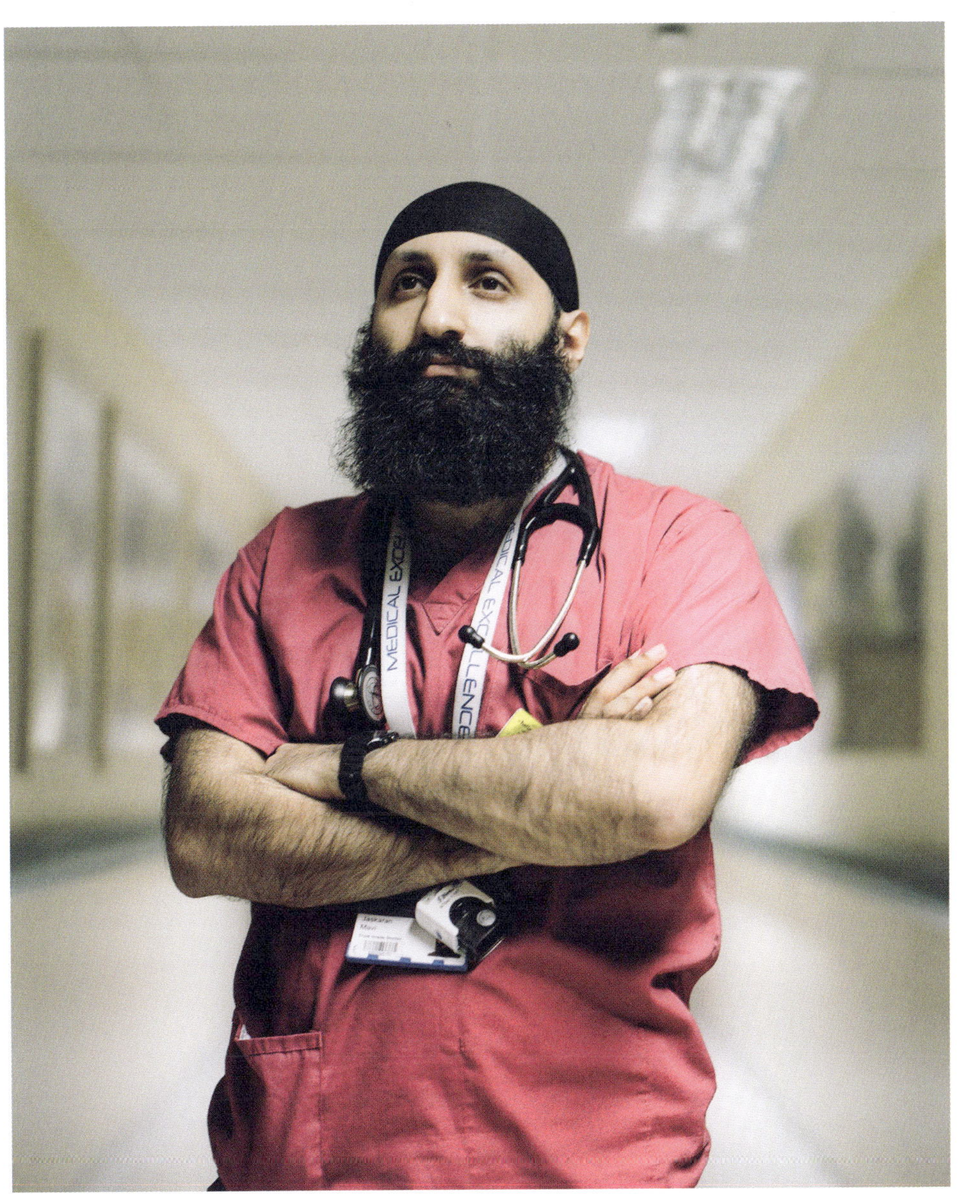

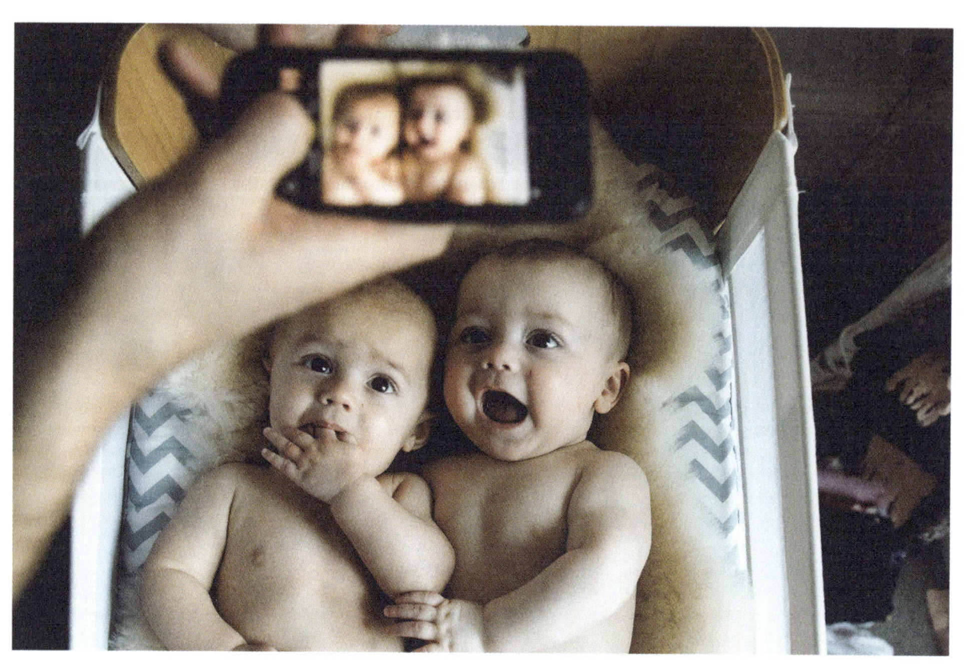

SAY HELLO
by Eleanor Church
Colchester, Essex

Our twin sons, Vincent and Gabriel, were born during
the pandemic. They still haven't met all of our family and
friends, who have mostly seen them grow up via Skype,
videos and photos. In some ways, it has probably made
life easier having an excuse not to be going out and about
with two young twins, but it still makes our hearts ache.

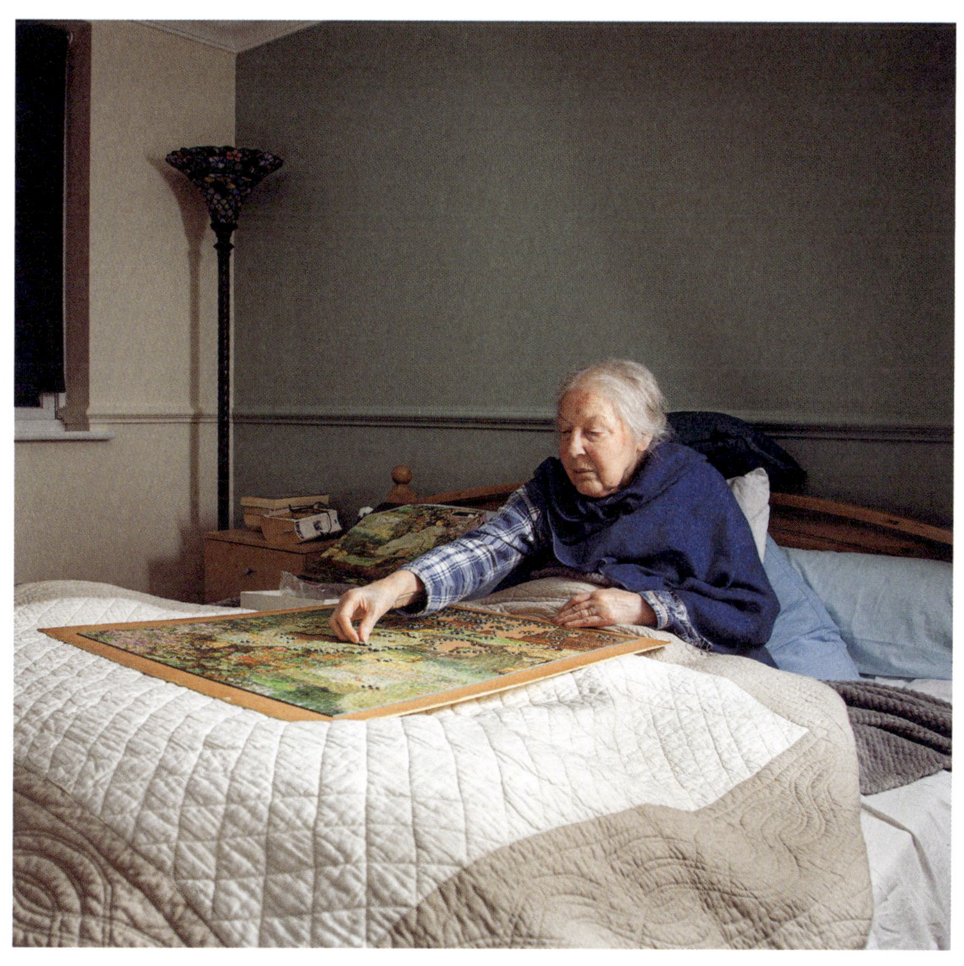

LIZ
by Roland Ramanan
London

My mother Liz came to live with us in January 2019.
Having lived in India, the Netherlands and France over
the years, her world has shrunk somewhat. But she
still goes out determinedly each day for a walk.

NORMA AT HOME
by Jonathan Clifford
Milton Keynes, Buckinghamshire

In May 2021, my mum Norma was diagnosed with
high-grade non-Hodgkin lymphoma. Although
considered treatable, the cancer had spread and
she had to start chemotherapy immediately. The news
came just as she and my dad were packing up their
home to move to Australia. Suddenly, their plans
for the sunny years ahead of them were undone.
Despite this, Mum has shown incredible resilience,
strength and good humour in the face of an
uncertain future. Her treatment is ongoing.

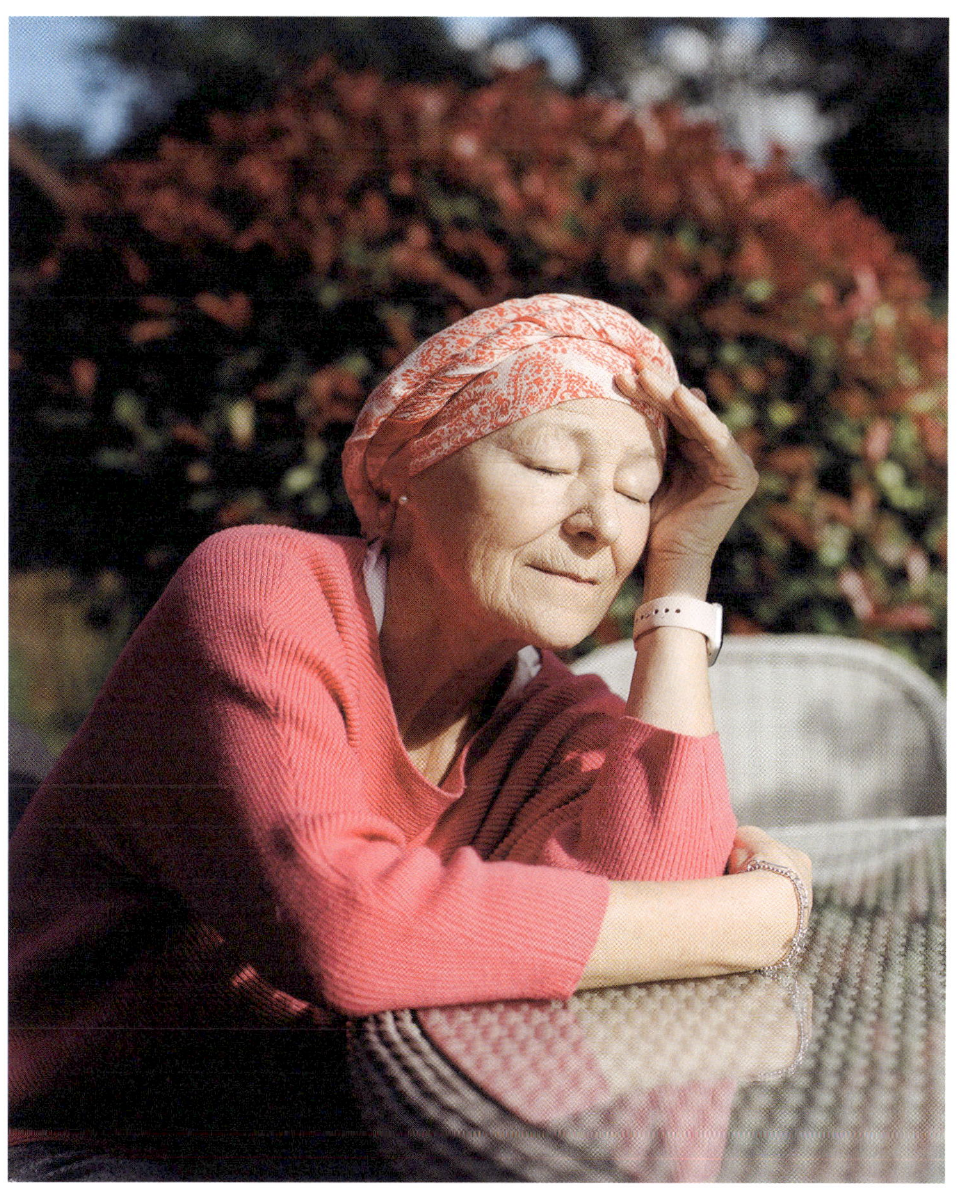

WREN AND HER FIRST SUNFLOWER
by Clare Hewitt
Birmingham

My two-year-old daughter Wren and I planted
a sunflower seed together in the first lockdown.
Each day, we went outside, poured a little water
on it and watched it grow. At a time when we needed
optimism, this small daily activity gave us hope.

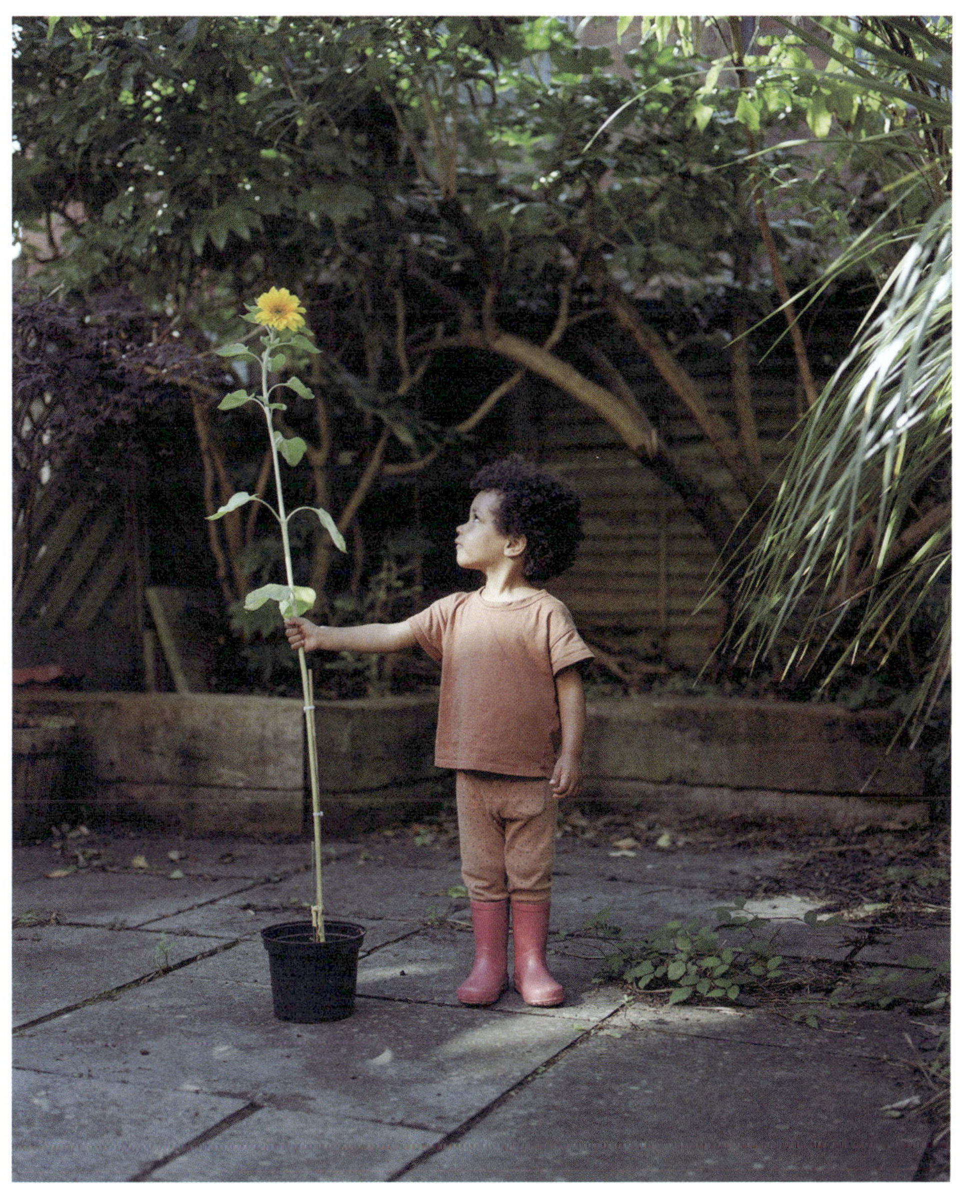

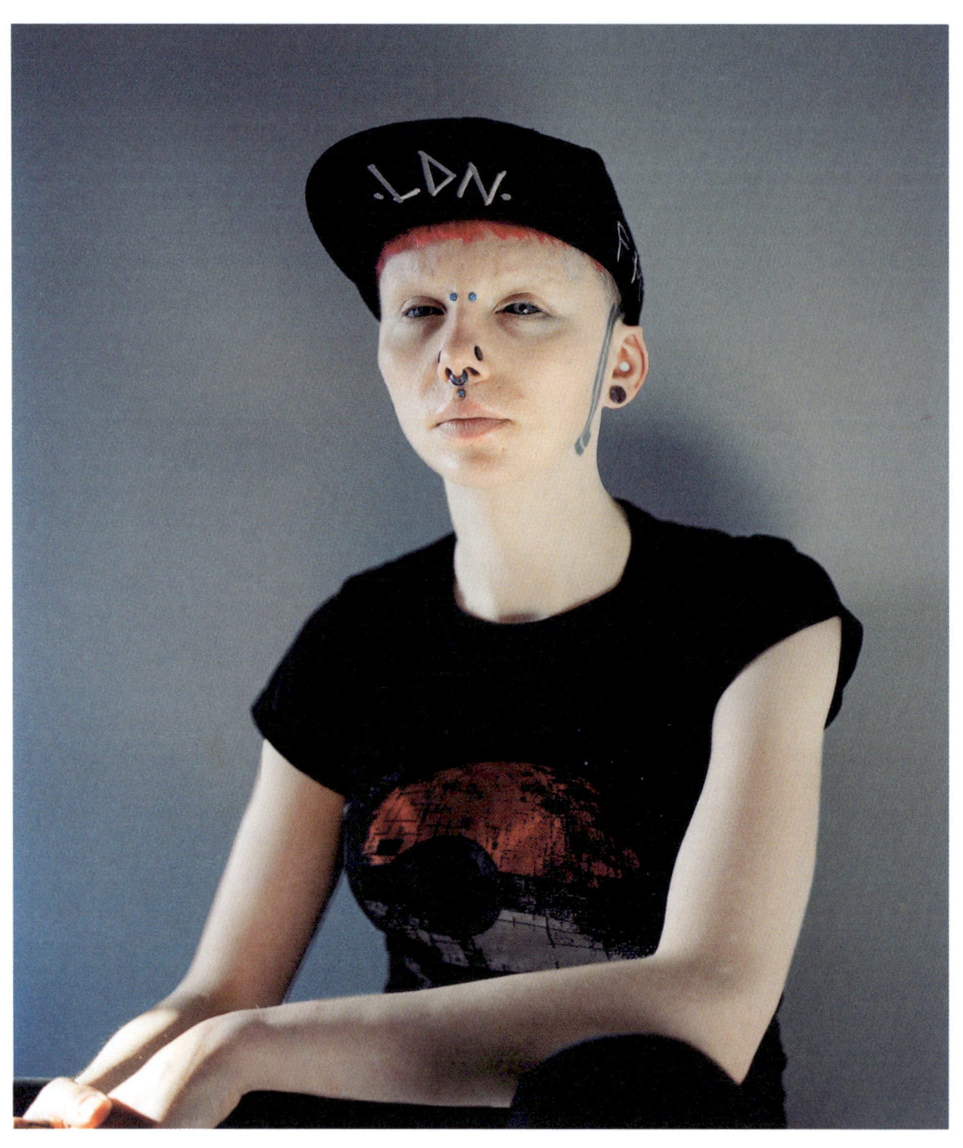

RONI AT HOME
by Daniel Keys
London

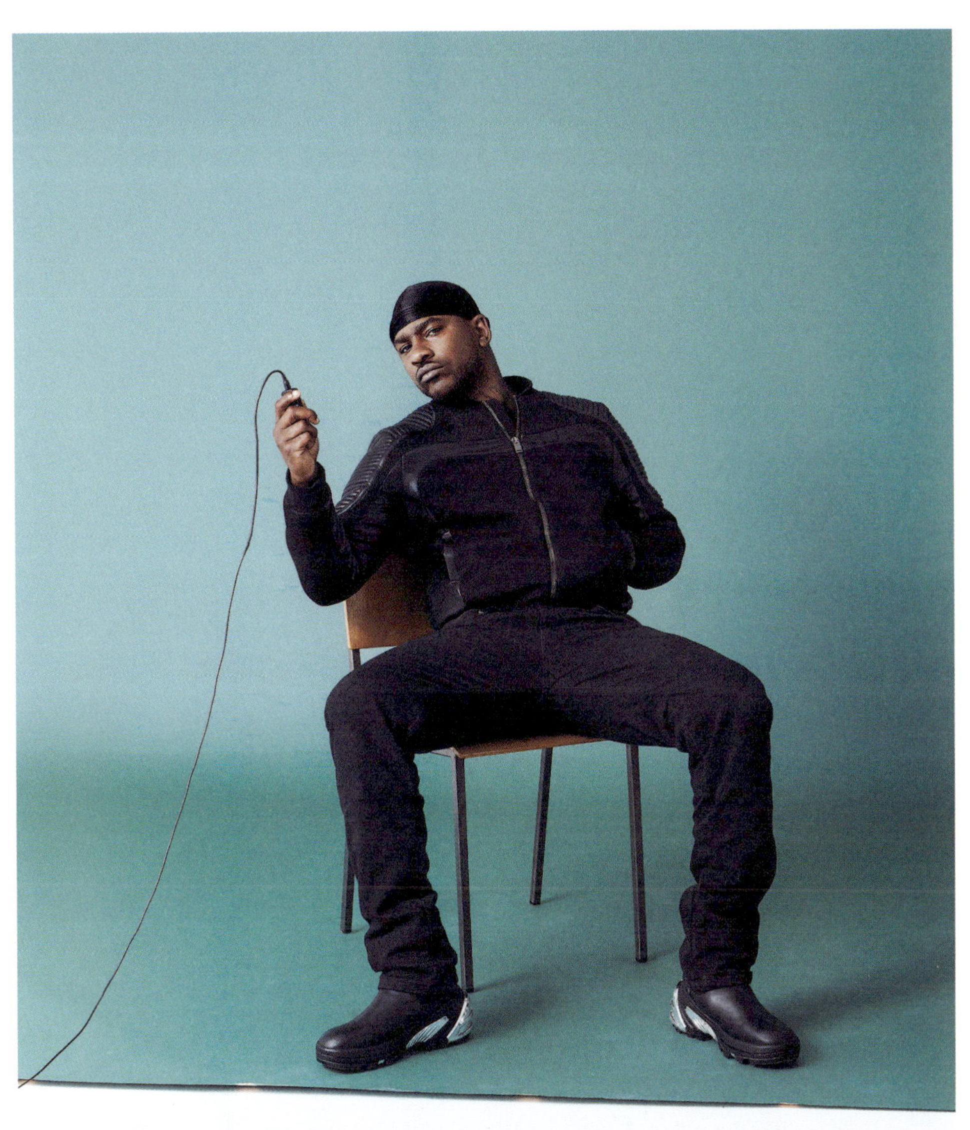

SKEPTA (SELF-PORTRAIT)
by Jake Green
London

MARTIN AND EMMA
by Phil Fisk
London

This image is part of a series where I invited people
on my street into my garden to take their portraits
during lockdown; I wanted to make a project about
the memory of touch at a time when it seemed
to be fading. When I explained to Emma that
I would ask her to hug her dad, she was initially
very shy, but when I asked her to squeeze her
dad's head this seemed to please her more.

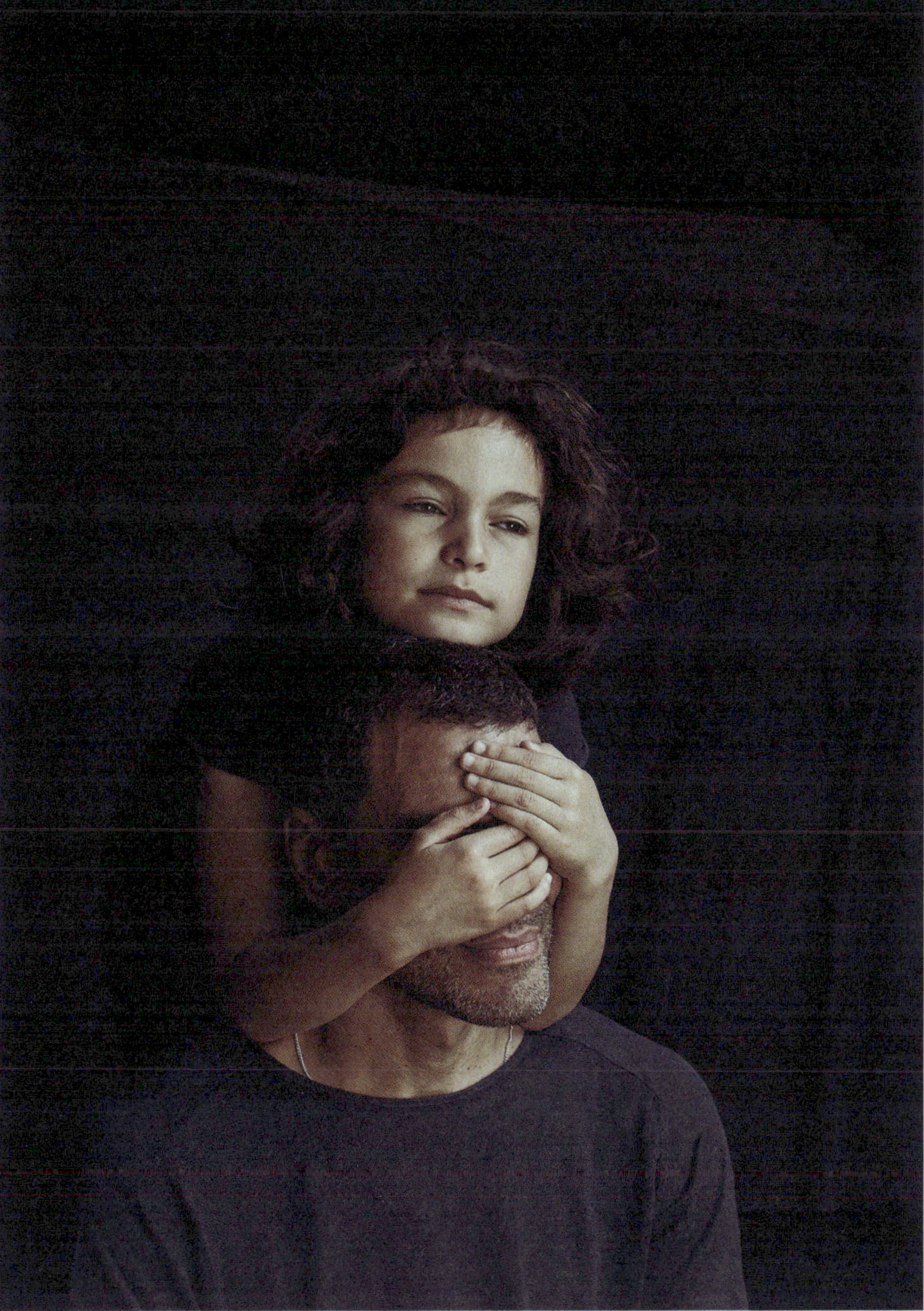

COEXISTENCE
by Sirli Raitma
London

Humans' relationship with technology is intensifying;
we spend more and more of our waking lives in digital
spaces. For my mother Eha (*pictured*), technology
enables her to stay in touch with distant family and
to feel connected. In 2020, in the midst of all the Covid
travel restrictions, Eha's grandchildren introduced her
to Virtual Reality and she has since been experiencing
all of the new possibilities this technology creates.

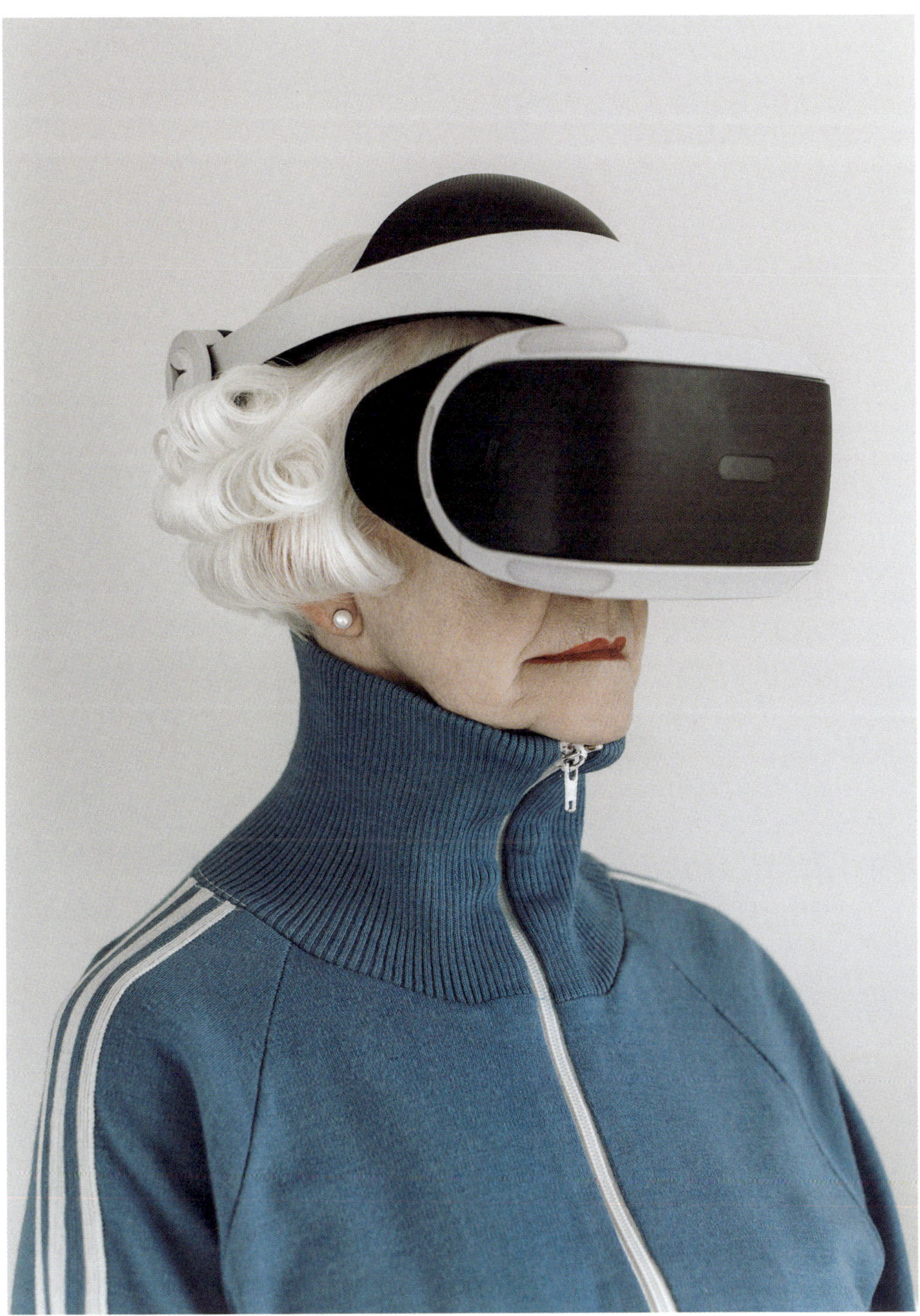

Index